Independent
SCHOOLS

Independent
THINKERS

Independent SCHOOLS

Independent THINKERS

Pearl Rock Kane
Editor

Jossey-Bass Publishers · San Francisco

For sales outside the United States contact Maxwell/Macmillan International Publishing Group, 866 Third Avenue, New York, New York 10022

Printed on acid-free paper and manufactured in the United States of America

The paper used in this book meets the State of California requirements for recycled paper (50 percent recycled waste, including 10 percent post-consumer waste), which are the strictest guidelines for recycled paper currently in use in the United States.

Library of Congress Cataloging-in-Publication Data

Independent schools, independent thinkers / Pearl Rock Kane, editor.
    p.   cm. — (The Jossey-Bass education series)
    Includes bibliographical references and index.
    ISBN 1-55542-398-1 (alk. paper)
    1. Private schools—United States. 2. School, Choice of—United States.   I. Kane, Pearl Rock. II. Series.
LC49.I53   1991
371'02'0973—dc20   91-27073
                                                  CIP

FIRST EDITION
HB Printing   10 9 8 7 6 5 4 3 2 1   *Code 9203*

The Jossey-Bass
Education Series

For Richard

Contents

Contents

Preface

The aim of this book is to convey the essence of independent schools and to stimulate reflection and dialogue on the purposes and possibilities of these schools. Those intimately involved with independent schools will, I hope, discover that the range of topics and the variety of opinions will enlarge ongoing discussions and provoke new thinking. Those unfamiliar with independent education will find an introduction to the nature and culture of the schools and learn about the ways independent schools may enrich the current public policy debate on school choice.

My own background has given me a perspective on public and private schools and a foot in both camps. After a public school education, from kindergarten through college, I received a fellowship for graduate study at Smith College, which carried a half-time teaching assignment in the Smith College Day School. On completion of my studies, I returned to work as a teacher and administrator in various public school systems in Michigan, Massachusetts, and New York.

My entry into independent schools was an accident of the New York fiscal crisis of 1975. The public schools were forced to lay off 14,000 teachers, and those most recently hired were the first to be let go. I lost my job. I was fortunate to find a job at the Dalton School, an outstanding New York independent school. My experience in the classroom at Dalton introduced me to an approach to schooling qualitatively different from what I had experienced as a public school teacher; it ignited my enthusiasm for independent education. I was eager to learn more about independent schools and to develop my skills as an educator. With my headmaster's encouragement, I accepted a fellowship at Teachers College, Columbia University. The fellowship was for a new program offered by the Esther A. and Joseph Klingenstein Center for Independent School Education, one designed to develop leadership for independent schools. My commitment to independent education continued, and after several years I returned to serve as the director of that center.

I have now been a student of independent education for over a decade. My knowledge of independent schools has come largely through intense and lively discussions with the nearly 700 exceptional educators from approximately thirty-five states who have participated in both the full-year Klingenstein Fellows Program and the Summer Institute for beginning teachers. The educators in the Klingenstein programs have taught me the most about independent schools. At the same time, I have been influenced by the ideas of my esteemed colleagues at Teachers College. The countervailing forces of public and private school ideology have shaped my thinking.

Private schools have suffered from negative labeling. They are sometimes considered undemocratic or unpatriotic institutions. This view may be a vestige of the crusade for the common school in the 1800s, when the champions of the common school thought that the moral vision of democracy could be realized only if all students were educated together, with equal opportunities extended to all, regardless of family background.

For a century, that view of private schools has pervaded our national consciousness. In the last few years, though, independent schools in the United States have come to a crucial moment in their development. For the first time, leading educators in these schools, educators in public schools, university scholars, and government policy makers are becoming conscious of the distinctive attributes of independent schools within the larger context of public policy for our national educational system. Instead of being perceived as antithetical to public education, independent schools are being seen as part of our national educational system, and even as models for the public schools.

My own education and teaching experience at the Dalton School and in various public schools, particularly in Jamaica Plains, outside of Boston, and in Harlem, New York, have given me a contrasting perspective and a sense of outrage at the disparities in schooling accessible to the rich and the poor. The quality of education available to a small percentage of American youth, mostly those who come from privileged families, is seldom accessible to those who would benefit from it most—children from impoverished families. Although independent schools are seeking to broaden the range of students they educate, the relatively small size of the private sector will allow them to make only a small (though not insignificant) difference. The burden of educating the vast majority of poor and disadvantaged children will continue to fall on public schools. Currently, there are practices in independent schools that may be beneficial to these children, and there are examples of private schools in impoverished neighborhoods where the results of these practices have been encouraging. Independent schools have opened my mind to what is possible in education; I want more educators to know about these possibilities.

In his book *The Creation of Settings and the Future Societies,* Yale psychologist Seymour Sarason has warned that even in establishing new organizations we are constrained by our own histories and experiences. In the absence of alternative models, more often than not we reproduce what we had before. This study of independent schools may present such alternative ways of thinking about public schooling.[1]

What can public schools learn from independent schools about democratic education? Many public school educators are unfamiliar with independent schools or disregard their usefulness as models because the schools are reputed to select the students they enroll. As Richard Barbieri points out in Chapter Three, many independent schools are nonselective "second chance" schools that accept students who have not succeeded or would not succeed in comprehensive public schools. Furthermore, although independent schools educate only a very small portion of American youth, and an even smaller percentage of the lower middle class or poor, their pedagogical and curricular practices may be more effective in ameliorating the inequities of class than public schools, most of which are organized around geographic residence, and the quality of whose schooling appears to reflect the income level of the community. As I point out in Chapter One, a child attending a public school in Greenwich, Connecticut, or Newport Beach, California, has a very different schooling experience from that of a child attending a public school on the South Side of Chicago or in Harlem. In contrast, among the diverse independent school types described in the chapters in Part One—boarding schools and day schools, highly academic schools and nonselective schools, coeducational schools and single-sex schools—one finds a commonality of mission: to provide the same basic education for all their students. Unlike public schools, independent schools resist differentiating programs and curricula to fit the estimated abilities of children. While the range of abilities in independent schools may not be as extensive as that in public schools, there is little of the tracking that predetermines the destinies of children deemed less able. Those with less ability or inclination are expected to work harder or are given extra help. They may decide not to take advanced or college-level courses, but all students are expected to meet the same basic curriculum requirements.

Public school educators can also look to independent schools for experience in moral education. In independent schools, the formation of character is considered as important as academic achievement. Since opportunities for character development are not confined to the classroom, teaching and learning occur in a variety of settings. As head of school Kendra Stearns O'Donnell emphasizes in Chapter Four, independent schools value the teachable moment on the playing field, in the dormitory (in a residential school), and in casual conversation. In Chapter Fourteen, sportswriter E. M. Swift describes the influence of athletics on his own development as a student at the Hotchkiss School. Swift claims that college athletes prefer their secondary school coaches to those at college because in the secondary school "most coaches are really educators who happen to spend their afternoons coaching." Teaching may be more effective in a variety of contexts, and it definitely is more exhausting.

Aside from the differences in mission, there are differences in the culture of public and independent schools. It may be that the most pervasive distinction, and the most elusive to describe, is the most powerful: It is culture rather than rules and regulations that defines standards and expectations, as well as how educators and students perceive their responsibilities and how they interact with one another. In Chapter Eighteen, Terrence E. Deal describes the way independent schools establish cultural bonds by reinforcing values, traditions, and history. The cohesive culture, according to Deal, gives independent schools a "competitive advantage."

In the context of school reform, the self-contained nature of most independent schools and the centrality of their teachers make them useful examples of what advocates for restructuring public schools are calling for: decentralization in governance, more autonomy for teachers, collegial decision making, parental involvement, and smaller, more personal environments. Their fundamental freedom from state and local government regulation has allowed independent schools to develop outside of the ferment that has rocked the public schools.

However, while independent schools have largely avoided the tidal wave of top-down reform, they have not completely escaped the influence of other external forces. College admissions offices have had a substantial effect on curriculum, a factor that compelled Z. Vance Wilson to pose the title question of Chapter Sixteen: "How Independent Is Independent School Curriculum?" Independent schools may, at the same time, miss some benefits that accrue from state mandates to public schools, such as required advanced coursework for teachers and administrators. Few independent school educators have formally studied pedagogy or been exposed to the growing body of professional knowledge available in schools of education. Most independent schools have not had access to the expertise of specialists such as curriculum coordinators and staff developers.

Both sectors, public and private, need to understand each other and to know what qualities of their own schools might contribute to useful professional dialogue. The scarcity of books about independent schools makes it difficult for educators in both public and independent schools to appreciate the factors that distinguish independent from public schools. Developing an understanding of private schools is the first step in opening communication and furthering a constructive relationship. This book is intended to address that need.

The authors represented in the chapters that follow are strange companions who seldom appear together in books about education. They are educational researchers such as James Coleman and Diane Ravitch, and policy analysts such as John Chubb and Terry Moe. They are also people who work and live in or attend schools—teachers, administrators, and students. They were selected to contribute to this book not only because of who they are but because they have something important to tell about a particular facet of life in schools.

Part One provides a description of the characteristics of independent schools, an introduction to the range of school types, and a justification for their existence in \merican education. The section ends with a look to the future, fc ising on the growing necessity for marketing and on questions about whether independent schools will—or even should—survive.

Part Two describes the culture of independent schools from the perspective of insiders and outsiders, those who study the schools as well as those who have experienced the schools directly as teachers, administrators, or students. An important part of interpreting the culture is understanding the way both the explicit and hidden curricula shape the academic, aesthetic, and moral development of children and adolescents. Maxine Greene sees the potential of the arts to stimulate images of a better social order, and Robert Coles challenges independent schools to take a more deliberate role in the moral life of children. In the last chapter of this section, Gary Simons, who has created a dynamic program for students of color in New York City's independent schools, addresses the public responsibility of independent schools.

Part Three examines the independent school in the context of the public policy debate on school choice. In the search for ways to improve public schools, some have advocated abandoning the long tradition of incremental reform of schools in favor of establishing dramatically new models of school organization. The authors debate the advantages and disadvantages of privatizing public schools or offering choice within the public sector.

A recurring theme in the essays that follow is a positive vision for the independent schools of the future—a belief that the schools have the capacity to be better than they are, and a conviction that independent schools are capable of making a greater contribution to society. For independent schools that face financial constraints and an expanding mission to educate an increasingly diverse clientele of students, this quest represents an enormous challenge and an unparalleled opportunity.

Acknowledgments

Four years ago, Lesley Iura, education editor at Jossey-Bass, visited me in New York and encouraged me to work on a book about independent schools. I welcome this opportunity to thank her and the many people who contributed to the book both directly and indirectly.

I extend gratitude to the contributing authors, all busy people who responded graciously to myriad requests for revisions of their manuscripts. I am indebted to John Klingenstein and his able associates James Koerner and Claire List and to the Esther A. and Joseph Klingenstein Fund for allowing me to learn about independent schools through their generous support of programs for independent school educators.

I was fortunate to have several outstanding Teachers College students who were willing to read and comment on various chapters. Walter Johnson reviewed early drafts of my own writing and made numerous thoughtful and sensitive suggestions that enhanced the final product. Lou Mandler, Penny Riegelman, Richard Davies, Polly Rimer Duke, and Diana Stafford carefully read and critiqued many of the chapters that appear in the book. Jane Mallison, William Bullard, and Betty Lies worked closely with me on individual chapters. Arthur Powell read the final draft and made recommendations for constructive changes. My office staff, Jill Steinberg Davis, Maureen Ford, and Delma Lopez, deserve special thanks. The staff of the National Association of Independent Schools graciously and patiently provided needed data. I am indebted to all these people for their important contributions.

My husband Richard is my resident cheerleader and the best of colleagues in all endeavors. Leslie, Lisa, Bradley, and Laura, my children, bring joy and a source of inspiration by their own accomplishments.

Note

1. Seymour B. Sarason, *The Creation of Settings and the Future Societies* (San Francisco: Jossey-Bass, 1972), pp. 18–19.

The Editor

Pearl Rock Kane is director of the Klingenstein Center for Independent School Education at Teachers College, Columbia University, where she is also an assistant professor of education in the Department of Educational Administration. Kane completed her undergraduate work at City College in New York and received a master's degree from Smith College and a doctoral degree from Teachers College. She has published journal articles on private schools and on faculty development and is editor of *The First Year of Teaching: Real Life Stories from America's Teachers.*

The Contributors

James T. Adams, an alumnus of The Lawrenceville School, where he is currently assistant head master, earned his A.B. degree in English from Princeton University and his M.A. degree in English from Boston College. He is the author of the article "Discrepancies in the Time-Scheme of *The Good Soldier,*" which appeared in *English Literature in Transition.*

Richard Barbieri is executive director of the Independent School Association of Massachusetts, a regional association of 145 independent schools in Massachusetts and other New England states. He holds a Ph.D. degree in English from Harvard University. Mr. Barbieri writes a regular column and frequent articles for *Independent School* magazine and has contributed to *Educational Leadership, English Journal, Shakespeare Quarterly,* and other professional publications.

Rachel Phillips Belash is currently head of Miss Porter's School, Farmington, Connecticut, having been previously a college professor and banker. Her major field of study is Latin American literature, and she holds B.A. and M.A. degrees from Oxford University and a Ph.D. degree from the University of Kentucky. She continues to translate from Spanish and is also conducting research on the development of adolescent females.

William Bullard currently is the academic dean at San Francisco University High School. He received his B.A. degree from the College of Letters, Wesleyan University, and his Ph.D. degree from Boston College. Since his year as a Joseph Klingenstein Fellow, he has been actively involved in developing interdisciplinary curricula, with a particular interest in science and culture. His perspective on teaching in the independent school comes from fifteen years as an English teacher at Montclair Kimberley Academy in Montclair, New Jersey.

Michael S. Cary, after seven years as dean of admissions and financial aid, has returned to the classroom at Deerfield Academy, where he chairs the Philosophy and Religion Department. He was a Joseph Klingenstein Fellow at Teachers College, Columbia University, in 1980–81 and is the author of "The Case for the Humanities," which appeared in *Independent School.*

John E. Chubb, a senior fellow in the Governmental Studies Program at the Brookings Institution, received his A.B. degree from Washington University and his Ph.D. degree from the University of Minnesota, both in political science. He has written numerous books and articles on bureaucracy and public policy, including *Politics, Markets, and America's Schools* (1990, with Terry M. Moe).

James S. Coleman, whose Ph.D. degree in sociology is from Columbia University, is professor of sociology and education at the University of Chicago. His research has covered a number of areas in education, with his more recent books being *Public and Private Schools, Equality and Achievement in Education,* and *Foundations of Social Theory.*

Robert Coles is professor of psychiatry and medical humanities at Harvard University. He received his bachelor's degree from Harvard University and attended medical school at Columbia University's College of Physicians and Surgeons. He has written over forty books and articles including *The Call of Stories: Teaching and the Moral*

Imagination, Privileged Ones: The Well-Off and the Rich in America, and *The Moral Life of Children.*

Terrence E. Deal received his Ph.D. degree in educational administration and sociology from Stanford University and is professor of education and human development at Peabody College of Vanderbilt University. He serves as co-director of the National Center for Education Leadership and senior research associate at the Center for the Advanced Study of Education Leadership. His publications concern various organizational issues including change, culture, management, reform, symbolism, theater, and theory.

Maxine Greene is professor of philosophy and education (emerita) at Teachers College, Columbia University, where she still teaches courses in philosophy and the arts. She has her M.A. and Ph.D. degrees from New York University and holds honorary degrees from Lehigh University, Hofstra University, the University of Colorado, and Bank Street College. A past president of the Philosophy of Education Society and the American Educational Research Association, she has published numerous articles and books, the most recent of which is *The Dialectic of Freedom.*

Richard A. Hawley is the headmaster of Cleveland's University School, where he has taught since the fall of 1968. In addition to his work at the school, Hawley has taught and lectured extensively in the United States and Canada. He has written numerous works of poetry, nonfiction, and fiction, including the novels *Headmaster's Papers* and *Shining Still.*

Bill Honig is Superintendent of Public Instruction for the State of California. Reelected to his third four-year term in 1990, Honig is spearheading the state's massive educational reform effort. He received his B.A. and J.D. degrees from the University of California, Berkeley, and a master's degree in education from San Francisco State University. Honig is the author of *Last Chance for Our Children.*

John Irving is a renowned contemporary American novelist. His latest prize-winning novel, *A Prayer for Owen Meany,* was published in 1989. His earlier novels include such celebrated works as *The Hotel New Hampshire* and *The World According to Garp*. He currently lives in Sagaponack, Long Island, and in Toronto.

"Ishmael" is the pen name of a currently sitting headmaster who wishes to remain anonymous. This individual holds a B.A. degree from a prominent midwestern college, a master's degree from Dartmouth College, and the M.Ed. degree from Teachers College, Columbia University.

John B. Mason, dean of the faculty at the Tilton School, New Hampshire, was a Joseph Klingenstein Fellow at Teachers College, Columbia University. He earned degrees in mathematics from Manhattan College and Michigan State University and an M.A. degree in educational administration from Teachers College. His interests include organizational aspects of schools, leadership, faculty development, and educational philosophy.

Deborah W. Meier is the principal of Central Park East Secondary School in the East Harlem community of New York City. Meier has been instrumental in creating three alternative schools in New York City's District 4. She is dedicated to working to reform America's secondary education system. The Center for Collaborative Education, which she helped to create, is a coalition of New York City public schools that share a common goal: creating democratic and effective communities.

Terry M. Moe is professor of political science at Stanford University. He graduated from the University of California, San Diego, and pursued graduate work at the University of Minnesota in political science. His research is generally concerned with American political institutions, and he has written extensively on public bureaucracy, interest groups, the presidency, and the education system. Among his more recent publications is *Politics, Markets, and America's Schools,* which he coauthored with John E. Chubb.

Meg Milne Moulton, a graduate of Wheaton College, is a marketing and enrollment consultant specializing in independent schools.

Moulton has worked with individual independent schools and national organizations in understanding their marketplace and developing marketing, communications, and planning responses. She authored a National Association of Independent Schools–sponsored report entitled *Summary of Market Research Themes* and contributed to that organization's *Next Marketing Handbook.*

Kendra Stearns O'Donnell is the principal of Phillips Exeter Academy in Exeter, New Hampshire. O'Donnell graduated from Barnard College and holds an M.A. and a Ph.D. degree in English from Columbia University. Prior to becoming a head of school, she was an assistant professor at Princeton University and was involved in foundation work.

Diane Ravitch is assistant secretary for educational research and improvement in the U.S. Department of Education. She received a B.A. degree from Wellesley College and a Ph.D. degree in the history of American education from Columbia University. She has written or edited eleven books, including *The Troubled Crusade: American Education, 1945–1980* and *The American Reader: Words That Moved a Nation,* and has published numerous articles.

Bella Rosenberg is the assistant to the president of the American Federation of Teachers. Formerly a researcher at the National Institute of Education, Rosenberg has written about a variety of education policy issues. She graduated from Queens College in New York and completed graduate studies at the Harvard Graduate School of Education.

Kathryn S. Schiller is working on her Ph.D. degree in sociology at the University of Chicago. Her special interests are methodology and the sociology of education. She received her master's degree from the University of Chicago and her bachelor's degree from the University of Southern California. Before beginning graduate studies, Schiller covered local school boards and education issues for daily newspapers in Louisiana.

Albert Shanker is president of the 750,000-member American Federation of Teachers. A former schoolteacher, Shanker pursued his

graduate studies in philosophy at Columbia University and holds
a number of honorary doctorates. For twenty years, he has written
a weekly commentary on education that appears in the Sunday *New
York Times,* as well as numerous articles for popular and academic
journals and magazines.

Gary Simons is the founder and the executive director of Prep for
Prep, an organization that identifies talented minority students and
prepares them to succeed in competitive private schools. He earned
a B.A. degree in history from the State University of New York,
Binghamton, and an M.A. degree in psychology from Teachers College, Columbia University. He was a fellow in the Graduate Leadership Education project in the area of education for gifted and
talented youth and taught at a public elementary school in the
South Bronx for ten years.

E. M. Swift is a senior writer for *Sports Illustrated.* He attended the
Hotchkiss School in Lakeville, Connecticut, from 1965 to 1969,
where he was active in hockey, baseball, and football. He graduated
from Princeton University in 1973 and now lives in Carlisle,
Massachusetts.

Johanna Vega attended the Groton School from 1984 to 1989 and
is a recent graduate of Columbia College, where she majored in
comparative literature. Her future plans, yet undecided, might include journalism or teaching and graduate work in the fine arts.

Z. Vance Wilson is a novelist and an English instructor at Madison
Area Technical College in Madison, Wisconsin. He formerly taught
at two independent schools and holds degrees from Yale, the University of Virginia, and Trinity College, Dublin. He has written
Paths to a New Curriculum (1991, with Stephen C. Clem), *The
Quick and the Dead* (a novel, 1986), *They Took Their Stand* (1982),
short stories, and critical articles.

Independent
SCHOOLS

Independent
THINKERS

Part One

DIMENSIONS OF
INDEPENDENCE

A UNIVERSAL CHARACTERISTIC OF INDEPENDENT SCHOOLS, SINCE THE establishment of the early academies, is a romantic vision of the malleability of youth and a belief in a school's capacity to transform. Inherent in most mission statements and curricular requirements is an optimism about youth and a positive view of the power of schooling. Where the schools diverge is in their idea of the optimal setting for enacting that vision.

The chapters that follow focus on the characteristics that distinguish independent schools from public schools and on the different types of schools that have emerged to serve the needs and preferences of families. The authors, through their justification of the various kinds of schools and a description of their advantages, reveal that there is no one type of school that is best for all children. The availability of different kinds of schools allows parents to decide what is most suitable for their children.

In Chapter One, Pearl Rock Kane discusses the distinguishing features of contemporary independent schools—self-governance, self-support, self-defined curriculum, self-selected students, self-selected faculty, and small size. She describes the recent challenges to the financial viability of the schools, which affects their ability to fulfill a moral commitment to greater socioeconomic and ethnic diversity among students. The need to stay financially afloat has resulted in increased efforts to promote independent schools through sophisticated marketing techniques. The chapter addresses

1

the tension that can exist when schools seek to be both moral communities and successful businesses.

Writing on the role of nonpublic schools in the United States, Diane Ravitch, assistant secretary of education, describes the political and social changes that have precipitated a reassessment of the democratic rationale of public schools and created a favorable climate for private schools. Ravitch argues that decentralization and competition between schools are advantageous and that private schools have a special place in American education because they have the freedom to be different.

Richard Barbieri, executive director of the Massachusetts Association of Independent Schools, explores the differences among independent schools. Barbieri notes that the significant advantage of independent schools lies not in the fact that they do not have to conform to state mandates but in the fact that they are not obliged to please a wide audience. Since schools can determine their own mission, they can offer a special kind of education and need only find a sufficient number of students to fill the classrooms. The author traces the genesis of independent schools that do not fit stereotypical patterns and offers a theoretical justification for a diversity of schools. His article shows that the best-known schools may be the least representative.

Among the school types, boarding schools represent the quintessential independent school. What most distinguishes boarding schools is also most obvious: students live away from home, with adults who are not their parents, and with a large number of peers. To Kendra Stearns O'Donnell, head of Phillips Exeter Academy in New Hampshire, this basic difference illuminates the nature of life in these schools and their inherent challenges. Boarding schools can accomplish their objectives best, according to O'Donnell, if they are transformed into pluralistic communities. She urges schools to make use of the special opportunities for teaching and learning that communal living affords by becoming diverse.

Which environment is more suitable for the education of boys and girls, a single-sex or coeducational setting? Although gender is only one factor to be considered in selecting a school for a particular child, it is an important one. The four chapters on this subject provide different perspectives on the optimal environment. Recent research on the psychological development of girls and female adolescents has brought attention to the advantages of schools for girls. The case for girls' schools, according to Rachel Phillips Belash, head of Miss Porter's School in Connecticut, rests on a recognition that what is taught in schools and how it is taught have direct implications for self-image and personal development.

Richard A. Hawley, head of University School, an all-boys' school in Ohio, addresses the advantages of single-sex schools for boys. The issue of boys' schools has been virtually unexamined by scholars in recent decades, an oddity considering that most single-sex schools at the secondary and university levels have chosen to become coeducational institutions over the past two decades. Belash and Hawley's elucidation of the issues related to girls' and boys' development may influence families and schools considering coeducation.

Recently, two prestigious boys' schools that had resisted the movement to coeducation, Lawrenceville in New Jersey and Deerfield in Massachusetts, have opened their doors to girls. The Deerfield director of admissions, Michael S. Cary, traces the events that led to the decision to become coeducational and describes that transformation. The effects on the Deerfield community are still being felt. Cary notes that a sense of loss among alumni and some students is balanced by indications of increased self-awareness among students in the classroom and by the institutional benefit of an unprecedented number of students interested in admission to the academy.

The process of introducing coeducation at Lawrenceville lasted for two years, but the debate that preceded it preoccupied the school more than any other issue in its 175-year history, according to Lawrenceville's assistant head master, James T. Adams. The final decision to become coeducational was made with a genuine commitment to educate girls, not merely to enhance the education of boys, and involved a myriad of faculty committees to consider both obvious changes and concerns such as preserving traditions without alienating girls. The chapter describes how the school's hopes for an increase in applications for admissions were realized and how their fears about a deterioration in their athletic program and reduced support from alumni have proved unfounded.

The range of schools presented in this section is evidence that given autonomy and the freedom to define themselves, schools will evolve in unique ways. That freedom, however, is conditioned by the marketplace. As predominantly self-supporting institutions, independent schools need to be viable as well as visible so that they can attract an appropriate student body. A marketing approach applied to schools views education as a service industry and prompts schools to examine their purposes in light of existing and potential markets. Marketing consultant Meg Milne Moulton describes the demographic changes that have fueled current interest in marketing and the increasing need for schools to present themselves to a broader cross-section of families. For Moulton, marketing is imperative to the survival and success of independent schools.

1

What Is
an Independent School?

Pearl Rock Kane

If asked about independent schools, most people in the United
States would respond with confusion. The term has virtually no
recognition value among the general public. So, since independent
schools constitute only a small proportion of nongovernmental
schools, independent school educators often resort pragmatically to
self-definition by exclusion: independent schools are schools that
are nonpublic and nonparochial.

Though the term "private schools" embraces both independent and church-controlled schools, the public has a narrower and
quite definite conception of private schools, an image formed by
reading popular fiction and viewing films such as the recently ac-
claimed *Dead Poets Society*. The media have succeeded in giving
these schools an aura of exclusivity and elitism more in keeping
with the Edwardian world of "Masterpiece Theater" than with current reality. Many still believe that only children of well-to-do
Anglo-Saxon Protestants need apply. The roster of graduates from
independent schools also contributes to their reputation. Accomplished professionals, well-known statesmen, and literary figures
such as Edward Albee, George Bush, John Irving, John Fitzgerald

This chapter first appeared in the spring 1991 issue of *Teachers College
Record* (vol. 92, no. 3). Reprinted with permission.

Kennedy, John Knowles, Franklin Delano Roosevelt, Arthur Schle-
singer, Jr., and Gore Vidal are only a few of such distinguished
graduates. The popular success of these schools is disproportionate
to their numbers: although there are approximately 1,500 independent schools in the United States, that is a small number in comparison to public or parochial schools. Moreover, the reputation is
formed from stereotyped images of a few prestigious northeastern
schools whose origins date back to the eighteenth and nineteenth
centuries. In fact, independent schools are quite diverse in their
educational missions, as diverse in character as any comparable
number of U.S. citizens—and like those citizens, most independent
schools were born in the twentieth century. It is that very diversity
that leads independent school educators to resort to definition by
exclusion, simply because it is easier than trying to create a definition broad enough to include all these schools and succinct enough
to satisfy the casual inquirer.[1]

This chapter has two purposes: to describe the characteristics
that distinguish independent schools from public and other private
schools and to point to both self-imposed and environmental challenges that are confronting the schools in the 1990s.

Characteristics of Independent Schools

Although the conditions of the marketplace shape independent schools, they have been relatively free to define themselves. A
tremendous range of schools has evolved, varying in philosophy,
organization, and style. Some schools are highly traditional, others
are progressive in outlook; some are boarding schools, some day
schools, some a combination of the two; some are single-sex, some
coeducational; some are highly academic and selective, others are
"second chance" schools for students who have failed elsewhere;
some are free or inexpensive, some have sliding scales of tuition
depending on the income of applying families, some have extensive
scholarship programs, and some are prohibitively costly, accessible
only to the affluent; some have the stability of generations of graduates, others have graduated only a few classes; some have impressive financial endowments and extensive resources in buildings and

grounds, others have recourse only to income from tuition and annual fund raising and operate in modest or even makeshift spaces.

However varied they are in their objectives and approaches, all independent schools share six basic characteristics: self-governance, self-support, self-defined curriculum, self-selected students, self-selected faculty, and small size.[2]

Self-Governance. A self-selecting and thus self-perpetuating board of trustees bears ultimate responsibility for an independent school's philosophy, resources, and program. Though an independent school may have a religious affiliation, it is the independence of the board of trustees that distinguishes it from a parochial school, which is ultimately subordinate to a church hierarchy. The trustees choose the chief administrator, to whom are delegated all aspects of the day-to-day operation of the school.

Self-governance results in responsiveness to the particular needs of the individual school and freedom from the bureaucratic intrusion by local, state, and federal governments that often comes with financial aid. A metaphor comparing the structure of public and private institutions is found in Gerald Grant's essay "The Character of Education and the Education of Character." Grant compares the contemporary public school to a watermelon: the thick rind represents the accretion of bureaucracy, court orders, union contracts, and measures of accountability that constrain the rightful use of power; the dispersion of such power is like the dispersion of the watermelon's seeds—there is no clearly definable center. He compares the private school to an avocado, where adult power and initiative are akin to the large seed at the center and there is only a thin skin of externally imposed policy.[3]

In independent schools, which are free of even the centralized bureaucracy present in denominational schools, there is significant autonomy in shaping the institution. The absence of bureaucracy has allowed a more fluid organization where the roles of administrators and teachers are less rigidly prescribed. Many administrators have regular teaching responsibility, and many teachers do administrative work as department heads, admissions officers, or college counselors. The blurring of lines between administrators and teachers may explain why most independent school teachers have not chosen an affiliation with a national labor organization. As a result, most independent schools have been unencumbered by the union-sponsored restrictions of tenure and collective bargaining.

Self-Support. Incorporated as not-for-profit, tax-exempt corporations, independent schools rely primarily on tuition for support, supplemented by gifts from parents, alumni and alumnae, foundations, corporations, and (for some) income from an endowment. Most independent schools are not eligible for significant financial assistance from local, state, or federal agencies. Although aid is sometimes available for books and equipment and, in many states, for transportation and mandated state services such as attendance monitoring, independent schools are cautious about accepting government subsidies because they pose a threat to self-governance.

That primary dependence on tuition is responsible for the high cost of independent schools, nationally averaging $7,700 a year for day schools and $14,700 for boarding schools.[4] Those figures reflect the expense of maintaining elaborate facilities, a commitment to low student-teacher ratios, and a recent impetus to increase faculty salaries.

Such high tuitions limit the ability of independent schools to shape the social composition of the student body, tending to favor the economically advantaged. This tendency leads to charges that independent schools are elitist. It is often overlooked that many public schools are less racially and economically diverse than independent schools. Since public school districts are organized within geographic areas, attendance at a particular school is determined by residence. In many affluent communities such as Greenwich, Connecticut, or Newport Beach, California, where the average cost of houses is over half a million dollars, only families that can afford to purchase these expensive houses can send their children to the local public school. The result is that the schools are white, upper-class institutions with little diversity. In affluent communities, private schools are often more diverse than the local public schools because the private schools recruit from a wider geographic area.

Even with public and private schools that are alike in student composition, dependence on tuition in lieu of funding from the government—that is, reliance on paying customers—adds an important difference to the way the schools operate and respond to constituents. Independent schools must satisfy their clients, and they are obliged to demonstrate successful outcomes. Driven both by such economic imperatives and by a philosophical belief in the primacy of the individual's development as an educational goal, independent schools make a commitment to nurture the students they admit. These schools give personal attention to each student and are determined to help each student achieve personal success. Faculty struggle with reluctant students, and, despite popular misconceptions, relatively few students are asked to leave. However, since progress with students is hard to assess individually, the educational achievement of these schools is often measured indirectly, and perhaps unfairly, by the record of admission of graduates to competitive colleges. To the degree that college admission is the dominant client interest, the tuition dependence of independent schools may pressure them away from individualization of instruction that does not directly serve this end.

Self-Defined Curriculum. Each independent school designs its own curriculum, and many independent schools use curricula or books espousing a particular value orientation—for instance, in moral education or in the theory of evolution. Such materials might not be permitted in public schools. The majority of those having a secondary division offer college preparatory programs.

Though free to experiment, most independent schools offer a curriculum that is highly academic and rigorous. Even the so-called second chance schools focus on preparation for college. There is a basic emphasis on English, history, languages, mathematics, and sciences, and because of the small size of most independent schools, a limited range of courses is available to students within these academic areas. The academic, college preparatory orientation allows for cohesiveness in the curriculum, but it usually confines electives to academic offerings and eliminates options for students to take technical and vocational courses, which are regular fare at public schools.[5]

In some states, independent schools are required to include mandated courses, such as the history of the region, or more conventional courses such as American history or algebra. While these are subjects that the schools would choose to teach on their own, most independent schools are not bound by rigid state regulations to teach a specified curriculum. The schools align themselves in state and national organizations to ensure that curricular freedom is maintained, and many schools ignore with impunity the requirements that do pertain.

One of the factors that stimulates faculty intellectually is the continuous assessment and discussion of curriculum that transpires within these schools. The autonomy of the individual teacher to select texts, alone or in consultation within a department, is a key advantage independent schools have over public schools in the attraction of academically oriented teachers. Putting curriculum in the hands of teachers in the school provides a kind of staff development that is not possible if the curriculum is both predetermined and decided outside of the school.

The explicit curriculum has two other facets that are equally emphasized and interconnected: physical development and the overriding goal of character development. Character, or moral development, is nurtured through academics, including courses in religion and ethics that public schools cannot offer. Moral education is also pursued through an extensive program of cultural and athletic activities. In many schools, particularly boarding schools, athletic competition is structured into the school day. Coaching is done by the academic faculty as a way to emphasize that the mind and body work together and that learning takes place on the field as well as in the classroom. [6]

Self-Selected Students. Although market conditions cause schools to raise or lower their standards of admission, independent schools are at liberty to select the kind of students the school believes will benefit from the type of education program offered.

Student selection implies mutual selection: the school chooses the student, but the student also chooses the school. There is a psychological advantage to such voluntarism. Although a study of attrition conducted in 1988 showed that only 2 percent of all students in independent schools were asked to leave for academic or disciplinary reasons, the knowledge that their independent school is not obliged to keep them is likely to have an effect on academic and social behavior. Conversely, the school knows the students may decide not to stay and finds that fact similarly motivating. Beyond the financial contract that exists between the family and the school, there is an unwritten agreement. As Otto Kraushaar has pointed out, "Both the patrons and the school have a stake in seeing that the contract is fulfilled satisfactorily." Mutual freedom of association by students and schools is fundamental to the sense of community that shapes the educational effectiveness of independent schools.[7]

Self-Selected Faculty. Each independent school develops its own criteria for hiring faculty, and, in all but a few states, independent schools are not bound by requirements for teacher certification. Independent schools have latitude in staffing, determining the background and competencies of faculty members they want. In keeping with the academic orientation of independent schools, there is a strong preference, particularly at the secondary level, for teachers with undergraduate and graduate majors in the liberal arts and sciences and for teachers who have demonstrated academic achievement by success at colleges with competitive admissions standards. Similarly, these graduates of highly academic colleges may be drawn to independent schools where students are preparing for college.[8]

Most independent school teachers have not taken the education courses necessary for certification to teach in public schools and may regard such courses as of lesser intellectual merit than courses in their academic fields. The schools, too, are not convinced that professional preparation in education is necessary. With the exception of training in early childhood education, many independent school administrators believe that pedagogy is a skill that can be learned on the job. Most schools supply only limited assistance in learning to teach, and young teachers learn the ropes informally from other teachers or by trial and error.[9]

This distinction between the preparation and academic orientation of public and independent school teachers, together with differences in working conditions and curricular freedom, may in part explain why teachers are willing to work in independent schools for less pay than they would receive in the public sector. It has certainly contributed to the reluctance of independent school teachers to affiliate themselves with public school teachers through unionization. Although a few schools have internal teacher associations that negotiate salary and benefits, the absence of union affiliation has allowed independent schools both to contain salaries and to maintain the freedom to dismiss unsatisfactory teachers without the elaborate procedures of public schools. That freedom of disassociation is seen by independent school administrators as essential to the educational effectiveness of their schools. The freedom to fail is, for independent school teachers, the price of the freedom to teach.

Small Size. Typically small, with a median student enrollment of 321, independent schools resist going beyond a specified size, regardless of the quality of the applicant pool or the number of candidates vying for admission.[10]

When the heads of New York City independent schools were invited to discuss ways to improve public schools with Mayor Edward Koch, they were unanimous in their focus on reducing school size. The average size of a public secondary school, for example, is more than twice the size of the average independent school, and class size is also significantly larger. Independent schools have, on average, six students for every full-time faculty member, fewer than half of the student load of public and Catholic school teachers. Despite having smaller classes and fewer students, independent school teachers report spending more time on the job than their public school colleagues, providing assistance to students, planning lessons, and grading papers.[11]

There is an important consequence of small size for the average student. Several researchers have argued that independent schools provide the optimal learning environment for such students, those who are neither top academic achievers nor in need of special support services. Public schools have accommodated those students with abilities on the ends of the achievement spectrum, or those with special needs. Independent schools provide the elements of "personalization" and "push," which are effective in motivating these "unspecial" students in the middle, who would not receive extra attention in a comprehensive public school.[12]

As Leonard Baird has pointed out, it is unlikely that students in independent schools can become like the "socially invisible nonpersons" who pass through large public schools.[13] Smaller schools also allow for increased student participation in extracurricular activities—athletics, clubs, student government, dramatic productions—which give students opportunities for leadership. Parents who claim to be sending their children to independent schools because of the personal attention afforded their youngsters and the opportunities to participate in the life of the school appear to be getting what they pay for.

Future Challenges

Critics of independent schools have argued that these schools are nothing more than "status seminaries" that furnish upper-class youth with the cultural capital they will need to assume elite-group membership.[14] Traditionally, independent schools have served a homogeneous, affluent stratum of the population, but there are indications of change. Independent schools are accepting the challenge to open their doors to a more ethnically and socioeconomically diverse student body. This could be a result of several factors: the economic imperative to fill seats at a time when demographic shifts have created a precipitous drop in the number of school-age children available; a desire to set up a more socially equitable school community that reflects American society; or a response to the threat that public school reform is imposing.

Demographic Change. Nationally, demographic trends have a great impact on schools. The number of school-age children in the population began to decline in the early 1970s. Despite two decades of declining population, independent school enrollment has been relatively stable. Although the population trend is beginning to reverse itself as a baby boomlet that started in the 1980s begins to increase elementary school enrollments, schools will face a new challenge. Demographer Harold Hodgkinson predicts that by the year 2000, America will be a nation in which one of every three people will be nonwhite and many will be living at the poverty level.[15]

A Commitment to Diversity. The number of students of color in independent schools has increased slowly but steadily over the past two decades, up from 5 percent to an average of 13 percent in 1991. In schools with greater financial resources available, the percentage is even higher. For instance, at Phillips Academy in Andover, Massachusetts, students of color represented 24 percent of the student body in 1991–92. One symbolic and important indication of the independent school commitment to diversity is the increased activity at the Office of Diversity and Multicultural Affairs of the National Association of Independent Schools (NAIS), whose responsibility it is to promote cultural diversity among the faculty and students of independent schools and to provide resources for the development of multicultural curricula. [16]

As the proportion of minority students has increased, many schools have come to understand that the responsibility for the students they recruit does not end at the admissions office door. Independent schools are becoming sensitive to the needs of students of color in schools that have been unaccustomed to having them and unprepared to meet their needs. Some schools have hired minority coordinators and counselors to assist students of color in adjusting to schools where pressure to achieve is great and social discomfort may be a reality. Attention is also being directed to modifications in the curriculum to allow for a multicultural perspective that includes different voices and a broader conception of education.

This more receptive outlook of the schools has attracted a small number of children of color from middle- and upper-income families. However, since most students of color are recruited from lower socioeconomic groups and must rely on financial aid, further confirmation that the clientele of the so-called elite schools is changing may be gauged by the overall amount of scholarship aid granted. Total financial aid granted by schools that are members of the National Association of Independent Schools increased by 72 percent (50 percent in constant dollars) between 1984 and 1989. In the academic year 1990–91, 33 percent of all need-based scholarships were granted to children of color, averaging $5,838 per student. In schools with greater financial resources, financial aid has been even more generous. At Phillips Exeter Academy in New Hampshire, for example, 30 percent of students receive aid, with grants averaging $11,300 per student. [17]

There is evidence that parents who send their children to independent schools are not merely motivated by the perpetuation of old school ties. According to Leonard Baird, who surveyed the most prestigious independent schools, students at the elite schools do not come primarily from "power elite" families, although most are clearly from upper-middle-class and upper-class homes, and there are not significant numbers of alumni children. [18] As the number of dual-career families increases and there is greater disposable income, independent schools may be attractive to a larger number of middle- and upper-income families willing to pay for the kind of education these schools provide.[19] With a greater commitment to both ethnic and socioeconomic diversity, there will be a need to increase financial aid while keeping the costs of tuition within the range families are able to pay.

Public School Reform. Since the early 1980s, improving our nation's public schools has moved to the top of the political agenda. Several widespread reforms—those specifically aimed at attracting higher-caliber teachers and giving parents choice among public schools—have direct implications for independent schools. Modifications in state teacher certification have made it easier for liberal arts graduates to enter public schools. In former years, liberal arts graduates who wanted to enter teaching—even graduates of highly competitive colleges—were forced to teach in private schools if they were unwilling to undergo the expensive and lengthy preparation for state certification. It turns out that public schools are now seeking the bright young people whose undergraduate preparation includes a focus on the liberal arts and a major in an academic discipline, the kinds of teachers who traditionally have been attracted to independent schools. Higher salaries and improved working conditions may make the incentives to work in public schools even more appealing. Independent schools have responded modestly to the challenge of increased public school salaries, but as the differentials increase, the schools will have to find greater resources to compete effectively with the public schools.

Choice among public schools—for example, in the magnet-school movement—may provide another challenge to independent school stability. Parents who can choose schools within or outside their district are no longer restricted to deciding between a neighborhood school and a private school. As the magnet-school movement grows, independent schools will be obliged to demonstrate that they are providing something different, or something special, to make the choice of paying tuition worthwhile.

Responses to the Challenge

The collective response in meeting a commitment to diversity in the face of a declining school-age population and a more positive outlook for public schools and public school teaching has been to increase efforts to promote independent schools. Many schools are producing expensive catalogues and videotapes, and some are hiring enrollment and admissions consultants or adding staff to admissions offices to do more intensive recruiting. Day schools estimated spending $400, and boarding schools more than $500, to recruit each new student in 1989 exclusive of the costs of admissions staff salaries.[20] Although many schools have found a consumerist approach objectionable in the past, the marketing orientation and the escalation of marketing expenditures may become a necessary approach to keep independent schools financially viable. Rick Cowan, director of boarding schools at NAIS, says, "It is a different, more competitive world and probably will remain so. . . . The 'market race' is likely to become a permanent feature of the educational landscape." The objective, according to Cowan, is to emerge with stronger enrollments and higher standards.[21]

If the description of independent schools offered here is accurate, then the popular conception of independent schools as exclusive, tradition-bound places that educate the aristocracy to take their place in society appears to be both inaccurate and untenable. The question of definition for independent schools in the 1990s may be reconciling, on the one hand, a profound self-conception as moral communities striving to institute social change through enhanced ethnic and socioeconomic diversity with, on the other hand, the pressures of marketing and the escalation of financial costs. The tension between moral mission and financial necessity has always been present for independent schools, but the moral mission has never been more demanding nor has the market been more unforgiving. Can independent schools be those moral communities and also be successful businesses, driven by a need to stay competitive in the face of multiple challenges?

As open systems, sensitive to environmental conditions, independent schools will no doubt be shaped in unprecedented and unpredictable ways in the next few decades. However, the characteristics that distinguish independent schools—self-governance, self-support, self-defined curriculum, self-selected students, self-selected faculty, and small size—provide a strong ethos of personalization and an orientation toward academic success that is not likely to be changed.

Notes

1. The independent schools described here do not include Montessori schools, special education schools, home schools, or street academies.
2. The National Association of Independent Schools lists five features of independent schools: governance, finances, curriculum, student selection, and faculty selection (*A Career in Independent School Teaching* [Boston: NAIS, 1984], pp. 5–7).
3. Gerald Grant, "The Character of Education and the Education of Character," *Daedalus* 110, no. 3 (Summer 1981): 135–49.
4. Median tuition costs are reported for 895 members of the National Association of Independent Schools (95 percent reporting) in National Association of Independent Schools, *NAIS Statistics 1990–1991* 1 (Boston: NAIS, 1990), p. 3.
5. James S. Coleman, Thomas Hoffer, and Sally Kilgore, *High School Achievement: Public, Catholic, and Private Schools Compared* (New York: Basic Books, 1982), pp. 73–78.
6. Pearl R. Kane, *Teachers in Public and Independent Schools: A Comparative Study* (New York: Esther A. and Joseph Klingenstein Center for Independent School Education, 1986), pp. 41–42.
7. Percentages of attrition based on a study of over 400 National Association of Independent Schools member schools, in NAIS Admission Services, "Survey of Student Attrition in Independent Schools: 1987–1988" (Boston: NAIS, 1989); and Otto F. Kraushaar, *American Nonpublic Schools: Patterns of Diversity* (Baltimore: Johns Hopkins University Press, 1972), p. 93.
8. Telephone survey conducted with administrators in independent schools in New Jersey, February to April 1988; and Kane, *Teachers in Public and Independent Schools*, pp. 21–25.
9. Kane, *Teachers in Public and Independent Schools*, pp. 31–35.
10. Median student enrollment based on a sample of 895 members

of the National Association of Independent Schools, *NAIS Statistics 1990-1991* 2 (Boston: NAIS, 1991), p. 7.

11.   Meeting with Mayor Edward Koch, January 12, 1988, New York City. For student-teacher ratio, see Coleman, Hoffer, and Kilgore, *High School Achievement*, pp. 78-81; for a comparison of the work life of public and private school teachers, see Kane, *Teachers in Public and Independent Schools*, pp. 36-48.

12.   Arthur G. Powell, Eleanor Farrar, and David K. Cohen, *The Shopping Mall High School: Winners and Losers in the Educational Marketplace* (Boston: Houghton Mifflin, 1985), pp. 207-32.

13.   Leonard Baird, "Elite Schools: Recent Research from the Outside and from the Inside" (Paper presented at the annual conference of the American Educational Research Association, Washington, D.C., April 1987), p. 3.

14.   Peter W. Cookson, Jr., and Caroline Hodges Persell, *Preparing for Power: America's Elite Boarding Schools* (New York: Basic Books, 1985), pp. 22-30.

15.   Harold L. Hodgkinson, *All One System: Demographics of Education, Kindergarten Through Graduate School* (New York: Institute for Educational Leadership, 1985), pp. 3-10.

16.   Statistics on students of color at Phillips Academy based on telephone interview with Robert A. Edwards, assistant director of admissions and director of recruitment of people of color, Phillips Academy, July 18, 1991; and national percentages of students of color reported are for 895 members of the National Association of Independent Schools, *NAIS Statistics* 2, p. 15.

17.   Barbara L. Schneider and Diana T. Slaughter, "Educational Choice for Blacks in Urban Private Elementary Schools," in *Comparing Public and Private Schools*, ed. Thomas James and Henry Levin (London: Falmer Press, 1988), v. 1, pp. 294-310; data on scholarship aid in Peter Aiken, National Association of Independent Schools Promoting Independent Education Project, *Briefing*, no. 4, 1991; telephone interview with Paul R. Mahoney, Director of Financial Aid, Phillips Exeter Academy, July 15, 1991.

18.   Leonard L. Baird, *The Elite Schools: A Profile of Prestigious*

Independent Schools (Lexington, Mass.: D. C. Heath, 1977), p. 10.

19. There has been a rising mean income in real terms and more families in which spouses are working. Adjusted to 1989 dollars, family income has increased for families in the 60 percent to 80 percent quintile: 1970, $42,230; 1980, $43,775; 1989, $49,213. There has also been a steady stream into the work force of wives with children: 1970, 39.3 percent; 1980, 50.2 percent; 1989, 57.7 percent. Data compiled from the following three publications of the U.S. Bureau of Census: "Money, Income and Poverty Status in the U.S., 1989" (Series P-60, no. 168) (Washington, D.C.: 1990), p. 30; "Income in 1970: Families and Persons in the U.S., 1971" (Series P-60, no. 80) (Washington, D.C.: 1972), p. 33; "Money Income of Households, Families, and Persons in the U.S., 1980" (Series P-60, no. 132) (Washington, D.C.: 1982), p. 81.

20. Maguire Associates, Enrollment Management Consultants Division, "National Survey of Independent School Admissions Officers" (Concord, Mass.: Maguire Associates, 1990).

21. Rick Cowan, "The Marketing Race," *Administrative Forum,* Spring 1987: 1-3. Marketing costs based on estimates reported by a national sample of 84 independent schools in Maguire Associates, "National Survey of Independent School Admissions Officers."

2

The Role of Private Schools
in American Education

Diane Ravitch

When I was growing up in Houston and attending public school, I hardly knew anyone who went to nonpublic school. There were two kinds of students who attended nonpublic schools: the rich and the incorrigible. For the rich, there were two private schools in town; the incorrigible were sent away to military schools, where, according to local lore, they got "straightened out." One of my five brothers was sent away to military school, but he didn't get "straightened out." Perhaps there were religious schools as well, but I was not aware of them. What I did know, because I heard it from my parents and teachers and in school assemblies, was that public schools were the best expression of American democracy and that deviations from that norm were only for snobs and misfits. So long as I lived in Houston, this seemed to be incontestable. I did not realize it at the time, but I was enmeshed in a world view that had a long history and many adherents. I later discovered articles written after World War II with titles like "Our Public Schools Kept Us Free," insinuating that those who did not attend public school were not really committed to a free society. Today one of my prized possessions is a large antique poster that displays a one-room red

This chapter first appeared in the spring 1991 issue of *Teachers College Record* (vol. 92, no. 3). Reprinted with permission.

schoolhouse and says, "Our Public School—the Bulwark of This Country."

Now, on the occasions when the relative virtues of public and private schooling are contrasted, one hears only faint echoes of that perfervid point of view. There are fewer true believers than there were a generation ago. The public schools continue to be an institution of great importance and value in our society, but seldom is it even hinted that nonpublic schools are divisive and that their graduates are unpatriotic. In part, the rise of demands for choice, tuition tax credits, vouchers, and other means to break the public school monopoly indicates a changed political climate. Partisans of nonpublic schooling no longer feel embarrassed to plead their case for tax dollars, and their appeal is clearly reaching an audience that goes far beyond the relatively small number of parents whose children are in nonpublic schools.

The reason for this change in the debate is that the public schools are no longer icons in the nation's civil religion. For many years, their supporters heaped extravagant praise on them, claiming that they and they alone had unified the nation, taught everyone a common language, prepared a work force for a mighty industrial machine, developed a high level of democratic citizenship, and provided equal opportunity to all. They were the guarantors of social stability and the path to social mobility. If the public schools had been able to deliver on all of these promises, no one would ever have challenged their dominance.

But the schools were effectively demythologized during the last generation by racial upheavals, by court decisions that held them guilty of intentional racial segregation, by a rising tide of ethnic particularism, by the declining legitimacy of a high school diploma in the workplace, by scholarly and journalistic criticism, and by the burden of their own claims. Free public education was an unquestioned boon for poor European immigrants, who came from lands where political and religious oppression denied many of them access to schooling. But large numbers of these immigrants stayed in school only long enough to become literate in English. The doors of opportunity were wide open, but the dropout rate (a modern invention) was high, as was the failure rate.

In the inflamed political atmosphere of the late 1960s and

early 1970s, the public schools were accused of every kind of evil: not only had they failed to do what they promised, but they were *designed* to fail, *designed* to oppress those who were failing. Instead of gaining credit for teaching a common language, they were lambasted for failing to preserve the native language and culture of their millions of pupils. Instead of winning applause for unifying a diverse nation, they were blasted for attempting to destroy ethnic diversity. Pity the poor public school: once the embodiment of virtue in our civil religion, it became a favorite target of neo-Marxists and other radical pedagogues, who characterized it as the instrument of a class conspiracy to repress the children of workers, minorities, and the poor. From archangel to archenemy in one generation!

There were many consequences of this harsh debunking of the public schools, some of which linger in our public policy debates. One was the rehabilitation of the reputation of nonpublic schools. To those who despised the bureaucracy, the uniformity, and the sameness of public education, the preferred alternative was schools that were not controlled by the state. In the early 1970s, the radical school movement created hundreds, perhaps thousands, of small alternative private schools. In poor inner-city neighborhoods, community activists opened storefront academies to vie with the public schools. Suddenly, private schools were on the cutting edge of change.

Meanwhile, certain sectors of the middle class abandoned public education. The growth of fundamentalist sects led to a corresponding growth in Christian day schools, mainly in the South. Also in the South, "segregation academies" opened in the wake of desegregation orders. In the Northeast, Orthodox Jewish sects created an extensive network of yeshivas, or religious day schools. Wherever there was a well-to-do black community, in cities like Washington, D.C., and New York, black parents took advantage of declining racial prejudice to place their children in good private schools.

At the same time, Catholic schools, which traditionally had enrolled the great majority of students in nonpublic schools, experienced declining enrollments. As Catholics became more prosperous and left the cities, urban Catholic schools had fewer Catholic children to draw on. Furthermore, the church had fewer religious teachers with which to staff the schools, and lay teachers drove up costs. But although Catholic schools struggled to maintain themselves, hostility towards parochial education abated, in part because tensions between Catholics and Protestants decreased, but also because it was evident that graduates of Catholic schools were just as civic-minded and just as well-educated as graduates of public schools.

By 1981, when President Ronald Reagan advocated tuition tax credits and others urged the creation of vouchers to subsidize the cost of private education, the support for these proposals was far broader than the 12-14 percent of the population that used private schools. Critics complained that it was wrong to permit tuition tax credits or to allocate funds for vouchers, and they offered a variety of reasons. It was wrong, they said, because such policies would violate the constitutional ban on funding religion; or because they would encourage racial segregation; or because they would favor the well-to-do over the poor; or because they would be too costly to the public budget. But scarcely anyone said that they should be defeated because public schools were better than private schools or because public schools were the apotheosis of American ideals. The most interesting aspect of the entire discussion was that the millenarian, patriotic rhetoric once associated with public education had virtually disappeared from the debate. To my knowledge, no one claimed that the American democratic way of life would be irreparably damaged if vouchers or tuition tax credits were approved.

At present, there seems little interest in government funding of private schools, largely because of the likelihood that the Supreme Court would not permit public funds to go to private schools. But a change in the membership of the Court could cause that issue to rise again. And potential changes in technology and in where schooling will take place in the future suggest that the present definition of a public school may once again be challenged.

I personally have doubts about the use of public funds for private education, but I confess that I waver in my convictions. I cannot rationally explain why tax dollars support college and graduate students who attend private institutions but cannot support students in private schools. Yet I worry that federal funding might someday lead to intrusive regulation of a sort that would deprive private education of the very qualities that give it value. Traditionally, there has been little regulation of higher education, no matter how many tax dollars it absorbs; and also traditionally, the secondary schools that receive public dollars are accustomed to close regulation by the state.

As it happens, many states already regulate important aspects of private schools, such as the qualifications of their teachers. But at present, private schools continue to enjoy a good deal of autonomy. Although there are exceptions, they are relatively free to design their own curriculum, hire the teachers of their choice (even if they don't have any education credits), select their own textbooks, create their own tests, and establish their own rules for student conduct. They may require their students to wear uniforms or they may have no dress code at all; if they have more applicants than places, they may admit whomever they wish, and they may suspend or expel students who violate the school's rules. Private schools are the exemplars of school-based management.

Being private precludes access to public funds, but it does have its benefits. When James Coleman compared private and public schools, he pointed out that the Catholic schools were less likely to have vocational programs and to track students, because they could not afford the equipment and the extra staff. So, for economy's sake, most children in Catholic schools are in an academic program, which produces higher achievement in the long run for children of comparable ability.[1] Catholic and independent schools do not have bureaucracies like public schools because they don't need them and can't afford them. Since they do not get public funds, they do not have administrators to coordinate the many different federal and state programs. In a private school, there are few staff members who do not teach.

But why should there be private schools at all? Why not require all children to attend public schools, so that none can gain special advantages from a private education and none can be excluded from the reach of public policy? If equity were the only value that counted in our society, then private schools might cease to exist. But equity is not the only value that counts in our society.

Down that path lies the danger of standardization, homogeneity, and uniformity.

The Supreme Court considered this issue in 1925, in the *Pierce* v. *Society of Sisters* decision. The Court invalidated an Oregon law requiring all children to attend public schools. The impetus for this law came from nativists who wanted faster assimilation of foreign-born children and feared that a private school education would allow them to remain "un-Americanized." The Court ruled that Oregon had unreasonably interfered "with the liberty of parents and guardians to direct the upbringing and education of children under their control." The Court further held that "the fundamental theory of liberty upon which all governments in this Union repose excludes any general power of the State to standardize its children by forcing them to accept instruction from public teachers only. The child is not the mere creature of the State."[2]

In a free society, parents and guardians have the right to send their children to schools that are not controlled by the state. Interestingly, as the democratic movement spread through Eastern Europe in the 1980s, democratic reformers complained about the complete monopoly of education by the omnipotent state. They realized that control of the schools by the state bureaucracy and imposition of the state's official ideology were linchpins of the Communists' efforts to regulate thought. As Poles and other East Europeans considered how to reconstruct their societies along democratic lines, one of the problems they confronted was the corruption of state schools into vehicles for political propaganda. As they go about the business of creating democratic institutions, it is likely that they will permit religious organizations to open their own schools, if they wish. They will do this not in order to promote religion but in order to promote divergent thinking, independent centers of thought and activity removed from state control.

Perhaps the most important lesson to be learned from the Communist debacle in Eastern Europe is that democracy flourishes when government power is broadly decentralized. A free press—free newspapers, free magazines, free television stations, free radio, and free publishing houses—is vital in order to inform public opinion and to encourage unfettered thought. Like a free press, the other institutions of democracy—an independent judiciary, independent religious groups, free trade unions, and so on—act as checks on the power of government.

In education, as in every other aspect of social life, competition and decentralization are positive goods. In this society, everyone has an obligation to support public education because it is provided on equal terms to all children. All are not, however, obligated to send their children to public schools. The public schools benefit by the diversity that private education encourages. We look to private education for the off-beat schools, for schools that are out of step with conventional thinking. Some private schools will be experimental and take risks. Some will offer a kind of rigorous academic curriculum that has virtually disappeared from public education. Others will find their own way of diverging from the mainstream.

It is, in short, their diversity that we value, for private education—whether religious or secular—has the freedom to be different. Whether it is a progressive school like England's Summerhill (and its American clones) or a traditional Catholic school staffed by old-fashioned nuns, the private school has a special niche in American education. Eliminating private schools, even if it were constitutionally permissible, would weaken American education.

Thoreau advised us to be tolerant of the man who hears a different drummer. In private education, there are many who hear different drummers—religious and secular, progressive and conservative, dogmatic and freethinking, odd and staid. For their own reasons, they do not wish their children to receive what the state offers them at no charge. For their own reasons, they choose to be different. It may be time to acknowledge that the private sector in education, in all its diversity, has helped to keep us free.

Notes

1. James S. Coleman, Thomas Hoffer, and Sally Kilgore, *High School Achievement: Public, Catholic, and Private Schools Compared* (New York: Basic Books, 1982), p. 78.
2. *Pierce* v. *Society of Sisters of the Holy Name*, 268 U.S. 510 (1925).

3

Different Forms of Independent Education

Richard Barbieri

From the pranksters of Owen Johnson's *Lawrenceville Stories,* through the fifties portrayals of Pencey Prep and Devon School by J.D. Salinger and John Knowles, to the more recent depictions in *The World According to Garp* and *Dead Poets Society,* Americans have ingested a picture of the independent school that is consistent and narrow. Most often a boarding school, this male institution is populated by jacketed-and-tied youths who exhibit varying degrees of arrogance over or rebelliousness toward their privileged state. Moving among playing fields, classrooms where literature or history are discussed in small groups, and dormitory bull sessions or illicit nighttime escapades, these young men rehearse for war or Wall Street, or for opposition to the cultural values of the American upper class.

Whatever truth this picture may have possessed in the first half of the twentieth century, its accuracy diminishes almost daily in the independent school world as single-sex and boarding schools continue to decline in proportion to coeducational and day schools, and as independent schools capitalize on their freedom to educate selectively in order to become more different from each other and from the comprehensive public school.

Describing the varieties of independent education must begin, unfortunately, with a clarification of terminology. The term *inde-*

27

pendent school is itself somewhat unclear. In theory, it applies to
any school governed by a board of trustees. The National Association of Independent Schools (NAIS), for example, uses the very
broad phrase "responsible governance" and explains that this term
is "usually interpreted to mean that it has a board of directors and
that it operates with authority independent of a religious institution."[1] But independent schools are commonly included as part of
a tripartite public/parochial/independent division, which confuses
funding methods, curricular content, and administrative structure.
Many independent schools are religiously affiliated, for example,
with Episcopal and Quaker schools clearly falling well within the
accepted independent school definition, while some Roman Catholic schools lie within the field and most lie outside it. Even less
likely to be considered in the independent school fold, despite similarities of governance, are Jewish, Lutheran, and fundamentalist
Christian schools. The National Association of Independent
Schools, for example, has 912 member schools, of which 27 percent
are religiously affiliated; exactly half of these are Episcopal
schools.[2] State and regional independent school associations, on the
other hand, although closely connected to NAIS, tend to have many
more members; the fourteen East Coast associations alone possess
over 1,000 members. Some classes of trustee-governed schools, such
as Schechter, Waldorf, and Montessori schools, are rarely represented in organizations of independent schools outside their own
national or regional networks. For this chapter's purposes, independent schools will be interpreted according to their governance and
will include types of schools represented within the national and
regional associations but widely found outside of these organizations as well.

     If categorizing schools as independent is itself complex, the
challenge of developing a taxonomy of independent schools' variety
is even more daunting, for the scalpel of division has so many lines
along which to cut. Schools can be divided according to what they
teach, both in the classroom and out, to whom they teach it, and
how they teach it. What is taught may apply to general curriculum
content or to a very specific set of goals for the education of young
people. Some schools choose to teach a particular set of pupils who
are similar in academic or intellectual characteristics, while others

cater to pupils from a single ethnic, religious, or racial background. (Among such schools I do not include segregationist institutions but only those that are either exercising protected religious freedoms or, like the recently retitled "historically black colleges," do not formally exclude majority individuals but appeal for a variety of cultural and historical reasons to a specific minority group.)

One problem with such a taxonomy is that who, how, and what are not independent variables. A school specializing in working with learning-disabled students, for example, will most certainly differ in pedagogical methods from one for students of average to above-average ability, and may or may not differ in curriculum as well. Schools with a religious or cultural mission will carry out that mission in determining who attends, what is taught, and how teaching proceeds—at least in theory. It is difficult to imagine, for examine, a Quaker school espousing a top-down educational model or a Jewish school agreeing with an African-American school on the content of a social studies curriculum. Nevertheless, stereotypical patterns here, as elsewhere, will prove misleading, as culturally focused schools may combine liberal politics with highly traditional academics, while church-related schools of many denominations may espouse educational methods that seem remarkably at odds with the common view of their church's hierarchical structure.

The variety within independent education is possible primarily because of the prime characteristic of an independent school's mission. The great advantage of an independent school is not so much that it does not have to conform to state norms for education as that it does not have to please all of the people all of the time. Rather than being required to educate the whole population, as public schools must, independent schools may choose a segment of the population who seek a special kind of education. And rather than needing to take care not to offend any significant constituency within the broader culture, independent schools need only find a sufficient constituency to fill their classrooms. The difference is roughly the same as that which obtains in the media between such mass entitites as a television network or a city's major daily newspaper and a cable station or special interest journal. A cable station may provide highbrow entertainment that would never suffice for a network or even a local station, and a small-circulation magazine may print polemics or publish photographs that would produce howls of outrage from the readers of the daily paper. (Within independent education, secondary schools tend toward greater uniformity as the pressures of college admissions and standardized testing militate against too wide a degree of nonconformity. Elementary schools, with several years between them and the onset of college pressure, are freer to consider a distinctive educational mission.) Let us examine a few of the special missions adhered to by some types of independent schools.

Climb the steps of a side entrance to a YMCA in a run-down section of Providence, and you will come upon a small school operating in some of the Y's vacant space. Community Prep's student body is over 60 percent children of color and includes a number of hearing-impaired students as well. Accepting children in grades four to eight, this school seeks to serve neighborhood children, specifically by giving them a strong foundation in the traditional subjects as well as in thinking and study skills, and then to place these students in strong secondary schools.

The curriculum at Community Prep is, then, quite traditional, and the teaching methods even more so. A poster featuring a quotation from Marva Collins hangs on the wall—the piece was created and donated by a local artist and is one of the many ways the school raises up to 95 percent of its income that comes from donations. Like Collins's Chicago school, the program at Community Prep focuses on standards of accountability and rigor that would be abhorrent to a progressive school and that would probably be seen as too pressured in many mainstream independent schools, where helping "hurried children" deal with the excessive demands on their lives is often a stated goal of teachers and administrators.

But as head Dan Corley explains, his students are used to a world in which there are few standards and in which they have never learned that their actions can make a difference to their futures. Therefore, frequent grades and reports—and strong sanctions for those who fail to perform to their abilities—are vital to the progress the school and its families seek. One of the school's sanctions illustrates the difference between its world and the world of students in other environments. Students participate in an after-school program that provides a wide variety of activities, including sign language for the hearing students. Those who are not working satisfactorily cannot stay after school but must go home instead!

My student guide, a sixth grader from the Dominican Republic, proudly shows me her workbooks and introduces me to her nearest seatmates, one of whom is white, the other African-American. As the class proceeds, she whispers to me, "I like this school better than my last school." "Why?" I ask. "Because I learn better here."

Schools like Community Prep exist all across the country, in Boston, New York, Baltimore, and other urban centers. Sometimes referred to as "storefront schools," they may be begun by parents of color or interested educators or clergy of many types. Some take a cultural heritage, particularly an African-American one, as a major part of their activities. Signs around the school may be in Swahili; the Seven Rules, which teach the value system (unity, self-determination, collective work and responsibility, cooperative economics, purpose, creativity, and faith) may be displayed; and maps and posters on the walls may introduce students to Marcus Garvey, Ida B. Wells, or "World History from an Afro-Centric Perspective." Financially struggling, with low tuitions and large amounts of financial aid, they perform a special community service by educating their students effectively within the children's cultural context.

Schools for students with learning disabilities, or for those with unsuccessful previous schooling experiences, are among the most common nonpublic schools. Though many of these are proprietary schools operated for profit (as are a vast range of institutions for those remanded by courts or youth service agencies, all of which lie well outside the scope of this article), and though others in accepting state funding are compelled to become quasi-public institutions, a significant number are fully functioning independent schools. In such institutions one of several theories of dyslexia, learning disability, or pedagogy may be a dominant force. At some, motor skill retraining is a vital element, and every aspect of daily life, from the organization of tasks and materials in the lunchroom to the use of unicycles in the athletic program, is intended to reinforce classroom learning. At others, outdoor education or indoor work on a climbing wall in the gymnasium may focus more on self-esteem and sense of accomplishment than on parallel skill building. Minuscule teacher-pupil ratios and closet-sized classrooms with two to four desks allow for the painstaking work of dividing reading, writing, and numeration into manageable units and of learning compensating strategies for various visual, auditory, or attention problems. In Bonners Ferry, Idaho, Rocky Mountain Academy—a proprietary school, but nevertheless recognized by the Pacific Northwest Association of Independent Schools—attends to both the academic and the emotional needs of students whose school failures are due to problems of emotional development. Combining a structured work setting as a farm with small-group soul-searching under professional leadership, Rocky Mountain, like other "second chance" schools, seeks to address the roots of a child's school failure rather than to simply provide tutoring and remedial academic work.

Another range of independent schools focuses not on the cultural background of its pupils nor on a select group of students with special academic needs but on a set of convictions about what is best for all children. Such schools tend to espouse a particular developmental theory and to emphasize the child over the academic discipline, often crossing subject lines or obliterating them. Oldest among these is, of course, Montessori education, but progressive schools, Waldorf schools, and the newest cluster, the members of the Coalition of Essential Schools based at Brown University, also share certain qualities.

Consider the methodology of Waldorf education, one of the largest, most distinctive, and least-known of school movements. Founded by polymath Rudolph Steiner in the years following World War I, and supported by the hotel family (schools often call themselves Steiner schools but define their programs as Waldorf education), this German-begun pedagogy is represented in countries throughout the world, with over 100 schools in North America alone. Of these, only about a dozen are high schools, and fewer than half that many belong to NAIS, though their representation in state and regional associations is growing.

Waldorf education, unlike Montessori, has not had a substantial impact on mainstream elementary schools. This is probably due to the movement's connections to theosophy and to some of the specific rigors of Steiner's theories. In a pure Waldorf elementary school, for example, a teacher moves through a class's full eight years of education, so that a forty-year career as a Waldorf teacher would ideally consist of nurturing five groups of youngsters through their entire elementary experience. Although this ideal is not always carried through in practice (and is not employed at all in the high school years), it clearly stands apart from the common practice of all other educational programs.

Curricularly, Waldorf education attempts to mold the child's whole environment. In a purpose-built Waldorf school, rooms will be designed without right angles and with flowing, curved windows. At each grade level through eighth, a different color is chosen for the whole environment, beginning with the gentlest pastels and gradually moving to stronger colors like brown. The curriculum too is precisely articulated and thoroughly integrated and is aimed at meeting the developmental needs of the children rather than exposing them to the world. The emphasis is on activity: writing comes before reading, the arts are used in an active way to underpin all disciplines, and a specific subject, eurythmy, which is defined as "giving visible expression to the arts of music and speech," takes its place among the traditional subjects. However, Waldorf education is also exceptionally academic in some of the most traditional senses: one spokesperson describes Steiner's program as "casual style and classical curriculum." Students are introduced to two foreign languages beginning in grade one, and the literature/social studies program follows a sort of "ontogeny recapitulates phylogeny" progression, beginning with myths, fairy tales, and legends and progressively descending to earth through a study of biblical, Near Eastern, Greco-Roman, medieval, and Renaissance materials until reaching the twentieth century in grade eight. At the high school level, students exemplify the casual/classical dichotomy in a startling way, as they wander the halls in fatigues and long hair, call teachers by their first names, and throw pots or move gracefully in eurythmy class, while knowledgeably discussing Shakespeare, Dante, and Goethe.

Although the very core of Waldorf education is to nurture children in an environment at odds with the stresses of the modern world—Steiner hoped to educate a new generation that would be incapable of perpetrating the horrors of World War I—the program is nevertheless moving into the modern world. High Mowing School, in Wilton, New Hampshire, America's only secondary boarding school run on the Waldorf model, has held conferences on the integration of computers into the Waldorf program, while both elementary and secondary schools are considering how to include multicultural education within the classical framework.

Sharing the developmental, child-centered, and interdisciplinary qualities of Waldorf education, but lying closer to mainstream secular America, are the Montessori and progressive movements. After a brief and politically charged appearance on the American scene in the period just before World War I, Montessori education returned to the United States to stay in the late 1950s. Although the vast majority of America's more than 3,000 Montessori schools are preschools, Montessori offers a process of multi-age group education clustered in units of three years beginning at birth and extending through age twelve. Montessori principles include a strong emphasis on cooperative and independent learning, with groups of even very young children working together and teaching each other under minimal adult guidance. The teacher is trained to observe the child's affect, always judging whether to intervene or not intervene in the learning process and adhering to Maria Montessori's dictum that "one is always teaching an inner child who is becoming."

Some of its practitioners feel that the Montessori movement has peaked precisely because it has been so successful that many of its principles, from its use of manipulatives to its stress on group and independent learning, have been accepted into elementary education as a whole. Ironically, although one of the oldest and strongest of school movements, Montessori is in many states today under considerably greater governmental threat than most other independent educational movements because of the age of children with which it works. Given the developmental nature of Montessori, its schools are educating younger children who fall within the state's oversight under offices for children and other noneducational agencies. These bodies are proving to be far more aggressive about prescribing the details of appropriate environments for children than are most public education hierarchies.

If Montessori has been absorbed into the mainstream, progressive education has in the past decade or more been suffering from a lack of congruity with prevailing notions of educational needs, at least among noneducators. Numerous progressive independent schools have closed or suffered declining enrollments as the movement's association with John Dewey and perceived permissiveness has raised opposition to it among politicians and parents. In public education, the near disappearance of progressive, open, or alternative schools has been a notable part of the educational backlash that followed the reforms of the sixties and seventies. Yet a number of progressive principles, such as empowering the school's faculty to design curriculum, integrating subjects along thematic lines, and allowing extended time for study instead of breaking the day up into rigid single-period units, are widely accepted as valid educational approaches. Today, new elementary schools such as the Atrium School in Watertown, Massachusetts, are following in the footsteps of the venerable Shady Hill School (Cambridge, Massachusetts), with central subject curricula and a strong adherence to progressive principles, while high schools such as the Cambridge School in Massachusetts and the Colorado Springs School organize themselves in four- to six-week modules in which students may study as few as two subjects intensively.

Beginning with the work of the North Dakota Study Group, significant efforts have recently been made to reestablish the credentials of the progressive movement. A series of conferences for progressive educators were held in the eighties, and the newly formed Network of Progressive Educators currently numbers forty-five schools as well as many individuals. Almost all these schools are independent, though the organization's goal is to attain a membership divided equally between public and independent schools. The independent schools form an established model, in some cases with more than fifty years of successful experience on which newer public school efforts can draw. Here is an interesting case in which independent schools, because of their relative freedom from the vagaries of public opinion, have been able at least partially to preserve an educational approach that was forced out of public education but may now be seen as offering a valuable alternative for educational reform.

Independent schools also have a role in the reform of teacher education. At the Shady Hill School and at the Little School in

Bellevue, Washington, for example, prospective teachers with bachelor's degrees enroll in a year-long training program that provides them with both on-site experience and course work in education and child development. Such programs are among the reform recommendations commonly made in the early 1980s, when attention was focused on the quality of teacher preparation in the subject areas in public schools.

Shady Hill's program, which provides a master's degree, has been in existence for over fifty years and has been a seedbed for prominent educators throughout the independent and public school world. The newer program at the Little School focuses on a totally developmental approach to children, who are assembled in small, multi-age groups of no more than thirteen in the primary grades and no more than sixteen through age twelve. According to the director, children at the school are engaged in "learning what their ways of learning are, and learning how to learn." Not only does the Little School combine the resources of its faculty with those of a post-secondary institution—the Pacific Oaks Institute in Pasadena, California—but it mandates parent involvement as well, requiring by contract that parents observe classes and attend education programs so that they may learn what is developmentally appropriate for their children.

Newest among the curricular reform movements is the Coalition of Essential Schools. Based on the model developed by Theodore Sizer in *Horace's Compromise*,[3] the coalition currently numbers eighty-seven members throughout the country, of which fourteen are independent schools. (Although the program began with a secondary focus, elementary and middle schools have been joining as well.) Based on a series of guiding principles, including "student as worker, teacher as coach," and the "exhibition of mastery" alternative to examinations, coalition schools seek to promote independent learners by a variety of methods. In a typical classroom, students will be set a task and given space and time to work on it as a group, with the teacher available for consultation, but with responsibility for both process and product resting with the students themselves. (One traditionally educated first-year teacher, on viewing a videotape of two classes working in this manner, blurted out, "But that was chaos! Where was the teacher?")

Among the principles of the coalition that seem particularly indebted to the independent school experience of Sizer and many of the early designers of the program are the notion of "personalization," which provides for a low teacher-pupil ratio so that individual needs may be addressed, often by having a teacher work with the same students in two subjects, and the notion of "intellectual focus," which defines school as primarily an academic rather than a vocational or life-preparation institution. The coalition is promising for many reasons, not least of which is its exceptional success in bringing independent, parochial, and public schools into closer cooperation than any other reform or alternative movement.

Most of the schools mentioned thus far are the product of some broad-based movement, whether educational or social. However, it is in the nature of independent education that the will of a founder can set a permanent stamp on an institution. Examples are too numerous and varied even to list, but one type deserves special mention because it cuts so sharply across the stereotype of independent schools as purely academic institutions. When Sarah Derby founded her academy in Hingham, Massachusetts, in 1784, she required all boys to take woodworking and all girls to take needlework in addition to the standard elementary curriculum. Derby Academy, which boasts of being the nation's oldest continuously operating coeducational elementary school, has retained this requirement for over two centuries, only modifying it in the 1970s by requiring both sexes to participate in both programs. On a larger scale, the Milton Hershey School in Hershey, Pennsylvania, was founded by the chocolate manufacturer to provide both trade and academic education for students from troubled homes. The school, which is in the process of refocusing its mission on college preparation, is so well endowed that it offers a full school and boarding program at no charge.

A similar focus and financial arrangement prevailed at the Lick-Wilmerding High School in San Francisco until the 1970s, when the school finally began charging tuition. Lick-Wilmerding, the result of merging three separate vocational schools, takes as its mission "education for the head, the heart, and the hand." Although all students go on to college, the school requires at least six semesters of woodshop, metal shop, drafting, design, and other mechanical and industrial arts. It hopes to instill in its pupils a "can do" confidence and a confidence about technology, regardless of whether they choose engineering or some other field or attend a traditional liberal arts college, as the majority do. In keeping with another of the school's mottos—"a private school with a public purpose"—Lick-Wilmerding spends more than 33 percent of its budget on financial aid and in recent years has worked with both the State of California and the City of San Francisco, which are seeking to restructure their own approaches to vocational education.

The centrality of the academic disciplines is challenged in a different way by schools that focus on the arts. These may endeavor primarily to facilitate the artistic aims of their students outside the school, as does the Professional Children's School in New York, or they may take on the central task of educating their pupils for the arts, as do such institutions as the Interlochen Arts Academy in Michigan or Walnut Hill School in Massachusetts. Independent schools are only a small fragment of the arts school world, constituting about 5 percent of the membership of the Network of Schools of Visual and Performing Arts. The majority are boarding schools, giving them a special advantage in scheduling rehearsals and performances, and they focus on preparation for four-year colleges and classical conservatories rather than on more immediate careers in the arts. (It is this vocational aspect that perhaps accounts for the fact that arts high schools have been relatively more common in the public school world.) Dedicated to a co-curricular model of arts and academic education, these schools represent a model for the recognition of the arts in a liberal education and of the artistic as a distinct "intelligence" in Howard Gardner's sense.

As John Chubb and Terry Moe suggest in the recent *Politics, Markets, and America's Schools,*[4] the route to educational reform may lie in the realm of school governance rather than in curriculum or teacher training. Here too the freedom of independent education leads to significant variety, as the running of a school may be profoundly affected by its theoretical base. The Quaker consensus model is an obvious example, but others may be more striking. At some progressive schools, for example, the principles of a democratic school and of students' ownership of their own educations extends to school structure as well. Schools that follow the "just school" model developed by Lawrence Kohlberg and his students, for example, will train students in ethical decision making by turning over to them every possible aspect of student discipline and other administrative functions. (Interestingly, though many independent school educators are disciples of Kohlberg, Carol Gilligan, or both, the just school model seems to have found more of a home among public school student governments and in prison or juvenile correctional settings.)

Other schools go even further. The Sudbury Valley School, an alternative independent school west of Boston that has been the subject of numerous profiles and has achieved full accreditation and a quarter century of continuity, has no administrators at all. Certain adults in the community are chosen as "clerks" for various duties, but all decision making is in the hands of what amounts to a committee of the whole. Once a week, all those employed by or studying at the school gather for an assembly. At this assembly, all decisions are reached by vote, with each individual, of whatever age or status, having a single vote. Students seeking to study a subject not currently offered will explain what they wish to study and why, what resources they have located, and how much will need to be appropriated. The school then votes this budgetary item up or down. Similarly, students wishing a diploma go before the community and explain why they feel ready to leave and what their plans are. The community then votes to grant or withhold the diploma. Other progressive or alternative schools go beyond administration to governance, seating elected student trustees along with those from the faculty, administration, parent body, and other constituencies.

All this is not to suggest that independent schools are the locus of innovation in American education, except administratively. It is probably fair to say that a majority are simply solid elementary and secondary schools, offering a familiar range of subjects taught in traditional ways to a clientele determined more by geography and economics than by a strong desire for a specific educational model. Indeed, it could even be argued that public schools contain more educational experimentation as a whole, for two reasons. First, their links with the educational research community make them more immediately aware of new theories than are independent schools, which, especially at the secondary level, have closer ties to liberal arts institutions, where pedagogical experimentation is relatively infrequent. Second, society's constant focus on the failings of public education and the desperate need to improve the condition of many of the nation's children make self-examination and new methods more pressing in such schools. Simply because of their relative success, many independent schools may find little need to reexamine either their means or their ends.

But the independent school offers a unique opportunity for employing an alternative model that functions throughout an institution, rather than in one classroom or one discipline. Needing no external authorization, and confronted with no entrenched interests, a new school may begin with nothing more than a small core of committed teachers and supporters and may survive on a budget that would be insufficient to hire the central office administrators, the consultants, and the professional evaluators who would be needed just to oversee such an experiment in the public sector. Particularly when the educational mission implies a thoroughgoing rejection of accepted norms, whether of secularism, preservation of academic disciplines, or educational hierarchy, independent schools may be the only places in which certain types of innovation can ever occur.

What is the value of all this independence? Is it an end in itself or a means to some clearly superior goal? Many justifications may be made, from Karl Popper's contention that an open society will invariably prove its superiority to a closed one by its ability to examine and therefore finally discard false ideas, to the congruence of independent education with the principles of the American republic. Chubb and Moe, for example, argue that the origins of American public education in a variety of local schools serving local needs were distorted by the professionalization and centralization of public schools early in this century into a false quest for the one best system. They contend that the decentralized, market-serving, and choice-based model of the independent school offers the best hope for educational reform for public education as well.

On a more humble level, we may recall T. S. Eliot's observation about Shakespeare. Eliot commented that about anyone so great we can never hope to be right, so it is good for us to change our way of being wrong from time to time. Our growing awareness that people learn in different ways and at different rates offers yet another theoretical justification for a diversity of schools, and curricula based on the theories of varieties of intelligence now being developed by Robert Sternberg and Howard Gardner may be among the most promising new avenues in education.

Some years ago, one of Jules Feiffer's cartoons sardonically suggested that every educational reform from McGuffey's reader to the open classroom works for a while and then fails because "the kids develop antibodies." In some sense, independent schools and those public schools that are free, whether as alternative institutions or as schools-within-schools, to follow a particular vision function like the genetic diversity that protects animal and vegetable populations from disease. In this regard it should be noted that genetic diversity may be enhanced in two ways: by developing new resistant strains of plants and animals and by preserving variations that would otherwise die out because, for example, they are not commercially viable. Either resource may prove to be just what is needed to counteract some problem affecting the main strain of a species. Perhaps those schools that demand jackets and ties, teach all boys, and require Latin for every pupil are as necessary for the survival of our educational enterprise as those that pursue critical language studies, teach entirely through computers or experiential education, or allow students relative or absolute choice in the construction of their educational experience.

Notes

1. National Association of Independent Schools, Memorandum to member associations, August 24, 1990.
2. National Association of Independent Schools, *NAIS Statistics* (Boston: NAIS, 1990).
3. Theodore Sizer, *Horace's Compromise* (Boston: Houghton Mifflin, 1984).
4. John E. Chubb and Terry M. Moe, *Politics, Markets, and America's Schools* (Washington, D.C.: Brookings Institution, 1990).

4

Boarding Schools:
Educating the Whole Child

Kendra Stearns O'Donnell

What is most obvious about boarding schools—that they are not only schools but residential communities—is what is finally most important in defining their collective character. Look first to their mission statements: in describing themselves, boarding schools invariably present the residential component as essential to their educational mission.

When the business of a school encompasses living as well as learning, the definition of mission expands. The mission statements of boarding schools articulate the widest and highest aspirations for education to be found in this country. Today, as traditionally, boarding schools connect their twenty-four-hour stewardship of students with a responsibility for educating the whole person. There is no part of a young person, no aspect of his or her development, that escapes the school's expansive mission. Boarding schools typically aspire to educate morally, socially, physically, aesthetically, and spiritually, as well as intellectually.

Some general conditions and assumptions follow from dedication to the education of the whole person. First and foremost, in boarding schools it is assumed that learning and teaching will take place outside the classroom. What happens in dormitories, on playing fields, in extracurricular pursuits, and in informal interactions between adults and students and among students has educational content. It is usual in boarding schools to hear the stuff of daily nonacademic, nonprogrammatic life spoken of by students and faculty in terms of what it teaches. The conditions and compacts that regulate communal life—rules, discipline systems, governance and leadership structures, processes and policies of all kinds, even as seemingly mundane a matter as scheduling—are assumed to have educational content and consequences and are devised and monitored accordingly.

Operating on these assumptions, the holistic approach to education at its very best means that the planning, thoughtfulness, and vigor that one associates with good, standard curricular work in any school, particularly in independent schools, is also applied to life outside the classroom in residential schools. This attention often shows up as an emphasis on providing a variety of experiences for the student, as though to make sure that no part of the whole child is neglected: social service programs, lectures, symposia, concerts, health education, sponsored discussion groups, religious services, outdoor challenge programs, and the like crowd the educational landscape at boarding schools.

This extraordinary degree of intentionality accounts, in my opinion, for two distinguishing features in the boarding school character. The first is a sense of security, a comfort flowing from the perceived interrelatedness of all the details and departments of life and the grounding of all in a consistent and well-understood sense of values. The second is pressure, the result of intensity or seriousness of purpose taken to an extreme. These two traits exist in counterpoint in most schools, with one or another dominating depending on the school's ethos, the phase of its evolution, or even the time of year. Nowadays, the energy of those managing boarding schools seems to be directed toward strengthening the sense of security and containing the pressure and unproductive stress.

Like the twin perceptions of security and pressure, there are other attributes of boarding school life that also rub against each other and also seem to be byproducts of a holistic mission. Numerous and varied offerings outside the classroom lend an air of plenty, of richness to life at school. New students may feel they've been let loose in an educational candy store. Recent graduates are given to regretting the opportunities they neglected to sample. Between the new student's awe and the graduate's regret lies the reality that continually leavens and sometimes deflates the expansive vision of holistic education: not enough time. Boarding schools are monuments to the truth that educating the whole person is uncommonly time-consuming for students and faculty. Typical school days—the stretch of time filled with requirements and commitments—last twelve hours. For students, study, sleep, socializing, play, and pizza consumption vie for the remaining hours. For faculty with dormitory responsibilities the school day seems never to end, and family, privacy, and social time are at a premium. Abundance of opportunities and scarcity of time—so much to do, so little time—are two fundamental attributes of boarding school life. Managing the tension between the two is a central, ongoing task for the institutions as well as for the individuals, young and adult, who make their lives at boarding schools.

Beneath generalizations about boarding schools born of their expansive mission are three homely truths that illuminate both the real experience of living, learning, and working in such schools and also the challenges that confront the faculty and administrators who run them. Boarding schools mean that students are living away from home; they are living under the care of adults who are not their parents; and they are living communally with their peers.

For students, the education of the whole person begins with the first homely fact of boarding school life: they are living away from home. For the young adolescent, living away from home can act as a catalyst to the various kinds of growth associated with the mission of boarding schools. To begin with, it offers the possibility of social and intellectual liberation. In the case of the well-loved child who comes from an advantaged—in the broadest sense—background, liberation is benign: it is being set free from family stereotypes about that child's gifts and weaknesses, prospects, and place in a sibling network or family system. For a child from a less advantaged background, it can mean liberation from damaging social, family, or economic circumstances.

For all children, leaving home to enter a boarding school is a chance to reinvent themselves, to be the authors and artists of their own lives. It is interesting that so many actually rename themselves as they enter their new world, accepting or announcing a nickname that is foreign to parents and friends at home. Labels acquired over the years fall away: in this new setting no one knows that Jan or Jake is supposed to be bad at this and good at that, serious or silly, cool or uncool. Moreover, Jan can make choices about everything from what to study to what to eat without reference to immediate parental reaction. She will begin to make those choices in reference to herself. Here, at school, Jake is apt to be treated as the expert on Jake; he must speak for himself, having left all the other experts at home.

It is in the nature of boarding schools to encourage the opportunities for self-discovery and taking responsibility for oneself that arise naturally from the mere fact and new circumstance of living away from home. Boarding schools do not engage in social engineering to the same extent that colleges do. They tend to see students entering as representing potential rather than product. It then becomes the business of boarding schools to help young people find their gifts, to discover all the ways in which they can become accomplished. The typical boarding school abundance of curricular and extracurricular opportunities, in combination with a structured approach that virtually forces students to become engaged with cultural, spiritual, athletic, and artistic pursuits, increases the chances that a young person will find a place to shine.

Despite their almost utopian aspirations in regard to liberating young talents, boarding school communities are subject to the same tendencies to value certain kinds of success over others that students encounter in any educational setting. One can handily define the ethos of a particular school by identifying the kind of success most valued—academic, athletic, social, artistic. Schools that take their missions seriously fight against these tendencies in the institutional and adolescent cultures. An increasing awareness among educators in boarding schools of current theories about what constitutes giftedness and about differences in learning styles reinforces a trend towards wider definitions of student achievement.

Living away from home can be experienced as loss as well as liberation. It is not unusual that the rules at school are more constricting than the rules at home and that students feel a loss of personal freedom. Many seem to feel even more acutely the loss of parental nurturing. While accepting that there is simply no substitute for parental nurturing, schools tend to take seriously their *in loco parentis* role.

Standing in for absent parents is considerably more challenging today than it was twenty years ago. There was a time when parents and schools were apt to agree on everything from manners to morals. In matters of values and conduct, in terms of what was *expected* of a young person, life at school was apt to be a continuation of life at home. This easy consensus was in part a consequence of homogeneity in student bodies. As efforts to bring racial and cultural diversity to boarding schools began to be successful, culturally based agreement could no longer be assumed. In a much larger sense, however, the old home/school consensus was simply a reflection of a general societal consensus about and support for parenting. The world has, in the space of a few decades, become dangerous for children and parents alike. Children grow up and parents parent in an environment that threatens rather than supports them.

Schools can no longer look to the home lives of their students and find there some virtually universal, well-established, and effective version of parenting on which to model their own efforts to compensate students for the loss of family that comes with living away from home. The challenge today is to provide parenting that at its best is more complete, more consistent, and better informed than is now the norm in the homes from which many students come and in society in general. The schools' parenting mandate stretches wider and deeper as the consequences for young people of neglectful, reluctant, or nonexistent parenting stretch to include physical and psychological disorders, substance abuse, racial and other prejudice, and—with AIDS—even death. Schools find they must add policies, programs, and specialized personnel to the old standbys of rules and codes, faculty advisers, and diligent deans. Student support services now typically include access to psychological counseling; curricula include courses that cover everything from nutrition to racism; student handbooks include policies on HIV-infected individuals and sexual harassment. Acting *in loco parentis* has become more clearly an educational as well as a caretaking function for boarding schools.

Seeing this evolution as an opportunity for further expression of the mission to educate the whole child, rather than as a burdensome necessity, will strengthen individual schools and the sector as a whole. Such a perception does not, unfortunately, characterize many schools today. The student support services that schools have needed to add in recent years tend to be regarded by teaching faculties as, at worst, a necessary evil, and, at best, expert backup for their own efforts with students. This is not surprising if we consider that these services have tended to be added piecemeal and to be housed in the inherently low-status surroundings of old infirmaries. Furthermore, those associated with the services are often excluded from places, processes, and positions that teaching faculty associate with power.

School heads need not simply accept an uneasy coexistence between what one could broadly define as the academic core of a school and the plethora of activities and functions that nowadays expresses the *in loco parentis* role of the school. Every school has processes peculiar to itself whereby faculty come to "own" aspects of the whole school enterprise: making sure that support services are run through these processes increases the chance that faculty will not see them as other, extra, or administrative but as belonging to them and therefore central. If policies related to, say, homework expectations and academic honesty are originated by faculty committees, debated and approved by faculty, so, too, should policies on drug and alcohol use and medical leaves of absence. If faculty play a role in new courses and new hires in the traditional academic disciplines, they should play the same or a similar role in regard to, for instance, a new health education course. School heads can step up to the challenge more explicitly if it seems appropriate and commission a thoughtful, schoolwide examination of the whole issue of how new parenting functions fit within the philosophy, the informal culture, and the daily life of the school. I believe that this issue has been left long enough to evolve on its own; it is particularly timely for schools engaged in long-range planning or preparation for an accreditation review.

A second homely fact of boarding school life, that young people are living with adults who are not their parents, also has important educational consequences. The adults who choose to live and work in boarding schools are extraordinary people. They are educators who make the commitment to the whole education of a child, a commitment which, with residence in a dormitory, encompasses a twenty-four-hour day. Moreover, it is customary that they take a number of roles: teacher, coach, dorm parent, adviser, administrator. Adults in boarding schools expect and are expected to be available to students. They offer for the developing adolescent the priceless gift of sustained adult attention, a gift that is increasingly rare in contemporary families. The value of the gift is increased when that attention is available from a number of adults who offer different personalities, different talents, different life experiences, and different connections or kinds of relationships to students.

The differences that now pertain in boarding school faculties, particularly differences in background and life circumstances, are bringing change to the compacts—formal and informal—that have governed adult life in boarding schools. In the past these compacts served faculties composed primarily of married men with wives at home, spinsters, and bachelors. These same faculties now include many more women, people with working spouses, and people who have made mid- or late-career changes into teaching. Boarding schools are, of necessity, paying attention as never before to meeting the needs of faculty. It is a new breed of faculty with new needs, everything from child care to opportunities for professional growth and advancement. What used to work for everybody now seems tailor-made for nobody. For example, two old standbys— long, even indefinite terms of dormitory service and the expectation that all faculty will coach a sport—strike many of the new breed of faculty as downright peculiar.

Schools have, quite rightly, begun to be very conscious of the need to present themselves as attractive places for teachers to work: it is no longer enough to point to the opportunity to teach students predisposed to learn, classroom autonomy, and the general pleasantness of surroundings in order to secure the good teachers every boarding school promises parents and students. Most schools have looked first to improving cash compensation. The harder work, in my opinion, is in the fuzzier area of improving the quality of professional and personal life for faculty. I speculate that change has come primarily as the accumulated weight of numerous administrative exceptions to longstanding, usually unwritten, policies. This may have improved the lot of individuals but is just as likely to have created confusion over what, after all, the school expects of faculty and what the faculty can expect of the school. At some point, fundamental review may be more helpful to a school than more and better individual problem solving. Such a review might consider questions of this sort: what needs of the school's must be met by faculty? What needs of the faculty's should be met by the school? What are the assumptions guiding the school's compensation and benefit plans? How do faculty view their careers? Those who lead by opening up these and similar questions may expect tensions caused by the usual perceived clash of interests between administration and faculty and differences among the various generations of faculty. They will also need to work with a marked tension between the desire for equity and the need for flexibility, a tension characteristic of recently diversified faculties.

In the decade ahead, then, we can expect that while students will increasingly benefit from the variety of role models represented on today's faculties, adults will continue working to build contemporary compacts around issues like compensation, workload, and quality of life. The end—the wholehearted and many-faceted participation of adults in the whole education of the child—remains the same; the means to ensure this end must change.

The boundaries of relationships between adults and students may seem to be constantly under negotiation in the boarding school setting: the usual rules don't apply when teachers are not just teachers but the people you live with, when those who parent you are not your parents. Boarding schools force an unusual intimacy between the generations. There is potential for confusion on both sides about roles and boundaries. This often shows itself most clearly when the faculty "friend" is challenged—as he or she inevitably must be—to take on the role of faculty disciplinarian. Behavior that simply goes with the parental territory, where a combination of nurturing and discipline is the norm, can feel unreasonable, inconsistent, and uncomfortable to one or both parties in a faculty-student relationship. Faculty who have no experience of parenting or who may themselves have no good parenting models need help. Schools, often with the help of various professional organizations, are becoming more active in providing faculty with training in parenting and education about adolescent development.

Interestingly, the emphasis in the last decade has been on giving faculty specialized training, in counseling, for instance, or in drug and alcohol abuse intervention. More needs to be done on the more fundamental level of educating and supporting faculty in their general role as adults in a community in which they are out-numbered by adolescents. Successful relationships between adults and students in boarding schools depend upon adult willingness to be adult—to accept responsibility for supervision, guidance, nurtur-ing—and students' acceptance of adults in this role. In healthy school communities the result can be relationships founded on mu-tual affection, respect, and trust that serve as models for young people.

It may be that the third homely fact of boarding school life is most significant for students: they live with numbers of their peers. Most boarding school students mention strong friendships as the hallmark of their school days. Friendship takes time and talent; among adolescents it involves extraordinary amounts of personal, often one-on-one support. Good schools tend to legitimize and build upon peer support networks with official peer counseling systems and leadership arrangements, such as proctor or prefect systems, that give older children responsibility over younger ones. It is an honor to be chosen as a peer counselor, for example, to work in a group that is trained in such things as listening skills and that receives ongoing support from a professional even as it offers sup-port to others. Since dormitory living virtually guarantees that young people will turn to each other for help, adults need to have safely distanced ways to help the helpers.

The bonding encouraged by communal living combined with the developing adolescent's drive to create an identity separate from adults and in relation to peers can be difficult to manage. Boarding schools run the risk of developing parallel cultures—a public or adult version of life at school and a private, hidden "kid-die culture." Divergent, or parallel cultures, one of which shuts adults out, have probably always existed and will always exist. Rot sets in when the hidden culture becomes so dominant that students generally agree that it is real and the other sham, when the hidden culture revolves around destructive behavior, such as hazing or drinking, and when students believe (rightly or wrongly) that adults know about destructive behavior and either won't or can't acknowledge its existence or importance.

Educators in boarding schools need not accept the existence of parallel cultures in extreme forms. They have to be willing, however, to expose the rot. Taking the initiative in naming the evil, putting it up for public viewing and discussion, can in itself be a way of disempowering a destructive culture and regaining control. Crises can be a gift when divergent cultures threaten a school. Again, adults have to be willing to make the most of the educational implications of a crisis. This can be tricky when the crisis is delivered, as it frequently is, in the form of a controversial discipline case. Although mindful of a family's right to privacy, adults can insist that the community extract general issues from particular instances; adults can explicitly and visibly lead in the community's processing of a crisis; and adults can be ready with plans for following up when discussion turns to a call for action.

Despite some hazards, communal living on the boarding school scale is above all an educational challenge for a young person. For many students, conducting one's domestic life with reference to the needs and desires of other individuals and of a group is a genuinely new experience. Dormitories are remarkably effective classrooms for learning skills like negotiation and compromise and for developing attributes like tolerance, empathy, and tact.

Communal living can exacerbate the tendency of young people to evolve sharply defined social structures that elevate some and leave others, often despondent, at the bottom. All schools must be societies of ins and outs with some splinter groups, but boarding communities are schools where these structures are hermetically sealed and the outcast must cope without the relief and the perspective provided by home and other community roles. Adults in boarding schools must constantly preach tolerance, empathy, and tact. Because their battle is of necessity so unrelenting and because schools explicitly value so many different things about a person, young people graduating from a boarding school often emerge more tolerant, more accepting, and less likely to judge, to dismiss, or to exclude than their peers at other schools who have not been compelled to exercise such vigilance.

The more diverse the student body, the more there is to teach and the more there is to learn from communal living. Differences that spring from diversity in the socioeconomic, geographic, racial, religious, and cultural backgrounds of students cannot be avoided in residential school settings. When diversity becomes a critical force in a boarding school, the life of the school becomes a more accurate representation of life outside the school, and the social learning that takes place as young people live with large numbers of their peers serves as a better preparation for the world outside.

Boarding schools are evolving institutions. If there is one priority that drives that evolution today, it is this very diversification of the student body. Building diversity, managing diversity, even celebrating diversity are all becoming familiar concepts, more familiar, perhaps, as ideas than realities. The word "diversity" has become a shorthand signifier for an indefinite, highly desirable state of affairs that involves considerable change and effort. It is high time, I think, to be realistic about diversity. We seem to have embraced the concept of diversity and to have begun the work of diversification without much consideration for creating the circumstances within our schools that ensure diversity will thrive. In my opinion, we can expect to see diversity transform independent schools in the next two decades to the same degree coeducation transformed those schools in the last two decades. And yet we have not begun this transformation by planning for diversity in the deliberate way we planned for coeducation.

Taking stock with the transformation well under way has the advantage of directing our attention to real rather than projected problems or issues. Some are very basic. It is clear to me, for instance, that those who are leading schools through this transformation cannot assume that those whose support is critical—trustees, parents, faculty, students—understand *why* a particular school might aspire to become a diverse community. Before those of us who lead charge ahead, we need to pause and allow debate around the fundamental case for diversity. We have to understand, too, that we will need to represent the value of diversity with the same patience, persistence, and tolerance of open conflict and unexpressed resistance that helped school leaders through the coeducation transformation.

Commitment to diversity at the institutional level should

begin with reference to a school's mission. It is not enough just to
refer to admissions and recruitment policies or to make vague asser-
tions about multiculturalism. The transformation through diversity in historically white independent schools will proceed with
difficulty, if at all, if its rationale is restricted to such factors as the
desire to be more socially equitable or the need to respond to a new
level of competition in the admissions market caused by improvement in public schools and demographic shifts. The only force
capable of sustaining the transformation, and the only force likely
to bring a school's various constituencies together to support transformation, is one that is rooted in a school's mission, its most basic
sense of purpose.

In educating the whole child, the time-honored goal of fostering intellectual, moral, and spiritual growth must, in this day
and age, include education liberated from stereotypes connected to
gender, race, or ethnicity. Prejudice in a young graduate should be
viewed much as we would view illiteracy—as a sign that we have
failed to educate the child. When, as in a boarding school, life is
school and school is life, then learning can be experiential as well
as didactic. The real experience of living in a diverse community
where racial, cultural, religious, and ethnic differences are explicitly
valued makes prejudice as unlikely an educational outcome as
illiteracy.

Boarding schools openly aspire to produce graduates who
can be counted upon to lead, to make a difference, to be good citizens, to live lives of service—the formulations differ but the basic
message is the same: we educate young people to be effective and
productive in their future lives. The stuff of those future lives—the
work to be done, the conflicts to be resolved, the opportunities to
be seized, the works of art to be created, the families to nurture—
crosses racial, cultural, religious, ethnic, and national boundaries as
never before. If boarding schools are to realize their historic calling
to educate youth who will make a difference in the future, they
must, within the little worlds of the schools, provide their students
with present lives of equal richness and diversity.

Rooting diversity in a school's understanding of its purpose
is critical, but it is only the first step. Schools have different personalities that are shaped by a dominant value or set of values. Leaders

need to attend to establishing the role of diversity in relation to these values, thus making it an integral part of a school's personality. Not to do so is to invite institutional schizophrenia. In a school, for example, that places a high value on academics, priding itself on a rigorous program, superior teaching, and gifted students, diversity will thrive only if it is seen as strengthening the academic life of the school. In a school devoted to the arts, diversity needs to be related to the pursuit of excellence in that realm. In both these cases, teachers' voices need to lead the discussion in making the case for diversity, not, as is frequently the case, the voices of admissions staff or the administration. Considering personality somewhat differently: schools with a strong aristocratic or autocratic streak might expect to have more difficulty integrating diversity than schools with traditionally pluralistic or democratic values.

As much of what I have said implies, I do not think it is too late for any school to reconsider and ultimately commit itself more strongly to diversity. I think that the individual and collective experiences of schools in recent years as they have set about some of the central tasks of diversity will move us quickly into a new level of strategic planning. The tasks have been defined as follows: expanding and diversifying admissions pools, recruiting and retaining faculty and administrators of color, building more inclusive curricula, and creating a school climate that supports diversity. I would like to comment on the last.

Assuming that leaders do not work for diversity in schools only to see it overwhelmed or driven into hiding by a still dominant white majority, they have to choose how to make use of racial, ethnic, socioeconomic, and other differences. Asking students simply to get along with others who are different from them is a good beginning, but in a holistic approach to education there is more than tolerance to be learned from differences. In boarding school classrooms, teachers ask more of students than just respect for the material being taught. They ask for engagement, for the kind of encounter with a subject from which a student emerges bursting with new information and insight and eager to make use of what has been learned. The great contemporary challenge for boarding schools is to create the conditions that will encourage the same beneficial engagement with diversity.

The conditions of a school climate that promote engagement with diversity include strong encouragement of differences and constant, active attention to building a common school culture. Encouraging differences can take the form of supporting various student organizations and activities that work as vehicles to explore and express racial, cultural, religious, and ethnic identities. My observation is that these vehicles begin as safe places for people who are a minority and feel themselves to be outside the mainstream school culture to get support and have fun. These private groupings gradually assume more public postures and, from a position of strength, begin to reach out to the community at large. What may begin, for instance, as an annual dinner or event for a club becomes, over time, something that involves everybody. When the soul food dinner cooked by students moves from a faculty kitchen to the main dining hall, when an international day festival appears on the school calendar, then differences nurtured in small closed settings become the stuff of whole-school celebration.

Finally, what about the common school culture; what happens to community in the transformation to diversity? The sense of community in a boarding school has traditionally sprung from a combination of shared backgrounds and shared experiences. One might expect that as backgrounds become more diverse, schools will feel some threat to their sense of community. It may be that certain hallowed traditions—I think, for example, of the singing of Protestant hymns on all-school secular occasions—come under fire or simply that what used to mean a great deal to everybody no longer means much to anybody. School leaders may rightly divine that this is not the time to cling to old school ties that no longer bind. However, they absolutely must compensate by strengthening present school cultures, those amalgams of shared experiences and shared values within a school that create the sense of belonging to a community. This is a time to make the most of what can be salvaged from traditional sources of school spirit; this is a time to invent new shared experiences, new traditions. Schools have lots of raw material, and what is old for one school maybe new for another. Here is a very partial list: ceremonies that open, close, or mark significant moments in a school year; dormitory or class-year-based activities like field days; camping trips; work or social service programs; holiday celebrations; all-school meetings. I am convinced that in time we will be able to measure a school's success in building, managing, and celebrating diversity by the extent to which differences located primarily in people—in their histories, hearts, and minds—are empowered to extend and enrich the common culture of a school.

As a new decade opens before us, we can see that boarding schools are places of tremendous opportunity. Their relative value in the spectrum of institutions that educate or somehow nurture young people is growing stronger as the efficacy of other entities like the church, the extended family, public schools, and community organizations is weakening. Perhaps their greatest opportunity lies in creating pluralistic, multigenerational communities that work: communities where people share values and goals; where differences enrich; where people grow and are productive; where work is constructive. There are fewer and fewer such communities that work in the world at large. Young people who live and learn in successful residential educational communities in the next decade will face their generation's task of remaking the outside world armed with both a vision and an experience of what is possible.

5

Boys' Schools:
A Progressive Case
for an Ancient Form

Richard A. Hawley

Clearing the Air

On trial for his very life, Socrates began his defense by pointing out to the citizens of Athens that it was not really he who stood
accused of impiety and of corrupting the city's youth, but rather a
vague yet nonetheless popular image of Socrates. The image had
been created by his most vocal critics and enemies and was given
wide currency in an uproarious stage comedy, *The Clouds*, written
by his friend Aristophanes. Socrates was not at all confident that he
could assert his reality—and, he believed, his innocence—in the face
of such a widespread adherence to an image he himself had never
cultivated. His concerns proved to be justified; the image was found
guilty, and the man was duly executed.

A similar difficulty tends these days to distort discussions of
all-male schools. Contemporary opinion and more than a century's
compelling fictions about boys' schools have combined to shroud
them in a vaguely dinosaurian aura. Many of the surviving boys'
schools are old and steeped in tradition, and this oldness carries
with it unexamined negative feelings. Whereas enduring unto old-

This chapter first appeared in the spring 1991 issue of *Teachers College
Record* (vol. 92, no. 3). Reprinted with permission.

ness often enhances the regard in which institutions or practices are held, the oldness of boys' schools tends, in the popular mind, to make them reactionary, "old-fashioned" in the most pejorative sense. Boys' schools, it is said, hark back to the days when only boys were prepared for universities and for the professions; as such they have been a principal instrument of male domination. To which it might be added: shame on them and good riddance.

This image of the boys' school as a cultural dinosaur does not, I believe, stand up to objective analysis. Boys' schools of former eras may well have maintained attitudes that today might deservedly be called sexist or oppressive, but identical attitudes were also maintained by those eras' boys and girls whether enrolled in coed schools, girls' schools, or no school at all.

It will be argued here that there are no objective data of any kind to support a negative appraisal of boys' schools qua boys' schools. The data suggest, if anything, the opposite conclusion. Objective data did not motivate hundreds of colleges and schools to convert from single-sex to coeducational student bodies over the past three decades. The great majority of coeducational conversions were driven by market considerations: coed schools were believed to attract more applicants, including more qualified applicants. For some schools on the brink of conversion, the motivating factor was a conviction—largely unexamined—that a coed student body is somehow more egalitarian. Stated simply, the assumption was that boys and girls together in school will be better people than they would be if segregated; they will be more understanding of, and effective with, each other. If that assumption is demonstrably true, schooling boys and girls together is clearly desirable. But is it true? A perhaps more important, and certainly more irritating, question is whether the current climate of opinion will allow anybody to find out.

Might there be inherently good, developmentally necessary qualities distinctive to all-boys' schools? That it is now possible to pose this reasonable question to the general public is due in good measure to the rising tide of feminist educational thinking. In their conviction that there truly are innately feminine modes of experience and feminine structures of thought, certain feminist theorists argue that those qualities will be nurtured and exercised best in all-girls' educational settings. The more pervasive the male domination of the larger culture, the more necessary it is to educate girls separately. Structuring schools so that they realize what is deepest and truest and best in females is currently regarded as a progressive educational attitude. Structuring schools so that they realize what is deepest and truest and best in males is not currently regarded as a progressive educational attitude (to put it mildly). This is unreasonable.

Good and various cases can be made that contemporary Western culture is skewed oppressively by male values and preferences. Males have undeniably enjoyed more social mobility, more political rights, and greater compensation for their work than females have. In the twentieth century, gender injustice has been resented and vigorously addressed by both sexes. It is obviously right to oppose gender-based unfairness, but it is a mistake to assume that boys' schools are a contributing cause. If females have been unjustly treated over the past century, and if gender composition of schools is to blame, the principal fault must lie in the dominant type of school: the coeducational school, in which over 90 percent of American schoolchildren have been enrolled. Far from being the culprits, single-sex schools, as some feminists have begun to suggest, may be the way out of the trouble.

What is the best school setting for promoting just and humane gender attitudes? This is a serious question. How and if it is answered will depend to a large extent on the climate in which it is discussed. Generous minds are required, minds willing to consider unfamiliar evidence and assumptions. Since serious people who favor single-sex or coeducational schools are likely to be motivated by a concern for the welfare and development of children, there is no need to address the issue in punishing, acrimonious tones. It might help, actually, to cultivate a little lighthearted playfulness. Socrates did—and while it did not save his life, it lightened its passing considerably.

Maleness and Boys' Schools

Is there an inherent "maleness" to boys and men? Are the distinctive biological features of males linked to deep psychological structures? If so, then maleness cannot be alienated from males without a fundamental loss of their humanity. If inherent maleness is also susceptible to development, the social structures that bear on that development—especially families and schools—should self-consciously aim to realize its fullest potential.

The American poet and mythologist Robert Bly has not only postulated an inherent deep maleness; he also argues that its suppression has been the root cause of a current masculine malaise. Drawing on the depth psychology of Freud, Jung, and the contemporary Jungian James Hillman, Bly attempts to document the late twentieth century emergence of a new male type: the "soft man." "Soft man" is not for Bly an altogether pejorative term. Soft men emerged, he believes, in the 1960s in response to feminist breakthroughs. As stereotypes of both genders were held up for critical appraisal, many conventional gender-related views and practices were altered. "As men began to look at women and their concerns," Bly writes, "some men began to see their own feminine side and to pay attention to it." For many this was genuinely liberating: to feel free not to like football if one happened not to, to engage energetically in domestic arts, in the nurture of children. Such men, Bly claims, found it "wonderful" to be more thoughtful and gentle, less reflexively macho. But there was also something wrong with the new condition.[1]

Soft men, while socially nicer and more acceptable to liberated women, are also, Bly has found, enervated and depressed: "They are life-preserving, but not exactly life-giving."[2] Forward-looking, sensitive, and intelligent as he may be, the soft man also feels rather a "wimp." He feels he is missing something. Some turn to women to get it back, but the women, whether mothers, sisters, lovers, or friends, do not have it to give back; they did not take it in the first place. The soft man—and indeed every developing male—needs finally to look beyond women for sustenance and direction. Discovering the feminine side of the male self is indeed crucial to self-realization, but it is not the ultimate discovery. For males the ultimate discovery, or rediscovery, is the deep male. The deep male, while necessary to male self-realization, may be a frightening, forbidding presence. He is not, Bly says, "a benign Asian guru" or "a kind young man named Jesus."[3]

The modern male's need to be reconciled with his lost deep

maleness is illuminated, Bly suggests, by the Grimm folk tale "Iron John." To summarize it briefly: a kingdom is troubled by the disappearance of hunters who enter a remote area of the royal forest. A stranger passing through learns of the problem and volunteers to help. When he enters the dangerous region, a great hand arises from out of a pond and pulls the stranger's dog down to the depths. The stranger then returns to the castle for help. With a number of volunteers, he drains the pond, bucketful by bucketful. At the bottom lies a reddish, rust-colored giant, covered with hair from head to toe. The giant, Iron John, is captured and carried back to the castle, where he is displayed in a cage. One day soon after, the king's young son is playing nearby with his treasured golden ball. When the ball rolls within Iron John's grasp, he grabs it. To get the ball back, the boy is told he will have to hand over the key to the cage. Since the key lies under the mother's pillow, a deception is required of the boy. He secures the key while his parents are away and releases Iron John, but as the giant heads off to the forest, the boy calls after him that his parents will be very angry when they realize what has happened. The giant agrees, and the two head off into the wilderness together.

The features of Iron John—hairiness, wetness, redness—are associated with primitive male sexuality; they are not easily acceptable, not nice. The pond, Bly suggests, is the subconscious mind, and emptying it bucket by bucket represents a patient, disciplined attempt to discover what lies at the bottom. The golden ball represents the boy's unity of spirit, positive energy, and destiny. The only way to retrieve the boy's imperiled wholeness and destiny is to come to terms with a previously submerged, monstrous reality, and to do this, to make this connection, the liberating key must be stolen from the mother. Indeed, the boy must break with both parents and reconcile himself with the primitive if he is going to make his own way.

What the soft contemporary man is missing, then, is his golden ball: a red, hairy primitive has it. Moreover, this primitive is his own deepest self, deeper than his haphazard childhood identifications, deeper than the expectations the culture has imposed, deeper even than his awareness of an unexpected feminine dimension. To be a man, the boy has got to do something very risky and very hard, and he must do it himself. In this regard the "Iron John" tale is consonant with other folktales and male coming-of-age rituals throughout history and all over the world.

Bly believes the modern male's alienation from his deep maleness is a consequence of industrialism, which has tended to remove fathers from their sons' company and thus to mystify a man's manner of work. With fathers only erratically present, their work is hard to imagine and harder still to like; sons have a difficult time conceiving their true manhood. The mother-acceptable view of manhood, the "nice" view, does not somehow ring true. Even in—perhaps especially in—the nicest households, the primitive stirs. "In the U.S. there are so many big-muscled high school boys hulking around the kitchen rudely, and I think in a way they're trying to make themselves less attractive to their mothers."[4]

Bly does not advocate male regression to the primitive, nor would he call for a pre-industrial economy. The reflexively macho man is as alienated as the soft man, only without the soft man's genuine appreciation of women and of the feminine dimension of himself. Bly favors a reconciliation with the primitive, not necessarily a blind surrender to its urges. If males are strong, if they are passionate questers; if they raise their voices sometimes, so be it. This does not mean they must be oppressive and cruel. It is also important, Bly suggests, to reverse the tendency to emasculate the male type in the popular culture. From the Dagwood cartoons of the twenties through the television sitcoms of Norman Lear, men, and fathers especially, have tended to be portrayed as hapless buffoons or benign eunuchs. Persistent denial of authentic masculinity is apt to produce eerie compensations—Rambo and his kind.

"In *The Odyssey*," Bly points out, "Hermes instructs Odysseus, when he is approaching a kind of matriarchal figure, that he is to lift or show Circe his sword. It is difficult for many of the younger males to distinguish between showing the sword and hurting someone."[5] Contemporary culture has by no means made it easy to draw such distinctions. The justifiable feminine imperative "Do not abuse me!" is too easily understood as "Do not be strong enough to abuse me!" Boys and men need to be reassured that the capacity to be forceful and the inclination to be destructive are not the same.

Other voices in depth psychology, particularly those in the

field of object relations theory, may help to explain more fully the male's need to discover his deep maleness. In her new study *Feminism and Psychoanalytic Theory*, Nancy Chodorow considers the developmental implications of the fact that women are the primary nurturers of both male and female infants. Unlike infant girls, infant boys must adapt psychologically to the gender difference between themselves and their primary love object. The mother's femininity is a daunting "otherness"; depending on and ultimately turning away from this otherness will cause a special quality of unease in the infant male psyche. Seen this way, the early (pre-Oedipal) male is launched "negatively" into subsequent development.[6]

This kind of feminist revision of Freudian child development casts mother-son relationships (also mother-daughter relationships) into greater prominence than is allowed by traditional psychoanalysis, with its father-driven Oedipal complex. Both the traditional view and the view offered by Chodorow, however, confirm a deep psychological motivation for males to set out on a distinctive developmental path. According to Freud, following that path entails the need to exceed, to triumph over, the father.[7] In imagination and dream this can be accomplished through satisfying symbolic victories over fathers and other giants—that is, chopping down a beanstalk bearing a thundering patriarch or, perhaps, as in oracle-beguiled Oedipus's case, simply bludgeoning one's father to death in a fracas on the open road. In reality, Freud hypothesized, boys overcome the mortal anxiety they feel about their competitor fathers by identifying with them: an act of psychic cannibalism. If Chodorow is correct, male children will have begun their journey of individuation before the onset of their Oedipal challenges. In fact, the latter may be a mere extension of an earlier, deeper need to swim free of the feminine "other" and to become a self. The key to self-realization may lie under the mother's pillow, as the tale of "Iron John" suggests.

It is probably not an overgeneralization to state that, throughout the history of civilization up until World War I, the answer to the question of whether there is an inherent maleness to boys and men would have been laughably obvious. Are males *male?* Is the sky blue? What has raised such questions? Such doubts?

The popular understanding of gender—of both masculinity

and femininity—has been traditionally determined by institutions organized by gender: priesthoods, armies, clubs, sororities, scout troops, teams, and, notably, schools. Gender-based organizations, whether the National Organization for Women or Eton College, risk stating not only what masculinity or femininity *is*, but also what a male or female *should be*. Neither gender has a successful record of making acceptable definitions of the other. There is some concern, however, that the soft man drawn by Bly may be a problematic consequence of males trying to define themselves in conformity to feminist prescriptions. A good or at least an acceptable man is thus one who does not attempt date rape; who does not assume that his preferences, activities, and employment are preeminent considerations when making mutual plans; who does not perpetuate gender stereotypes; who would not assume the male always pays the check or that women would not care for boxing; and so forth. No one, of either gender, should be defined negatively.

For better or worse, but probably forever, each gender tends to define its own nature and aspirations. When those definitions break down, when there is no social structure to affirm them and to pass them on, there is trouble. Gender definition and expectations have traditionally been a responsibility of schools, but schools have increasingly declined to set specific, positive expectations for masculine and feminine conduct. Schools typically define and prescribe good studenthood, good citizenship, but this does not solve a deeper developmental problem. Each student, each citizen, is a boy or a girl. There is that dimension of selfhood to be realized as well, and only a few schools these days are either structured or inclined to address the task. Does it matter?

For nearly all of Western history boys were educated and trained apart from girls. That structural fact, apart from reflecting a number of social assumptions that no longer prevail, was also accompanied by fairly clear conceptions of what a boy should be and do. Some of those conceptions are durably appealing. In the late twentieth century, by contrast, one would be hard-pressed to identify—except in certain boys' schools and other all-male organizations—a clear conception of male adequacy.

Questing, striving, leading, serving, adhering to ideals despite temptations not to—these values have rested at the heart of boys' schools and of boys' stories from the earliest recorded history. Summoning up one's wit and wiles and strength in the face of great danger or great adventure is a theme running from Hebrew scriptures through the great Victorian schoolboy sagas such as *Tom Brown's Schooldays.*

Boys schooled together have no trouble seeing the developmental point of teenage David facing the Philistine champion Goliath. David's story is developmentally important to boys, in fact, exhilarating. It is not unlike Telemachus's story, or even the story of his father, Odysseus. Not all the questing of boy heroes in the Western tradition is martial or regal. The individuating quests of Jesus and St. Francis are marked by the force and depth of their spirituality. In Peter Abelard's case the quest was intellectual. The Christian chivalry of the Arthurian stories prescribed highly specific expectations for boys and men, expectations that again, despite entailing hardships, personal restraint, and exposure to mortal danger, have for centuries been stirringly attractive to boys. Moreover, the hypermasculinity of the chivalric code was accompanied by an extraordinary veneration of women. Indeed, the women of the Arthurian cycle are more than objects of love and loyalty; they are also intelligent, resourceful, powerful, often formidable adversaries.

The masculine ideal in the West has rarely—and then at its peril—isolated itself from feminine influence. The very object of the masculine quest, as in Romeo's case, may be the love of a girl or woman. But Romeo, like Abelard and Dante before him, arises out of a culture of males to meet the exquisite otherness of his love. Juliet is no school or neighborhood chum. The common thread in the heroic stories of the male quest is the *subordination of the hero's welfare* to the object of the quest. Young David and Romeo and Robin Hood are not selfish. Even now that theme, if vividly evoked, as in *Chariots of Fire* (a semidocumentary film about the Olympic ambitions of two Cambridge athletes, Eric Liddell and Harold Abrahams), resonates with surprising power.

It is well beyond the scope of this chapter to isolate the precise causes of the break or warp in the tradition of masculine heroism in the West. Undeniably, however, that tradition has been massively countered by the post–World War I emergence of the antihero. Who is the paradigm case? Is it Holden Caulfield, gentle, sensitive, physically and sexually doubtful, on the verge of nervous collapse? Is it Willie Loman's disillusioned boys in *Death of a Salesman?* Is it James Dean's baby-talking portrayal of a conflicted teenager in *Rebel Without a Cause?* Conrad Jarrett poised on the brink of suicide in *Ordinary People?* Or is it the lost teenager become middle-aged, as in Jack Nicholson's characterization of Bobby Dupea in *Five Easy Pieces?*

These and legions of other lost boys compose a good part of the cultural backdrop against which boys are now expected to grow up. Whatever dark and worrying messages they collectively convey, the larger point is that they are not conveying enough. They are not conveying how to become a man. Again, very few institutions seem willing to take up this task. An exception is the boys' school.

The Data We Have Are the Schools We Have

Boys' schools have not disappeared. Many have not only weathered an era of coeducational conversion, they have thrived in its midst. When their scholastic and extracurricular performance is measured and compared, as Valerie E. Lee and Anthony S. Bryk measured and compared it among parochial school students, boys in boys' schools do better than boys in coed schools—never, apparently, worse.[8] Moreover, boys from boys' schools have not as a body registered special difficulties in adapting to the coeducational conditions of university life. A boys' school can, obviously, be poorly conceived, badly run, and resourceless. Herding boys together under the banner of a school is no panacea, but schooling them within a structure designed to realize and to celebrate their distinctive developmental features has resulted in a high count of the most longstanding and most demonstrably effective schools in the world.

There is little mystery in the fact that well-conceived boys' schools have turned out to be good for boys. From their preschool years through their late teens, boys reveal a number of gender-specific contours in their skeletal, motor, and neurological development. Boys generally develop language skills, the capacity for quantitative analysis, and large- and small-muscle proficiencies at a developmentally different tempo from girls. Child psychologist J.

M. Tanner has demonstrated that girls' skeletons and nervous systems are at birth more fully developed than those of boys, and the maturational gap increases somewhat through early childhood.[9]

Gender-based variations in the tempo and pattern of learning can be identified from the pre-kindergarten through the high school years. Primary school girls generally demonstrate reading and writing proficiency earlier than boys do; middle- and high school boys' mathematical-logical capacities accelerate more rapidly than those of girls. Girls generally develop fine muscle coordination sooner; boys develop large motor coordination sooner. Females tend to reach the peak of their pubertal growth spurt a year or two sooner than boys. Each gender-based physiological difference is accompanied by distinctive psychological and sociological adjustments.

If the learning styles and learning tempos of boys and girls are often at variance, a homogeneous school program—whether curricular or extracurricular—will unavoidably miss either the masculine or the feminine mark, if not both. Just as school programs tailored to gender-specific learning patterns should facilitate more learning, teachers adept at teaching boys or girls might reasonably be assumed to be, by virtue of their specialization, more effective than those who teach (developmentally variegated) boys and girls together. As maturational differences between the sexes level off in the late teens, there are fewer theoretical advantages for educating them separately. Coed colleges would seem to make more educational sense than coed schools, although A. W. Astin's massive 1977 study of 200,000 undergraduates in 300 colleges suggested otherwise.[10]

From the onset of adolescence, there are new, emotionally vivid gender issues afoot in classroom and corridor. Adult sexual potency is reached, and its attendant urges and manifestations must be managed by the executive capacity of a very recent child. Adolescents must address this demanding and dramatic task while, simultaneously, they are asked to do more and more difficult kinds of schoolwork. Middle- and high school students are challenged to progress from concrete to theoretical forms of thought. Higher mathematics is introduced. Students are asked to use language less literally, more symbolically. The performance expectations of athletes and artists and performers are dramatically elevated. Schoolwork and extracurricular performance are increasingly graded and evaluated, and the evaluations are increasingly consequential.

For deep biological reasons, schooling pubescent boys and girls together produces inequitable distractions. Only some of the erotic distraction experienced by boys and girls in school is active and visible—flirting, erotic looking, dressing, grooming, posturing for romantic effect. A substantial if not dominant part of the diverted energy goes into suppressing sexual interests and urges. The flattest adolescent appearances are likely to express intense arousal neutralized by equally intense suppression; apparent imperviousness to nubile gender opposites comes at some cost. Expressed or suppressed, however, sexual distraction is an undeniable impediment to focused activity, to learning and development. This is why Astin attributed the positive effects of single-sex colleges to "restricted heterosexual activity" and why Valerie E. Lee and Anthony S. Bryk's 1986 study of coed and single-sex parochial schools invited a reconsideration of learning environments where adolescent boys' and girls' "social and academic concerns are separated."[11] Or, as a colleague of mine put it recently, "I like boys' schools because the intersexual posturing that interferes with my work goes on somewhere else." That it does go on somewhere else is, of course, crucial to healthy adolescent development, but, despite the predominance of coeducational schools, there seems to be no demonstrable evidence that the experience of boys and girls together during school hours contributes positively either to cross-gender socialization or to learning.

Here the intuitive advocate of coeducation may well ask, "But what about the child who simply prefers going to school with the opposite sex?" There is a robustness, an agreeable weight to this objection, particularly if rounded off with, "It's a coed world after all." The question of the adolescent's own preference for coeducation deserves to be taken seriously. It will be an *adolescent* preference, incidentally, not a childhood preference generally. Preadolescent children, given the chance and mobility to do so, exhibit a powerful tendency to seek out their own gender for mutual or group activity—despite their placement in both-gender settings from preschool years onward. Indeed, possibly the most underexplored feature in the sociology of education is the persistence of same-sex structures within coed schools. There is, it might be demonstrated, a shadowy boys' school and girls' school underlying every coed school. Certain members of each make heady forays into the other, and from the rest there is a good deal of gawking, speculating, and general preoccupation with those of the opposite sex who are most proximate.

To return to adolescent preferences: what sort of school program would adolescents, as a body and unguided, prefer? Would they prefer more rigorous and more required courses or fewer? More homework or less? A longer or shorter school day, school year? Required or optional commitments? Classroom exposure to classical culture or to pop culture? Would adolescents prefer to sit through a performance of *As You Like It* or a screening of *Risky Business?* Systematically explore the historical record or discuss the events of the day? Read *Moby Dick* or *Jaws?* If most would opt for the latter alternatives over the former, is there a robustness, an agreeable weight to *these* preferences? It is hard to see why an adolescent preference for coeducation should be regarded as any more substantial than other, highly arguable youthful inclinations.

In the fall of 1989, a delightful bit of anthropological research was carried out by Julia Kennedy, a senior at the Buckingham, Browne and Nichols School, a coed independent school in Cambridge, Massachusetts. On special assignment from her school newspaper, Kennedy donned her brother's clothes, a friend's spectacles, and, in collusion with the editor of the student paper of Boston's Roxbury Latin School, set out to document the ethos of boys' school life from her disguised feminine perspective. Announced to the school as a visiting student journalist, "Justin" Kennedy proceeded through a day of exclusively male camaraderie and a scholastic program that included courses in English, contemporary American history, calculus, art, and chemistry. The day was understandably harrowing for her at times; she initiated, but could not bring herself to complete, a mission to the men's room. She carried with her certain expectations from her own well-established coed college preparatory school, and she reported as many similarities as differences to it in the all-boys setting. The Roxbury Latin School, founded in 1645 by the British divine John Eliot, is an academically rigorous, highly regarded school, and Kennedy knew it. But what about its *boy*-ness? The following is excerpted from her published account of her day.

> The bell rang after about twenty minutes, and we headed for English. During class, the all-male atmosphere became apparent. Here, although the class discussion was quite intelligent, the students seemed more relaxed than at B.B.&N., and ready to joke around.
>
> While analyzing Wordsworth's poem "Tintern Abbey," [the teacher] inquired, "Does he like his sister?" "I like his sister!" [a student] boasted. Mr. Randall laughed again, shook his head, and remarked, "This is a steamy little class here." Nobody looked at me to see if I was offended. Nobody expected me to be.[12]

While duly impressed, Kennedy was on balance less interested in the caliber of the boys' academic performance than in the behaviors that might bear on their relations with girls. A day in the midst of these boys' school boys seemed to alleviate her concerns that they might be missing something essential in gender relations:

> I dreaded unbearably crude jokes in class, guys slapping my rear in camaraderie, or else myself nearly getting into a fist fight by the end of the day. However, when none of these horrors happened, I wasn't too surprised.
>
> [Boys] may spend eight hours each day with hardly a female in sight, but this doesn't mean they don't know how to treat girls. In fact, all-boys' schools never [!] produce boys who behave differently from boys with a coed school education.
>
> They just make for a very interesting day.[13]

An interesting day, and then some. Speaking personally, I too can recall my sudden immersion into boys' school life. While, unlike Julia Kennedy, I entered the school (Cleveland's University

School) as a male and as a new member of the faculty, the composition and tone of the school made a vivid contrast to the coeducational high school and college I had attended. I had chosen the school because I needed the job, not for its all-boy composition. I had liked my earlier visits and was impressed by the directed liveliness in the classes I observed. What I had admired, I thought, was the vigorous, down-to-business tone of the school, which I attributed to the quality of the students enrolled and to an especially effective faculty. I was, if anything, unfavorably disposed to the idea of an all-male student body. Again, boys' schools had played no part in my own (far from exemplary) education, and I wondered whether boys without girls might not evolve into forms of barbarism unfamiliar to me. As it happened, my prejudices were unfounded. I was not unpleasantly surprised by the boys' approach to school life, but I was surprised. In each class, at each baseball practice, at the luncheon table, but most vividly in the continuous stream of light and serious conversation with them in the hallway, after class, or on the way to and from the fields, I was aware of something altogether new to me. There was an unaffected directness, an authenticity I had not experienced before in a school and that I had not thought possible between students and their teachers. Attempting to describe it to my wife, I used the term "edge." There was a special edge to boys' school life, a positive edge.

Twenty-two years have passed since I registered those initial impressions. I have now dwelled professionally in a boys' school, the same one, so long and so agreeably that I find it hard to imagine deliberately deciding to school children otherwise. I find it continually, renewably inspiring that my colleagues and the boys they teach set such staggeringly high goals for their intellectual, athletic, and artistic performance. The striving after these creates the edge I sensed years ago. Until I observed it in a boys' school, I never saw adolescents so self-directed or so resourceful. Life has never been easy in my school. Challenges are real, consequences are sometimes hard. Even gifted boys are unlikely to succeed without tenacity and courage. It is possible to fail. Despite, and in some respects because of, the fact that their school life poses real challenges, the boys express more straightforward support and affection for one another than I had ever thought possible among schoolchildren.

Whatever I expected from the teaching life in my twenties, I do not think it included a sustained infusion of inspiration and hope, but that is what happened. That is what the edge has produced. I am grateful, but no longer surprised, that I learned this lesson in a boys' school. It is a durable lesson.

Notes

1. Robert Bly, "What Men Really Want," *New Age,* September 1982: 31.
2. Ibid., p. 32.
3. Ibid., p. 34.
4. Ibid., p. 37.
5. Ibid., p. 33.
6. Nancy J. Chodorow, *Feminism and Psychoanalytic Theory* (New Haven: Yale University Press, 1989).
7. Sigmund Freud, *An Outline of Psychoanalysis* (New York: Norton, 1969), pp. 46–47.
8. Anthony S. Bryk and Valerie E. Lee, "Effects of Single-Sex Secondary Schools on Student Achievement and Attitudes," *Journal of Educational Psychology* 78, no. 5 (1986): 381–95.
9. J. M. Tanner, "Sequence, Tempo, and Individual Variations in Growth and Development of Boys and Girls Aged Twelve to Sixteen," in *Twelve to Sixteen: Early Adolescence,* ed. Jerome Kagan (New York: Norton, 1971), pp. 1–24.
10. A. W. Astin, *Four Critical Years: Effects of College and Beliefs, Attitudes and Knowledge* (San Francisco: Jossey-Bass, 1977).
11. Ibid.; and Bryk and Lee, "Effects of Single-Sex Secondary Schools on Student Achievement and Attitudes," p. 381.
12. Julia Kennedy, "I Was a Boy for the Vanguard," Roxbury Latin School *Tripod* (Boston: 1989), p. 10.
13. Ibid.

6

Girls' Schools:
Separate *Means* Equal

Rachel Phillips Belash

Milford Haven, where I was born and raised, is a small town on the west coast of Wales. It is plebeian in caste, energetic and boisterous by nature, like the blustery gales it weathers on more days a year than its inhabitants like to admit. Deeply egalitarian at heart, it only rarely produced a family that looked elsewhere for education; everyone else "mucked in," as we used to say, making the best of the state system, which for years streamed eleven-year-olds into "grammar," "technical," and "normal" schools, and later, under the Labour Government, into "comprehensive" schools modeled, perhaps ineptly, on the British idea of the American system.

Here I battled my way through six years of unself-conscious, examination-driven, and determinedly coeducational schooling. I scoffed at the few girls I knew who went away to places with names like Cheltenham Ladies' College and came home for holidays in uniforms that invariably included cloaks instead of our standard gabardine raincoats. Since I did poorly in the ongoing girl-boy popularity contest, I learned instead how to get the better of the boys in class—if you did your homework, answered questions, and fed the teachers back what they had told you, it was easy to get good marks and come out top of the class. Where student leadership was concerned, the system preserved a rough justice by having boy prefects and girl prefects, a head boy and a head girl, and so on. As head girl of my year, downtrodden I was not—but smart, good girls were not social hits, and high grades were chilly compensation on a dateless Saturday night. Life was a battle—tough, unrewarding, and grim.

Almost three decades later and three thousand miles across the Atlantic, working in a bank's corporate headquarters, I was pondering my flight from the academic world when I received a phone call from a former colleague. Why didn't I consider running for the headship of the place where she was now teaching, a girls' boarding school as a matter of fact? Returning to education in *any* school felt like going home, and there seemed little to risk, as my chances of getting the position were certainly thin. Yes, I had started teaching years before in a girls' day school, but that had been a very part-time commitment, sandwiched in between having and raising babies, and undertaken to get out of the house and preserve sanity, not as a career move. More recently I had had a brief experience at a large coed school that was amalgamating its two single-sex halves into a new whole where, at least at that time, "coeducation with a difference" was the watchword. With real knowledge neither of boarding schools nor of girls' schools, I had nothing to lose, and the interest of the application process to gain. So why not enjoy the experience and become a candidate?

The first interview was enough to make me realize how badly I wanted to be back in the world of schools. Having reassured myself that the much touted dichotomy between the "ivory tower" and the "real world" was a myth at best, a dangerous slur at worst, I knew where I belonged. And miraculously, the doors reopened for me. Blessing whatever fates had conspired in my favor, I accepted the offer when it came, with alacrity and in the same spirit in which many of its students seem to enroll—the love affair with the school was instantaneous and, on the surface at least, had nothing to do with its being for girls only. I felt, in short, that I accepted the position despite the school's being single-sex, not because of it. Thus, for me to make the case for girls' schools from conviction is in fact to chronicle a conversion.

What appealed to me so strongly, even on a first visit during a February blizzard? An unknown adult walks through the door, and girls smile and say, "Hi." Even, sometimes, "Can I help you?"

An instant friendliness I have never experienced on another campus, certainly not back home in Wales, nor at my children's coed schools. A sense of spontaneity that doesn't disappear in front of adults but seems a perfectly natural part of life. A sense of respect and affection from students to teachers and vice versa. A deep sense of belonging—this is the girls' place, they like it here, and they like each other. A feeling of complete freedom to try their hand in any area that appeals to them, and an underlying confidence that they can do anything. Lots of kidding around, jokes, laughter, some tears, easy self-expression. Classrooms filled with girls' voices, questioning, discussing, arguing, *learning* in any number of ways. Girls competing for leadership positions, proud to win them and comfortable with the exercise of authority. And lots of friendships, made, broken, remade, betrayed, realigned, but always with great concern for each other and deep awareness of the importance of this part of their lives.

Still starry-eyed from finding myself once again involved in what I consider the most important work of all—educating kids— and in such a propitious environment, I was jolted into reality the first time I spoke off-campus as the head of a school. "Why a girls' school?" seemed to be the question on everyone's mind, from alumnae uncertain how to guide their daughters' school choices, or just nervous about the school's future, to prospective parents not sure if girls' schools should be taken seriously, to professional colleagues looking at enrollment statistics and demographic realities. Frankly, like many other people I had simply assumed that girls' schools had as much right to exist as coed schools and would go on existing ad infinitum. Only as head of one such school did I realize that the issue really at stake was survival. Needless to say, my attention became riveted on the problem, and the first thing to explore was the depth of my own conviction, to this point almost completely unscrutinized. I had for years been a passionate advocate of women's issues. How did girls' schools fit into the big picture? I began clinically observing the day-to-day scene around me and reprocessing my own experiences in light of my new circumstances and of the books and articles I was reading. What I found available in the early 1980s that had not existed ten or more years earlier was a growing body of psychological and socio-pedagogical research. The research is accessible and by now generally well-known, or at least known about. Personal experiences are also important, I think, because when intellect and emotions fuse together realization becomes rooted and therefore powerful. Indeed one of the first such moments of fusion occurred soon after my return to schooling, when, like many other women, young and not so young, I read Carol Gilligan's *in a Different Voice*,[1] and experienced what Martin Gardner calls the "aha" phenomenon of deep recognition.

In fact it was Gilligan whose work initially led me into the area of psychological research that has had the most direct implications for the education of young women. Following the growth of feminist studies from the 1960s on had always been important to me, and here was a direct bridge to the life of an all-female community. What the body of new scholarship has achieved is an understanding of female psychology as an area valid in and of itself, not merely of interest because of its degree of deviation from a male-defined norm. What Carol Gilligan did at Harvard's Graduate School of Education in the early 1970s was to take a fresh look at Lawrence Kohlberg's work on the development of moral decision making from childhood through adolescence and to ask some deceptively simple questions: "Why has this and other theory-building research been based only on the experience of males?" and, even more devastatingly: "Why hasn't someone noticed this before *and done something about it?*" At once powerful and radical like all strokes of genius, the blinding simplicity of Gilligan's premise (that psychological theories of human development have heretofore excluded the experience of half the human race) has tended to obscure its revolutionary consequences. Like Jean Baker Miller and her colleagues at the Stone Center for Developmental Services and Studies at Wellesley College, and Peggy McIntosh and others at the Center for Research on Women, also at Wellesley, Carol Gilligan, Nona Lyons, and their co-workers have made it their business to take the study of women seriously and to ensure that mainstream thinkers take it seriously too. Much of this work has been done with the help and backing of institutions traditionally devoted to women's advancement. Should it surprise us that it is Wellesley that has provided the base for the two groups I mention, or that two recent foci of research for Gilligan and her team have been schools devoted to the education of girls—the Emma Willard School in Troy, New York, and the Laurel School in Cleveland, Ohio?

In a Different Voice, Gilligan's first book, had spoken powerfully to me as a woman, a mother, and an educator. In the latter capacity I find even more pertinent the results of the more recent longitudinal studies, whose subjects were girls in grades ten through twelve at Emma Willard, and from grade five on at Laurel. The studies show that female adolescence cannot be neatly matched to previously accepted (and male-based) norms, and that for girls adolescence is an especially critical period. Gilligan describes it with an image that lingers in the reader's mind: "As the river of a girl's life flows into the sea of Western culture, she is in danger of drowning or disappearing."[2] She continues: "To take on the problem of appearance, which is the problem of her development,[3] and to connect her life with history on a cultural scale, she must enter—and by entering disrupt—a tradition in which 'human' has for the most part meant male."[4] Since the tradition of liberal education certainly involves leading young people to "connect . . . with history on a cultural scale," the problem hits the high school educator squarely on the jaw. By forcing adolescent girls into this new connection, do we force them also into emotional alienation? And if so, do girls' schools do any less damage than other schools?

My life for the past few years has been spent in the company of adults who work, in one way or another, to minimize this alienation. When the student body is female and more than half the teachers are women, there is an unspoken validation of female norms and their consequences. It is understood instinctively that adolescent girls are alienated by a sense of disconnection and that strengthening the sense of self goes hand in hand with a strengthened sense of relationship with others.[5] Teachers are willing to accept that these psychological truths have implications both for what girls are taught and for how they are most likely to learn. Hence, girls' school faculties are more invested than are their colleagues in coed schools in making changes in form and content if these may be of benefit to girls—gender-balancing the curriculum, for instance, or downplaying competitive behavior in the classroom. It is interesting and heartening that educators are beginning to recognize that these insights, first seen as relevant only to girls, are in fact conducive to boys' education and development, too. As we should have known all along, when we enlarge our world view to include any previously excluded segment of humanity, we enrich our concept of humanness itself.

For myself as a school head, one of the most pertinent chapters in the account of the study at Emma Willard is that in which a group of the teachers involved with the study from start to finish talk about their reactions to its findings. A comment that strikes a female reader with great poignancy is made by Paul Lamar, an English teacher, who has become acutely aware of how a female student may be approaching an issue from a perception totally different from his own: "That always struck me as such a profound mismatch, what one person was seeing as being the issue and what the other person was seeing as the issue. And actually I play out in my own mind the frustration that the girl must feel because she is saying exactly what she sees as the problem and, I guess by extrapolation, what it is like not to have your point of view validated and how frustrating that would be over the long haul, never to be taken seriously."[6] For many girls an alternative to not being taken seriously is "disappearing," in Gilligan's terminology.

Drawing upon the model of the "connected" or "separate" knower used by Mary Belenky and her colleagues[7] and described by Nona Lyons,[8] Emma Willard teachers talked about their responses both to curriculum content and to teaching styles. The last decade has produced much evidence that a collaborative approach to teaching, particularly of math and science, is often extremely effective, not only with young women but also in other "at-risk" situations (such as the Undergraduate Math Workshop established in the late 1970s by the Professional Development Program at the University of California, Berkeley, to shepherd students of color through introductory calculus and science courses). Here is the testimony of Anne Riendeau, a math teacher at Emma Willard: "All my life I have known that I learned math by doing homework with my friends, comparing answers on the telephone, in the dorms, or on the way to school. This included male and female friends in high school and classmates in an all-female college. It was never something we would admit. If anyone ever found out we hadn't 'done our own work,' we felt wrong and accused of having cheated. Yet all intellectual pursuits and learning take place with exchanges of information and ideas. We do not learn in a vacuum. There is as much learning that takes place in the small groups of two or three as there is that takes place at the individual desk."[9]

During the last decade other reformist efforts have joined feminist scholarship in creating a climate more propitious to non-traditional teaching methods.[10] Furthermore, the fact that a school's student body is all-female does not in and of itself guarantee enlightenment. Yet a sense of crisis powerfully focuses the attention, and the heightened consciousness of the defenders of girls' schools has produced an increasingly alert and dynamic group of schools. Thus, many girls' school teachers (though not they alone, of course) have profited from understanding that girls develop their sense of self through relationships and that learning takes place more naturally in cooperative than solitary situations. By legitimizing collaboration in class over projects, even in producing papers, as well as by including material that speaks to the female experience in all subject areas, girls' schools have, in the past ten or fifteen years, brought themselves dramatically to the forefront of enlightened pedagogy.

Over these same years, gender differences in math and science have been endlessly debated. A report from the 1983 Conference on Girls and Women in Science and Mathematics organized by the Council on Women in Independent Schools of the National Association of Independent Schools analyzed the causes for the lagging performance of females. The report opens with categorical directness: "To succeed in mathematics and science, students must be risk-takers; that is, they must be willing to ask questions, to hazard guesses, to learn to use unfamiliar equipment, to take on challenging spatial and conceptual problems." Describing student patterns in coed schools, the report tells us, "Women teachers of both science and math see girls and boys behaving differently when faced with risk. . . . Girls, from the junior high years on, often try a helpless, flirtatious approach to challenge rather than leaping in with the fearless bravado characteristic of boys." After outlining the problem and prescribing possible remedies, the report's last paragraph opens thus: "The fact that girls in single-sex schools seem to face math and science with equanimity and even enthusiasm leads to an inference that single-sex math and/or science classes might be profitably employed, either at all or at certain stages of development." Ah, yes, say those of us who recognize from our own experience that the effectiveness of the girls' school does indeed derive from the creation of an environment where female adolescents can develop an assertive, risk-taking, questing attitude toward learning, while at the same time maintaining the connectedness in which the sense of self is strengthened. [11]

A recent statistical study documents in quantitative terms the value of an all-girls' school education. Valerie E. Lee, of the University of Michigan, and Anthony S. Bryk, of the University of Chicago, completed a longitudinal study of about 2,500 students— half of them girls—in seventy-five Catholic high schools, both single-sex and coeducational. The study showed that girls from the girls' high school were more likely to enjoy math, do more homework, have higher test scores in vocabulary, reading, math, and science, and have more ambition as well. [12] Follow-up research, as yet unpublished, focusing on the same 2,500 students once they went to college "showed that the gains girls made in their single-sex schools continued, even though more of them chose coed colleges. The alumnae of girls' high schools went to 'more selective' colleges; they were more interested in politics, reported being more satisfied with their college experiences and were more apt to apply to graduate schools and choose non-traditional careers, according to Lee." [13]

As the psychology of the student affects learning, so that of the teacher affects pedagogy. In the last few years, interesting facts about how teachers handle males and females in coeducational classes have come from two sources in particular, the work of Catherine Krupnick at Harvard and of Myra and David Sadker of American University. What we learn is illuminating but may be discouraging to many an earnest practitioner. A team of teaching consultants at the Harvard-Danforth Video Lab led by Catherine Krupnick has spent many hours videotaping a broad range of instructors at Harvard College and elsewhere. Given our culture's emphasis on class participation and on articulateness in general, the team wished to find out how men and women fared in classroom discussions. The results were categorical: male students dominate coed classrooms. In classes with a male instructor and a majority of male students, the men spoke two and a half times longer than their female peers. Worse yet, in classes taught by male teachers with a majority of female students, males dominated discussion by a ratio of nine to one; and worst of all, if a female teacher was teaching a class that was predominantly male, male students talked almost thirteen times as much as the female students. Krupnick then goes on to say, "The only conditions under which male and female students talked in proportion to their numbers was approached by having a female teacher and a predominantly female class, a situation which is, of course, natural in female colleges or female independent schools with all-female student bodies, but is actually fairly atypical in situations elsewhere."[14] Even the scenario of the predominantly female class and female teacher may prove overoptimistic. Asked to observe classes at Wheaton College in its second year of coeducation, Krupnick found a situation that should give educators pause. In classes where they made up one-tenth of the students, male students would do a quarter of the speaking. Though female students at Wheaton tend to do better than their male classmates on written papers, they are losing their chance to develop an ability to speak articulately in public, in itself an important aspect of many of the careers they may subsequently choose. It would seem that in the vast majority of cases, young women will fully develop that ability during their school or college careers only in all-female classrooms.

Lest we in schools unduly pride ourselves on avoiding the pitfalls of college teachers, it should be noted that two professors of education, Myra and David Sadker, have produced similar results for primary and secondary schools. After a three-year study of coed classrooms, with teachers many of whom thought they were even-handed in their treatment of boys and girls, the Sadkers found class discussions dominated by boys to a ratio of three to one, "at all grade levels, in all communities and in all subject areas."[15] Boys are eight times more likely to call out answers—and be listened to—and twice as likely to demand help from the teacher. Teacher behavior is very significant: teachers give boys more attention, praise them more often, and are more likely to have extended exchanges with them. In other words, "Boys receive more specific teacher reaction and benefit from longer, more precise and intense educational interaction.''[16]

Pondering these relatively recent statistics, I am haunted by a classroom scene in Chicago Hall, the language building at Vassar College. I had started teaching there in 1970, the first year the freshman class included males. Either that year or a year later, I interrupted my Latin American literature class to point out that anyone overhearing it from the corridor would assume it was made up of male students with a female teacher. Actually there were ten young women and four young men with me in the room, but the women were almost totally silent. In those days I saw myself as a standard-bearer of the Western tradition. I knew nothing of female psychology except in some vague sense my own, and the notion of women's studies raised my suspicions and my hackles. My response to what I noticed about that class was to blame the young women: why did they take a back seat? Why did they let the boys dominate? Didn't they know I was ashamed of them? My suppositions would have been shaken had Catherine Krupnick or the Sadkers trained their video cameras on me and forced me to examine my own teaching! And how different an experience both I and those young women would have had at the Vassar of ten years earlier (at which time I admit that my male-trained intellectual snobberies might well have discouraged me from accepting a position in a woman's institution).

It would be seven or eight years after this experience of mine that Adrienne Rich would give her great speech to teachers of women, "Taking Women Students Seriously." There were many of us who needed to hear Rich's challenges: "Listen to the women's voices. Listen to the silences, the unasked questions, the blanks. Listen to the small soft voices, often courageously trying to speak up, voices of women taught early that tones of confidence, challenge, anger, or assertiveness are strident and unfeminine."[17] Once again, it must be said that true listening can take place—or not—in any kind of classroom. Had I back then had the benefit of Rich's message I would have had to realize that my own teaching methods in that coed classroom were at fault. I did not hear the women's voices because I was not creating spaces in which they could have their say. I was going along with the rapid-fire dialogue at which the men excelled. The fault was mine.

Similarly, an all-female classroom has not, in the past, ensured that women would be taken seriously, either as objects of study or as subject learners. Nevertheless, given today's more gender-conscious world, in an all-female classroom the odds are certainly vastly higher that young women will receive the attention Rich demands: "We can refuse to accept passive, obedient learning and insist upon critical thinking. We can become harder on our women students, giving them the kinds of cultural prodding that men receive, but on different terms and in a different style. Most young women need to have their intellectual lives, their work, legitimized. . . . We need to be hard to please, while supportive of risk-taking, because self-respect often comes only when exacting standards have to be met."[18] In a girls' school, teachers are responding to no demands but those of young women. Yes, indeed, they get a better deal.

When we shift to the issue of training women for leadership, we have facts (the scarcity of women at top levels of government, the professions, corporate management, educational institutions), anecdotal evidence from those who were encouraged and from those who weren't, and some statistical research to back claims that the presence of female role models plays a crucial role in adolescent women's development. Girls' schools, few as they are, certainly provide such role models in greater abundance and variety than coeducational institutions have yet been able to do. Individual testimony and the available data make clear that awareness of forerunners broadens young women's sense of what is possible and fortifies them in exploring their own capabilities, whether these seem orthodox and traditionally female or not. Taking into account the varied alumnae bodies of women's institutions as well as the female teachers and staff members, this seems indubitable, especially in cases where the head of the school and the board president are also female. (The message sent in girls' schools—too many, alas—where these positions are filled by men should be carefully examined by those responsible.)

In the late 1960s, M. Elizabeth Tidball, a professor at George Washington University Medical Center, undertook "large-scale studies on the baccalaureate origins of women . . . who have attained a substantive intellectual or career accomplishment." Focusing on the achievers' backgrounds, not on women's colleges, Tidball found that "women's colleges appear and reappear . . . by every measure available as the institutional type most productive of achieving women."[19] Tidball correlates this in part with the much higher percentage of adult women achievers in the environment of single-sex colleges, and with these women's degree of satisfaction with their personal and professional lives. The statistical data clearly show that "the number of women faculty and the number of women achievers were highly and positively correlated; their dependence was not a matter of chance."[20]

As the number of women's colleges has declined and the number of women at coeducational institutions has correspondingly risen, research of this sort needs constant updating. Also, we must show due caution in assuming that research on college achievement presents a direct analogy to high-school-age girls. Yet in dealing with critical issues of female psychology and development, all evidence is important. Furthermore, having corresponded with and talked to many of our own alumnae now at coed institutions or making their way in the world, I, like other heads of female schools and colleges, have a storehouse of moving tributes paid to the inner strength these young women felt their single-sex experience had given them. It seems that experience in an all-female environment, be it school or college, does have a bolstering effect on a young woman's confidence in her own abilities.

Since the theme of role models is a constant motif for supporters of female institutions, it was disconcerting, recently, to hear one of the few women heads of an independent coed school cast doubts on their efficacy (during over a decade of my colleague's tenure, the school has never had a girl elected as head of student government). Thinking back on my own experience, however, I would argue that role modeling can often, perhaps most often, have delayed effects. As a student, I found myself at Oxford University (coeducational, I thought, while actually deeply male chauvinistic) but perforce a member of a woman's college, namely Somerville (still single-sex, now fighting for survival). It was not till years after my graduation that I realized the tremendous security, intellectual and psychological, that I had derived from that base of powerful, modest, unself-conscious women dons. Perhaps the very nature of role modeling is to seep into the psyche unperceived, not calling for immediate imitation but, like an underground river, ready to flow to the surface when conditions are right. Older, more scholarly, more experienced than I, these women accepted me into their community of learners without approving or disapproving, without condescending, making no allowances, always demanding compliance with the highest standards, by their respect forcing me to respect myself. Probably only women who at some time in their lives have been part of a similar community, school, or college will understand. But from these ranks come those of us who wish to see female institutions not merely survive but flourish.

Finally, relying now on anecdote and observation, two interrelated characteristics of girls' schools inspire not only mention but celebration. The first is the development of close personal relationships that lead to lifelong friendships; the second is the playfulness that single-sex schools seem to foster. I will not dwell on the former—the importance to girls and women of connectedness with others is emphasized in all the sources mentioned earlier. The ability to play, however, is less often noted in school catalogues and magazines, and yet it is a very important part of the life that girls develop for themselves in schools of their own. There are the rites of passage by which newcomers are made members of the group— this is play as ritual, taken seriously and handed on as hallowed tradition; there are skits and parodies of school life written and acted by students; dressing up is a constant source of fun, especially when teachers can be persuaded to join in the game. Serious study is punctuated by spontaneous outbursts of high spirits, of sheer silliness, sometimes even horseplay, especially among the younger girls. In an era when we deplore high-pressure parents and the early advent of adulthood,[21] we should appropriately foster environments that allow teenagers to let childhood linger a bit and learn to distinguish between being childish and childlike. Before they enroll in a single-sex school, girls seem unsure that anything worth calling "fun" can take place without the opposite sex. Once acclimatized, they become aware of new possibilities, of a freedom to deal with their own changing self-image, to explore who they are and who they are becoming. And behind it all is the camaraderie, the relationships, and the encouragement of creative, productive play.

When all is said and done, the case for girls' schools rests on the importance for young women of a place of their own. In the early to mid-nineteenth century it took women—in this country Mary Lyons, Emma Willard, Sarah Porter—to take women seriously enough to educate them beyond the eighth grade (something we now take as a basic democratic right). Yet the history of the female institution in more recent times has been a troubled one, especially since progress towards gender equality was for many years, and to a large extent still is, defined in terms of storming the male bastions of power—elite schools, colleges, clubs, boardrooms. Thirty years ago several girls' academic high schools flourished in major cities. In 1972, Girls' Latin School in Boston changed its name and opened its doors to males. In 1986, the New York City Board of Education compelled the Washington Irving High School, the last single-sex public school in the city, to go coed. None other than Diane Ravitch said of that event, "The Board of Education was wrong. . . . The advantages of single-sex education, especially for girls, are well known. . . . Something about the atmosphere of an all-girls school or college encourages women to excel."[22] Yet in the private sector, where choice is the clarion call, women's colleges have decreased in number from 228 twenty years ago to 94 today, and of the 870 NAIS schools, only 109 are for girls alone. In 1963, 166 of 682 members were girls' schools.

In 1928, Virginia Woolf spoke for women's full inclusion in the tradition of the liberal arts and sent her challenge to the female undergraduates recently admitted to Oxbridge to give voice in themselves to "the dead poet who was Shakespeare's sister."[23] But in 1979, Adrienne Rich still felt impelled to ask teachers, and teachers of women at that, "to think of ourselves seriously, not as one of the boys, not as neuters or androgynes, but as *women*";[24] this only a few short years after Carol Gilligan had asked the question that may ultimately change, more dramatically than any other, society's attitudes to theories of human development. It can be argued that girls' schools and women's colleges have existed all along: why, therefore, has change been so elusive, so minimally incremental? My answer would be that the kind of changes necessary fully to incorporate women and all marginal others[25] into a global and inclusive society are monumental because they call into question the whole of the Western Judeo-Christian tradition; that if one considers the time that has elapsed since Plato advanced his immensely radical and instantly forgotten vision of genderless education in book five of *The Republic,* great strides have been made in a very small percentage of those almost two and a half thousand years. Without the determination of our foremothers, who found the female academies both a source of support and the only power base available to them, and without those academies themselves, progress would have been slower still. During my own journey from youthful skepticism to considered conviction, I have sometimes found it tempting to feel that with a few more forward strides we will reach a world that will no longer call for centers of female solidarity.[26] In retrospect, however, I now agree with David Riesman, who takes a contrary and, I think, wiser view: "My own inclination is rather to think that the slight genetic differences and the unlikelihood that fathers will ever take fully equal responsibility for child-rearing in the American grain make girls' schools not transitional."[27] I now feel that girls' schools provide an environment that not only is good in and of itself but that also, in its redefinition of competitiveness and collaboration, of autonomy and connectedness, presents a model that other schools do well to emulate.[28]

So my defense of girls' schools is also the record of some of the stages of my own journey from those early, unaware days, through the battles for equal rights and equal access, to a recognition of and respect for difference. Yet the world is much with us, and we must be ever on our guard. As head of a girls' school, I am received with a respect that derives from respect for the position I hold; does the big, wide world accord more respect to a woman head of a coed school? One wonders. And old habits die hard. Searching for an appropriate conclusion for this chapter, I was about to give David Riesman the last word, in deference to his stature and his scholarly worth. One of my daughters saw only recidivism in my closing a case for girls' schools with a male stamp of approval, no matter what that male's reputation. Accused, and feeling guilty, I take credit vicariously for her reaction. I silently hope that when the time comes we can still find a selection of good girls' schools for her daughters, so we can consolidate these generational gains!

Notes

1. Carol Gilligan, *In a Different Voice* (Cambridge, Mass.: Harvard University Press, 1982).

2. Carol Gilligan, Nona P. Lyons, and Trudy J. Hanmer, eds., *Making Connections: The Relational Worlds of Adolescent Girls at Emma Willard School* (Cambridge, Mass.: Harvard University Press, 1990), p. 4.

3. See Gilligan's discussion of the musical as opposed to the linear interpretation of the word "development" (Ibid., pp. 318-20). Of course, an inevitable extension of the work of Gilligan and her colleagues is a broadening of the definition of human development, both male and female. The need for inclusion, however, belongs specifically to women and other marginalized groups.

4. Ibid., p. 4.

5. Ibid., p. 10, where Gilligan cites her own work and that of other researchers.

6. Ibid., p. 286.

7. Mary Belenky, Blythe Clinchy, Nancy Goldberger, and Jill Varule, *Women's Ways of Knowing* (New York: Basic Books, 1986).

8. Gilligan, Lyons, and Hanmer, *Making Connections*, pp. 64-69.

9. Ibid., pp. 294-95.

10. Collaborative learning is an inevitable result in student-centered as opposed to teacher-centered classrooms. It is interesting to note that the discovery of the pertinence to girls of collaborative classrooms has coincided with the growth of the Coalition of Essential Schools under the aegis of Theodore Sizer. One of the principles of the essential schools is "student as worker," which in practice produces not only active learners but much group participation.

11. An interesting comparative study of girls' and boys' performance in mathematics classes both coeducational and single-sex has been done by Rena Subotnik, coordinator of Gifted Programs at Hunter College, using students at Hunter College High School and at the Brearley School. See Rena Subotnik,

"Coeducation or Separate Schooling?" (Progress report read at Brearley Alumnae Day Panel, 1989, and printed in the *Brearley Alumnae Magazine,* Summer 1989: 11–15).

12.   See Valerie E. Lee and Anthony S. Bryk, "Effects of Single-Sex Secondary Schools on Student Achievement and Attitudes," *Journal of Educational Psychology* 78, no. 5 (1986): 381–95.

13.   Quoted by Alice Digilio in "Classrooms of Their Own," *Washington Post Education Review,* August 6, 1989: 4.

14.   Catherine Krupnick, "Equalizing Classroom Discussions: Gender Differences" (Proceedings of the Sixty-Seventh Annual Meeting, National Association of Principals of Schools for Girls, Colorado Springs, 1988), pp. 150–51.

15.   Myra and David Sadker, "Sexism in the Schoolroom of the '80's," *Psychology Today,* March 1985: 54–57.

16.   Ibid., p. 56.

17.   Adrienne Rich, *On Lies, Secrets and Silence* (New York: Norton, 1979), p. 243. See also Michael Gorra, "Learning to Hear the Small, Soft Voices," *New York Times Magazine,* May 1, 1988: 32.

18.   Ibid., p. 244.

19.   M. Elizabeth Tidball, "Women's Colleges—Seven Decades of Women Achievers," *Sweet Briar College Alumnae Magazine,* Fall 1986: 2–3.

20.   M. Elizabeth Tidball, "Academic Women and Affirmative Action," *Educational Record,* Spring 1973: 130–35.

21.   Neil Postman, *The Disappearance of Childhood* (New York: Delacorte Press, 1982).

22.   Diane Ravitch, "Coed Schools Aren't Necessarily Good," *New York Daily News,* May 1990: 42.

23.   Virginia Woolf, *A Room of One's Own* (London: Harcourt Brace Jovanovich, 1929), p. 199.

24.   Rich, *On Lies,* p. 240.

25.   An illuminating example of how working to broaden the curriculum to include the experience of women logically leads to an awareness of and concern with the experience of all marginalized groups is seen in the development of Peggy McIntosh's writing. As associate director of the Wellesley College Center for Research on Women, Peggy McIntosh has guided

many schools and colleges towards a gender-balanced, or at least a less gender-biased, curriculum. Yet her most recent article in *Independent School,* Winter 1990, entitled "White Privilege: Unpacking the Invisible Knapsack," moves towards even greater inclusiveness.

26. Rachel Phillips Belash, "Why Girls' Schools Remain Necessary," *New York Times,* February 22, 1988: "Yes, some people think girls' schools are anachronisms, but they succeed, better than most people realize, and remain necessary in a world where men and women still do not work equally together as professionals" (p. A19).

27. David Riesman, personal letter to the author, March 3, 1988.

28. For an interesting and analogous treatment of how gradual integration of female values into top-level management is producing a more collaborative kind of leadership and changing the definition of strong leadership, see Sally Helgesen, *The Female Advantage: Women's Ways of Leadership* (New York: Doubleday, 1990), part 3.

7

Becoming Coeducational: A Report from Deerfield

Michael S. Cary

> You may say what you want to, but in my opinion she had
> more sand in her than any girl I ever seen; in my opinion
> she was just full of sand. It sounds like flattery but it ain't
> no flattery. And when it comes to beauty—and goodness,
> too—she lays over them all.
> —Mark Twain, *The Adventures of Huckleberry Finn*

Huck Finn's words about Miss Mary Jane Blodgett are a revelation—a teenage boy's discovery of the depth and strength of character in a young woman. The world of the Widow Watson, an uncomfortable place of form, order, and propriety, was as strange to the boy as it was confining. The freedom and fraternity of the raft bring their own reassurance that the world can be observed safely at arm's length—but the view comes with a price. Even with a good moral compass and a hawk's eye for foibles, Huck, while he remains on the raft, suffers from a fundamental ignorance about the way the world works.

The argument for a boys' boarding school is an argument for viewing the world from the raft. Economy of purpose and certainty of task, the ability to address the needs of a particular group of

This chapter first appeared in the spring 1991 issue of *Teachers College Record* (vol. 92, no. 3). Reprinted with permission.

young people at a complicated time in their lives, are the warrant for all single-sex schools. Simplicity, clarity, straightforwardness in a school community enable young people to appropriate knowledge more effectively. Deerfield could make the claim that it was a rigorous but not a complicated place. Still, by the 1986–87 academic year many faculty, together with the academic affairs committee of the board of trustees, were recommending that, after a hiatus of twelve years, the coeducation issue be revisited. Among the faculty a view was emerging that, while the academy did many things well, important dimensions of education were missing in a single-sex environment. At its April 1987 meeting the board charged the headmaster to undertake a full and thorough study of coeducation with a trustee-faculty committee as the mechanism for that study.

The ninety-four page report of this committee addressed every facet of school life: curriculum, faculty, athletics, extracurricular activities, school traditions and ethos, social life, admissions, college matriculation, medical and health issues, and finances and facilities. Admissions data, alumni office annual support records, alumni letters to the headmaster, the results of a faculty survey, a report on meetings with the student body, interviews with five boarding school heads—all became part of the official record for deliberation. Additionally, the study committee read Carol Gilligan's *In a Different Voice*, Lionel Tiger's *Men in Groups*, Valerie E. Lee and Anthony S. Bryk's University of Michigan study "Effects of Single-Sex Secondary Schools on Student Achievement and Attitudes," and the "Bender Report" of the Harvard Admissions Office.[1]

The writers of the coeducation report acknowledged the importance to the board of "hard" issues—the financial costs of coeducation, the effects on admissions and college acceptance, alumni support, and faculty hiring and retention—but urged equal consideration of philosophical issues like the values inherent in a Deerfield education and the identification of the most important pedagogical goals for a contemporary boarding school. When the trustee vote came in February 1988, it had been preceded by three letters from the headmaster to the alumni body detailing the substance of the coeducation debate. Alumni disapproval of the nearly unanimous trustee vote in favor of coeducation was less than had been anticipated and was countered by new alumni interest in admission for daughters.

A four-year, $336 million capital campaign came to its conclusion in the year following the coeducation decision, surpassing by $6 million the campaign goal. The year following the vote was taxing. A third of the campus lay under construction with projects planned before the coeducation vote, including the renovation of two classroom buildings and the building of a new fine arts center, three new dormitories, and new athletic facilities. A planning process that was to involve virtually all members of the school community was under way with the formation of six student-faculty committees and a steering committee. Their charge was to develop policies and make recommendations for implementing coeducation in 1989. Each Tuesday evening during the school year was set aside for committee meetings to plan for changes in curriculum, admissions, athletics, institutional resources, and student life. Committee decisions became public record in three reports to alumni and the school community from the assistant headmaster.

A coeducation speaker series brought to the campus several educators whose views on teaching and residential life were to inform discussion and planning. Addressing the faculty in the winter and spring of 1989 were George Fleck of the Smith College chemistry department on the subject of a nonsexist science curriculum; Rachel Belash, head of Miss Porter's School, on women in power; Ronald Green of the Dartmouth religious studies department on men's issues in coeducation; Marilyn Schuster and Susan Van Dyne, Smith College curriculum consultants, on gender issues in curriculum redesign; Robert Bain, professor of sports psychology at York University in Ontario, on coaching in women's athletics; Ruth Solie of the Smith College music department on women in an arts program; and Dr. Robert Maslund of Harvard Medical School on adolescent development and sexuality. Three former Deerfield faculty members who had gone on to teach at coeducational boarding schools also offered their views in a panel discussion.

Alternating between heady philosophical discourse and choosing the design and colors for the girls' field hockey kilts, coeducational planning became all-consuming. Many believed that perfection lay in the details, others that too much planning would leave the school community enervated and edgy and inhibit the joyful spontaneity of the first year. Virtually all were ready to get on with it by the end of the 1989 school year. One faculty member offered the metaphor of becoming a parent for the first time: all that could be planned for had been; the rest was to be learned by doing. That would require the professionalism of the faculty and the enthusiasm of the student body.

Two important directives from the trustees were to shape the experience of the first coeducational year. The first was that coeducation was not to take place by accretion. Academy enrollment was to remain substantially unchanged. The second was that a "normal" coeducational experience in the first year would require the enrollment of at least 100 girls: Deerfield was not to be a "a boys' school with girls." An enrollment of 100 girls through all four grades would ensure the presence and participation of girls in all facets of school life from the outset.

The academy commenced the 1989–90 school year with 123 girls, the majority of whom were enrolled as ninth and tenth graders. Eight of their number were African-American or Hispanic. Another eleven were international students. Eleven alumni daughters and twenty-one younger sisters brought with them a familiarity with the school and its traditions. More than half of the 212 new students, including day students, were girls. Still, the girls were to be a distinct minority in the first coeducational year.

Admissions experience had suggested a high degree of self-selection in the first girls' applicant group, and, not surprisingly, the admissions yield for girls was several points higher than that for boys. The decision to reserve for girls a number of leadership positions in school organizations and to offer eleven girls' interscholastic sports teams proved to be incentives for many girls in choosing Deerfield from among several offers of admission. Of course, equally appealing was the notion of being one of the "first girls." In spite of campus construction, a national decline in applications to boarding schools, and uncertainty about the transition, Deerfield's applications soared from 640 the previous year to nearly 1,040. Conscious of the fact that both the successes and failures of the first females would be conspicuous, the admissions committee gave careful attention in candidate evaluations to evidence of strength of character and leadership promise.

Evidence of the impact of a coeducational student body on the academic program appeared even before opening day. The dean of studies reported that over half of the prematriculation inquiries about the academic program came from girls, though they constituted only slightly more than one-fifth of the student body. Foreign-language enrollments shot up, with all levels of French and introductory Russian posting new highs. Likewise, enrollments in non-Western-studies courses and advanced placement science courses increased. The academy's new dance program generated enrollment for both academic and athletic credit.

An important policy decision addressed gender balance in Deerfield classrooms. Whenever possible, three or four girls were assigned to a particular section. A gender balance in some classes with no girls in others was thought preferable to a thin distribution of girls across the maximum number of sections. The girls were spared the awkward responsibility of speaking for their gender as a lone voice, but the sacrifice came in senior courses, several of which contained not a single girl. Additionally, girls' academic schedules were structured to include at least two female teachers out of five, a feat made possible with a female representation on the faculty of 30 percent.

In the opening weeks of the first coeducational year the transition seemed to most to be effortless and uncontrived, almost seamless. Deerfield girls entered without fanfare into extracurricular life as tour guides, class officers, editors of student publications, proctors, musicians, actors, and debaters. Librarians reported an increase in the noise level at the library during study hours, perhaps an indication of a more collaborative pattern in study. Boys complained about new parietal regulations and more stringent sign-out procedures for dormitories. In fact, resistance to coeducation has taken the form of resistance to a perceived increase in the structure of community life. The academy became, in the minds of several older male students, more complicated, more regulated, and less casual.

At the same time, the camaraderie that male students had taken pride in was extended to include girls. The mixed reactions to coeducation among students have not been directed ad hominem. The sadness or anger among some boys is a result of a perception of loss. The Deerfield they know is gone, and a new community is taking shape, one whose characteristics are still uncertain in their minds. The fact that several of the changes in community life have been mandated by adults exacerbated their unease. A half-serious "men's club" that formed in the spring term was more a defiant gesture toward the administration than a statement to female students.

What is clear is the student concern that coeducation not mean a homogenization of school life. Enclaves where friendships among boys and among girls can be strengthened are important, in students' minds, to the health of the school. Yet even as they sought time and space for single-sex friendships, students of both genders obviously enjoyed each other's company. One faculty member commented, "I'm struck by the good humor and joking that crosses gender lines. It is a humor with less malice or sarcasm than I have seen in the past." Another noted that students more often lingered in the dining hall for conversation after meals and recalled hearing a cheerfully stated but challenging question, "Well, would you curtail your career for your children so that your wife could take a challenging position?"

"I find the campus more relaxed, open, and accessible," remarked a woman faculty member. "There is more merriment and laughter in my class." For a school community that many faculty believed took itself too seriously, the more relaxed, lighter tone of campus life came as a relief. "Our schizophrenia of intensity in work and play has subsided," noted a history teacher. "The girls' presence has made for a more humane place."

In the classroom the effects were more tangible. Many had wondered about the conservative argument that coeducational classrooms would bring with them a heightened, inhibiting self-consciousness. A member of the English department conceded, "Yes, coeducation has forced greater self-consciousness," but added, "In many if not most cases the self-consciousness creates the possibility, even the likelihood, of self-awareness. . . . There seem to be more students this year who have revealed, assessed, accepted, or reconsidered themselves than I've noticed in previous years. A comment or reminder from a peer of the opposite gender is a wonderfully accurate and unavoidable mirror." "There is no loss of candor in my classroom," wrote a drama teacher. "If anything the candor is more ready."

Anxiety about a bifurcation of male and female voices in the classroom appears to have been unfounded. One science teacher noticed a change in the dynamic of classroom discussion from student to teacher to student to student. "I'm hearing articulate young people speak about issues that literature engenders," wrote an English teacher. "Granted, many girls argue a critical point from their own experiences and perceptions, but I have yet to hear rancor, vindictiveness, or animosity in any female voice in my classes to what might once have been a particularly male point of view."

Some speculated that tension about the coeducation transition played itself out more among the adults in the community than the students: "Perhaps we as faculty at Deerfield are too uptight about issues of sexism. The girls openly resent what often appears as a search for controversy." "The issue of equity between boys and girls in every facet of school life is more valued by adults than by students. Many girls do not like rocking the boat and prefer to moderate dissonance by agreeing, complying, or deferring. This extended the life of some vestiges of chauvinism. I hope and suspect this will change with the increasing number of girls."

Many believe, as does the assistant headmaster, that the issues of equity and parity are related. Deerfield opened in 1990 with more than 200 girls, approximately 37 percent of the student body. The following year was slated to bring the school close to parity in male-female numbers. Coeducation, within the classroom and without, is a matter of balance. The consensus at Deerfield now is that the school should not settle for any status less than fully coeducational. That commitment assumes change in faculty through hiring and retention that parallels change in student enrollment. Unprecedented admissions interest in the academy has confirmed the wisdom of proceeding boldly. There is no halfway point between Huck Finn's raft and the shore with its greater ambiguity, complexity, challenge, and reward.

During the 1990 spring term all Deerfield students were given time in English class to write their reflections about the year and their place in the school. At the end of that school day a special school meeting was called to enable students to share their thoughts with each other. Two weeks later at another school meeting several faculty read excerpts from those student essays. The combination of hopefulness and pointed institutional criticism was striking. Students wrote of the need for greater tolerance, better communication, improved opportunities for school service, more time for reflection. At the same time, they revealed immense pride in their school and impatience with complacency. The institution has, by virtue of coeducation, set its sights higher because mediocrity is more conspicuous now.

Notes

1. Carol Gilligan, *In a Different Voice* (Cambridge, Mass.: Harvard University Press, 1982); Lionel Tiger, *Men in Groups* (New York: Random House, 1969); and Valerie E. Lee and Anthony S. Bryk, "Effects of Single-Sex Secondary Schools on Student Achievement and Attitudes," *Journal of Educational Psychology* 78, no. 5 (1986): 381–95. The "Bender Report" is an internal unpublished Harvard Admissions Office document.

8

Becoming Coeducational:
A Report from Lawrenceville

James T. Adams

In the 1960s, when no less of an authority than the Fifth Dimension announced the dawning of the Age of Aquarius, even those least inclined to consult the zodiac to determine their future saw the light. The clubby world of the great boys' boarding schools, sustained so enthusiastically and generously by their own scions— those blue-blooded old boys exchanging the secret handshake in boardrooms across America—was turned inside out, and before the sun set on the decade of the sixties, it revealed a landscape thickly dotted with freshly coeducational schools. Exeter, Andover, Northfield-Mt. Hermon, Choate, Hotchkiss, and St. Paul's—the New England elite—one by one and within one short decade had become coeducational, and a new era in the history of boarding schools was begun.

Happily for Lawrenceville, a little south and a bit west of New England, dawn came later in the day, about twenty years later in the day to be precise. By the time our alarm went off, the pioneers up north had turned terra incognita into navigable terrain, and the record of their successes and misadventures proved a reliable beacon for us Johnny-come-latelies. The debate over coeducation, which alternately raged and smoldered for twenty years, preoccupied Lawrenceville more than any other issue in its 175-year history.

The idea of coeducating Lawrenceville was first conceived in the late sixties. The established New England schools had gone or were at least on their way to coeducation. The women's movement was gathering momentum, and student opinion at the time supposed that the school's administration hadn't done much right lately anyhow, so radical change made all sorts of sense. In the spring of 1969 the Turning Point Committee, a long-range planning committee formed to midwife the birth of the new post-sixties Lawrenceville, undertook a feasibility study about coeducation at Lawrenceville. Their tepid recommendation for "some form of coeducation at Lawrenceville" was just enough to fuel the debate.

Trustees, faculty, and students were invited to participate in the debate by writing position papers, and the *Lawrence,* the school's newspaper, became vehemently involved. While the debate included some serious discussion of practical issues, among them the admissions picture, it was generally philosophical in nature, and no compelling consensus emerged. Students, predictably enough, were largely for coeducation, but the faculty was somewhat divided and the trustees more so. By the winter of 1971, the board had quietly issued a resolution affirming single-sex education for Lawrenceville.

The resolution was received as quietly as it was issued, but it did not end the debate. The student council invited alumni consideration of the issue by publishing an open letter to the board in the *Lawrentian,* the school's alumni magazine, and they were joined in that forum by the vice-president of the board. In the summer issue of the magazine in 1973 the board announced again the school's determination to remain single-sex for the time being.

That equivocal rejection hardly discouraged proponents of the change. The debate boiled on. Massive but peaceful student demonstrations, a new feasibility study, and the recommendation for coeducation by Bruce McClellan, the headmaster himself, ensued but, alas, were not enough. In 1978, ten years of preoccupation with the topic ended temporarily when the board voted 14 to 11 against coeducation and requested a moratorium on the subject, which was by and large respected. The 1978 class gift, a full set of girls' field hockey uniforms, however, reminded everybody that the issue would not go away forever.

There was a practical flavor to the various reasons to reject coeducation. "If it ain't broke, don't fix it." "What will the alumni say?" "It will cost too much." "Our admissions picture doesn't require it." These considerations waxed and waned over the course of the debate with a whimsical illogic that finally betrayed their ultimately secondary importance. The theme that remained constant throughout the debate, the theme that finally carried the day, was philosophical: a growing sense that the school had not really been honestly debating a commitment to educate girls so much as a commitment to ensure the best educational environment for boys. If the history of schools that coeducated early in the game teaches us anything, it teaches us that that fine distinction may be everything.

The character of the debate, when it resumed in the early eighties, was decidedly different. Practical considerations abounded, most of them familiar, but the difficulties of recently coeducated schools, the legitimacy of the women's movement, and the greater sophistication about the process of coeducating generally had combined to shift the emphasis from the question "How can we better serve our boys?" to "Do we want to educate girls?" The real question then was finally understood, and the answer, delivered by yet another long-range planning committee, the Directions 2000 Committee, was a resounding yes, despite the passionate and articulate opposition of the incoming president of the board. The faculty in 1984 were 95 percent for coeducation; the students as always were overwhelmingly in favor of it; the alumni, if some opposed it, sensed its inevitability; and the board, whose constitution had changed recently to include nonalumni and women, was behind it—behind, that is, the commitment to educate girls, not merely to enhance the education of boys.

In short, we like to believe we coeducated out of philosophical commitment, and we did it with universal enthusiasm and a profound confidence derived from twenty years of study of other schools that coeducated before us. Do it for the right reason and do it with enthusiasm and confidence. Forget everything else. Well, on second thought, don't forget everything else; there's plenty of work to do. We do believe this, however: all the work in the world would have ended badly had it been undertaken by a divided faculty, alienated alumni, a disenfranchised student body, and a board not thoroughly engaged in the process.

That commitment to make girls equal partners in the opportunities and demands of the school informed every preparatory task, and there were many. Twenty-seven months were allotted between the vote and the arrival of girls, and they were well used. A steering committee was established, which promptly begat a litter of other committees devoted to specific issues: rules and regulations, faculty transition, student transition, traditions, athletics, medical and counseling issues, student activities, security, student government, and curriculum.

Parietal rules had to be decided, and certain policy issues had to be resolved: would violation of rules related to sex, for example, be a disciplinary or a counseling issue? (The school decided on the latter.) Campus security was beefed up and campus lighting radically improved. Obvious physical changes were made in the athletic facilities, locker rooms were added, and new fields were created for a doubled athletic program. Faculty had to be sensitized to the needs of girls, the curriculum was reexamined in anticipation of female arrivals, and the infirmary was expanded and a gynecologist added to the staff. Current students had to be prepared emotionally and psychologically, and social implications had to be explored. There were implications for student government (how do we guarantee leadership opportunities for girls, or should we?) and questions of tradition to resolve (how do we preserve treasured rituals without alienating the girls, and how can we help the girls establish their own traditions?). These and other issues preoccupied the school for two years, and each deliberation was driven by one thought: making girls in every way equal partners in the school's opportunities and demands. Timetables had to be established and publications changed. Admissions implications were studied intensively. Alumni had to be informed—and in some cases placated. Over two years of frantic but wildly enthusiastic preparation ensued.

Preparation for coeducation wasn't the only activity going on at Lawrenceville during that period. The school had decided to reduce the population of each of the boys' houses and to introduce a five-course curriculum. That meant considerable construction— $20 million worth—and a dramatic increase in the number of faculty members. When Lawrenceville finally opened its door to girls in 1987, there were four brand-new houses and a faculty much expanded with a variety of female faces among them, including one female senior administrator.

Once the buildings and the faculty were in place, once the program was systematically adjusted in anticipation of the girls, once the steady stream of guest speakers on various topics of education had ended, there was a collective sense that Lawrenceville was as ready as it could be. And then finally they came.

A week later the girls' casual presence all over campus made it seem as though Lawrenceville had always been coed. Now, four years later, having reached a 40 percent target of female enrollment, that seems naturally the case.

Nevertheless, despite all the extensive preparation, it was still impossible to prepare for all the implications of coeducation. There were high hopes for the admissions picture, grave worries about the school's athletic future, and acute anxiety over alumni support, especially as it manifests itself in the green currency of the realm. Only time would tell. Time has told. Here are some figures. Admissions: the year before coeducation Lawrenceville had 828 applications for 231 places. In 1990 there were 1,100 applications for 246 places. And the applicant pool has become much stronger as some inevitable anticipation of more rigorous acceptance standards has set in. Five years ago, for example, the median SATs of a Lawrenceville student were 527 verbal and 620 math. In 1990 they were 571 verbal and 657 math, a combined rise of over 80 points. The consequences in the classroom have been profound. The year the board voted to go coed, 38.6 percent of the student body earned dean's list averages. In 1990 66.9 percent did, even though the curriculum went from four to five courses in the interim. Students took 330 Advanced Placement exams in 1985 with 288 earning a 3 or higher. In 1990 Lawrenceville students took 438 Advanced Placement exams with 380 earning 3 or higher.

One of the best measures of success in the admissions office, paradoxically, has been a modest decline in the percentage of accepted students who choose to come to Lawrenceville. For the first time in a long while, Lawrenceville is competing head to head with some of the most competitive boarding schools—St. Paul's, Choate,

Exeter, and Andover—and not depending upon a diminishing self-selected pool of students who prefer, or whose parents prefer, a single-sex education. A new era in admissions has begun as the number of parents with personal experience of single-sex education diminishes. The decision to coeducate Lawrenceville was not driven by admission concerns, but those interests have proved a powerful vindication of the change.

Athletics: it was widely feared, especially among alumni and the coaching staff, that Lawrenceville's rich athletic tradition would be threatened. Nothing could have been farther from the surprising reality that ensued. During the first year of coeducation the football team had a modest record, but it soundly defeated the three all-boy schools we played, two of which subsequently decided to become coeducational. And girls, despite their initially sparse numbers, have excelled in sports. In the fall of 1990, all five of the girls' varsity squads captured state championships. The local sports pages publicize Lawrenceville's achievements, and girls have contributed disproportionately to that publicity.

Alumni support: the most unsettling anxiety about the move to coeducation has centered on alumni reaction. The year prior to coeducation 37 percent of the alumni contributed $1.3 million to annual giving. Three years later, over 50 percent contributed over $2 million. And the future board president mentioned earlier who argued so passionately for remaining a boys' school? He donated the first girls' house, naming it appropriately after retiring headmaster Bruce McClellan. Even if some alumni were permanently disaffected, many of those who announced they were are returning to the fold, resoundingly affirming the decision.

Perhaps the most encouraging news is the sense that the new alumni are even more enthusiastic than the old alumni. Evidence is sparse and anecdotal, but it is compelling. One hundred members of the class of 1988 contributed to the annual fund last year, even though they are still in college. They return for reunions, organized and spontaneous ones, in astounding numbers, and the new captains' boards in the field house honoring the girls' varsity captains have been largely donated, at $1,000 apiece, by male alumni still in college. These kids are recklessly enthusiastic, and that can only augur well for Lawrenceville's future.

So much for the implications of coeducation for those who would like to come and for those who have already left. What about the ones who are presently on campus? Our commitment, implicit in every preparation and every policy, to treat girls as full-fledged, equal partners in all things Lawrentian has led to a smooth and full assimilation of girls into the life of the school. The house system ensured that girls would meet with leadership opportunities immediately; the admissions office ensured that girls would be strong and self-confident; and the enthusiasm for the change on the part of the faculty and students alike ensured that they would be welcome.

Perhaps the best measure of the success of coeducation at Lawrenceville, more compelling than any statistic, is the report of the 1989 Middle States Evaluation team: "So complete is the transition that a visitor to campus unaware of its history would easily conclude that the School had been a coeducational institution for many years." And, most important of all, the Middle States team commented that the students were "a happy and almost joyous group of young people."

9

Marketing Independence:
Ensuring Survival in the 1990s

Meg Milne Moulton

Woody Allen would most likely divide schools into the same three categories he uses for people: "Those who make things happen, those who watch things happen, and those who wonder what happened."[1] The independent schools that will succeed in the 1990s will be those that "make things happen"; they will be the schools that will not only monitor changes in their landscape but respond to them. Sound marketing strategies will characterize these schools. Those that watch and wonder will struggle for survival.

Marketing is not new to independent education. Consciously or unconsciously, independent schools have been practicing marketing for years. Identifying successful outcomes of an independent education was very much on the mind of one distinguished headmaster in the 1940s, for example, as he promoted his school by sharing with prospective families the names and number of school alumni listed in *Who's Who*.

Often, as the costly alternative to the "free" public school, independent schools have had to keep a watchful eye on maintaining the value of their educational product without losing sight of the needs of their student and parent consumers. In an ever-evolving society, independent schools have exhibited both constancy of purpose and receptivity to change. Both activities are at the core of successful marketing.

During the 1980s the increasing pressures of a competitive marketplace, demographic constraints, and limitations on both personnel and financial resources forced many independent schools to consider a more formalized marketing posture. For some schools, marketing has become a necessity—a matter of institutional survival. Without students and sufficient tuition revenues, educational programming and fiscal well-being at these schools are threatened. The market research and resulting strategies endorsed by the Coalition of Girls' Boarding Schools, for example, were prompted by a concern about the visibility and viability of girls' boarding schools. The coalition's recent marketing efforts have reversed group enrollment trends and, in 1989, resulted in a 2.5 percent increase in enrollments.

For other schools enjoying relative stability in enrollment, marketing has made the difference between mere survival and success. The focus of the marketing effort for these schools is not solely on maintaining bottom-line enrollments but on attracting an academically appropriate and diverse student body and ensuring educational excellence. The focus of the marketing efforts of the Thacher School in Ojai, California, for instance, is not on increasing enrollments but on fine-tuning outreach efforts to create the best possible match between the school and the most diverse and capable students possible. Tremendous effort has been put into the campus visit experience and into developing a current-parent network to help broaden geographic and socioeconomic diversity.

Regardless of an institution's fiscal and enrollment health, it is of paramount importance for all independent schools in the years ahead to pay close attention to both balance sheets and educational outcomes. By employing sound and respectful marketing practices (practices that link institutional strengths with the educational needs of the student), independent schools will be able to preserve and promote their learning experience and realize a more measured fit between the needs of the families they serve and the distinctive attributes of their educational product. It is not enough for independent schools to be unique—they must continually strive to remain unique. A marketing orientation will provide the needed direction in planning, management, and implementation to make that happen.

What delineation of marketing is most appropriate in this context? In their book, *Strategic Marketing for Educational Institutions,* Philip Kotler and Karen Fox extend a useful definition of marketing: "Marketing is the analysis, planning, implementation, and control of carefully formulated programs designed to bring about voluntary exchanges of values with target markets to achieve institutional objectives. Marketing involves designing institutional offerings to meet the target markets' needs and desires, and using effective pricing, communication, and distribution to inform, motivate, and service the markets."[2] As this definition implies, marketing is both a concept and a process. At the very foundation of the marketing concept is the premise that education is a service industry. It is user-centered, not exclusively product-driven. Marketing does not rely on "the sell" but rather on a carefully calibrated strategy directed at effecting meaningful and satisfying exchanges. Unlike sales, marketing "listens"—it listens to the needs of the consumers and seeks to align their needs with the distinctive attributes of the product. The purpose of marketing, suggests Peter Drucker, "is to make selling superfluous."[3]

Taking on a marketing mentality will prompt independent schools to examine, clarify, and confirm their educational purpose, as well as listen to the needs of their existing and potential markets. With an emphasis on quality exchanges, independent schools will be able to encourage higher levels of "customer" satisfaction and institutional loyalty and, ultimately, achieve greater enrollment stability.

The Macro Environment of the Independent School

Demographic trends have fueled the current interest in marketing among independent schools. Nationally, the 1980s saw a decline in the total number of school-aged children (1.6 percent), despite the growth in elementary school enrollment (5.4 percent).[4] Noticeable population shifts occurred (and are continuing to occur) away from the northeastern and midwestern states toward the south, southwest, and west. These trends were reflected in independent school enrollments as well.

The 1990s present a different landscape. Over the course of

the decade, elementary and secondary school enrollments (kindergarten through twelfth grade) will increase by more than 7 percent[5]—with public school enrollments growing at a slightly faster pace than private schools (7.5 percent versus 6.6 percent).[6] The aging 1980s baby boomlet will result in a growth of almost 17 percent[7] in secondary school enrollments by the year 2000, and America will be a nation in which one out of every three residents will be nonwhite.[8]

The economy has not been a friend to independent schools in the past ten years, nor is it likely to be one in the coming ten. Despite increases in median and disposable family income during the 1980s, the American family does not appear to be enjoying a newfound prosperity. The high interest rates related to chronic federal deficits and an inflationary economy continue to eat away at discretionary income. Proportionately more families are in the lower rather than the higher income brackets. Mean income for white families continues to be substantially higher than that of African-American and Hispanic families.[9]

In order to retain a socioeconomically diverse student body, independent schools in the 1990s will be called on to commit more financial aid dollars to ensure diversity and/or be more creative about identifying new sources of funding. For those families who can afford the independent school option there is no question that investment issues will enter into the choice process. Independent schools are costly compared to public schools. More questions concerning value relative to cost will arise as independent schools market themselves to these families.

Changes within the American family and in the fabric of society have also occurred. Traditional families are no longer the norm, comprising only 7 percent of all families.[10] The divorce rate continues to increase (tripling since 1970),[11] and with it the number of single-parent and newly configured homes. Twenty-two percent of all children in this country live in single-parent families (91 percent of which are headed by women).[12] The number of dual-income families is on the rise, as is the percentage of working mothers with school-aged children. Drugs, alcohol, and changing ethical standards have had a profound impact on the teenage population and on the role that schools (both public and private) play in the lives of teenagers.

The marketing implications of these trends for independent schools are considerable. In the broadest sense, independent schools in the 1990s must be prepared to:

- Respond strategically to regional and national demographic shifts
- Plan creatively for decreases in elementary school enrollments and concomitant increases in secondary school enrollments
- Maintain enrollments by defining more precisely and communicating more persuasively their unique, independent nature to a broader cross-section of families
- Allocate financial aid dollars to support greater socioeconomic diversity
- Behave in a fiscally conservative manner and, at the same time, take calculated investment risks to ensure academic substance and quality, encourage diversity, and provide funding to attract and retain capable teachers and students
- Continue to nourish caring and supportive communities that foster high ethical standards of behavior and academic performance
- Become more aware of the competitive environment (in particular, identify distinctive strengths that distinguish independent schools from publicly supported schools)
- Develop a stronger consumer orientation—one that focuses on investment issues and educational and personal outcomes

Obstacles and Opportunities

How can independent schools heighten their visibility? How can they create a greater awareness of who and what they are? How can they deepen marketplace appreciation for their value and accessibility? How can they attract students of quality and diversity without compromising enrollment or fiscal stability? The challenge for independent schools in the 1990s is to frame answers to these questions.

The process begins by looking inward to rediscover and define those enduring qualities that make independent schools unique (from one another and from the public school). Looking to a school's past is often helpful. It sometimes does not make sense, as R.M. Pirsig writes in his book *Zen and the Art of Motorcycle Maintenance,* to "look at where you're going or where you are . . . but then you look back at where you've been and a pattern seems to emerge. And if you project forward from that pattern, then you can come up with something."[13] Reflecting back on the enduring values of a school's past and looking forward to determine how those same values can be translated to equip students to participate in their world will be critical activities as independent schools seek to remain viable and valuable educational alternatives.

Once schools have identified their unique qualities, they must then, as John Esty put it, "proceed to do those things uniquely well, and . . . make sure everyone in sight knows that they are."[14] As independent schools begin to design effective marketing strategies, they should be mindful of the following issues:

Exclusivity. A private independent education is thought to be exclusive and apart from the so-called real world. In numerous research studies conducted by independent schools and organizations, academic quality surfaces as a major calling card. The reputation of independent schools for educational excellence appears to be well grounded. Less well understood and less appreciated is the nonacademic component of the independent school milieu relating to the climate and culture of independent school communities.

Families of prospective students have a very different impression of independent schools than do families of currently enrolled students. Words and phrases such as "exclusive," "homogeneous," "removed from the real world" surface frequently as families of prospective students describe the independent school experience. Those more familiar with independent education use a very different vocabulary—"inclusive," "diverse," "involving," "fostering," "friendly" are common descriptions. Families of prospective students are much more likely to associate a "good ethnic balance," "the real world," and "a variety of people and ideas"[15] with a public school rather than a private independent school. A definite gap exists between perception and reality. In order to realize their full marketing potential, independent schools will have to be more aggressive in their efforts to deepen the public's understanding of the positive realities of their world.

Independence. In the recent National Association of Independent Schools focus group research, the very word "independent" appears to be a source of confusion and misrepresentation. Participants in the focus groups defined independent education as being synonymous with home schooling and self-study and as having "an unstructured educational philosophy."[16] Ironically, the word "private" appears to be a more recognizable descriptor—one that the NAIS studiously steered away from in the 1940s when it fastened on the word "independent" in an effort to highlight freedom from regulation and to downplay elitism.

Cost. Independent schools are perceived to be prohibitively expensive. Regardless of family income, the cost of an independent school education is substantial—especially when compared to the public school. With median 1989–90 day tuitions hovering around $6,000 and boarding tuitions approaching $14,000,[17] few of our nation's families have the financial resources to make an independent education a realistic alternative. In order to serve those families who most want and would benefit from the experience, independent schools will have to creatively and strategically distribute limited funds.

The cost of an independent education and the lack of awareness of the availability of financial aid appear to have a significant impact on the ability of many schools to broaden their inquiry and applicant pools. Despite impressions of high value and a willingness to finance an independent education, the stark realities of the bottom line deflect the interest of many prospective families. If independent schools are to realize gains in enrollment, they must emphasize value, communicate affordability, and make a substantial commitment to financial assistance programs.

The independent school market can be divided into three family groups: those who are predisposed toward independent education and have the resources to afford that education; those who have the income to invest in an independent education but need assurance as to its value and evidence of its worth; and those who have expressed an interest and require financial assistance. Each family group brings a different set of variables to the school-choice equation.

All families (regardless of their incomes) place high importance on the quality of a school's academic product. Families differ, however, in the value they assign to other attributes of the educational experience. Traditional independent school families, for instance, are much more likely to appreciate the benefits of community, belonging, and personal growth within an independent school setting. Families with the income to afford an independent school education but who are not personally familiar with that education are more likely to focus on tangible outcomes and physical evidence of quality and value such as college placement record, academic and athletics facilities, computer programs, and numbers of courses and extracurriculars. Size, structure, discipline, and attention to a child's moral and ethical development are also of interest to this family group. To the lower-income families, tuition costs and the availability of financial aid are overriding concerns.

Competition. Public schools are notable competitors of independent schools. There is strong support for public education in this country—especially when personal tax dollars are involved. Public schools, particularly in high-income suburban areas, provide stiff competition for many independent schools in terms of educational quality, college placement, academic and athletic facilities, number of curricular and extracurricular offerings, and ability to tailor academic programs to an individual student's needs.

A number of public schools have launched their own marketing campaigns directed at preserving their share of the budgetary pie. The public schools of Tarrytown, New York, for instance, recently released an ad that lists the colleges their graduates are attending. "Comparing high schools with college on your mind?" their ad reads. "Come to Sleepy Hollow, You'll find us in all the best places."[18] The Minneapolis–St. Paul public school system has a four-color brochure that advertises the strength of the school system. The brochure highlights educational excellence, comprehensive curriculum, facilities, teaching quality, counseling, and resource centers—all issues of concern to parents as they select a school setting for their child. In the face of such competition, independent schools literally cannot afford to be complacent.

Consistently high academic standards, a capable faculty, successful educational outcomes, challenge, individualized attention, a sense of community, attention to moral and ethical values, and the existence of a structured, safe, and caring environment are all competitive strengths of independent schools. These strengths are highly attractive—and marketable—features, particularly in today's society, and ones that public schools (simply because of their size, funding, structure, and student body) are often unable to deliver with the same degree of consistency.

Lack of Publicity. The competitive strengths of an independent school education are not widely known and appreciated. Research indicates a strong interest in independent education but comparatively low levels of familiarity. In one research study, 70 percent of the inquiring parents surveyed expressed a moderate to high level of interest. Approximately the same percentage considered themselves not at all familiar to moderately familiar with independent education. The general marketplace is surprisingly unfamiliar with those characteristics of an independent education that are considered to be its greatest strengths—namely those that define academic quality and relationships. Raising levels of familiarity and helping families identify the valuable outcomes of an independent education represent a distinct marketing opportunity.

Applicant Pools. In order to increase enrollments, independent schools must seek to stimulate and sustain the interest of more nontraditional independent school families. These families represent the majority in many independent school inquiry pools. The inability of independent schools to sustain their interest through to the point of application represents a major marketing challenge. Nontraditional families bring to the school search a different set of impressions of an independent education and concerns about costs and financial assistance.

A clearly articulated case in support of an independent education is required if independent schools are to attract these families. Specific tangible and intangible outcomes of the experience must be communicated in publications and through a school's network of contacts. Currently enrolled students and their parents are often a school's most effective and persuasive communicators. One-on-one contact on campus or off will help to boost the interest of the nontraditional family in an independent education.

Good News for Independent Schools

The challenges faced by independent schools are not the whole story, however. Independent schools have a strong reputation for academic quality and successful educational outcomes orchestrated by capable, caring, and committed teachers. The learning environment of an independent school is seen as one that sets high standards for academic excellence and personal behavior. It is one with a focus on the individual and an emphasis on community.

Size, governing structure, and a more easily identifiable bottom line (financial income and educational outcomes) also make independent schools better equipped than a majority of public schools to reset their sails and, if need be, chart an altered course. Unencumbered by stultifying bureaucracies, independent schools rely heavily on consensus to effect change. Cooperative community involvement in the educational process appears to speed up the rate of positive change rather than to slow it down. Flexibility and responsiveness are two marketing strengths that will serve independent schools well in the years ahead.

In addition, independent schools are not troubled by the magnitude of problems that afflict many public schools. Unlike the public school, attendance at an independent school is voluntary. Families participate in independent education because they recognize the value of the experience and have the financial reserves or support to make that experience possible. These families are vested in their educational choice, interested and involved in school activities and educational outcomes. As a result, independent schools are relatively untouched by the problems that confront many public schools such as high attrition rates, discipline problems, disjointed academic programs, poor teacher morale, and low levels of parental involvement.

Independent schools should take full marketing advantage of their different climate. They should also strive to remain the "moving target that public schools aim for, but never quite hit"[19] (as Governor Thomas Kean of New Jersey urged independent school administrators at the 1988 NAIS annual meeting in New York). Setting the pace and being the moving target without upsetting the delicate balance between learning as a demanding exercise and learning as a delightful process is a tremendous challenge for independent schools as they reach out toward the new millennium.

The Art and Science of Marketing

Marketing is both an art and a science. As an art form, it requires a sensitivity to people and the creativity to look at the present and the future through different sets of lenses—"to continually scramble the familiar and bring the old into new juxtaposition."[20] As a science, marketing requires keen observation, careful research and record keeping, logical planning, and constant evaluation. Among the ingredients that contribute to successful independent school marketing are a high-quality product, strong leadership, an entrepreneurial spirit, organization, a marketing plan of action, teamwork, introspection and market assessment, and a focus on people. Each of these is worth examining in more detail.

A High-Quality Product. First and foremost, successful marketing relies on the quality of a school's educational experience. Without quality, the most sophisticated marketing strategies will go awry. The tangible and intangible qualities of a school's educational "product" must be identified, nurtured, and communicated. A school cannot promise preparation for college and advantageous placement in college unless it has the records to support that claim. Neither can a school market the strength of its community when disgruntlement and dissatisfaction exist. Retention is one clear indicator of the quality of a school's educational product. If a school is unable to retain students for reasons within its control (whether they relate to academic program or community life), a marketing campaign built on quality will be difficult to orchestrate.

Strong Leadership. Leadership at the highest level is required to provide guidance and support for the marketing effort. Because the marketing process entails an examination of mission, an assessment of institutional strengths and weaknesses, and strategic planning, the participation and commitment of the leadership is essential.

An Entrepreneurial Spirit. A "nothing ventured, nothing

gained" philosophy in many ways characterizes the entrepreneur. It is this same pioneering spirit that resulted in the formation of many of today's independent schools. The most innovative, most vital independent schools continue to pioneer and experiment with new approaches to learning, new ways to introduce students to the independent school experience. Student internships, team teaching, outdoor challenge courses, community service outreach programs, multicultural awareness, financial aid prepayment plans, direct mail campaigns, and collaborative marketing all represent new ventures.

A belief in a vision or idea, an intense desire to succeed, a willingness to take calculated risks, persistence, an eye for opportunities (as well as pitfalls), and the ability to reconfigure different pieces of the same puzzle are all a part of the entrepreneurial personality. In order for independent schools to transform the challenges of the 1990s into opportunities, they must continue to exhibit an entrepreneurial spirit. Independent schools must continue to be change masters—continually questioning new ways of doing what they are currently doing well.

Organization. Organization and structure are necessary ingredients of a successful marketing program. To succeed in a competitive environment, today's independent school must be organized in such a way as to be both reactive and proactive. While decision making must be shared, there should be a clear line of command. Channels of communication must be in place so that key individuals and constituencies can share important information and ideas.

A Marketing Plan of Action. Planning is of the essence. A successful marketing program rests on carefully stated goals and objectives. A good marketing plan seeks to develop a road map that will guide a school as it aligns its offerings and resources with the needs of prospective families. The four P's of marketing (product, price, promotion, and place) all come into play in formulating an effective marketing plan. Planning should be recognized as an ongoing process.

Teamwork. Marketing must be a schoolwide effort. While leadership provides the necessary impetus for a successful marketing program, the entire school community must be the sustaining force. Ensuring a high-quality product and attracting and retaining students is everyone's business—administrators, teachers, students, parents, alumni, and school support staff alike. The ultimate success of a school's marketing effort will rest on its ability to create a coalition of supporters.

Introspection and Market Assessment. Sherlock Holmes once remarked, "It is a capital offense to theorize in advance of the facts."[21] In much the same vein, it is a mistake to market before collecting and analyzing information about a school's internal and external environment. Important questons relating to institutional strengths and weaknesses, competitive position, image, perceptions of quality relative to cost, decision-making patterns, financial aid, and enrollment trends must be asked and answered before an effective marketing plan is framed.

A Focus on People. Successful marketing is user-centered. For independent schools this means not only satisfying the needs and wants of students and parents but also enlisting the support of the school community. The most effective marketing plans for independent schools focus on people. Personalizing the school experience for the prospective family by enhancing campus visit programs and developing a contact network of students, parents, and alumni are two examples of successful marketing activities that are people-centered. One school, recognizing the importance of the link between current and prospective students, developed audio training tapes for its tour guides to heighten their responsiveness to school strengths and a family's information needs. Another school enlisted the help of current parent volunteers to make welcome calls to inquiring prospective parents.

Marketing is a matter of survival and success. It provides independent schools with the tools to shape their future. While offering no magic solution, sound marketing practices will encourage independent schools to clarify mission, focus on institutional strengths, identify receptive markets, enhance quality, and build community support. No one marketing solution exists, as each school remains unique. There rests the challenge *and* the opportunity.

Notes

1.   Pacific Crest Outward Bound School, *Book of Readings* (Portland, Ore.: Pacific Crest Outward Bound School, 1989), p. 105.
2.   Philip Kotler and Karen F. A Fox, *Strategic Marketing for*

Educational Institutions (Englewood Cliffs, N.J.: Prentice-Hall, 1985), p. 7.

3. Peter F. Drucker, *Management: Tasks, Responsibilities, Practices* (New York: Harper & Row, 1973), p. 64.

4. U.S. Bureau of the Census, *Current Population Report, Series P-20, 429, School Enrollment, Social and Economic Characteristics* (Washington, D.C.: U.S. Government Printing Office, 1988), p. 12.

5. Ibid., p. 12.

6. Ibid., p. 12.

7. Ibid., p. 12.

8. Harold L. Hodgkinson, *All One System: Demographics of Education—Kindergarten Through Graduate School* (Washington, D.C.: Institute for Educational Leadership, 1985), p. 7.

9. Statistics drawn from other sources as reported by *Memberanda, Secondary School Admissions Test Board,* Winter 1990, p. 2.

10. Statistics drawn from other sources as reported by *Memberanda, Secondary School Admissions Test Board,* Fall 1988, p. 3.

11. Statistics drawn from other sources as reported by *Memberanda, Secondary School Admissions Test Board,* Fall 1989, p. 2.

12. *Memberanda* (1988), p. 3.

13. Pacific Crest Outward Bound School, *Book of Readings,* p. 101.

14. John C. Esty, Jr., "Report from the President," in *NAIS Annual Report* (Boston: NAIS, 1989), p. 5.

15. Focus group research results on eight parent groups conducted in Atlanta, Denver, San Francisco, and Stamford, Conn., with families having school-age children not enrolled in an independent school and with incomes sufficient to afford an independent school; research sponsored by the National Association of Independent Schools and supervised by the Independent Education Fund. NAIS Promoting Independent Education Project, *Briefing,* no. 1, May 1990: 2.

16. Ibid.

17. Tuition costs are reported for 984 members of the National

Association of Independent Schools, *NAIS Statistics,* Spring 1990, p. 31.
18.   Public schools of the Tarrytowns, North Tarrytown, N.Y., 1990.
19.   *New York Times,* March 2, 1988, p. B7.
20.   *Advertising Age,* October 31, 1960.
21.   William S. Baring-Gould, ed., *The Annotated Sherlock Holmes* (New York: Clarkson N. Potter Books, 1967), p. 311.

Part Two

CULTURE, CURRICULUM, AND ACHIEVEMENT IN INDEPENDENT SCHOOLS

FROM *TOM BROWN'S SCHOOLDAYS*, PUBLISHED IN 1857, TO *A PRAYER FOR Owen Meany*, published in 1988, some of the best-known fiction-alized accounts of school life have been set in independent schools. Because of their small size and unified culture, independent schools lend themselves to the kind of vivid description novelists seem to prefer. The great school stories set in private schools have an indel-ible effect, in positive and sometimes disturbing ways. Because one attends school during the formative period of one's life, the years of schooling linger in adult memory, and the ethos of private schools appears to have an enduring quality.[1]

Much has been written about the way the ethos or culture of a school shapes individual and group behavior. Culture influences human interaction and the values, beliefs, and assumptions people hold about education and schooling. In independent schools most faculty members have similar academic preparation, making it more likely that they will share basic values and beliefs. Because most independent schools have remained relatively unencumbered by the dictates and vicissitudes of the external political environ-ment, they have been allowed to develop a clear and unifying mis-sion and have regularized ways of doing things, enforced more by ritual and tradition than by rules and regulations.

This section attempts to convey the realities of life in inde-pendent schools and is written from the perspective of people in the schools—administrators, teachers, and students—and from the per-

121

spective of those who are intimately familiar with independent schools in other ways. The diverse views presented in the chapters that follow attempt to capture the essence of school life, revealing strengths, blemishes, and opportunities.

The first chapter offers a philosophical account of the work of a headmaster in a Massachusetts boarding school; he sees as his central task the development of human beings. His thesis is that because most problems in schools are unsolvable, any action is dissatisfying, and thus most heads of schools appear to fail. To elucidate his thesis, the author provides brief case studies that demonstrate the array of problems that confront independent secondary schools and suggests a general resistance to rational problem solving. The chapter also illustrates the extent to which teaching occurs in different contexts, outside of the classroom. Because of the nature of these cases, the author uses the pen name Ishmael. His school will remain anonymous.

What administrators do may be different from what they say they do. Pearl Rock Kane and John B. Mason report on a study conducted by "shadowing" the heads of schools and division directors in independent day schools in New York City. Researchers found differences in roles that gave the school head latitude to define the job, while the division director's work was shaped by the school's day-to-day needs and required constant availability. The absence of rigid hierarchies in independent schools, the similarity in the educational backgrounds of teachers and administrators, and the fact that almost everyone in the school teaches make an authoritarian relationship unlikely. The authors conclude that independent schools may provide an example of a leadership style that is more collaborative and less predetermined than is traditional in public schools.

William Bullard, academic dean at San Francisco University High School, describes how small classes, the multitude of roles a teacher must perform, the relative autonomy teachers enjoy in designing and teaching courses, and an emphasis on the quality of human relationships make independent schools seem more like communities than institutions. Bullard analyzes the way people teach and interact in an independent school. He cautions that the spirit of community and the family ethos that nourish excellence in teaching have the potential to compromise professionalism.

Celebrated author John Irving was a poor student at Phillips Exeter Academy in New Hampshire. Irving claims that the prep school subject of his novels *A Prayer for Owen Meany, The Hotel New Hampshire,* and *The World According to Garp* is not specifically Exeter but may reflect his anger and frustration at having been a struggling student there.[2] It was not until Irving had published several novels that he stopped feeling he was stupid, and it was not until his younger son, Brendan, was diagnosed as slightly dyslexic that he recognized the same problems in his own learning. Irving's personal story serves as a humbling reminder that the effects of schools on children can be deleterious.

The only distinction John Irving felt at Exeter was his success in wrestling. Athletics at Exeter, as at most independent schools, is integral to the curriculum. Competitive sports belong in the curriculum because they are about "the pursuit of excellence," according to *Sports Illustrated* writer E. M. Swift, who claims to have learned as much about life as about athletics playing hockey, baseball, and football at the Hotchkiss School in Connecticut. Swift elaborates on four enduring tenets of high school sports: "The rules of the game were unassailable. The purpose of the game was to win. My teammates were people who depended on me. My coach was a man I could trust."

Although philosopher Maxine Greene acknowledges that the arts occupy an integral role in the independent school curriculum, she envisions a larger purpose for the arts. Greene wants independent schools to broaden their canon beyond the cherished Western cultural tradition to include images and voices ordinarily omitted. Literature, visual arts, music, drama, and dance have the potential to stimulate students' imagination to consider cultural and social realities not usually represented. Skillfully taught, the multiple perspectives presented through the arts have the potential to evoke a vision of a better social order.

Do independent schools use their independence in determining their curriculum? Z. Vance Wilson, a writer and former teacher at the Asheville School in North Carolina, describes the prototypical secondary school curriculum in independent schools as being structured along the lines of traditional liberal studies and including the arts, athletics, and attention to values. Wilson argues that the schools' freedom from the dictates of political structures and their ability to choose students and teachers have not resulted in curricular options that distinguish the schools from one another. Despite their claims to uniqueness, the schools are more alike than different. Wilson challenges schools to use their independence in developing curricula that take risks, that fight back against the external forces that are unifying curricula, and that incorporate what is known about learning theory and pedagogy.

University of Chicago professor James S. Coleman and researcher Kathryn S. Schiller report on public and private school comparisons of eighth graders, concluding that students in private schools achieve higher scores on standardized tests. Parents whose children attend private school have more positive attitudes toward the school. The social milieu of independent schools appears to encourage children to have higher aspirations for attaining higher levels of education than does the milieu of public schools. The authors observe that private schools may be more effective because parents often share a common set of values or beliefs, and in some communities values are reinforced because people know each other and interact in a variety of contexts.

All the chapters in this section seek to demonstrate that independent schools exert a powerful influence on members of the school community—more by tradition and belief than by rules and regulations. These cultural forces may bond people together and increase their commitment to the school, but they may also cause discomfort among those who perceive themselves to be outside of the culture. Terrence E. Deal of Peabody College, Vanderbilt University, perceives the cultural bonds of private schools as a distinct advantage in distinguishing the unique characteristics of each school. He encourages school leaders to preserve the cultural patterns that make them unique by articulating values, practicing rituals, and offering celebrations. Deal warns leaders to proceed cautiously in reshaping tradition as new challenges present themselves.

Johanna Vega, a young woman of Puerto Rican descent, graduated from the prestigious Groton School in Massachusetts four years ago, but she continues to struggle with the effects of the experience on her own identity and her relationship to her family and community. Vega finds herself uncomfortably situated between two worlds and feels alienated from both. She came to Groton from the South Bronx at a time when independent schools were just beginning to open their doors to ethnically and socioeconomically diverse students. Vega's painful experience was portrayed in a film produced by the Smithsonian Museum and aired in a national television broadcast. The film shocked the independent school community, but it may have served as a catalyst in making schools aware that a commitment to diversity requires modifications in all facets of school life and a larger representation of students of color. Vega's story is presented as an oral history that she helped to edit.

Independent schools represent the most extreme denial of equal access to high-quality education, according to Gary Simons, which gives them a particular responsibility to serve a public purpose. Simons is director and founder of Prep for Prep, a program that identifies and develops talent among minority youth and prepares them to enter competitive independent schools. He argues that a diverse student body will enhance the role of the independent school in society and further the schools' mission. First, academic excellence requires critical thinking and a consideration of moral and ethical issues that can best be addressed in a school with a significant level of students whose cultural backgrounds and life experiences vary. Second, since the graduates of independent schools are more likely to achieve leadership positions and become policy makers, it is essential that they develop a sensitivity to divergent needs and views among those who are least able to influence policy. Finally, these schools can increase the number of leaders from minority groups in the pipeline—people who will have an unusual breadth of experience and awareness of different points of view.

This section concludes with an interview with Robert Coles, the well-known educator and child psychiatrist. The editor poses questions about independent schools and their role in the moral development of children. Coles, an independent school parent himself, discusses many issues of concern to independent educators, including community service, distinctions between noblesse oblige and social responsibility, broadening the nature of the student body, and using the curriculum to transcend the immediate life of students. Coles values the intensity of independent education and the dual emphasis on character development and academic rigor. The powerful existential questions that still haunt a significant number of faculty in independent schools may, according to Robert Coles, be their greatest strength.

Notes

1. Richard A. Hawley, ed., *Coming Through School: School Life Through Fiction* (Wellesley Hills, Mass.: Independent School Press, 1982); Thomas Hughes, *Tom Brown's Schooldays,* (n.p., 1857; reprint ed., New York: Penguin, 1984); John Irving, *A Prayer for Owen Meany* (New York: Morrow, 1988).
2. Irving, *Owen Meany; The Hotel New Hampshire* (New York: Dutton, 1981); *The World According to Garp* (New York: Dutton, 1976).

10

Revelations of
Boarding School Life:
A Headmaster's Perspective

Ishmael

Philosophy

I am the headmaster of a boarding school in New England.

The final responsibility for its 500 students and 140 staff, stretching from hiring faculty to evaluating instruction in three levels of Greek, from judging the chemical qualities of fertilizer to choosing the composition of roofing materials, from traveling the country to address groups of alumni to working on the design of catalogues, is mine. Most of these judgments concern things other people know more about than I do.

Routinely, I make decisions about asbestos removal, transportation to the senior prom, menus for alumni luncheons, the function of laboratory experience in freshman biology, and the literary value of the student skit night (from which I removed what I feared might be offensive references to "kielbasa" for a parents' evening presentation). I must envision the school of the future and discuss the condition of damp chasers in our practice pianos.

At Christmas, I send a thousand personally signed cards to alumni and friends of the school. The normal work week exceeds seventy-five hours.

Occasionally, when people are talking with me about my work, they say, usually in a generous and well-meaning way, "That's a big job."

And it is true that there is plenty of size to it, in terms of hours of labor, or diversity of responsibility, or multiplicity of personality. I tend to nod in agreement about the bigness of the job, but not because of its diversity or its hours—which are, at any rate, about the same as those for anyone leading an organization, large or small. For me, the haunting immensity of the job is the shadowy, shifting, ironic nature of the central task: to develop human beings. In that sense, the job seems to me infinite.

The center of this work is, I think, an abstraction: shifting like the light in a Monet painting, impossible to pin down, elusive in some eternally tantalizing way, like trying to describe the scent of a hay barn with language. The reality of it is always just beyond what can be understood, like whispers of crucial things heard always in snatches.

What I think I do is live intimately with the problem of objectivity; I live with what people describe as "the truth"—but from their point of view. I live with the question of whether or not their point of view has, in fact, created the situation in need of solution. In reality, the situation isn't the question I need to answer, but its deeper causes are. And they are rarely in front of me or, perhaps, even knowable: a parent tells me his child is "devastated" by a coach's decision to cut him from the varsity team and wants him reinstated. The coach tells me "the kid doesn't care and doesn't work." The boy tells me his dad is tough on him, and he doesn't see how he could live up to what he's been. A senior faculty member tells me I'd "better take a stand" on this one. "A lot of people are watching how you handle it."

In *Philosophy in the Twentieth Century*, A. J. Ayer summarized the "perennial problems" of philosophy: "Chief among them perhaps is the problem of objectivity. . . . The fundamental question is whether, and to what degree, it is possible for us to describe things as they really are, independently of their relation to ourselves."[1] In this job, our wonder at the impossibility of knowing "what things really are" has a human face, and it is invariably a face requesting a resolution.

I act, knowing that all action is tentative and often misses the deeper point. I act, knowing my actions dissatisfy—and they seem to dissatisfy someone at almost every turn—because failure to act is weakness, while all action is flawed.

Finally, I content myself with knowing that the nature of the central problem rather than the nature of the solutions is more truly the source of dissatisfaction. The removal of asbestos, mandated for the health of students by a law with which we comply at a cost of $250,000, is later suggested by an authority to create greater risk than keeping it in place. The student who "had to be expelled" sticks in my mind longer than ten who moved smoothly through to graduation.

Benighted adolescents who don't know, yet, why they act out, relentlessly remind me of the sometimes savage cruelty inherent in my quintessentially "establishment job" with its high expectations for rational and responsible behavior. I am haunted always by the look on a young man's face who knows, in some powerful but inarticulate way, that there is a contradiction in the fact that although I've preached publicly about the energy rising out of interest and self-esteem, when he was really lost I sent him back to his destructive family because the school "couldn't continue him." Or perhaps I really helped him "face reality" in some way we are both helpless to understand for another ten years. But I doubt it.

In an age when stories about the problems with education are offered constantly and when both scholars and politicians continuously offer solutions to these same problems, my thesis is, perhaps, more grim. The job is to offer—and, indeed, enforce—solutions to fundamentally insoluble problems. The question may be a conundrum; it may be shadowy, shifting, and ironic. But the solution must be action. And, because the problem is often unsolvable, any action is, by definition, dissatisfying. There is a fundamental philosophical reason why those in schools appear to fail. The soil they cultivate is part shadow, part water, part quicksand, part compost, part mirage. It is the stuff that gives philosophy its name.

I would like to illustrate my thesis with case studies. My cases demand anonymity, as will be readily apparent, and names and other details have been changed to preserve confidentiality.

Rooming

In the fall, the father of one of our students appeared in my office to protest the room to which his child had been assigned. In

China, families of ten occupy such spaces, and, in my opinion, few adolescents anywhere have a healthy place like it. The room looks out on great open spaces. But it was not, true enough, the room originally chosen.

He was furious with me for the thoughtlessness of such provisions for his child's welfare. This kind of thing, after all, he told me, had happened here before. We met for over an hour, during which time I was expected to take his child's rooming situation— and the undoubted stunting of her development from insensitive rooming tactics—with utmost seriousness.

Then, two months later, the man sued for divorce and left the family without a penny, disappearing without a forwarding address.

He had fought with me, with real anger and bitterness, over his child's room. I had said I thought the real job was for the child to learn to accept reality. He had told me, as I am often told by those who don't agree with me, that I didn't care about his child.

Irony, in one form or another, is the centerpiece of a boarding school headmaster's work.

Financial Aid

We give financial aid based on statements of need made to the School Scholarship Service in Princeton, New Jersey. But giving aid is a tricky business. During the middle of the year, a student's family says they have fallen on hard times and would need more tuition remission to continue throughout the year. We oblige. At graduation, the boy is tooling around campus in a new sports car. It was, he said, a graduation present from his father.

Contrast

Once, I spent nearly an hour with parents whose son had been caught smoking in the dorm—his fifth discipline offense in two years at the school—and was about to be separated from the school. They were plenty angry—at him, at the school, and at me. He wasn't a bad boy—but school rules on smoking in buildings tend, for a very good reason in my view, to be inflexible. We were caught, and, though I was more familiar with the sensation, no one was happy about it. The hour was interspersed with the father's shouts and could, I suppose, only be called "difficult."

As they walked out the door and I stood in it, feeling ragged, in came a salesman—he'd been waiting for his appointment—to try to get the school to take on free television sets in exchange for watching news and advertising from his company. We'd get a whole closed-circuit system for the school, and all I had to do was promise that our kids would watch ads by McDonald's and Coke—and just two minutes a day. Actually, he said, who would know if they really watched it or not? All I had to do was sign that they would. One more siren's song—but so fast on the heels of an entirely different dance.

We didn't take the TVs, and we did expel the smoking student whose grandfather, it shouldn't be necessary to add, had been one of the school's top ten benefactors.

Discipline

The day after Thanksgiving vacation, Nick, a sophomore in a small dorm of eleven boys whose dorm master is in his second year of teaching, comes to the dean's office. He has returned from vacation to find his sports coats slashed. Every one of them—and none belonging to his roommates—has been ripped, "viciously," he feels, with something very sharp.

Nick is angry and not a little frightened. His parents have called the dean's office to emphasize how distressed they are over this incident. Clearly, Nick says, he has been singled out. Further, there is other damage in the dorm. Another boy has obscenities written in marker on his desk, his walls, and his mattress.

Some boys report compact discs missing. There is an expensive Walkman gone, too, although this may have been missing before Thanksgiving.

This is unusual and seems odd.

There is some initial thought that the dorm was broken into over Thanksgiving. No one was around. The police are called, and they question boys and investigate for signs of forced entry. Nothing very certain emerges.

As he continues to investigate, the dean feels more and more strongly that it is an inside job. One boy, also fifteen, a smaller lad named Muhammad from Saudi Arabia, whose parents currently live in this country, was in the dorm for a day after the other boys left. Further conversations reveal he is angry with the boys in the dorm, particularly with Nick.

Slowly, over several days, his story emerges.

Over the fall term, three or four boys have been "after" him, he says, "relentlessly." Nick, he says, is the ringleader. They call him "Mo," and sometimes, they say "Moo" when they see him. Once, they spray him with a fire extinguisher. Nick holds it. They tip him upside down and threaten to put his head in the toilet. They set a kind of firecracker to explode when he opens his dorm room. They lock him out. One takes a sandal and hides it above a light. When the boy asks repeatedly for his sandal, no one knows its whereabouts. His clothes are knocked to the ground when he showers.

He feels, he says, that he should be able to handle this on his own. His adviser is the art teacher, with whom he meets weekly, but never once does he tell her anything that is going on. The young dorm master is aware of "horseplay" in the dorm, he says, but, although he has spoken to the boys, he is unaware that anything more than boys "goofing around" is afoot.

Muhammad denies for more than two weeks that he is guilty of slashing the jackets or writing the words. Yes, he is angry, but he would not do anything like this.

Finally, after many days, he relents.

The other boys say they did not know how upsetting their actions were. They do not admit doing what he says they have done, and in their version it is less dramatic. Plus, Muhammad emerges as a stealthy and nasty figure in their telling. He walks into their rooms uninvited and will not leave. He stands near them when they are on the phone. When one of their mothers is in the dorm, he pointedly ignores her. He is sullen and "haughty," they say. We don't really trust this kid. Sometimes you find him where he shouldn't be. Further, they have never done anything to him that is really hurtful, they say.

It is, we say, the classic response of the bully—to deny culpability, to try to spread the blame.

Feeling angry, the dorm empty, Muhammad goes to Nick's room and takes a knife that Nick keeps illegally in a chest and slashes Nick's clothes.

Finally, two days before Christmas vacation, all four boys appear before the disciplinary committee—students and faculty—to review the situation.

There is a long, long debate, and the case comes to me: the discipline committee of students and faculty has recommended that Nick be expelled from school; the other boys are to be suspended, and Muhammad is to have a warning.

I ponder. Can these boys learn from this experience or is this the time to "put a stop" to "this kind of thing" by throwing them out? Is it quite as racial or religious as some would say? Is it just plain bullying—or worse? Is the viciousness of the harassment—on both sides—clearly established?

I decide to suspend all the boys at the end of Christmas break: Muhammad for a day and a half for his violent destruction; Nick for a week, the other boys for lesser periods. They can learn, I decide, all of them. Muhammad's father calls me on Christmas Eve to protest any punishment for his son. Nick's parents feel that he has been threatened by this clothes slashing and want him taken out of this dormitory. Muhammad's adviser writes me a note asserting that I do not understand what it means to be oppressed but that she, as a woman, does. My decision, she says, has a "holier than thou" quality to it. Do I really know what emotional pain is?

A month later, after he gets into a fight with a normally calm boy from Korea, it is discovered that Muhammad had been stealing in the dormitory throughout the fall. He has the material in his trunk. We thought he might be the crook all along, says the Korean lad.

Muhammad's father arrives to appeal his son's case. He actually bought the radio, he says, and we should have discovered that. He has witnesses. His son has told him there are witnesses.

The dean says, yes, Muhammad tried to produce a witness. Would the father like to hear the witness's letter? It read: "Yesterday, Muhammad came to me to get me to say that I'd seen him buy a radio at the mall. But I wasn't with him, and I didn't see him buy the radio."

Muhammad's father is silent.

Then he says, "Well, I must believe my son. Wouldn't you?"

Muhammad is expelled.

A faculty member says to me, "Well, you called that one right. I really didn't believe those boys before Christmas."

Another writes me a note. It says, in part, "Stronger action with those boys before Christmas, even if incorrect, was still the better thing to do. Now, you are taking a stronger stand over property than over the importance of human emotion."

Faculty

A faculty member has been having a very difficult time with his marriage—"mostly my fault," he says—and we have made an appointment at 7:30 one morning to talk about it and his future at the school. The volume of argument in their dorm apartment has been the subject of talk, and more than one person has suggested their relationship is affecting the students..

We talk in the office for about half an hour about the darker sides of life; impulses and anger. He supposes that he has a darker side; he'll think about that, he says. He gazes off to the view out the office window. He is a good teacher whose students respect him. Plainly competent but now, at fifty, wondering about his future in a boarding school "where everything you do is everybody else's business."

We agree to get back together again. "I have a hard time talking about this," he says.

As he leaves, another faculty member catches me at the door. "Can I see you for just two minutes?" Yes. "Are you aware," he says, solemnly, "that you can get only one piece of chicken at the Saturday evening meal? I think I'm an adult, and I know how much I can eat, and they will only give you one piece of chicken. That is treating us like children. I know that the students throw their food away sometimes. But I eat everything I take. I wish you'd look into it, because the kitchen has this very rigid policy."

Academic Life

The director of studies and I have proposed a schedule change that would lengthen our current forty-minute periods on

Mondays, Tuesdays, Thursdays, and Fridays to forty-five minutes. We would change our thirty-minute periods on Wednesdays and Saturdays (when we meet all eight class periods in four and a half hours) to fifty minutes. We would hold four classes on Wednesday and four on Saturday.

The plan is complex and takes a lot of time in faculty meeting to discuss. The intent of the change is to make a somewhat less disrupted day and to provide something we call "more flexible" academic time. Under the proposed schedule, the total academic time is, in fact, slightly higher for each class, but the number of periods is fewer.

A senior faculty member writes me that he will now have some twenty fewer class periods and that while total time may well be the same he believes his courses will suffer grievously. We are losing our center, he tells me.

With fewer classes, another faculty member remarks, there is less total fooling around because you have fewer beginnings and endings. "I'll bet we'll gain ten or fifteen minutes a week this way," she says.

"I'll have to redo all my assignments," says the senior man. In a month, he retires, citing health reasons after more than forty years in the classroom.

Parents

Stan has been separated from school for the year. He has sold some marijuana to a couple of students. He comes to my office to discuss whether he will be allowed to return. "My mother," he says, "only gives me this school or public school as a choice."

Perhaps, I suggest, there are other options?

He begins to cry.

"Do you know what happened when I called my grandfather to tell him what happened? He hung up on me. He's never done that."

He cries more.

Stan's brother is also a student here. Their father was killed in an accident several years ago. He was a graduate of the school.

Stan's mother has not remarried. Each year, the family donates flowers to the chapel for graduation.

His mother comes in to talk with me. I relate that Stan feels he has only one choice of school for next year and that he feels he must prove something to his grandfather.

"Oh," she says. "His grandfather was upset with him. But that isn't why he hung up. Stan just reminds him of his own son— who was always getting into trouble too." She pauses. "He hung up because he has such a hard time thinking about that." She pauses again. "He sees Stan's father in him. Do you understand?" She pauses. Tears come into her eyes. "We all have a hard time thinking about this school."

The Arts

It is the Friday afternoon of the winter musical, *The Sound of Music*. The faculty member who serves as drama coordinator comes to my office door. She is visibly upset. The director of the musical, another faculty member, has omitted the name of one of the students from the program. "This girl has worked with the show all winter," she says. "The director left her off on purpose, and I have told her to put her back on the program!" She is angry. "I want your support on this," she says. "I'm in charge of the drama program."

I respond that I will go and talk with the director, who is, in fact, in the copying room, running off the programs.

Yes, she says, she did leave the girl's name off the program. Why? "Because," she says, "she quit the show early on—didn't want anything to do with the show—and we needed her. Then she went to work for *her* [the drama coordinator] and I'm not going to put her name on the program because she did quit the show!"

I tell the drama coordinator that it is her responsibility to work these things out before the eleventh-and-a-half hour. Her job is to find a solution; the problem now hasn't one. At this date, I can't see changing the program.

The girl comes to see me the next day. "I don't think either of them is being a very good role model," she says to me.

The Mitchell Scale

John Mitchell brings a car onto campus against all school regulations. Around supper time one afternoon, he drives to the local McDonald's—about twenty minutes from school—where he is seen by a faculty member, quite serendipitously. The rule against cars is a very strict one. In the McDonald's the boy tells the faculty member that his brother has driven him to get dinner and has just gone shopping.

It sounds fishy to the faculty member. Before he can check out the story, the young man calls his brother so they can straighten out their stories. Details are left out. When the boy is questioned and the brother questioned, many discrepancies emerge. Finally, after many hours, the boy reveals the truth.

After meeting with the discipline committee, he is separated from school for being away from campus without signing out, for having a car on campus, and for lying.

When we meet with the father, he becomes so angry with the dean and with me he stands up in my office and fairly shrieks at us: "I hope you men are proud of yourselves—if you can call yourselves men."

When he leaves, there is a moment of silence, and we turn to each other. Neither of us has ever seen a parent so angry. A reason, I say, why the boy may be very used to lying.

"That is the angriest I have ever seen a parent," says the dean. "That was a ten on the anger scale—the Mitchell Scale."

After that, we gauge every parental reaction by the Mitchell Scale. "Just a six. He didn't stand up, and he didn't swear at me."

"How was it?" "Nine point five. He punched a pillow on the sofa and swore—but he didn't stand up. I think you have to stand up to get a ten."

Trustees

The chair of the board comes to see me. A letter from the school's business manager has gone out to the parents of our newly accepted students. It is about the fee payment schedule. But, unlike the letter he wrote last year, this one neglects to mention the tuition figure, which is some $1,200 higher.

This, says the board chair, doesn't reflect well on the administration. I agree.

We discuss the matter. We are sending out a bill a few days later that does have the figure on it. Still, he says, you should have caught this error.

Later in the conversation, he says that I am doing too much. "You really have to have some people you can count on explicitly. That's the key to effective administration—being able to delegate."

An Afternoon Off

My wife and I have been invited by a trustee to visit a Monet exhibit at the Museum of Fine Arts in Boston. Our host is a trustee at both institutions. My wife is glad we have been invited to see this exhibit by a trustee because otherwise, she said, we wouldn't have had the time to go.

The exhibit collects many of Monet's series paintings from the 1890s. Some of these are familiar: *Rouen Cathedral, Grainstacks, The Water Lily Pond*—but most are entirely new to us: *Ice Floes, Spring Meadow, Cliffs at Pourville.*

From the same vantage point, Monet painted views of each scene, in different lights and different seasons. He sought the "richness of light," writes the curator; sought to see wherein reality lay as each scene was transformed by light and season. Sought to find that place in the human spirit somewhere between "objectivity" and the human imagination.

The tour guide notes that people familiar with Monet's paintings of Rouen Cathedral are quite startled when they see the place "in reality." "It doesn't look anything like the paintings," the voice says. Monet's work lies in a landscape of the imagination as much as a landscape of reality; it celebrates the French soul and, finally, human vision. After Monet, in Boston, I look at "the big job."

A divorce and Saturday chicken servings seem about the same in their intensity for some. A trip to McDonald's, a death, a history of kids in a dorm, an academic direction, a line left out of a letter; I took action on all of them. Did I, I wonder, do what I ought?

At the moment, it is, oddly, Monet's light that consoles. In the arena of the day, situations must come to conclusion. But, their inability to rest easily, to conclude in the soul, arises from our gift of vision. Ayer and Monet touched that deeper irony: our limited sphere of reality in an infinite universe. If that sphere for me comes as chicken servings or "free" televisions or confused parents, the shade of light out my window cheers me.

Cheers me because, in time, my actions, too, will change, will dance into some other kind of perception, will become, in their momentary intensity, also ironic and therefore hopeful. Hopeful, because they will have about them the possibility of some other interpretation than the one I gave them at the time, or the one they were given.

It is the creative possibility in life, then, that both mocks us and—finally—saves us. It is that possibility that makes "objectivity" a philosophical problem. Because the choice comes down one or the other—creativity or knowing things for "certain." It is the creative possibility in the dancing light that beguiled Monet and that sends us out of his vision reminded that there are, after all, other lights.

Action in my cases doesn't satisfy because they are moments in time rather than permanent monuments. But there are successive moments in the twilight of contemplation—that place where, to this day, I do not know what combination of hazing, theft, smugness, cruelty, selfishness, self-deception, hope, and charity brought controversy to the surface—or acted upon it.

The large dimension of the job is to wonder, all the time, about other possibilities. I acted as I did "at the time," I say; "it's how it looked at the time. In that light. From my point of view."

Notes

1. A. J. Ayer, *Philosophy in the Twentieth Century* (New York: Random House, 1982), p. 3.

11

The Role of Administrators

Pearl Rock Kane and John B. Mason

It is no secret that teachers in independent schools are similar to public school teachers in at least one respect: they tend to view administrators with suspicion. Characterized all too often as "distant," "frazzled," or "superficial," independent school administrators suffer, rightly or wrongly, from an image that makes them and their work unappealing, at least to many faculty members.

How much of this image is based in reality? What styles of leadership guide school administrators? How do these styles mirror or diverge from corporate models? How does the relation between the school head and division heads play out? And how do these men and women, charged with carrying out the missions and molding the temperament of their schools, see their own roles?

Intrigued by such questions, a group of twelve graduate students along with their instructor conducted on-site research, known more modestly as "shadowing." The graduate students were experienced teachers from independent secondary schools who were

Note: The authors wish to express special appreciation to Klingenstein fellow Peter Herzberg for his comments and suggestions as this chapter was being written. This chapter was first published in the spring 1990 issue of *Independent School* (vol. 49, no. 3) and is reprinted by permission of the National Association of Independent Schools, publisher.

spending a year on a fellowship at Teachers College, Columbia University.[1]

Each researcher spent at least three days in the field logging the day-to-day activities and interactions of school administrators. We were aiming for something beyond mere observation of "days in the life" of each of our subjects. We wanted to see how administrators felt about their work and to gain a sense of their concerns and beliefs.

Researchers spent a total of fifty days with thirteen administrators—seven school heads and six division heads—in ten different New York City independent schools, ending each visit with an interview that allowed the researcher to ask directed questions evolving from the visits.[2] Although conclusive findings cannot be claimed on the basis of such a small sample, unusual consensus among the researchers did give rise to some intriguing ideas about school administration that directly challenged old prejudices.

The Head and the Job

Not surprisingly, school heads spend the majority of their time communicating with the varied constituencies of the school, opening conduits for further communication, and monitoring the pulse of the school. What was surprising was the collaborative nature of that process—it is not lonely at the top. The head's office appears to be a forum for consultation, not the apex of a rigid hierarchy so often associated with more traditional corporate models.

Generally, school heads seem to operate in the belief that distributing authority increases power, a concept that is advocated by those who would empower teachers. Every school head appears to have established decision-making systems that empower many different people. In arriving at decisions, they rely a great deal on information and advice provided by many members of the school community. This observation corroborates research on managerial decision making showing that managers rely on information from others to make decisions and indeed may make few decisions on their own.[3]

The type of school and its financial viability necessarily

shape the job of the chief officer. Yet even in schools of similar types having similar problems, we found that how heads perform their jobs and allocate their time are matters of personal choice. In general, heads of schools appear to have great latitude in defining the job. To use Donald Schon's phrase, the school head "frames the role" according to his or her personality, strengths, beliefs, and vision of the job.[4]

One characteristic of the seven heads we studied is a high degree of self-knowledge, a trait that allows for the successful collaboration and clear framing of the role that we observed. The heads seem comfortable acknowledging their strengths and weaknesses and do not hesitate to delegate aspects of their job to those with greater expertise. One observer commented on the personal self-awareness of the head he was following in this way:

> He is aware of his strengths: "Smart, energetic, organized; concerned with the big picture and with small details as well; supportive of others and committed to the enterprise." He is equally aware of his weaknesses: "I can get too anchored to my desk; I have to be less impatient with chitchat; I'm often fleeting in my attention—I zip in and out of focus; I alternate between avoiding confrontations and provoking them, and as a result I sometimes miss the 'teachable moment.'"

School heads seem to have the opportunity to exercise enjoyable aspects of the job. For example, one head, who sees her job as largely "pastoral," feels that she is most effective operating in a counseling role. She maintains an open-door policy and spends much of her day meeting with faculty members, parents, and students. She is able to do this because the work of public relations and development is successfully carried out by other administrators.

Several heads were adamant about continuing to teach as a way of satisfying scholarly interests and establishing themselves with the faculty. Another head, however, said simply, "I don't teach because I'm not very good at it."

One school head summed up what appeared to be how heads

function by saying, "The best way to handle things you're not good at is to ask somebody else to do them for you."

The presence or lack of people and resources to share the job may foster or curtail the opportunity for shared leadership. Where financial problems exist, the head's energy is directed at alleviating them, with more time devoted to development work, alumni and alumnae activities, and fund raising. In the schools we studied, heads' estimates for time spent on development activities ranged from a low of 4 percent to a high of 25 percent per year. In addition, heads of schools having financial problems estimated that they allocate as much as 10 percent more of their time to business matters than their more fortunate colleagues.

One aspect of financial health is enrollment. Where enrollment is strong, the head is often the person in the school who enforces values and standards. Where enrollment is a problem, the head's energy is directed toward examining the school's mission and spending much time on public relations and promotion. Declining enrollments also require the head to get directly involved with admissions activities and to work more closely with trustees.

What is unusual here—and contrary to most research on leadership—is that, while an institution's situation affects the way the head allocates time, it does not dramatically modify the head's managerial style. Each of the heads we studied had created a consistent style of operating. Even the degree of emphasis on human relations appeared to be a matter of personal conviction rather than one of institutional determination. Whether this connection between personal conviction and operating style is viewed as possible demagoguery or humane efficiency is another story, but the latitude and freedom in the job are greater than we expected to find.

Freedom to shape a job has meaning only when the head of the school has the power to get the job done. The boards of trustees of our ten schools set policy but do not seem to have a heavy hand in the way their schools are managed, and the absence of bureaucracy appears to allow the heads to do their work. Independent school heads, unlike so many of their counterparts in public schools, are not stifled by chains of command or legislative dicta. They can set priorities and goals and have the authority to accomplish them.

Clearly the heads are aided in reaching their goals by the power networks of the parent body, an asset that should not go unmentioned. One school head expressed it well: "Access to power is energizing. I can pick up the phone and talk to people who will make things happen. That's a heady feeling. Sounds grandiose, but I have the feeling that I can make the city work for me." In a large city like New York, at least, the power of connection to the community of influential people may increase the power of the school head and the satisfaction that comes with accomplishing objectives.

The Head's Vision

Just as intriguing as the head's freedom to shape the job was how the head's own vision of schooling helped to make each school distinctive. Each head we talked to mentioned the importance of keeping the big picture in mind at all times.

In part, that vision directly reflects the school's stated philosophy, but it also extends beyond the school. As school heads go about their work, they appear to be responding to a broader mission that transcends the immediate school setting. Are they subscribing to a somewhat romantic notion of using their position to improve the human condition?.

Perhaps this notion explains the fearlessness the heads seemed to demonstrate in their daily interactions. They were not afraid to confront sticky issues, and they appeared confident in the face of adversity. Since three of the seven heads had been in their jobs for less than two years, we could explain this fearlessness only by assuming that they saw themselves as people of strong personal conviction motivated by a purpose transcending the immediate job. Perhaps this also explains why these heads are good at putting the vicissitudes of daily leadership into a broader context. Clearly, they relish what they do, and their satisfaction accrues from their ability to undertake challenges in a variety of ways.

For several of the teacher-researchers who had dismissed any notion of becoming an administrator, shadowing a school head shattered their stereotypes. "His enthusiasm for his job was almost contagious enough to get me to think about administration," one said. For others, the act of getting to know the inside life of the head of an urban school was humbling: "By the end of the second day I was wondering how he possibly kept track of all those people, ideas, problems, and things. I still don't know." There is probably more (and less) than meets the eye in the head's role, if we view it in terms of the predominant stereotypes. That much, at least, our research suggested.

Division Heads and the Job

Whereas the school head has latitude to define the job and choose a leadership style, the division head's job is comparatively constrained. The division head's style and responsibilities tend to be shaped by the school's needs, by the culture of the school community, and by the expectations of the head of the school. If we view the head of the school as the chief executive, the division head may be described as a manager of operations.

Division heads react to circumstances, situations, and needs across a vast spectrum of activities. The observers marveled at their resilience in performing varied tasks and duties while doing what was needed to keep the school in full operation, so that perhaps within the space of a single day they would be coordinating curriculum, evaluating colleagues' classes, covering unprotected light bulbs, and calming frazzled tempers during a student pizza sale.

Much of the time transactions are handled by direct communication, in person or by telephone—a method that division heads distinctly prefer. They tend to resent time spent at their desks doing paperwork, perhaps because such work impedes the personal interactions they seem to cherish, and they arrange their jobs so that they do as little desk work as possible. In fact, it seemed to the observers that while division heads have little of the school head's powers to shape the job, they exercise considerable latitude in shaping the way they approach the varied dimensions of their work.

One way to interpret that work is to ask division heads to describe their role within the school. With striking consistency the six division heads we observed used terms such as "climate person" and "consensus builder." One said that his central role is "reminding students that we are a community." Another envisions himself as a "moving lightning rod" who tries to use his presence "to draw lightning away from others in the school so that they may accomplish their missions."

Others described their roles as "enabling faculty" in curriculum planning and in other ways. Division heads saw themselves as a symbolic presence in the school, helping students and teachers alike to formulate and solve problems. If school heads are energized by freedom and power, division heads seem to be motivated by connecting with other people.

But the division head's presence is not just symbolic. The upper and middle school directors we observed, partly by virtue of how they conceive of their roles and partly because they have to react to almost everything, were among the most aware people in the school. One observer described the division head being studied as a person on whom "everyone in the school is absolutely confident of being able to count for trust, support, wisdom, security, and validation."

The head of one of the ten schools said that the upper school head is the one who always knows where every student in the school is, what each student is doing, and how each student is feeling. To varying degrees, all the division heads we observed seemed to recognize their role as central, all accepted it, and most embraced it— even though there was nothing in any job description about this kind of nurturing.

The Division Head's Day

We were often amazed by the unconditional availability of division heads to students and staff. When they were not in private meetings, their doors were always open, and they were constantly with other people. The observation that much of one division head's day included purposely unscheduled time for "affirming, stroking, coaching his staff and kids" applies equally to all those we observed. The people we followed acknowledged that they are strongly people-oriented. That is what they most enjoy and what the job most calls for.

The way the division heads approach their work reminds us that leadership is no less masterfully accomplished when it appears to blend in with a situational or organizational context or because it takes its cues from the needs of others. As one researcher observed, "A leader is part of a context, a kaleidoscope of styles. Leadership must not only strengthen the specific territory over which it has control, but it must provide a dialectic with other leaders in the school so that the overall mission succeeds."

Although we sensed that each of the division heads could be action-oriented and decisive if a situation warranted it, all seemed to prefer working behind the scenes, helping rather than initiating. What they seem to do most of all is ensure connectedness in their schools. The enabling and consensus building that come about in hours of talking with students and teachers, roaming halls, and dropping in on classes—in their awareness of almost everything that is going on in the school—result in connections between people that reinforce the underlying mission of the school. Division heads are the ethos builders of the school.

Administrative Roles

People in schools bring a wide range of beliefs, values, and styles to their work. Although the image of the efficient American organizational structure most often implies strict systems of accountability, rigid hierarchies, and established organizational frameworks, the reality in schools is usually very different.

In independent schools, distribution of power does not depend on the rigid hierarchies of most corporate models. The limited bureaucratic structure of independent schools and the similarity in the educational backgrounds of teachers and administrators makes an authoritarian relationship less likely to develop. [5]

In the schools we observed, the division heads appeared as key players in a shared power structure that extended throughout the school. Karl Weick has proposed the concept of "loose coupling" to describe organizational life in schools, a concept that was corroborated by our observations. Although formal organizational relationships do exist, according to Weick, staff and faculty in practice possess considerable autonomy and independence as long as their activities remain consistent with the school's policies and underlying mission. [6]

Thomas Sergiovanni and others suggest that schools actually represent a combination of tight and loose coupling—loose in the management sense but tight (that is, more focused) in a cultural or philosophical sense, a description that appears to fit the independent school model. "What matters most are the norms of the work group and individuals' beliefs, values, patterns of socialization, convictions, and commitments," writes Sergiovanni. "Management systems and related patterns of control are less important in a school. The theories that often drive school improvement efforts are based on the opposite premise: They give too much attention to managerially oriented systems of control and not enough to the human factors."[7]

The role of the division head appears to be judiciously targeted at shaping those human forces in schools. Perhaps that explains why teachers in independent schools, even though they complain about administrators, say that what they like best about their schools is the pervasive sense of community.[8]

Our research was not intended to be a study of effective leadership or effective management patterns in independent schools. Our intent was simply to look at how heads of schools and division heads spend their time, how they frame their approach to their jobs, and how they perceive their work.

But we came up with unintended findings as well. In looking at the character of leadership in the school, a balance between the roles and style of the head of the school and the division head was often apparent. Abraham Zaleznik has suggested that marked differences in behavior exist between leaders and managers. Whereas leaders operate from a global perspective, focusing on ideas and an institutional mission, managers function in a shorter-range context that tends to emphasize people and tasks. Managers aim to anticipate and respond to constituent needs; leaders generate entire new sets of needs and goals. Managers solve problems; leaders create new ones.[9]

Our findings suggest that successful school leadership calls for a balance of management and leadership. Beyond being shaped by the dimensions of the job, division heads and school heads tend inherently to have very different styles, and in most cases the division head's style balanced that of the school head. This revelation by us came as no surprise to either group. When asked, most said they were aware of it and that often this arrangement has been made by design. The school heads and division heads we observed appeared to acknowledge intuitively that leaders need managers and that managers need leaders.

Our observations imply that such a complementary structure may even be requisite for organizational health. It is not clear from this research, however, whether the distinction between leaders and managers is determined by the demands of the job and time constraints or by personal factors associated with the individual.[10]

Some of our observations may confirm what students of independent school leadership already sense, while others may shatter preconceived notions, particularly on the part of those who have always dismissed administration as an unpleasant necessity of the school workplace. In our research, administrative roles came across as being both more appealing and more complex than they had seemed from the outside. Independent schools, like other institutions in American life, are undergoing soul searching about what leadership means in the last years of this century. But it might just be that they offer a distinctive opportunity for soul searching of a kind that other institutions do not allow: a focused view of the assets and liabilities of a more collaborative, less predetermined approach to leadership and management.

Notes

1. The researchers were recipients of the 1989 Klingenstein Fellowship, which provides for a year of study and research at Teachers College, Columbia University. They included Robert Bandoni, Vail Mountain School; Joan C. Countryman, Germantown Friends School; Martha Bein, Laurel School; Peter Herzberg, Rutgers Preparatory School; Betty B. Lies, Stuart Country Day School; John B. Mason, Tilton School; William S. Mayher, Hackley School; Nancy Melser, Dwight-Englewood School; Christina Moustakis, Friends Seminary; Paul M. Ness,

Concord Academy; Jere Aubrey Wells, the Westminster Schools; Erland Zygmuntowicz, Packer Collegiate School; and Pearl R. Kane, director of the Klingenstein Center for Independent School Education.

2. Schools included in the study are Brearly, Browning, Collegiate, Convent of the Sacred Heart, Dalton, Friends Seminary, Horace Mann, Riverdale Country, St. Hilda's and St. High's, and Trinity. Seven of the administrators were heads of schools and six were divisional directors. Six of the schools were coeducational, two were single-sex boys' schools, and two were single-sex girls' schools. Four of the schools had a religious affiliation: one Catholic, one Quaker, and two Episcopalian. All of the schools were well-established college preparatory institutions (kindergarten through twelfth grade) and were relatively traditional schools. The size of the schools ranged from 300 to 1,237 students, with a median enrollment of 580.

3. John P. Kotter, *The General Managers* (New York: Free Press, 1982), p. 127.

4. Donald A. Schon, *The Reflective Practitioner: How Professionals Think in Action* (New York: Basic Books, 1983), p. 210.

5. Leonard L. Baird, "Elite Schools: Recent Research from the Outside and from the Inside" (Paper presented at the annual conference of the American Educational Research Association, Washington, D.C., April 1987), p. 9.

6. Karl Weick, "Educational Organizations as Loosely Coupled Systems," *Administrative Science Quarterly,* March 1976: 1–19.

7. Thomas J. Sergiovanni, "What Really Counts in Improving Schools," in *Schooling for Tomorrow,* ed. Thomas J. Sergiovanni and John H. Moore (Needham Heights, Mass.: Allyn & Bacon, 1989), p. 2.

8. Pearl R. Kane, *Teachers in Public and Independent Schools: A Comparative Study* (New York: Esther A. and Joseph Klingenstein Center for Independent School Education, 1986), p. 60.

9. Abraham Zaleznik, *The Managerial Mystique* (New York:

Harper & Row, 1989); and "Managers and Leaders: Are They Different?" *Harvard Business Review,* May/June 1977: 66–78.

10. W. Warner Burke, "Leadership as Empowering Others," in *Executive Power,* ed. Suresh Srivastva (San Francisco: Jossey-Bass, 1986), pp. 51–77.

12

On Teaching
in the Independent School

William Bullard

It is the Sunday before school starts, time for one of the inevitable rites of Labor Day weekend—reporting the bad news about American public education. National Public Radio is interviewing a burned-out teacher who recently left the classroom, no longer able to face the Sisyphean struggle of managing twenty-five bored, unruly fifteen-year-olds while conducting discussions about the meaning of love. In the front section of the *New York Times,* a two-column article explains the "continuing morale problems and mounting frustrations among teachers," detailing their discontent with the failure of reform movements, with the complacency of their students, with spending cuts by school systems, with their lack of participation in decision making.[1] In the same paper, CBS News has a full-page ad for a series of newscasts called "Project: Education." The ad features a school bus heading across the page under the banner: "Are they really going nowhere?" and the ad's copy begins: "Across the country, entire school systems are going to pieces . . ."

My reaction to this annual rite is a mix of relief and guilt. I teach in a good independent school; my students are ambitious and energetic; I enjoy enormous academic freedom; neither I nor my students lack for paper and pens, books or computers. The bus that my students are on *is* going somewhere—to the best colleges in the country—and my colleagues and I who drive that bus are respected and appreciated accordingly. Yet I also recognize that money and privilege fuels it. Like many of its kin, the school where I teach occupies the highest ground in town and literally looks down upon the flatlands where the bad news originates. Every morning on my way to work I drive past the huge high school beset with racial tensions, past the parochial school where teachers are paid more of an offering than a wage, up to the avenue of Gatsby-like estates and on to our campus, where children arrive in coats and ties and BMWs. Catch phrases from the sixties echo accusingly: "You're either on the bus or off the bus." "If you're not part of the solution, you're part of the problem." Despite the means we fabricate to ease our discomfort—community service programs, curricula emphasizing social responsibility, scholarships set aside for the underprivileged—there is no question that my colleagues and I, many of whom spurned our parents' wealth and materialism twenty years ago to take up teaching as a calling, are empowering the powerful and contributing to the ever-greater spread between the rich and the poor. The issue of privilege is not one that I will address specifically in this chapter, but, like the background noise on an old record that we learn not to hear, it is the constant reality behind much of what I will describe as distinguishing the experience of teaching in independent schools. The obvious benefits to teachers working in these schools—small student loads, motivated pupils, self-determined school missions—are simply those provided by parents able to place a high value on their children's education.

However, it would be facile to define this experience by contrasting it absolutely to the public school counterpart. Although I will use some data from public school research to frame an argument about professional relationships in private schools, the distinctions I make are really about teaching in a collegial school rather than in a bureaucratic one where lines of responsibility and authority are strongly hierarchical and rule-governed. There are signs, too, that public and private schools may be converging.[2] Public schools are learning, at least on a systemwide basis, the benefits of decentralization, of moving the locus of authority down the ladder, while private schools are responding with new sensitivity, if not with a great deal of wisdom, to perceived marketplace pressures by becoming more professional in their management practices. We now hear heads of school referred to as "CEOs" and their division heads as "managers," a discourse that places both real and symbolic distance between administrators and teachers and threatens the very culture that, as I argue in this chapter, accounts for their spirit of enterprise.

As diverse as independent schools may be in their varied missions, policies, and clientele, universals do exist that distinguish the experience of teaching in them from that of teaching in their large public and parochial counterparts. Small classes, the multitude of roles a teacher is called on to perform, the relative autonomy a teacher enjoys in designing and teaching courses, the closeness of his relationship with students, and the collegial tone of his association with other teachers and administrators combine to make many independent schools feel more like communities than institutions. And because values stressing mutual respect, tolerance, cooperation, and service are so important to these schools, their policies emphasize the quality of human relations more than bureaucratic regularity. For the teacher this means that his work takes place in the context of both demanding and invigorating relationships with two groups of people—his colleagues (the faculty and administration) and the school's clients (parents and students). The ethics of these associations form a culture that exerts a number of conflicting and frequently covert pressures on the teacher. This chapter will examine each in turn: the collegial ethos that is responsible for much of the professional endeavor of independent schools, and the family ethos that, while it creates a spirit of community that nourishes excellent teaching, may also act to compromise that professionalism.

I

In their 1973 article, "The Social Realities of Teaching," Ann Lieberman and Lynn Miller make a number of useful generalizations about the complex experience of teaching. Their point of view is that of field workers in public schools undergoing the improvement projects of the 1960s and 1970s, and their aim is to "develop an understanding of the social reality of teaching from a teacher's perspective."[3] Although the article makes few value judgments about schools or teachers, it does identify a number of conditions and feelings that detract from the rewards of the profession. Theirs is a useful discussion to summarize because many of these negatives stem not from the reality of teaching per se but from that of teaching in a highly bureaucratic, hierarchical, and politicized school culture. While these afflictions are potential within any teaching situation, they arise more rarely in the collegial culture of most independent schools.

Lieberman and Miller discern two informal rules that govern their subjects—"being practical and being private." To be practical is to be realistic, to be a part of the adult world. It means knowing your place, accepting the school as it is, not making waves, adapting to rather than fighting the system, and "learning to keep quiet when private principles are violated by public practice."[4] "Being practical" governs not only a teacher's association with the system but also his attitude toward students. To believe in students or to be self-critical is idealistic; to accept their limitations or to blame their failures on their effort rather than the teacher's is practical. Lieberman and Miller conclude that "in essence, the value placed on practicality is a value placed on resistance to change and to expanding the possibilities of teaching."[5] It is thus a negative value, one designed to protect the territory of the teacher against the encroachments of colleagues or administrators eager for reform. It is exactly the attitude satirized in such popular films as *Conrack* or *Dead Poets Society* in which the innocent and idealistic young teacher prevails against the self-protective negativism of his pragmatic, hard-boiled colleagues, who proclaim righteously that "they shouldn't" or "they can't."

Following from the practicality rule is the privacy ethic, for it too serves to protect the teacher's independence. "Being private" includes not talking to your colleagues about your teaching, your students, or your role in the school, and most definitely it includes not inviting colleagues into your class or visiting others. It is a code that protects teachers from each other's professional judgment and safeguards the teacher's control of his domain. As one of Lieberman and Miller's subjects confessed, "It is safer to be private. There is some safety in the tradition, even if it keeps you lonely."[6]

Combined, these informal rules create an ethos that feels cyn-

ical and unprofessional to administrators and teachers energized by
new ideas. However, as Lieberman and Miller indicate later in the
article, both stem from a condition that is natural to teaching in
schools where teachers have little authority outside the classroom.
Within the classroom the teacher's authority theoretically puts him
in full control; outside of the classroom, the teacher's loss of authority means loss of control and feelings of powerlessness. When
teachers act to protect their authority in a classroom, it is not just
power they are seeking to maintain but their professionalism as
well, for the classroom may be the only context in a school where
the teacher is treated as an authority. If the school bureaucracy
renders teachers powerless outside the class, then it has to expect
that they will protect their authority within, for their professional
self-esteem depends on it. As easy as it is to denigrate teachers for
resorting to the rules of pragmatism and privacy, these rules are not
part of the natural behavior of teachers but a result of a system ruled
by rigid hierarchies and lines of authority.

　　　For a number of reasons, the culture of independent schools
tends to be collegial rather than bureaucratic, their hierarchies more
homogenized than stratified. Their size, their freedom from external
constraint, and the relative simplicity of their operations mean both
that they do not require a massive bureaucratic shell to make education mandates out of public policy and that those who perform
administrative duties need not be specialized in those tasks. A spirit
of collegiality is likely to prevail in the small independent school
because almost everybody in the workplace does the same things.
Division heads, deans, department chairs, and teachers alike teach,
advise, coach, and work with parents. Teachers serve on innumerable committees generally charged with turning broad policy into
sound practice. Most importantly, they often do most of the screening and interviewing of job candidates, so that they have a powerful
role in selecting their future colleagues and thus in perpetuating the
academic culture of their departments.

　　　Not only do administrators teach, but teachers administer,
assuming and shedding any number of leadership roles over the
course of their career in a school. Teachers serve as department
heads, curriculum coordinators, master teachers, faculty, student
and class deans, admission officers, guidance counselors, and so on.

The collegial atmosphere is powerfully enhanced by the simple fact that teachers and administrators share the same background; both are likely to have graduated from selective colleges, have strong academic interests, perceive themselves as reasonably expert in their discipline, and identify themselves with intellectual pursuits.[7] Sharing the same assumptions, the same values, and the same discourse, teachers and administrators, even if they acknowledge in the abstract that one has authority over the other, are likely to perceive their interchange as more on the level of advice and consent than of command and obedience.

The collegial ethos in independent schools is, in part, a product of an enlightened spirit of amateurism, not unlike the concept of citizenship that H.D.F. Kitto praises in his famous short work, *The Greeks*. Kitto embraces Aristotle's notion that the Athenian citizen was more fully human than the *barbaroi* outside because he was expected to participate in all of the city's institutions, each of which—the assembly, the gymnasium, the theater, the army, even the marketplace—contributed to the full spectrum of his human capacities.[8] In all of their roles, independent school teachers are, in fact, amateurs in the root meaning of the word—"lovers" of study, or athletics, or leadership, or any number of activities and avocations. And most of them are, in the strict sense, amateur teachers, having learned their craft more by observing models than by professional training. Recent research indicates that, compared to their public school peers, independent school teachers made the decision to enter teaching late in their academic careers and did little to plan or consciously prepare for it.[9] Most come from competitive colleges and decide to become teachers in order to enlarge their own academic experience in a school preparing students for the kinds of colleges that they themselves excelled in.

This background has two consequences. First, independent school teachers tend to view their school as a small extension of their college, where their professors enjoyed academic freedom, where academic values prevailed, and where, most importantly, they came into their own as intellectual beings. Naturally they want to create a similar experience for their young students, so that they are not only well educated in a discipline but value a liberal education as an end in itself. Second, they view their colleagues as fellow scholars with whom it is commonplace to talk about books, ideas, and teaching methods. For reasons that I will pursue later, the curriculum in independent schools tends to be unprescribed and fluid. Teachers have as much responsibility in developing it as they do in delivering it, a fact that is central to independent schools' favoring of young scholars who choose to teach over graduates of teachers' colleges trained to teach. Thus a teacher's intellectual collaboration with his colleagues is vital to his job and a natural consequence of his background, reasons again why the rule of privacy is little obeyed in independent schools.

Even if independent schools are not actual democracies, the personal scale of their operations allows them to avoid the relationships of power and self-protection that more rigid hierarchies tend to breed. Themselves granted a large degree of autonomy by their boards, school heads are freer to delegate their authority to other members of the school community possessing particular talents. In turn, division heads and deans select the most trusted and respected teachers as department chairs because their stature allows them to run their departments more by consensus than decree. This practice creates a professional climate—mutual trust, a belief in collaboration, and a willingness to subordinate personal interests to group needs—that neutralizes the conditions leading to the rules Lieberman and Miller see governing the culture of many public schools.

Because independent schools depend upon their teachers to perform administrative functions and to provide academic leadership, the tension created between authority in the classroom and powerlessness in the school is less serious, if it exists at all. In many schools, the faculty is called on to vote on almost every issue, great and small, that administrators need to decide on—from disciplinary action taken against a single student to the exact wording of the school's philosophy. From an administrator's point of view, this empowerment of faculty has a price, for it tends to encourage dissent and protracted political struggles to get even simple projects completed. However, it also creates a highly entrepreneurial, collaborative, and creative faculty who, on or off duty, naturally turn to talking about their students, their classes, and their roles in the school—that is, a faculty that collectively could not imagine succumbing to the rules of privacy and pragmatism.

II

In both boarding and day schools, we often use the image of a family to describe the school community. The metaphor is double-edged; on the one hand, it conveys the warmth and personal responsiveness of these school communities; on the other, it conveys the loss of professional distance and authority that comes when children and parents expect, if not friendships with teachers, at least a good measure of personal accommodation. One of the most remarkable and attractive features of independent schools is the casual intimacy that forms between adults and children. While students and teachers may acknowledge the final authority of the teacher, they often speak to each other in the tone and language of equals or friends—a fact that contributes powerfully to the sense of shared goals and responsibility that makes these schools such healthy communities in which to teach and learn.

The family metaphor also conveys an attitude of personal accountability that underlies the policies and climate of these schools; teachers and students feel personally responsible to each other and relate as much to each other's character as they do to their formal roles in the school. However, the metaphor also conveys the independent school's implicit promise to guarantee, within limits of course, the child's success and enhanced self-esteem by providing extraordinary measures of adult support, attention, and empathy— a promise that places a number of hidden pressures on teachers to create different standards for different students.

Not only does the family metaphor convey the positive and nourishing aspects of the independent school community for students, it does the same for the faculty, whose self-esteem often comes from the success and gratitude of students with whom they have grown close. Again, there are two faces to this ethos, for as much as the independent school provides in emotional security and support for its teachers, it takes away in professional distance. My peers who teach in public schools gain feelings of security and stature through their relationship to a system—they are granted tenure after so many years of teaching, they ascend a published salary scale, they gain titles or positions by earning graduate credits, and so on. Teachers in independent schools gain security and stature in their human relationship to a community—they grow close to families, form friendships with generations of alumni, become respected "institutions" in their school. In the public school, the teacher is protected or represented by his union, and his relations with the school administration are mediated by well-known rules and formalities. In the independent school, the teacher is only protected by the good will of the head, on whose personal discretion she relies to gain raises, promotions, teaching assignments, and so forth. The public school teacher knows what is negotiable and what is not; the system grants her a degree of job security, but it also renders her relatively powerless to change the system. The life of the independent school teacher is much less determined; she may lose her job more easily, but the one that she has generally grants her as much influence over the policies of the school as her talent and energy permit. In short, the dynamic of the independent school is, as the family metaphor suggests, fluid and mercurial simply because it is so contingent on its human chemistry.

Compared with the public and parochial schools I've been in, the independent high school where I teach seems like a disorderly place. In those schools a bell rings, large groups of students make their way quickly and efficiently to the next class, another bell rings, and one could hear a pin drop in the hallway. Every student is someplace; every student is accounted for. By contrast, the atmosphere of our halls is more like that of an outdoor market. There may be a surge of students in the halls between classes, but the hum of activity never stops. Sitting on benches and floors, students study, talk, and cavort. A teacher walks down the hall to get her mail and is met by dozens of greetings and two or three impromptu conferences. There is little formal courtesy and a good deal of noise. To the casual observer, the tumult can seem chaotic, a sign that students have too much freedom, too much spare time.

Every spring when our defenses are down, the pandemonium gets to us, and we threaten to promulgate new rules. At that point we have to remind ourselves that this absence of formal order is, in fact, the presence of trust. In the classroom, we trust that students can think for themselves, so we restrain ourselves from giving them the answers, from succumbing to easy authority. In the halls, we trust that they share our values of responsibility and achievement, so we don't have to account for them because they will account for themselves. This makes for a messier school, for we are asking each student to keep his watch set rather than listen to a bell that tolls for all. But what counts, whether measured in the halls or in the classroom, is not the control of children but the building of responsible relationships between adults and students.

This was brought home forcefully to me in our Middle States Evaluation a few years ago when the committee members took what they termed an "unprecedented action" in reporting their "admiration and respect for the high quality of caring and commitment . . . for the encouraging and unthreatening atmosphere . . . [and for] the high degree of trust and mutual respect [between students and teachers]" in a special citation that prefaced their report. True, this sounds like language out of the admissions catalogue, but in my school, like so many others of its kind, that language describes a reality that the independent school has, perhaps uniquely, the power to create. The focus on the individual child, long the hallmark of private school education, really means creating meaningful and lasting relationships between children and adults. Many deliberate policies foster this—small classes, the insistence that teachers take on advising and coaching duties, the inclusion of students on committees, and so on. However, these relationships are also the unconscious effect of something more elusive—the climate created when teachers relate to the school not as a place to work but as a place to be; that is, when they see the school as a functioning community that sustains their growth as they sustain that of the students around them. At that point students become much more than empty vessels into which teachers pour their wisdom; they become necessary partners whose very activity is a gauge of the teacher's success and value.

While a student's relationship to a teacher is typically mediated by rules, formal courtesies, duties, and expectations, one of the finest aspects of independent school teaching for me has been witnessing or experiencing the daily transcendence of that contractual relationship. It expresses itself in the easy intimacy and banter between faculty and students, in the intense colloquies in the department lounges over the meaning of life or books or last night's Mets game. It shows itself in the ease with which teachers become devoted to or even identified with their students, often to the exclusion of any personal time during the school day. It is not that these teachers are more self-sacrificing than others, but that the quality of their relationships with students is more personal and thus both more demanding and rewarding on that scale. What the Middle States team reported as "caring and commitment" was really the fact that students and teachers take pleasure from each other's company and so naturally and continuously migrate into each other's space.

Immersed in these relationships, it becomes difficult to do in the classroom what comes easiest to many teachers—talk at students. The reason that the "teacher as coach" model—as well as most of Theodore Sizer's other "essential principles"—often seems like folk wisdom to many working in independent schools is that these ideas come with the territory. Certainly a teacher can succumb to giving only lectures or multiple-choice tests to ten students as easily as to thirty, but when a teacher feels personally responsible to an individual student, the only thing that will satisfy the human demands of that relationship, that will make it reciprocal, is the meaningful activity of the student. The excellent teachers I know are the ones who feel that responsibility the most keenly and as a consequence practice a kind of "negative capability." They do not tell or give answers or regard themselves as the intellectual authority. Rather, they deflect the work back to the students so that their ideas and revelations become the intellectual currency of each day's work. They do this by asking good questions (what Sizer calls "essential questions") that reveal the central ambiguity of an issue, by listening carefully enough that they can orchestrate the answers into some kind of symphonic whole, and by making certain that the work students do—papers or tests or projects—is built, not on some abstract expectation, but on the class's actual insights and discoveries. As soon as the teacher does anything to render the student passive, the human relationship is broken and the contractual one—the one ordered by rules and duties—takes over; responsibility is replaced by obligation, with a corresponding loss of intellectual energy. Reduced to instruments who merely serve each other, both the teacher and the student suffer, and the school, in that relationship at least, stops functioning as a community.

Of course good teaching of this kind is not the sole province of independent schools (nor is lecturing obsolete or dangerous), but it comes more naturally to them because the family ethos not only fosters responsible relationships between teachers and students but also provides the external conditions that prevent their frustration—small classes, a large degree of latitude for teachers in the classroom, and the opportunity for teachers to work with students in many different capacities.

The benefits of small classes are not limited to the mechanical advantages of small student loads. Certainly being responsible for sixty students instead of a hundred or more should mean that individual students receive more attention in class and more help outside, that more assigned work is read scrupulously and returned quickly. Small student loads also mean that the most important promise a private school makes to the parent—that the school will work with the child as an individual—is, in fact, a reasonable expectation for the faculty. It is axiomatic that the fewer students a good teacher has, the more sensitive and imaginative he can be in recognizing and responding to the needs of each student. However, the more lasting and meaningful benefits of small classes can be seen only after we examine the role of the class in the larger community of the school.

When one thinks of a class, one usually imagines an entity that lasts forty-five minutes or an hour. It may have a lesson plan constructed by the teacher and homework that the students did to prepare for it. It has a beginning and an end, a block-like existence in the midst of a schedule card, a designated place in a particular classroom. Teachers and students think in terms of having a good class or a bad class on a particular day. Administrators usually evaluate teachers by observing a class. In other words, we think of the class as a discrete unit, a thing with a particular lifetime and character. Of course, classes function very differently. Their actual lifespan is a semester or a year; they persist in the teacher's and students' consciousness in between their meetings; and, most importantly, they exhibit a kind of organic existence, maturing over their lifetimes with every individual changing in relationship with every other. Their life histories are extremely complex and unpredictable with small causes—a word to a student in passing, a response to a question, a comment on a paper—having large effects. A class that is dynamic and brilliant at the beginning of the year can go rigid with silent rivalries by the middle, or, as I often find, a class of mean-spirited boors that I can barely suffer in September learns so much good humor and tolerance by the end that I can hardly bear to leave them. Classes are not just the organizing instrument we use to educate children; they are, in fact, human communities, each with its own collective character, needs, and talent.

Although what constitutes the "smallness" or "largeness" of a class depends on many factors (twenty seniors may be a small math class but a large English class), its relative size is second only to the skill and personality of the teacher in determining its character as a community. Although great talent in the teacher can overcome this, large classes tend to be teacher-centered, the geography of the classroom necessitating rows of desks facing a blackboard and the maintenance of decorum requiring the teacher constantly to lead and dominate the discussion. The lines of communication move in two directions only, to the teacher and back to the student. Students can hear each other but rarely talk to each other. Whatever healthy community there is in the class is largely silenced by the formality of its structure, since all the potential reserves of character and leadership in its student body go largely untapped.

Although there is nothing guaranteeing that a small class will have a different life, since an unimaginative teacher can render a small group passive as easily as a large one, a circle of twelve or fifteen students sitting around a table allows the teacher to exercise what I referred to above as "negative capability," that is, the deliberate diminishing of his own power and visibility in favor of the students'. In this kind of class, the lines of communication change radically; students not only talk to each other but listen to each other talk to each other. Their ideas become the substance of the class, while the teacher inserts the critical language that gives those ideas shape and value. And when students talk to each other earnestly and passionately in class about intellectual matters, they are much more likely to carry that discussion on outside, either with each other in the halls, or with the teacher in his office, or with their parents at home. When that happens, the classroom becomes the center of the class but not its boundary, and the school takes a major step toward becoming a community that has internalized academic values and views education as an end in itself.

If small class size is the essential logistical element to instilling these values in the school community, then the freedom of the teacher to manage curriculum is the necessary structural one. For a number of reasons, independent schools have traditionally granted teachers a large degree of freedom in the classroom. Collegial hiring practices generally mean that departments choose their own members and place a large degree of trust in their educational background and experience. Moreover, the traditional academic orientation of most independent schools makes them relatively resistant to educational dogma and skeptical about any best way of teaching. Furthermore, the liberal values of many independent schools lead them to appreciate personal diversity in their faculty and make them willing to sacrifice the benefits of conformity to those arising from the unfettered exchange between a group of students and the personal styles of a varied array of teachers.

The most important reason, however, stems directly from the family ethos. Because the relationship between the individual child and teacher is at the heart of the whole enterprise, teachers are given a great deal of latitude in orchestrating curriculum to meet the needs of their classes and to exploit their own strengths as scholars. As I argued before, the most pressing need a teacher feels within a school that fosters responsible relationships between adults and children is that the student be active and responsive, the subject rather than the object of his education. And when teaching becomes student-centered, that is, focused on the needs of the child rather than on the conventional demands of a discipline or department, the teacher ceases to be the vehicle of a fixed curriculum ordained by powers outside the class and becomes, instead, the creator of a dynamic one whose details vary according to the progress and discoveries of his students. This shift in emphasis from the acquisition of facts to the process of disciplined inquiry requires supple, responsible pedagogy and a minimum of external restraint.

But a child in a school is more than just a student, and independent schools have long recognized that the building of responsible relationships in the classroom must be reflected in their nourishment elsewhere. Again, the Athenian concept of citizenship is relevant; just as a man was not fully human for Aristotle unless he lived in a *polis* where his full potential could be developed through amateur participation in a complete culture, so the independent school celebrates its ability to educate the whole child. Of course, public schools offer many (if not more) of the same extra-curricular programs that make such a promise plausible, but there is at least one condition that distinguishes the experience of the independent school student: the whole student is taught, coached, and mentored by whole adults, that is, by teachers who are strongly encouraged—if not required—to play as many roles with students as students play in the school. Nothing distinguishes the experience of teaching in an independent school more than this spirit of ama-teurism, and teachers, particularly young ones in boarding schools, may find themselves coaching sports whose rules they barely under-stand, leading activities that they have never before participated in, or advising students barely four years younger than themselves. Equally, however, a teacher in these schools finds myriad opportu-nities in the context of teaching to pursue interests and develop talents that, in the public arena, would require official forms of training and certification. This may appear unprofessional to the cold eye looking for accountability and conformity. But the bonds that this faith in amateurism creates between students and teachers is largely the source of the trust and spirit of mutual enterprise that distinguishes the climate of so many independent schools.

III

As good as this ethos sounds, it is also the root of a subtle paradox largely absent from the public sector. While we may think of our schools as extended families, they are, unlike public schools, businesses and are often governed, at their board levels at least, by business people who look on teachers, not as the surrogate uncles or parents of their children, but as employees of a private enterprise hired on one-year contracts. In the modern independent school, the fabled attention to the whole child or the individual child (as if there were something else) is really an implicit promise made to prospective clients that their child will be treated on his own terms.

This pledge to parents becomes a condition of employment to teachers. Not only should the faculty perceive and meet the individual needs of the child, but it should also establish a rapport with students that will make them feel esteemed and nurtured and, most important, that will lead to academic success. In short, the business of the private school is built on the promise of familial bonds between teachers and children. In contrast, the bargain struck between a parent and a public school is that the child will receive an *equal* education based on only a broad determination of his needs (for example, special education or placement on a fast track).

In a strong and stable school where these expectations are shared by all constituencies, this understanding can lead to a powerful and nourishing sense of community, since the individual regard that teachers bestow on children returns to them in ever-increasing showers of esteem from students, alumni, and parents. However, the agreement that the individual child is the center of the school may force other values to the periphery. We may hesitate to fail a student who has abused even the most minimum academic standards. Believing that we are uniquely qualified to teach a student to learn from his mistakes, we may keep a child in the school who continuously violates its rules. We may ignore our own policies by removing a student from a course after a deadline or voting not to report his grade on the transcript because he was badly placed. And then we may turn around and do exactly the opposite for another child, all because operating on precedent or rule violates the real policy of an independent school and its strongest promise to the parent, that is, doing what is best for the child. This practice transforms school policy from what it pretends to be—the constitution of the school defining its professional identity—into a set of guidelines, readily subordinate to circumstance, which often fails to hold students accountable to any absolute standard.

Although it is rarely felt as an obligation, this expectation that teachers should form a familial relationship with students leads to an unconscious social contract between the adult and student communities that may make the cooler, more instrumental relationships in large public and parochial schools seem refreshing by comparison. Because of independent schools' academic and college preparatory orientation, the kind of tacit negotiation between a child and a teacher to limit their expectations of each other that Theodore Sizer describes in *Horace's Compromise* may be relatively rare in independent schools; however, another kind of deal is continually being struck and was implicit, for us, in the affection and mutual trust that the Middle States committee found so praiseworthy. On the one hand, the students agree to comply with the whole achievement-oriented, college-bound ethic of the school. They agree to be positive, alert, responsive, to greet their teachers warmly in the hall, and to dress and generally behave like young adults and their teachers' intellectual peers. They agree to seek their teachers out when they need help, and they agree to attribute their successes to the school and faculty. Most importantly, they agree to enjoy doing what they are told to do, to maintain a good attitude, to take pleasure in learning. In return, the teachers agree to be tolerant, accessible, and generally accommodating. They agree to treat the children according to circumstance and, to some degree at least, according to the child's intentions as well as his deeds. This may mean tailoring different punishments for different children committing the same offense, or it may mean deciding questions of academic honors not on the actual record but on subjective criteria (the major one in my school is "loving knowledge for its own sake") so that we can reward or punish students, not on the basis of their actual accomplishment, but on how well they have kept their side of the bargain (that is, appearing to enjoy doing what we ask them to do).

That such an agenda exists in my school becomes clear every time foreign teachers enter the school who are used to more formal relations with students. They see the friendliness and warmth of the students but, more revealingly, perceive a systemic lack of respect for the faculty's professional status. The students may admire their teachers' knowledge or wit and regard many of them as friends, but the very familiarity of their relations is more characteristic of children who have never learned to acknowledge the autonomy of their parents, so conditioned are they to special treatment. Foreign teachers who try to maintain a professional distance from their students are often seen as cold or hostile. This year an advisee of mine was bewildered by her relations with a new foreign math teacher. "I have such a hard time learning anything in her class," she sighed.

"All my other teachers have been my friends, but Mrs. M. doesn't even greet me or smile at me in the hall. I guess she doesn't like me." Her attitude is typical of the ways that our students have unconsciously identified being able to learn with the personal responsiveness of their teachers. On the other side of the coin, students who remain aloof from their teachers are rarely the ones honored by the school, regardless of their actual achievement.

The family ethos and the resulting compact with the parent that the success and self-esteem of the individual child form the dominant agenda of the school also raise complex questions about what the needs of a child are and who determines them. In private schools where parents choose to spend upward of $10,000 a year in tuition, the needs of the child can be confused with those of the parents—for example, the parents' need to have their child be given special attention or the parents' need to send their child to an Ivy League college. The old notion that privileged children should be sent to private schools to learn the values of service in spartan surroundings from uncompromising teachers is no longer the operating standard. More and more, parents see private school tuition as an investment in the financial futures of their children. And the return on that investment is often measured, not in preparation for the appropriate college, but in admission to the prestigious one. While the faculty perceive the needs of the child in terms of learning necessary academic skills and internalizing positive intellectual values, needs that might only be met by establishing and respecting rigid academic standards, the parents are more likely than ever to perceive the needs of the child more narrowly and pragmatically— acquiring the grades and using the reputation of the school to move up as many rungs as possible on the college admissions ladder. The old faith in the process that students would naturally end up in colleges that were suitable for them has been largely superseded by a pervasive anxiety over grades, SAT scores, and college essays. Because it is irrational, the parents' effort to alleviate that anxiety by sending their children to private schools with good college admissions records is not enough, and the continual pressure many place on their children, once there, to get good grades becomes pressure on their teachers either to give good grades or to so structure the curriculum that they are a real possibility for everyone.

As much as the family ethos may subtly corrupt the mission of the school into serving the pragmatic or even narcissistic needs of parents, it also confuses the relationship between the faculty and the governing powers of the school. Teachers who have developed familial relationships with students may tend to project those into unexamined expectations about their relations with the school's administration, looking to it as a kind of benign parental authority that should protect and nourish them. This feeling is often enforced by the head's public language, which may refer to the faculty as "my" teachers, to his own role as ministerial or nurturing, or to the willingness of his faculty to sacrifice their time out of pure love for children. Salary negotiations may consist simply of a talk and a handshake, with no accounting of details. Teachers may be asked to take on extra duties as a sign of the head's trust and good opinion, with only the vaguest indication that they will be remunerated in some fashion.

In more direct ways, as well, the school may take on a parental role in a teacher's life, providing housing, food, monies for education, and so forth. Over time, this practice can infantilize a faculty, making them dependent on the school and individually unwilling to risk fracturing this parental bond by acting collectively as adult professionals who have a valuable service to sell. Although independent school teachers may excuse their reluctance to organize by arguing that professionals don't join unions, the real reason lies deeply embedded in the family ethos of their schools. The familial trust that the school environment conditions them to have in their students is naturally, and often naively, assumed to exist at all levels of the school hierarchy; to act in blatant self-interest—to join a union or bargain collectively for higher wages or better working conditions—would be a crude betrayal of that trust unbefitting their commitment. Thus the family ethos ultimately breeds a kind of perverse elitism that places subtle but powerful strictures on a faculty's willingness to act as independent professionals.

It is fair to say that I have drawn an ideal picture of the independent school, both in its strengths and limitations. But if the description is not literally true for all such schools, it should have heuristic value for most. As much as good teaching depends upon the act of educating students through responsible relationships with adults, so strong schools depend upon a faculty empowered by a professional ethic that values collegiality and consensus over hierarchy and authoritarianism. Because they are self-determined, independent schools have the best chance to create communities in which these dual but mutually dependent beliefs govern, yet there is much in the current climate endangering this process. Their fragile economies, the ever-present peril of declining enrollment, and their need to position themselves appealingly in relation to the competition press incessantly on boards and threaten to make questions of market and management dominate over the less tangible issues of community and morale. If the education that independent schools offer becomes a commodity that is sold, and thus packaged and modified according to a market, it will no longer be the faculty who decides what that product is, although it will remain their responsibility to deliver it. When and if that happens, the most independent school in town may be the public one.

Notes

1. *New York Times,* September 2, 1990: 24.
2. Chester Finn, "Are Public and Private Schools Converging?," *Independent School,* Winter 1989: 45–55.
3. Ann Lieberman and Lynn Miller, "The Social Realities of Teaching," *Teachers College Record,* September 1978: 54.
4. Ibid., p. 59.
5. Ibid., p. 60.
6. Ibid.
7. Pearl R. Kane, *Teachers in Public and Independent Schools: A Comparative Study* (New York: Esther A. and Joseph Klingenstein Center for Independent School Education, 1986), pp. 49–51.
8. H.D.F. Kitto, *The Greeks* (Harmondsworth, U.K.: Penguin Books, 1957), p. 78.
9. Kane, *Teachers in Public and Independent Schools,* pp. 20–30. Kane reports that 55 percent of independent day school and 68 percent of independent boarding school teachers in her study come from "very competitive" to "most competitive" colleges,

and that 60–80 percent of them majored in academic subjects either in college or graduate school. Comparatively, 15 percent of public school teachers come from the same range of colleges, and 45 percent and 19 percent of them majored in academic subjects in college or in graduate school, respectively.

13

On Being "Shafted":
Memories of
an Exeter Graduate

John Irving

I have converted to fiction the best of my observations of Phillips Exeter; most recently, and most obviously, in *A Prayer for Owen Meany* (1989)—my seventh novel—the fictional town of Gravesend is clearly Exeter, where I was born and grew up, living usually in sight of the Academy and always within hearing of the bell in the Academy Building. In *A Prayer for Owen Meany*, even the street names are as accurate as my memory of Exeter allows; and my late grandmother's house, where I lived until I was six, will forever be 80 Front Street, both in the novel and in so-called real life. The prep school in *A Prayer for Owen Meany*—called Gravesend Academy— is much more consciously modeled on Exeter than The Steering School was modeled on the Academy; although, when *The World According to Garp* (1978) was published, everyone *said* that Steering was Exeter. . . . Exonians even said that Dean Bodger was Dean Kesler, that Ernie Hom was Ted Seabrooke, that Steward "Fat Stew" Percy was Bill "Barney" Cox. I disagree; I was merely generalizing: The Steering School was all prep schools, the fictional faculty were just representative types—they were not even developed characters. I was only warming up to the prep school subject; in 1978, my memory of Exeter was a muscle suffering from disuse.

John Irving's chapter is reprinted from *Transitions: Exeter Remembered 1961-87*, copyright 1990 by the trustees of Phillips Exeter Academy.

Then, in *The Hotel New Hampshire* (1981), I wrote about a prep school as opposite to Exeter as I could imagine—another type of school, another generalization, but this time the subject was a deliberately third-rate school, a school so conventionally mediocre that it knew it was third-rate. The students knew they were bad—they were often thugs and miscreants who'd been fired from other schools—and even the faculty were aware that *they* were inferior. The Dairy School, it was called—a bastion of shoddy values, a zenith of mediocrity; the faculty were wardens, not teachers, and the students were inmates.

To be sure: even at a good school, a student can feel like an inmate; even with good students, a first-rate teacher more than occasionally feels like a prison guard. I suppose that The Dairy School allowed me to indulge in my less favorable impressions of Exeter—the few bullies, the few lunkheads on the faculty, and the overall aura of claustrophobia at *any* boarding school—but The Dairy School is not Exeter.

In *A Prayer for Owen Meany*, I allowed myself to close in, much more concretely, on my memories of my Exeter experiences; yet I was careful to keep out of the vocabulary of the novel a particularly dated word. Who remembers being "shafted"? Someone was always "getting shafted"; it was also common usage to say that one had been "given the shaft."

Well, I wanted to tell a story about a good boy in a good school who is given the shaft. And the so-called shaft he is given in that school precipitates a far greater tragedy than being thrown out of school; *because* this boy is thrown out of school, he misses out on getting a scholarship to college; because he needs a scholarship to go to college, he signs up with the Reserve Officers Training Corps—thereby graduating from college with the rank of second lieutenant (unfortunately, during the Vietnam War).

Everything about Gravesend—the town and the school—in *A Prayer for Owen Meany* is a much better piece of writing about my memory of Exeter than any actual memoir I could write. Perhaps because it's my business, as a novelist, to imagine, I am not a reliable provider of *any* memoir; but if my memory of an experience is inaccurate, the resultant fiction best illuminates what was important in that experience for me. If I alter the reality of Exeter in writing fiction, I also make the experience more crucial and vivid than most memories are; details we invent are often visualized more clearly than the details we only think we remember. After all, with invention comes total responsibility; I am responsible for everything I make up. In my experience, I'm not very responsible for what I remember.

Of course, I was not "shafted" at Exeter in any way that resembles how the main character in *A Prayer for Owen Meany* is shafted; I was not thrown out of school; I didn't go to college on an R.O.T.C. scholarship—I was never even drafted. I was married, and a father, before I graduated from college; my student deferment turned immediately into a more lasting deferment—"married, with child."

But, in fact, I *was* shafted at Exeter; and I suppose that my anger and frustration at having been given the shaft has—in no small way—contributed to my imagining the character of Owen Meany. My true story simply isn't as interesting—and it certainly isn't as dramatic—as Owen's. At the time, I don't recall even knowing I was being shafted; I simply accepted the conventional wisdom of the day—I was a struggling student; therefore, I was stupid.

I was such a poor student, I needed five years to pass that three-year foreign language requirement; and in my fifth year at Exeter—in my second "senior" year—I was taking Math III for the second time (I had already taken Math II twice). I was such a weak student, I passed Latin I with a D- and flunked Latin II; then I switched to Spanish, which I barely survived—so barely that one of my Spanish teachers was moved to remark that grades like mine would not qualify me for admission to Wichita State. It was presumed at Exeter that such a place as Wichita State was a bad place to be; and this presumption lies at the heart of how I was shafted at Exeter. I was led to believe that colleges and universities *not* in the Ivy League (or the almost-as-good equivalents, such as Stanford, Duke, Amherst, or Williams) were rusticated beyond redemption; and that an Exeter education set standards for higher learning that could be met by only these name-brand schools. With my C- average and a college-board score—in English—of 475 (my score in math was below 400), I couldn't even apply to the esteemed institutions. I went, with my head down, to the University of Pittsburgh, the only place I could get in. Naturally, I hated it; no Harkness tables, very uncool habits of dress.

I had a wonderful English teacher at Pitt—one of the best I ever had—but I was too much of a snob to believe that anyone could teach me anything in the company of several *hundred* other students who *all* attended this particular teacher's lectures. I was not used to lectures; at Exeter, we had discussions. I left Pittsburgh. I went to the University of New Hampshire, an institution that my fellow Exonians were highly contemptuous of—"the local cow college," they called it at Exeter. Naturally, I hated it, too. I left Durham.

I went to Vienna, to the Institute of European Studies and the University of Vienna. I think I needed to leave the United States in order to get far enough away from Exeter to discover that there were things to learn, and people to teach you, wholly outside the accepted "better" colleges and universities where most Exonians went.

Eventually, I graduated from the University of New Hampshire, where—in my senior year—I discovered excellent teachers who taught me more about writing than I'd managed to learn at Exeter (or *have* learned since leaving Durham the second time); I even graduated cum laude, prompting one of my former teachers at Exeter to call me "a late bloomer." (At forty-seven, I find this appellation more endearing than it seemed at the time it was bestowed upon me.)

I received a graduate degree from the University of Iowa (an M.F.A.), but the so-called Writers' Workshop was not a school in any formal sense; it was a two-year loan of time—time to write and to meet real (or at least grown-up) writers. I say this truthfully: I needed to publish three or four novels before I stopped feeling I was stupid. I do not blame Exeter for this; I state this as a no-fault fact— Exeter made me feel stupid, and I didn't get over that feeling until I was thirty-six or thirty-seven.

It wasn't until my younger son, Brendan (now a prep school graduate), was diagnosed as learning-disabled—as slightly dyslexic—that I realized how I had been given the shaft. They said that Brendan comprehended everything he read but that he didn't comprehend a text as quickly as his peers; they said that he could express himself as well as, or actually better than, his peers but that it took him longer to organize his thoughts on paper. This sounded familiar to me. As a child, Brendan read with his finger following the sentence—as I read, as I *still* read. Unless I've written it, I read whatever "it" is very slowly—and with my finger.

It wasn't until Brendan's so-called learning disabilities were diagnosed in concrete terms—grade-level of perception equals time taken to perceive—that I realized I had always been so "disabled." I never knew it wasn't normal to follow a sentence with my finger. I wasn't diagnosed as learning-disabled or dyslexic at Exeter; I was just plain stupid. I failed a spelling test and was put in a remedial spelling class; because I couldn't learn how to spell—I *still* can't spell!—I was advised to see the school *psychiatrist!* This advice made no sense to me then—it makes no sense to me now—but if you were a poor student at Exeter, you would develop such a lasting sense of your own inferiority that you'd probably be in need of a psychiatrist one day.

I don't mean that a single faculty member ever ridiculed me or humiliated me. I would not have survived my struggles in math without John Warren's patient tutoring; he was my adviser, and he saved me. I was so insecure about my writing that I showed everything I wrote to George Bennett before I handed anything in to my many English teachers—I never had George in the classroom, but, for five years, he read everything I wrote, and he encouraged me. And my wrestling coach, Ted Seabrooke, kept me in school; he gave me enough confidence in myself—through wrestling—that I was able to take a daily beating in my classes and keep coming back for more. An ironic blessing of my needing to repeat my senior year at Exeter was that I finally got to be captain of the wrestling team— my sole distinction, my only honor, in five years at the Academy.

That my father was in the History Department, and an extremely popular teacher with my fellow students, also made me very proud. From my father I learned to elevate my language, to expand my vocabulary, and to take pride in a hard-earned C-, the grade he gave me in Russian History. He is a Harvard man, a Phi Beta Kappa man; yet he never made me feel stupid: he made me feel like a hero for just barely passing Spanish III.

I wish I'd known, when I was a student at Exeter, that there was a word for what made being a student so hard for me; I wish I could have said to my friends that I was dyslexic, or learning-disabled. Instead, I kept quiet, or—to my closest friends—I made bad jokes about how stupid I was. My son Brendan knows he's not stupid; he knows he's the same kind of student I was. With Brendan's diagnosed learning disability, of course Exeter would have been too hard to him; we both knew that. My elder son, Colin, who—ironically—won the Ted Seabrooke Memorial Award for the Outstanding Wrestler in the 1983 New England Class "A" Tournament, is not dyslexic or learning-disabled; but I wouldn't let him even *apply* to Exeter. I thought he would have to work too hard, and that he'd suffer at Exeter as much as I had. (Colin went to Northfield-Mt. Hermon, instead; the year he won the New England Class "A" wrestling title, he pinned an Exeter boy in the finals—even Ted Seabrooke would have appreciated the irony in that! Brendan, as a senior at Vermont Academy, also won the New England Class "A" Championship—demonstrating no sign of a learning disability in wrestling.)

I'm sure you can detect something angry in the tone of voice with which I remember Exeter; but I'm proud to have graduated. As hard as it was, the Academy didn't exactly hurt me; or if the Academy hurt me, it hurt me inexactly. Besides, anger and frustration are useful emotions to novelists; feeling inferior doesn't hurt a novelist, either—too many novelists suffer from far too much self-esteem. But anyone can understand why I would rather imagine Exeter than remember it.

14

Sports in a School Curriculum:
Four Postulates
to Play By

E. M. Swift

I can remember sitting at Mr. Gurney's table—the late Dick Gurney, the Hotchkiss School's revered and somewhat irreverent English teacher—my first week of boarding school in 1965. I was a prep, which is what freshmen were called at Hotchkiss. As such, I was the low man on the totem pole in this place so far from home, and while I do not remember being timid, or homesick, I must have been a little in awe.

Mr. Gurney had taught and coached my father some twenty-five years before. He had a raspy voice and great bushy eyebrows that made him seem—to me, a prep—like God Almighty. As a youngster I had always pictured God Almighty wearing robes and a turban, a figure with great bushy eyebrows, like the man on the Hills Brothers coffee can. Suddenly, here was Mr. Gurney, a dead ringer for that fellow, except that he wore a rumpled tweed coat instead of robes and a turban. He had a perpetually amused expression on his weathered face and smelled of pipe tobacco.

"I knew your father. Did you know that, Mr. Swift?" Mr. Gurney asked.

"Yes, sir," I replied. "He asked me to say hello to you for him."

"I'm pleased to hear it. Your father was a hockey goalie. Do you play hockey, Mr. Swift?"

"Yessir."

"Are you a hockey goalie like your father?"

"Yessir."

He chewed his mouthful slowly and mulled that information over. "Your father played goalie like the Ancient Mariner," he said with a wry expression.

This was interesting news. It was not, however, enlightening. It did not sound like much of a compliment. "Do you play goalie like the Ancient Mariner?" Mr. Gurney continued.

"I don't think so, sir. I've never heard of him."

"No, but you will," Mr. Gurney said. " 'It is an ancient Mariner, And he stoppeth one of three.' "

I must have looked pretty bewildered, which delighted him. "That's not very good goaltending, is it, Mr. Swift?"

"No, sir."

"I daresay you'll do better."

Two years later, after I had studied the Romantic poets, and Samuel Taylor Coleridge, under Mr. Gurney, I better appreciated his little joke. I remember it now as my first exposure to the interrelationship between sports and academics at boarding school, two worlds that conspired to round my personality into something like the shape it is today.

I am a sportswriter by profession, so I am not an unbiased voice in the debate over the role of athletics in a school curriculum. Naturally, I believe that sports are worthwhile, and can be important, less for what they teach you than for what they allow you to discover for yourself. I happen to agree with golfer Mike Reid, who, after frittering away his lead in the 1989 PGA championship, observed: "Sports are like life with the sound turned up."

The good moments are blown way out of proportion. That is not just true when they happen. Years later, at unexpected times, we replay our heroics in our minds. The bad moments leave nicks and scars in our psyche that never fully heal. I write this from the perspective of someone to whom sports came relatively easily, at least at the high school level. Athletics were a source of great pleasure and self-confidence for me. But I know they can also lower self-esteem, and I wonder about youngsters who lack a certain level of coordination, who find athletics a trial, a chore to be dreaded every afternoon. The dark side of school sports is that they can be a young person's first exposure to rejection.

It will not be their last one, however. One can grow through failure just as easily as one can become stunted by success. The youngster who understands that, who is not afraid to give his or her all and fail, who can learn to laugh through that disappointment and see it for what it really is, has really discovered something.

I doubt there was ever a four-year period in which sports were quite as important to me as those four years I went to boarding school. Things were different then, of course. Hotchkiss was an all-boys school, for one thing, so love interests were on the back burner. Campus rules, by modern standards, were pretty strict. You were expelled from the school the first time you were caught drinking alcohol or smoking marijuana. You were put on probation for smoking cigarettes, and kicked out for a second offense. You were sworn to an honor code. Daily chapel was mandatory, and coats and ties were worn to all classes and meals. Weekend passes were practically nonexistent your first two years.

Sports were an outlet. They were one of the things that made prep school life tolerable, even fun. Not just the organized sports, but the games of touch football on Sunday afternoons in the fall, pond hockey in the winter, and after-dinner stickball in the spring. Sports were a way for us to blow off steam, to bond with classmates, to interact with upper- and lower-classmen, and to get to know the teachers on an informal basis.

It was an opportunity to live life with the sound turned up. The subtleties of the boarding school experience were stripped away in the white glare of athletic competition. The phonies were exposed as being phony. The quiet, shy types had the chance to come into their own. The bullies bullied; the hogs hogged; and the truly exceptional personalities emerged as future class leaders. It is true that competitive sports can teach character, but what they really do best is reveal it.

At a time when I, like most of my classmates, was trying to find myself, sports offered me both clarity and focus. How welcome that unambiguousness was. The rules of the game were unassailable. The purpose of the game was to win. My teammates were people who depended on me. My coach was a man I could trust.

Those four simple truths, I think, are what is enduring about high school sports. All the practices and games, the friendships and rewards, the disappointments and successes would be fleeting if those four basic tenets weren't behind them.

1. The rules of the game were unassailable.

The sports world is, essentially, black and white. There is a winner and a loser. A runner is safe, or he is out. A foul shot is made, or it is missed.

There is very little gray in all of that, and it is the same with the rules. They are either obeyed, or they are broken. Black and white. In football, offside by one inch is still offside, even if the player involved does not have a tinker's damn to do with the play. A batter who has been hit by a pitch is awarded first base whether the ball barely nicks him or strikes him full on the buttocks. In basketball, a three-second violation means three seconds, not four.

Unassailable. There is no compromise involved; no interpretation; no extenuating circumstances. And when a rule is violated, there is a price to pay. Small violation, small price. Big violation, big price.

Young people understand black and white. They have lived with do's and don'ts all their lives. However, it is here, on the athletic fields, that they get some of their most potent lessons in accountability, because they cannot charm, lie, bawl, or plead their way out of their mistakes. Their actions are all that matter. The referee is deaf to excuses in a way that no adult in their lives has been deaf before. The referee does not care who your father is, whether you are feeling sick or well, what your motives were, or whether the infraction was accidental or intentional. All that matters is the integrity of the rules of the game.

Players who are tempted to break the rules must therefore learn to weigh risk and reward on a split-second basis. A hockey defenseman considering hooking an opponent who is breaking in alone might wonder if the action is worth the possible price. Will the coach approve? Will the goalie make the save? There are smart penalties and dumb ones; careless penalties and thoughtful ones. I did not say the rules of the game were sacrosanct, merely unassailable.

Of course risk and reward are also weighed in an average student's everyday life, say when he walks into a math or English class unprepared. But in such an instance, the risk is strictly personal. Will I flunk if the teacher gives us a test? Playing a team sport, players soon discover that their mistakes have an effect on others, and the mistakes of others have an effect on them. They are ensnared in a web of accountability, much as they will be in marriage, or on the job.

It should probably be noted that if the rules are unassailable, then the arbiter of the rules—the referee—should be unassailable, too. That certainly is not the case at most high school basketball games I have attended, but the primary violators seem to be the parents, and one of the educational advantages of a residential boarding school is that parents are usually not around to interfere. At Hotchkiss we were not allowed to argue with the referees. That was another unassailable rule. I suppose that was because it looked unseemly, but, from an educational perspective, I would like to think it may also have had something to do with this accountability business. By arguing a player is saying, in effect: it's not my fault, it's *his*. That is not an adult way of facing up to things, on the field or off.

One of the most vivid memories I have from my rather nondescript Hotchkiss baseball career was the time I got called out on strikes in a preseason scrimmage on a pitch that was over my head. I was a sophomore, trying to make the varsity, and that was my only at-bat in the game. I turned incredulously to the umpire, an elderly man who was the coach of the other team, but bit my tongue and turned back to the bench, the tears welling up in frustration. Life had never seemed so unfair. (I had lived a sheltered life.) As I stomped angrily toward the far end of the bench, our baseball coach, Art White, told me not to worry about the strikeout, and that he was proud of me for buttoning my lip. Life all of a sudden was fair again.

You remember such things. I think of it every time I see a videotape of some enraged manager kicking dirt over the shoes of a major league umpire. At what stage was that man's emotional development arrested, I wonder, while silently acknowledging that there, but for the grace of unassailable rules, go I.

2. *The purpose of the game was to win.*

This is a thorny issue with a lot of people who link competitiveness with poor sportsmanship and being a bad loser. Competitiveness is facing up to the fundamental truth that the purpose of the game is to win.

Any game, any level. Otherwise, it would not be a game, it would be an activity, like walking or fishing. I like activities. I like both walking and fishing, and I particularly *dislike* people who try to turn fishing into a competitive sport by keeping score of fish hooked and landed. But if I am playing a game with rules in which score is kept and at the end there will be a winner and a loser, I don't feel I should apologize for trying my best to be the winner.

Pretend, for a moment, that there was such a thing as non-competitive chess. Winning or losing doesn't matter, you're just in it for the fun. Players attack recklessly. They don't plan or anticipate or defend. They just move pieces willy-nilly about the board, no strategy, no passion, no care. In the process they have ruined the essence of the game.

Most people accept that argument when it is made about chess, because chess is a cerebral game. But for some reason people do not see that physical games, like tennis and baseball and soccer, are also destroyed in a fundamental way if the participants are not carefully trying to win. That does not mean that winning is the only thing, as Vince Lombardi once said. It does not mean you cheat to win, or behave obnoxiously, or go into a deep funk if you lose. It just means you respect your opponent and the sport enough to try your hardest, to attempt strategy, and to exploit strengths and weaknesses.

If the effort to win is missing, then none of the rest of it matters. Obeying the rules does not matter. Being a reliable teammate does not matter. Having a good coach does not matter. All these matter only if both sides are trying to win. If no one really cares, if everyone's just out there fooling around, what is the value in that? Why should that be part of any school curriculum? We learn something from winning and something different from losing. But what do we learn from not caring? We should care. We have to care, whether at the varsity or the intramural level—or else everyone is wasting their time.

3. My teammates were people who depended on me.
You hear a lot about the friendships and bonds that develop

between teammates, but what is just as significant are the petty jealousies, rifts, and personality conflicts that are part of any team. Somehow, if the team is going to succeed, these must be overcome or suppressed. Thus do competitive sports provide some of our earliest lessons in learning to work with people that we do not really like.

Most students arrive at boarding school from fairly homogeneous backgrounds. They are used to going to school and playing on teams with kids they are comfortable with and who, in many ways, think as they do. They grow up rooting for the same professional football team as their friends and wearing the same style of sneakers. They all go to the same beach in the summer and chase the same girls. Everybody pretty much accepts everybody else, warts and all. Childhood friendships are not the type that require very much work.

Suddenly, at boarding school, that unflinching support is gone. Everyone's warts are held up to inspection. Judgments are passed on schoolmates one barely knows on the basis of clothing, accent, hairstyle—you name it. Cliques appear. Friendships are formed overnight, and fall apart just as quickly. Classmates of wildly different backgrounds behave in strange and intimidating ways.

In a dormitory situation, or in the classroom, that can be finessed. If you do not like someone, or do not understand him or her, it's a relatively simple task to avoid him or her. If that person happens to be on a sports team with you, and if winning is important, well, his or her successes became your successes, and vice versa. You have become mutually dependent on one another, like it or not.

This is a powerful bond, sharing a common goal—more powerful than stereotypes or predilections. Actions on an athletic field do not just speak more powerfully than words. Actions replace words. Teammates gain and lose respect, not on the basis of what they are (white, black, funny, sad, rich, poor) but of what they do.

Furthermore, it is not just what they do on game days. It is the whole scene—how your teammates are in the locker room, at practices, on the team bus. Every member of a team has a role within that team, and, if it is a good team, truly formed, all those roles should merge into a single personality. Not the starters' personality and the substitutes' personality, but one personality. The basis by which we judge our teammates is not how good they are but whether they fulfill their roles. Are they there when they are called on? Do they try? Do they care about the team?

One of the worst feelings in the world is the feeling of having let your teammates down. Therefore, you try to be dependable, but the nature of sports being what it is—one person's success is another's failure—you sometimes fail. Your teammates sometimes fail. Do you point fingers at one another, or ask the more difficult question, What more could *I* have done? You learn the shared responsibility of true teamwork.

That is not something that can be taught in a classroom situation, in which every student is ultimately on his or her own. If John flunks, does Jim feel responsible? Of course not. However, if one of the goals of a boarding school education is to turn out good citizens and prepare young people for life (as opposed to merely preparing them for college), then teaching students about shared responsibility, about being dependable, about suppressing the ego in pursuit of a common goal, should be pretty high up on an educator's priority list.

It may just be coincidence, but none of my teammates were expelled from school while I was at Hotchkiss. Several classmates were, but no teammates. Team members would have felt betrayed if a teammate had been caught drinking or smoking during the season, so not many of them did.

During my junior year I was in a school play, *Inherit the Wind*. It was directed by two seniors, who were also starring in the roles of William Jennings Bryan and Clarence Darrow. It was an enjoyable experience, and I thought of the cast as a team. You did not want to be late for rehearsals because of all those other people involved, people to whom you had become attached through sharing this common goal. You did not want to let them down.

A few days before the play was scheduled to be performed, the two directors were caught smoking marijuana and were expelled. The play had to be cancelled. I don't remember much about those two, except that neither of them played on a sports team, and I cannot help thinking, wrongheaded as it might be, that if they had, they would have better understood that we had entered into a sort of pact of voluntary interdependence. They would not have risked letting us down.

4. My coach was a man I could trust.

I never met a college athlete who preferred his college coach to the coach he had in high school. Some must exist; I just never happened to meet one, and I spent most of my time around jocks. I have wondered about it many times.

Obviously a high school athlete is at a more malleable age than his collegiate counterpart, but there has to be more to it than that. I certainly remember college professors whom I preferred to some of my teachers at boarding school. The only theory I can come up with is that, at the secondary school level, most coaches are really educators who happen to spend their afternoons coaching.

College coaches are professionals. That is what they do for a living: coach. Their self-esteem rises and falls with the won-lost record of their teams, and since not all teams have winning records, not all college coaches have enormous self-esteem. The players recognize this—and sometimes lose respect for them.

My coaches at Hotchkiss, by contrast, made their living by teaching. They were good teachers and, generally speaking, had loads of self-esteem. Coaching was something they did in their spare time. They took it seriously, and they coached to win. But they had the games in perspective, which, strangely, made them better coaches.

It also rounded the athletic/academic experience into something of a whole. My American history teacher was also my junior varsity football coach. My baseball coach was also a math teacher and the dean of students. My hockey coach taught twelfth-grade English.

It had a synergistic effect on my development, both academically and athletically. For instance, I worshipped my hockey coach, Blair Torrey. He, too, had been a goaltender. He had started at guard for the Princeton football team while weighing 165 pounds. He had been a Marine. As a coach he was compassionate, tough, fair, enthusiastic, and open-minded. He inspired and, when aroused, terrified us.

I am not a big fan of analyzing dreams, but one of my teammates once had a dream that defined our feelings for Mr. Torrey. It went like this: Mr. Torrey created a drill in which half the team lifted a teammate on their backs and skated across the rink, up and back, up and back, up and back—until they all collapsed from exhaustion and died. The surviving players then hoisted the dead bodies on their backs and skated up and back, up and back, until they, too, died. That was the end of the drill.

The thing was, Mr. Torrey could have gotten us to do it. No question. We both feared and trusted him.

Yet this same man would become misty-eyed when discussing the poetry of John Keats. "Some shape of beauty moves away the pall / From our dark spirits." And since it was important to him, it became important to me, because I had already established a compelling connection with this man through sports. If he believed that Keats's "Ode to a Grecian Urn" was "great stuff," then I would lift that volume on my back and skate with it until I understood it, or died of exhaustion trying. I wanted his respect.

This was true of my other coaches, too. Seeing them in the classroom rounded out their personalities and humanized the entire boarding school experience. A dour French teacher might be a veritable laugh riot during an intramural soccer game. The screaming, tyrannical football coach might be an old softie in the biology lab.

You came to realize that these men, too, had good days and bad ones. They had days when they could not wait for class to end so that they could get outside, and days when they could not wait for practice to end so they could get back to grading tests. The overriding message was that everything has its own time and place, because all of it matters. Your work matters. Your play matters. Your enthusiasm, time, friendships, loyalty, goals—all of them matter. Latin matters. Rules matter. So does art history. And junior varsity football.

All of it. It matters because you're doing it, not the other way around. It is the attitude that is important. That is the lesson of sports. That is where the educational value of an athletic program lies. Sports, at any level, is about the pursuit of excellence in a medium that is, essentially, trivial. It is the *pursuit* that matters, not the attainment of excellence as embodied by wins and losses, batting averages, track times, or points per game. The pursuit of excellence is the only game a school should be willing to play. So it follows that a school that fields four league champions but has only 50 percent of the student body involved in organized sports has a poorer athletic curriculum than a school with no league champions and 98 percent involvement.

Because the pursuit is not trivial. Once a young man or woman starts trying to be the best that he or she can possibly be, it's difficult to stop.

15

The Role of the Arts
in Independent Schools

Maxine Greene

At first glance, and certainly from the vantage point of public education, the independent schools provide green fields for the arts. They appear as sophisticated places where creativity can be nurtured, the sense of craft encouraged, and personal expression of many sorts affirmed. For all the emphasis on the formal and the cognitive, there seems to be a regard for the imagination. Not only is this the capacity that brings, as Virginia Woolf said, "severed parts together";[1] it allows people to reach beyond themselves, to summon up alternative possibilities. It seems to be widely recognized in independent schools that informed engagements with the arts are what enable the young to explore and play in this way. Awakening the young, they can move them to wonder and the posing of questions; and most independent schools are reputed to be hospitable to such questioning in the recognition that this is where learning begins. There is no need here to seal off the arts as frivolous or merely affective. The feelings they evoke can be perceived as responsive to understanding; and the understanding that is sought excludes mere conventionality. At a moment of general thoughtlessness and carelessness in society at large, this cannot but lead to a hope for the invention of exemplars accessible to public schools. What happens in the privileged space of independent schools ought some day to move beyond them and around them, radiating outwards into the community, touching a diversity of hitherto untouched lives. It may be that, by example and support, the independent schools will communicate the possibility of a deeply educative role to be played by the arts in the lived situations of many, many children, no matter what their class or origin.

It is clear enough that utilitarianism and a peculiarly American moralism have accounted for the relative neglect of the arts in the public schools over time. The primary object of those schools, after all, was to train the young for work in an industrializing society, to make it possible for them to "pursue wealth,"[2] to prepare them for citizenship and compliance with the laws of righteousness. Traditional pieties rendered anything associated with play or frivolity in some manner sinful, a waste of time. There is a telling metaphor to be found with regard to this in Nathaniel Hawthorne's story "The Maypole of Merry Mount,"[3] where the dancers of the maypole colony are contrasted to the citizens of the colony whose emblem is a whipping post. The action of the story involves Governor Endicott and his fellow Puritans moving through the woods to "establish their jurisdiction over the gay sinners" and make New England a land "of hard toil, of sermon and psalm, for ever." It is not only that the maypole colonists are flower growers, impractical men who have "sported" with life. They include among them minstrels no longer tolerated in London, wandering players, mummers, mirth makers "discountenanced by the rapid growth of Puritanism." Of course they are defeated; the maypole is cut down; the young men's hair is cut into the "proper pumpkin" cut; the dancing bear is shot through the head. At the end, the Lord and Lady of the May (favored because they were about to be married) join the other colony and go heavenward "supporting each other along the difficult path which it was their lot to tread, and never [wasting] one regretful thought on the vanities of Merry Mount." The ironies are multiple. Neither colony, in truth, is defensible; and the questions go unanswered. What is clear, however, is the threat to law and order felt by the Puritans. The threat lies in the masks the others wear, the mirth they communicate, the sweetness and the gaiety they embody in their very uselessness.

For many years, when art appeared in classrooms, it was used for didactic purposes. (Who can forget the McGuffey readers and

"The Boy Stood on the Burning Deck"?) Later on, it was frequently trivialized into the making of pumpkins and Christmas cards and Valentines. It is true that at certain moments, when spontaneity and free expression were valued by an Emerson, or a Francis Parker, or by the "romantic" Progressives,[4] art making was brought into young children's classrooms. But, as in the case of the early progressive schools, this was most likely to happen in private settings, even as such pioneers as Viktor Lowenfeld[5] and Hughes Mearns[6] had most of their successes in museums, private schools, or colleges. Art education under such auspices was primarily concerned with creativity, free expression, a kind of Blakean innocence. The cognitive, the critical, the sequential, and what some have come to call the aesthetic were thought to belong in another realm. At certain moments, as in the 1950s,[7] there were bursts of interest in discipline-based art education, in links between the arts and the humanities, even in the teaching of art in historical contexts. On rare occasion, such approaches made inroads in certain public schools. Today, however, for all the programmatic innovations of large foundations,[8] the participation of numbers of public and private arts councils and the like, technological preoccupations and budgetary difficulties are daily making the arts more marginal in public schools. Because of the desperation of many men and women concerned about their children's future, it has not been difficult to justify the elimination of the arts in favor of the practical or the technical, something that may some day "pay off." Learning in the arts is simply not viewed as integral to what school learning is supposed to be.

Parents and patrons of independent schools, in contrast, do not usually need convincing that acquaintance with art and high culture has something to do with status or at least the look of success. Many parents, moreover, like the teachers in these schools, are themselves graduates of fine colleges and universities. There often tends to be a tacit agreement that all are members of a cosmopolitan, sophisticated world, one in tune with the world of art galleries, ballet companies, orchestras, and theaters. There is often a kind of cachet that goes with some acquaintance with "the latest" or the avant-garde, even among those who would far prefer to attend a football or baseball game. (Of course there may be many fathers like the one in *Dead Poets Society*, people who cannot tolerate the idea of their sons' *becoming* artists of any sort. But this is quite different from contributing to an orchestra fund or being thought *au courant* where the arts are concerned.)

The soil, therefore, seems to be prepared for the rich programs in the arts proposed by the National Association of Independent Schools Arts Planning Group.[9] The arts curriculum, as that group presents it, should not only reach every student; it should involve every one of them personally, introduce each one to the nature of the arts and the way they function in the culture. Quite obviously, the report stresses the knowledge and skills to be gained; but it also talks about valuing perceptions and emotions as it sheds light on the importance of critical thinking and interpretation. The teaching patterns suggested do systematize the teaching of particular disciplines, but they do not underestimate the importance of developing creative power—of learning *in* the arts, *about* the arts, and *through* the arts. This means that the familiar dichotomies—between affective and cognitive, right and left hemispheres of the brain—are to be set aside in favor of integrated, transactional approaches. The writers are sensitive to special talents and to the diversity of talents, as well as cultures, to be found in the schools. All told, the report offers an exciting, insightful, and inclusive accounting of what art education and independent schools can and ought to be.

There still exists a need, given the unfairness and the lack of care so characteristic of our society, to search for a more far-reaching way to talk about the arts in relation to human existence itself. It seems unlikely that any independent school teacher would be gratified by the prospect of inhabiting an enclave, a refuge from the clattering, unaesthetic world. The resources for the arts are often so great that marvelous experiences can be offered to students. Frequently, students are taught by visiting artists of the highest quality: a ballet dancer from the Joffrey Ballet, a horn player from the local orchestra, a scene designer from a downtown theater, a percussion quartet on its way through the city. A consciousness of discipline, of well-honed craft is communicated. Taken seriously, as each art form is taken by the practitioner, it no longer seems like play. Because the artists come so often from outside the school, they bring with them a feeling of the risks and realities of the real world.

It is not uncommon for there to be an illusion on the part of both teachers and students that, through their participation, they have left their privileged world behind. Studio, atelier, salon: art, whether intentionally or not, becomes art for art's sake. This, in some odd way, makes it easier for the art forms to become subjects, like other discrete subjects, in a liberal arts curriculum. This may happen even when the art teachers are in no respect product-oriented or performance-oriented.

This can all be carried on so long as there is consideration given to how the art world enters the school and finds a place in the school in relation to the culture's systems of commodification and against the background of popular culture or the media-derived representations that are more real for many people than reality itself. What is understood by an art world? How does it relate to established traditions, to the canon that is under so much attack today? Does the art world as recognized by the school allow for shapes and images and voices ordinarily left out by those who constructed that world? Arthur Danto, philosopher and critic, has been much interested in how things become art works and in how we can tell the difference.[10] When he talks about theories of art, he says that an art world is always dependent upon a theory. An art theory, he says, can be powerful enough "to detach objects from the real world and make them part of a different world, an *art* world, a world of interpreted things." Much depends, of course, on whether the interpretation given is an artistic interpretation; but it is important to see that it is an interpretation, a human judgment of (for example) certain paintings.

Once we recognize the part played by human choosing and intention in determining what *is* an art work, we need also to take into account what Terry Eagleton says with regard to literature and the literary tradition.[11] The so-called literary canon, he writes, "the unquestioned great tradition of the national literature," must be recognized as "a *construct*, fashioned by particular people for particular reasons at a certain time. There is no such thing as a literary work or tradition which is valuable *in itself*, regardless of what anyone might have said or come to say about it." Later, criticizing the philosopher Gadamer's view of tradition, Eagleton challenges the assumption that "there is indeed a single 'mainstream' tradition; that all 'valid' works participate in it . . . and that the prejudices which 'we' (who?) have inherited from the 'tradition' are to be cherished." He finds this view complacent and accuses Gadamer of projecting on the world at large "a viewpoint from which 'art' means chiefly the classical monuments of the high German tradition." Whether this is true or not, the implicit questions are significant.

We are provoked to critical thinking with respect to what indeed is to constitute the art world in the school. Once reminded of the human involvement in determining what is to count as art at any given moment in history, and in any given place, teachers and planners may be opened to the provisional character of existing categories and canons. Not only might there be less orientation to self-sufficient works existing within timeworn and burnished frames, there might be openings to voices, forms, and articulations excluded over the years. By now, we are familiar with the gradual and then climactic opening of the tradition first to women's literature and then (far more slowly) to women's painting and sculpture and musical compositions. The entry of Kate Chopin's *The Awakening* into reading lists; the discovery of Charlotte Perkins Gilman's "The Yellow Wallpaper"; the recognition of Tillie Olsen's triumph over years of "silences": all these are signs of traditions in the making and of the significance of perspectivism. Where women's paintings are concerned, we have come to recognize the impact of prejudice and misunderstanding on women's opportunities to discover themselves as artists; we have found out, for example, what it meant for women to be excluded from life classes and from numerous studios. Considering this, considering what happened in the domains of music (from composition to conducting), we cannot but realize how many dimensions of the subject matter called "art" are intricately bound up with social history, gender issues, and economics, as well as with the many facets of art history and the humanities.

We have had kindred, although often more difficult, experiences with what we have thought of as "minority" art, long excluded in places focused on classical monuments of one sort or another. Attention was drawn to Black literature when Richard Wright, James Baldwin, and then Ralph Ellison were recognized as first-class artists. Because of the peculiar influence of Afro-Americans on popular culture in this country and abroad, the interest in Black literature expanded to a new interest in gospel music, blues, jazz, ragtime, and rhythm and blues. Not only did these feed into the rock revolution and what followed after, but they have become significant influences on so-called serious music today, even as some of the graphic images of popular culture have been absorbed by paintings in museums and galleries. Beginning to pay heed to all this, independent schools must come to terms as well with the challenges posed by Hispanic arts and cultures, what Lucy Lippard calls the "mixed blessings" of works long thrust to the margins of our lives.[12] By now, we are aware of great writers like Marquez, Fuentes, Borges, Cortazar, Allende, Vargas, and Neruda; we are only faintly aware of the great visual traditions throughout South and Central America. A recent Metropolitan Museum of Art exhibition, entitled "Mexico," revealed a tumultuous, still unresolved history of shapes and images reaching from the Mayan and Aztec past to modern Mexico. Grand and complex though that is, it cannot be said to exemplify or include the almost infinite variety of Hispanic art forms. When it must be pointed out, as it recently was by the Mexican novelist and statesman Carlos Fuentes, that the popular television series called "Civilization," produced by the British art historian Kenneth Clark, omitted the Hispanic contributions for Clark's own reasons, we are reminded again of the need for a continuous critical and questioning approach to what we often take for granted, particularly where art worlds are concerned.

There has been, in many of the art fields, a break with formalism. That means a skepticism when it comes to treating works of art as autonomous universes, complete unto themselves in closed-in enclaves. Even as the day of the "new criticism" has ebbed in English teaching, so have formalist or objectivist approaches to the visual arts, dance, and music. On all sides, scholars and critics are stressing the importance of treating created works in relation to their contexts and with reference to larger social realities.[13] There is, on all sides, what has been called a "blurring of the genres"[14] as scholars and artists in particular disciplines incorporate or connect with the perspectives of other disciplines. Philosophers like Richard Rorty[15] and Martha Nussbaum[16] are exploring the peculiar illuminations literature can make possible for philosophy. John Gilmour, like Heidegger and Merleau-Ponty before him, explores painting for philosophical understandings.[17] John Berger, in the tradition of the critical theorists like Adorno and Habermas, examines art forms and other cultural artifacts for clues to the meanings of western socioeconomic life.[18]

In independent schools, opportunities abound for crossing boundaries in these ways, and it seems clear that the study of art can feed into—and be fed by—ongoing dialogues, seminars, and study circles that examine consciousness and cultural realities. Nevertheless, and perhaps paradoxically, efforts must be made to open distinctive spaces for the study of the arts—literature, visual art, music, drama, dance. The critic Denis Donoghue, troubled by the impact of bureaucratic cherishing and overanalytic examination of the arts, writes that it does not bother him to say the arts are marginal: "I want to say that the margin is the place for those feelings and intuitions which daily life doesn't have a place for, and mostly seems to suppress."[19] Even as we work to incorporate the arts more meaningfully in curricula, we need to cherish that special marginality. For Donoghue, there are moments of freedom and presence in the domains of the arts that cannot be experienced anywhere else, especially if people are caught through most of their lives in conventions, habits, and routines.

Imagination and the possibilities opened by imagination may be at the heart of a conception of the role of the arts. Imagination is a cognitive capacity that not only allows us to apply thought to things but is the means by which, as Mary Warnock reminds us, we see into "the life of things." Imagination, moreover, is that capacity that allows us to realize that there is always "*more to experience and more in what we experience than we can predict.*"[20] Art forms are imaginatively created forms; they bring into being unreal worlds that reveal themselves to us to the degree we can encounter them imaginatively. Imagination, then, reaches beyond the actual; it enables us to summon up alternatives and to look at things as if they could be otherwise. There are multiple examples to be found in literature to clarify what this means. One comes from the opening of Melville's *Moby Dick*;[21] reading it for many of us becomes an enactment of what imagination can do in a human life. Melville wrote about the "insular city of the Manhattoes, belted round by wharves as Indian isles by coral reefs—commerce surrounds it with its surf." And then: "Right and left the streets take you waterward. Its extreme downtown is the Battery, where that noble mole is washed by waves and cooled by breezes, which a few hours previous were out of sight of land. Look at the crowd of water-gazers there."

Melville was not only depicting the city where he once had lived. He was bringing into being a transfigured city, a created world, offering to readers a vision of people: "of week-days pent up in lath and plaster—tied to counters, nailed to benches, clinched to desks"; yet reaching outward towards the sea, towards another space, an alternative reality. Melville provides an instance of what imagination can do when it comes to moving people to reach beyond themselves, to break free of the counters, benches, desks of the ordinary. This is an instance, too, of how an art form can reveal the ordinary qua ordinary, taken for granted and therefore unseen.

The images of constraint, of a kind of commercial crucifixion (people "tied to counters, nailed to benches, clinched to desks") are contrasted to the images of water-gazing, looking to the masts, the keels, the harbor, the sea beyond. Reading it summons up thoughts of Dewey opposing the artistic-aesthetic to the mechanical and the routine;[22] it summons up Warnock's notion of there being "more to experience" than anyone can predict. It evokes as well the last stanza of Wallace Stevens's poem "Six Significant Landscapes":[23]

> Rationalists, wearing square hats,
> Think, in square rooms,
> Looking at the floor,
> Looking at the ceiling,
> They confine themselves
> To right-angled triangles.
> If they tried rhomboids,
> Cones, waving lines, ellipses—
> As, for example, the ellipse of the half-moon—
> Rationalists would wear sombreros.

In this case, it is an opening from the one-dimensional, an opening to alternative or even multiple realities. The moments of expansion we associate with imaginative engagement with a work of art are suggested here in a way that resembles and yet differs from Melville's imagining. But both suggest an imaging of the absent, of what remains to be experienced. In a time of technicism, of a narrowing of frames, this may be of great importance, certainly for education. Without some sense that experience holds more than it appears to, that there is something truly worth reaching towards, people (even privileged young people) are unlikely to take the initiative for learning to learn.

There are multiple examples of the importance of the imagination in grasping the possibilities of transmutation—possibilities made suddenly clear in a dance movement, a dialogue, a gesture, a montage in a film, a change in tonality. Attending to a Martha Graham performance, let us say, or paying heed to what King Lear calls out through the storm, or watching Laura limp heavily across a stage in *The Glass Menagerie*, we can experience—and allow students to experience—a kind of expansion in consciousness, a growing density of texture as we allow past encounters to feed into present ones. Dewey wrote that experience becomes fully conscious only when meanings derived from earlier experiences enter it. "Imagination," he wrote, "is the only gateway through which these meanings can find their way into a present interaction."[24] He meant that we become more acutely aware of what is happening to and around us at the moment when what is given to us is extended by meanings drawn from what is past or absent. They are the meanings that can be summoned up imaginatively. Reading *Moby Dick*, for example, we may become aware of grasping the text at the present moment of reading with the help of meanings funded from past readings, and not only of this particular novel. One person reading about a "damp, drizzly November" in Ishmael's soul, and about his desire to go off in order to save his own life, may be influenced by memories of her or his own Novembers, thoughts of suicide, efforts to survive. Someone else may summon up lost fishing stories, lived ones perhaps, or those from novels like *The Old Man and the Sea*, or even a grandfather's storytelling. Enlarging what is presently discovered, rendering it increasingly resonant and meaningful, the reader may go on to confront her or his own White Whale.

It need not be *Moby Dick*. Nor need it be *King Lear* or *Swan*

Lake or Mozart's *Clarinet Quintet* or *Citizen Kane*. Independent schools ought to be able to find ways of moving in and out of the canon, of entering alternative cultural traditions, looking at the familiar from diverse vantage points, until the familiar is defamiliarized and can be seen afresh. The obligation of the teacher, it would seem, is both to make available a variety of possibilities and to contextualize those possibilities. This means to initiate students into the ways of knowing, the ways of seeing associated with history and ethnography and psychology and criticism, permeated by the ardor and energy of imagination. To do that ought to enable them to multiply the perspectives through which, for example, they look at Velasquez's *Las Meninas* or Manet's *Luncheon on the Grass* or Picasso's *Woman Ironing*.

It is not simply learning how to notice what is there to be noticed, significant though that is. The philosopher Michel Foucault, in a noted essay on *Las Meninas*,[25] enables a viewer to see what that viewer might never see without him: the painter's arm bending towards the palette; the hand in the air; the design created by the back of the canvas turned to the spectator; the flood of light through the window; the mirrored images; the little Infanta with her pink and grey dress and the ladies in waiting hovering over her. Provoked into gazing, into perceiving with a kind of haunted intensity, the spectator cannot but find a field expanding over which her or his imagination can play. The more a person knows, after all, the more that person can see; the more that person sees, the more she or he can imagine; and the walls of Stevens's "square room" break down. It happens that Foucault develops a complex explanation of Velasquez's painting and the way it exemplifies a traditional view of representation. He ends: "But there, in the midst of this dispersion . . . is an essential void: the necessary disappearance of that which is its foundation—of the person it resembles and the person in whose eyes it is only a resemblance. This very subject—which is the same—has been elided. And representation, freed finally from the relation that was impeding it, can offer itself as representation in its pure form." Whether or not a student or any viewer agrees about the importance of the absent spectator and the problem of who is being represented in the painting and to what end, the very wondering that may take place after the perceptual journey through the painting may help to make it an event in consciousness.

Whatever the painting or work of art, and no matter how lengthy and abstruse the explanation made available, the living, conscious being must be present to the work if it is to be realized. No essay *about* nor discussion *of* the Velasquez can provide an aesthetic experience of the work. Foucault's pages might be tacked to the wall next to the painting and next to a long account of Velasquez's remarkable fame and career; but in the night, or whenever the museum is closed, that painting does not exist as a work of art. It is simply a large piece of canvas hanging on a wall in the Prado, with paint strokes on it, odd glimmers coming from it, nothing more. An attentive, grasping consciousness is required if the painting is to be brought into human time, if it is to exist as a work of art. It must be the *object* of someone's experience if it is to exist in that way. Someone has to enter into transaction with it, let her or his energies pour into it (just as a reader necessarily must lend a text her or his life). *Las Meninas* will realize certain of its potentials in a space between the viewer and the wall; it will be, to some degree, *achieved* for a person as a work of art. Much depends, of course, on the quality of the noticing. Much depends on the number of perspectives brought to play. Much depends upon the degree to which imagination can be released so that the lived world of the viewer can open up to what is, after all, an unreal world.

What seems to be so important in these times has to do with the kinds of encounters that are informed enough to permit the percipient to transmute an art work (poem, painting, sonata) into an aesthetic object, again an object of a human experience, something grasped by a wide-awake consciousness. Of course there must be some instruction in the concepts and processes intrinsic to the subject; but that instruction is validated, not by a test or even a performance, but by the way it informs awareness and provokes the perceiving and imagining that bring works of art alive.

Contributory to the process of realizing works of art are the kinds of engagement with the material (the medium) that acquaint students directly with the "language" of each form.[26] This means, very often, to move with a dancer in order to learn the language, let us say, of Martha Graham—the pelvic movements, the reaching from the ground. If this can be experienced after some work with classical ballet patterns, the complexity and emotion of Graham movement may be grasped in a piercing fashion. Students may begin to resonate to the expression of what Graham called an "interior landscape" through tension and the release of tension, through the making of kinetic metaphors. Say, for example, we wanted to introduce the dance called "Lamentation" as a movement text. We would point, of course, to the movement inside the drapery, to the embodying of the particularities of grief. Solitary, centered, it is "a dance of anguish, expressed through stress lines on the fabric, much as the passage of emotional waves leave their stress lines on a face."[27] Particular though they are, the possibilities of meaning are inexhaustible. To witness a performance after having worked, however awkwardly, with its rhythms and shapes is to know something not solely with the mind, but with the body, the nervous system. Not only will there have been a dance experience; students may discover new modalities within their own reach, an alternative kind of intelligence, or what Howard Gardner calls "frame of mind."[28]

We are most familiar with this approach in programs that integrate writing with reading. Many of us know that an effort to shape experience in the form of a sonnet—to seek out the words, the images that will catch what we perceive or feel—is to understand a sonnet in a personal way. We know somewhat the same thing when it comes to drawing, using watercolor, and then looking at pictures. There are programs in aesthetic education that make fundamental the relation between what is called "doing" (moving on different levels, composing an abstraction, writing a poem) and what is called "attending" to what is thought to be a work of art. Vincent Van Gogh, writing to his brother about his struggle to find the depth of color he needed for a certain painting, said, "I perceived for the first time how much light there was in that darkness."[29] The point seems to be that the very effort to render intensifies perceiving. We might carry this over to analogous experiences: striving to find the right figure of speech; looking for the slant of light that might frame the child's softly painted head; gazing at one's own hand to discover the shape it might take in the dance. Not only do the art works on hand take on a new immediacy, but the perceiving made possible ("for the first time," as Van Gogh said) may feed into the informed noticing we want to attain and, as well, into new ways of being in the world.

Crucial to all this is the development of a sense of agency. With that may go the capacity to undertake the kinds of actions that open spaces in consciousness and disclose possibilities to be explored. That is one of the remarkable things about encounters with the arts: the Elizabeth Bishop poem, the Toni Morrison novel, the Cezanne landscape, the Bach cantata can never be used up. There is always more to be discovered in them by the active, probing consciousness; and *what* there is to be discovered is contingent upon the kind of knowing, perceiving, feeling, and imagining the living being brings. To view it this way is to resist product orientation, commodification, preoccupation with the finished and complete. To view encounters in this way may make more likely the kinds of critical attentiveness that can resist both mystification and hype.

There are, according to this view, multiple roles for the arts in independent schools. Opportunities exist for many kinds of exploration, many kinds of clarification. Because of the part so many independent school graduates are likely to play in the society at large, there may be special responsibilities for them to shoulder—particularly when it comes to consumerism, privatism, and vulgarization in our world. On the one hand, experiences with the arts can open all sorts of spaces for them, connecting them with the shapes and sounds around, linking them to the human condition. On the other hand, because the arts in society can have so much to do with the health and integrity of the way people live together and create community together, the study of them ought to turn attention to cultural and social realities ordinarily not seen. These realities have to do with censorship and free expression, with multicultural diversity, with the protection or rejection of old canons. They have also very much to do with a flawed and fragmented society. They have to do with violations of human beings, old and young, with injustices and neglect. Unleashing dialogues, opening new visions, the arts may move some of the young in independent schools to reach out to those whose plight they have only begun to imagine. They may even be provoked to ponder images of better social orders. Jean-Paul Sartre wrote once about how the vision of a better order of

things makes people recognize, very often, what is intolerable in
their lives. He spoke of how important it is for people to be able
to imagine that they can exist otherwise, that they can be different.[30]
It is this kind of imagining that may move the young to think of
transforming what they see around them, even as it moves them to
dream of changing themselves. If this occurs, even here and there,
independent school teachers will be discovering ways of releasing
the young to renew.

Notes

1.   Virginia Woolf, "A Sketch of the Past," in *Moments of Being*
     (New York: Harcourt Brace Jovanovich, 1976), p. 72.

2.   Horace Mann, "Tenth Annual Report (1846)," in *The Repub-
     lic and the School: The Education of Free Men* (New York:
     Teachers College Press, 1959), p. 74.

3.   Nathaniel Hawthorne, "The Maypole of Merry Mount," in
     The Scarlet Letter and Selected Tales (New York: Penguin,
     1979), pp. 287-98.

4.   See Lawrence A. Cremin, *The Transformation of the Schools*
     (New York: Knopf, 1961), pp. 205-15.

5.   Viktor Lowenfeld, *Creative and Mental Growth* (New York:
     Macmillan, 1956).

6.   See Cremin, *Transformation of Schools*, p. 206.

7.   Manuel Barkan, *Through Art to Creativity* (Boston: Allyn and
     Bacon, 1960).

8.   *Discipline Based Art Education*, "New Voices, New Perspec-
     tives," in *Multiple Perspectives* (Los Angeles: Getty Center for
     Education in the Arts, 1990).

9.   National Association of Independent Schools, *Arts Planning
     Group Report* (Boston: NAIS, 1984), pp. 1-27.

10. Arthur Danto, *The Transfiguration of the Commonplace*
     (Cambridge, Mass.: Harvard University Press, 1981), pp. 45,
     135.

11. Terry Eagleton, *Literary Theory: An Introduction* (Minnea-
     polis: University of Minnesota Press, 1983), pp. 11, 72.

12. Lucy R. Lippard, *Mixed Blessings: New Art in a Multicul-
     tural America* (New York: Pantheon, 1990).

13. See, for example, Wayne C. Booth, *The Company We Keep: An Ethics of Fiction* (Berkeley: University of California Press, 1988) and Thomas Docherty, *After Theory—Post Modernism/Post Marxism* (New York: Routledge, 1990).

14. Clifford Geertz, *Local Knowledge* (New York: Basic Books, 1983), pp. 19–35.

15. Richard Rorty, *Contingency, Irony, and Solidarity* (New York: Cambridge University Press, 1989).

16. Martha Nussbaum, *Love's Knowledge* (New York: Oxford University Press, 1990).

17. John C. Gilmour, *Picturing the World* (Albany: State University Press of New York, 1986).

18. John Berger, *Ways of Seeing* (London: Penguin, 1984).

19. Denis Donoghue, *The Arts Without Mystery* (Boston: Little, Brown, 1983), p. 129.

20. Mary Warnock, *Imagination* (Berkeley: University of California Press, 1978), p. 202.

21. Herman Melville, *Moby Dick* (Berkeley, Calif.: Arion Press, 1979), p. 3.

22. John Dewey, *Art as Experience* (New York: Minton, Balch, 1934), p. 40.

23. Wallace Stevens, "Six Significant Landscapes," in *The Collected Poems of Wallace Stevens* (New York: Vintage, 1982), p. 74.

24. Dewey, *Art as Experience*, p. 272.

25. Michel Foucault, "Las Meninas," in *The Order of Things* (New York: Vintage, 1973), pp. 3–16.

26. Nelson Goodman, *Languages of Art* (Indianapolis, Ind.: Hackett Publishing, 1976).

27. Don McDonagh, *Martha Graham* (New York: Popular Library, 1975), p. 70.

28. Howard Gardner, *Frames of Mind: A Theory of Multiple Intelligences* (New York: Basic Books, 1983).

29. W. H. Auden (ed.), *Van Gogh: A Self-Portrait*. Letters revealing his life as a painter. (Greenwich, Conn.: New York Graphic Society, 1961), p. 171.

30. Jean-Paul Sartre, *Being and Nothingness* (New York: Philosophical Library, 1956), pp. 434–35.

16

How Independent Is
Independent School Curriculum?

Z. Vance Wilson

I

Jennifer Williams, a senior at an independent school, sits across the desk from a highly selective college's admissions officer. Jennifer's parents and teachers have been lecturing her since middle school that her education pointed toward this end: get into a "name" college.

Jennifer and the counselor begin with her transcript. She has taken four years of English, math, history, and foreign language, three years of science. She has also studied art, and in the ninth grade she took a physical education course.

The admissions officer asks some clarifying questions.

"Emily Dickinson and Wordsworth," she answers. *"The Great Gatsby* and *Tess of the D'Urbervilles*—and *Macbeth* of course. Geometry came between my algebras. This year I took calculus, but French instead of physics, because I started French in the eighth grade and wanted to take the Advanced Placement exam to get college credit. Yes, they changed modern European history to world history when I was a sophomore, but U.S. history is still a junior-year course."

Jennifer has an A- average and is in the second quintile of her graduating class (most of the students in the last quintile have

B- averages). She has made either the dean's list or the headmaster's list (honors and high honors) all four years of her high school career, she has won a number of book awards for the highest grade-point average in individual courses, and her junior year she was given the Yale Book Award for qualities of scholarship, character, and leadership.

After reviewing her academic transcript, the college admissions officer and Jennifer discuss her board scores. She has taken three years of nationally administered tests: the PSATs her sophomore year, followed by three shots at the SATs, an increasing number of Achievement tests, and Advanced Placement tests in May of her junior year.

Now Jennifer asks her question.

The admissions officer shifts in his seat. "Well, we never like to think of a cutoff score per se," he answers. "No one wants to reduce education to a bunch of numbers."

She is relieved when he doesn't ask a question her best friend was thrown by another college counselor. Her independent school had provided a noncredit SAT review course, which she had taken in addition to a Stanley Kaplan review course, but she preferred not to talk about either. "You weren't supposed to prep for an aptitude test," she thought to herself.

Then the conversation becomes less structured. In the hotel the night before Jennifer had glanced over her "brag sheet," a list of her extracurricular activities she had prepared for the school annual. She sang in the chorus and has a leading role in the current play. As an athlete she had won a series of awards—"most valuable" in field hockey, "most spirited" in softball. Her student government responsibility was to coordinate the recycling program. There was a potful of clubs, some hardly active, and two service organizations, one of which ran the Thanksgiving food collection for the across-town poor.

She explains other awards: she always helped clean up after the proms and didn't get busted by the honor council—these were some of the factors she assumed the faculty used in nominating her for that civic club's character award. The college admissions officer points out that every teacher recommendation checked off either "top 5 percent of my career" or "top 1 percent"—most impressive numbers. And her adviser wrote a glowing letter documenting her successes and her crucial role in the community. In sum, she is truly a fine candidate, another outstanding graduate of an independent school.

II

There are 896 members of the National Association of Independent Schools.[1] It would appear, by the use of the word "independent," and by being single entities freed from the dictates of a city or county school system and a politically determined tax base, that these schools would present a wide range of intriguing curricular and pedagogical options distinguishing them not only from public schools but from other independent schools. In a recent edition, subtitled "Reflections on Uniqueness," of *Private School Monitor,* a publication of a special interest group of the American Educational Research Association, many of the writers claim such diversity for independent schools.[2]

In my opinion, however, it does not matter whether Jennifer Williams is a student at a day or boarding school, a single-sex or coed school, whether she is Asiatic or Hispanic or black, or even whether she has a documented learning disability: her curricular experience narrated in the first part of this chapter is the rule and not the exception. This is *not* to say that the five major and two or three minor courses; the nationally administered tests; the competitive or collaborative athletics; the art, music, and drama; and the extracurricular activities make an inferior curriculum. On the contrary, as Art Powell writes, independent schools present "reasonably high academic standards . . . applied to . . . a fairly wide range of student ability levels."[3]

But this *is* to say that among independent schools there are perhaps more similarities than differences. Though independent schools work hard to protect their self-governance, their means of financial support, and their teacher and student selection, they are too easily forsaking their responsibility to be independent academically.[4] The curriculum at independent schools, in fact, would profit by some serious political risk taking, some standing up to colleges and state legislatures, some education of parents, and some in-depth research into what the educational community has discovered about learning theory and pedagogy.

Let me summarize the similarities among independent schools' curricula, and in doing so try to concisely describe the basic curriculum (which most independent schools, sidestepping the questions of "hidden" and "null" curriculum, would describe as every planned activity in a school). The individual courses in an independent school are structured along traditional liberal studies lines and are assumed, though not always articulated to be, major and minor subjects; in addition, nationally administered tests are widespread; athletics—usually competitive and interscholastic—are important and often considered part of the school's mission; art, music, and drama are also offered and encouraged; other extracurricular pursuits, usually organized into clubs, exist; and an adviser system, centered around an official relationship between a teacher and a student, is a highly publicized characteristic of the curriculum. And finally, the independent school curriculum intends to foster educational values having to do with the importance of the individual, academic standards, moral behavior, and community service.

III

At the center of the independent secondary school stands an essential definition: it is college preparatory. Teachers prep the preppies. The curriculum is not intended to train students for the immediate job market, nor to be a collection of individual and random educational experiences like adult life, where the burden of making connections and seeing patterns rests solely with the individual. It is a hierarchy of fairly clear content areas and skills intended to be recognized as built upon one another, algebra to trigonometry to calculus, writing sentences to paragraphs to essays—one grade (or form) after another until college. If a student at graduation chooses not to attend college, on the graduation program under his name the school doesn't write "the workplace" or "U.S. Marines" or "travel" or "has decided to gain maturity." The school writes "undecided."

If, then, the independent school curriculum can be described and understood as college preparatory, what lessons does it teach students?

Prepare. Obviously. Sometimes teachers and students speak of the "joy of learning" or the "delight of scholarship," but their language constructs are more frequently "if-then" sentences: if your language skills are good, then we will put you in first-year language in middle school; if you do well in math, then you can start Algebra I in eighth grade, which will make it possible for you to take calculus as a senior; if you have a C average or better, then you can place out of study hall; if you study, then you'll get into the college of your choice.

Only separate. Unfortunately. The epigram to E. M. Forster's novel *Howards End* is "only connect." It portrays the essential moral act as one of making connections among ideas, cultures, and people. The independent school curriculum's carefully landscaped path into the future, however, does not easily translate into students understanding the connections that sequential and spiral learning ought to provide. On the contrary, students see subjects as separate academic pursuits. They frequently defend the separateness not only of content but also of skills, and not only from one year to the next, but within the same year. To some students even alluding to Charles Darwin in both biology and English class somehow seems a violation of the essential sanctity of each course, as a chemistry teacher showing concern for writing skills in a laboratory report violates the sanctity of that skill.

Such an attitude is not surprising. In 1988, while sitting on the Academic Services Committee of the National Association of Independent Schools, I read over 500 curriculum surveys that the committee mailed to member schools. One question on the survey was: what are the obstacles to curriculum reform in your school? Two answers were overwhelming: that there was not enough time in the school calendar to seriously review the curriculum and that academic departments blocked any change. The monoliths of the independent school are these academic departments. As in any political system, each one protects its own turf and in doing so fails to free students from the prejudice that their education is like the post office wall, where each course has a box with a separate combination to the mail. (The last letter, of course, is from a college and is an either-or proposition: acceptance or rejection.)

The stereotypical independent school curriculum gives other messages also. *Numerical assessment is essential* is one. The curriculum acknowledges that there are many ways to assess intellectual processes, though it concentrates on testing the verbal and logical modes of thought and categorizing the results by numbers. It seldom assesses the visual, auditory, metaphoric, and synesthetic modes. And though admitting the national tests' flaws and at times strenuously objecting to their stranglehold on secondary education, independent schools buy into the predominantly multiple-choice tests, teaching their students that perhaps the most crucial assessment tool of all is this: if you can eliminate any one of the five answers, it profits you to guess.

Breadth is more important than depth. Jennifer Williams, our mythical independent school senior, took five or six courses a year for four years of high school. In her junior year, for example, she was enrolled in a stunning array of intellectual pursuits: American literature, U.S. History, chemistry, French, math, and art. Her physical education came from her competitive athletics. She also had student government, the chorus, the school play in the winter, and five clubs she belonged to. Her day was divided into seven or eight periods of approximately forty minutes in length. The breadth of the academic and nonacademic activities in the curriculum and the pace of the school day (and night—since she came back to school at least two nights a week) only encouraged her to see education as a hodgepodge of disconnected activities under one roof, and tests as activities for the day—do well, get the right number, and then forget everything. There was not the time nor the quiet for her to face an intellectual problem and chew on it—to divide and classify, to research, to compare and contrast, to write and revise, and so on, with the hope that the knowledge gained would become part of her life.

Win. The independent school curriculum also teaches some subtle and usually unarticulated lessons about winning and losing. First, there is a premise that all independent school students are winners. Anything that could be construed as solely the province of the public school, such as vocational programs (which, because they might cause students to bypass or delay college, make for "losing" propositions), has been left out. On the contrary, the current vocation of an independent school student is to get into a selective college first and then find a profession. In the independent school curriculum prizes are overabundant—not prizes for the kind of teamwork most adult professions will require, but prizes for individual excellence: in each individual course, in each year's grade-point average and in cumulative grade-point averages, in every sport, in innumerable school-sponsored activities, and in what sometimes seems like any other human pursuit this list has left out. And yet the final prize—acceptance at the most selective colleges— makes many of the students feel like losers. Somewhere in this maze of being number one and not being number one the independent student and her family find their place. At graduation there is often the talk and indeed the sense of class unity and loyalty to the school, as well as a deeply felt relationship between some students and teachers, but there remains the overwhelming lesson of the past four years: that competition is the essence of education and adult life.

Serve. At the same time the independent school curriculum includes service programs. Some schools go so far as to require that their students work at centers for the disadvantaged or in hospitals. Other schools require service on campus. But all schools have programs that at least encourage volunteerism. Given the socioeconomic background of the students, the emphasis on service can't help but teach noblesse oblige, but whatever complications arise from this attitude, the fact remains that the curriculum teaches that service to the community should be a concern of the educated person.

IV

The independent school curriculum boasts many successes. Some are accomplished because of the nature of the curriculum (its content and organization). Others are owed to size—only 9.3 students in a classroom, on average, and 396 students per school;[5] still others grow out of organizational structure (a school-based administration responsible to a board of trustees). Many of these advantages are portrayed in Sara Lawrence Lightfoot's *The Good High*

School and Powell, Farrar, and Cohen's *The Shopping Mall High School*,[6] but they bear repeating.

The first great success of the curriculum is that it prepares students for selective colleges. Enrollment in independent schools makes up only 0.8 percent of the total enrollment in elementary and secondary schools in the United States,[7] but at some Ivy League institutions (to pick on a favored group of highly selective colleges) a disproportionate percentage—between 40 and 50 percent—of the graduating classes are independent school graduates.[8] Institutions such as the Ivies like independent school graduates, finding them easy to retain and a pleasure to educate.

Teachers are given a large measure of curricular freedom in independent schools. Instead of being given a countywide syllabus geared to a committee-approved textbook, independent school teachers often choose the texts for their courses. These books might even differ from those used in a course with the same title taught by another member of the department. Teachers also set the syllabus and determine what methods of assessment they will use. And many schools encourage teachers to create their own courses, believing that the students will profit by teachers teaching their own expertise and passion.

Though many independent schools create tracks according to ability (usually labeling the advanced track "honors" or "Advanced Placement"), all the students in the school take the same basic curriculum—Jennifer Williams's course load is stereotypical. Though the Advanced Placement students might advance to calculus their senior year, for example, the other students will not be directed toward business math or even out of mathematics toward a course in shop—they will follow the same mathematics curriculum but simply not advance as far.

The independent school curriculum particularly excels in teaching the humanities in great breadth. Consider some of the courses offered: Latin, French, Spanish, and even German in some schools; modern European history, Western civilization, world history, United States history and government; British and American literature; history of art; and more. In four years of high school students might take as many as twenty full-year courses in the humanities. Though many independent school faculty violently disagree with the recent work of E. D. Hirsch,[9] because the independent school curriculum offers such a wide array of content-oriented courses covering a long span of history, it pushes its students toward literacy in Western culture. It also makes them capable of scoring high on College Board achievement tests.

Some of the other distinctive aspects of the independent school curriculum produce excellence. Because the schools are so small, a high percentage of independent school students have the opportunity to play sports and keep them within a reasonable perspective. They may develop characteristics that the better side of sport can produce: a profound sense of teamwork, hard work, resiliency, and love of play. The service programs of independent schools also make a burgeoning sense of community possible.

Finally, independent school students spend an exceptional amount of time in the company of adults. Classes are small and manageable. Teachers also coach, sponsor activities, advise, and are available to be informal counselors. All of an independent school's bureaucracy is located in one place. Students even directly address the board of trustees, the final decision-making authorities.

If education should always be centered on the student, as I believe it should, then the size of an independent school is important because it allows educators to easily keep an ongoing dialogue with the pupils. This not only allows educators to test the efficacy of their work quickly and efficiently, but it gives a student a potentially stronger voice in his own education.

And perhaps most importantly, change can happen quickly. A single teacher, for example, can make a radical change in the nature of the school's curriculum by addressing a committee of peers or, in some schools, by convincing a dean and the school head of the importance of the change. Thus the independent school curriculum can be immensely flexible and can quickly improve itself with new research and new insights.

V

There are some questions, however, about the independent school curriculum.

Using Ivy League admissions figures to prove the superior

quality of an independent school education is a debatable point, for example. Independent schools gear their curriculum toward these colleges, carefully following the recommendations that originate in admissions offices; they do not have the public schools' obligation to accommodate radically divergent backgrounds and educate a wide range of abilities. And, even more crucially, independent schools get a disproportionate percentage of their graduates into selective colleges because they begin with a selective talent base and cater to a socioeconomic group that has been historically associated with these colleges and expects that association to continue. The nay-sayer would ask this simple question: would the same talented independent school kids placed in the local public school at the ninth-grade level also reach their goal of getting into a selective college?

Art Powell makes a similar point:

> What strikes me as most significant is . . . the relatively modest ways in which private schools have capitalized on [their enabling conditions] for the benefit of students. At one analytic level—that of public and private student achievement on certain tests—one can point to the conclusions of Daniel Levy and Richard Murnane that . . . show that neither [the public or private] sector has a decisive advantage and that even the largest estimates of a private school advantage are small. . . . Given all the enabling conditions private schools enjoy, one would have hoped for more decisive data about their educational benefits. [10]

But the data are not more decisive. Powell doesn't mention other evidence showing that in certain subjects the enabling conditions make no difference: in *High School Achievement,* for example, James Coleman, Thomas Hoffer, and Sally Kilgore argue that independent schools do not demonstrate superiority to Catholic or public schools in teaching their students math and science. [11] Important educational research, such as the recent Curricular and Evaluation Standards published by the National Council of the Teachers of Mathematics, has come slowly to the independent school classroom. Not one independent school, for example, has been in touch with the National Center for Research in Mathematical Science Education.[12] The culture of many independent schools simply seems skewed toward the humanities. The books previously mentioned (Sara Lawrence Lightfoot's *The Good High School*; Powell, Farrar, and Cohen's *The Shopping Mall High School*), as well as Theodore Sizer's *Horace's Compromise,* confirm that independent schools produce a disproportionate number of professionals such as doctors, lawyers, historians, literary critics, writers, linguists, and other scholars of the humanities, but a lower percentage of scientists and mathematicians.

Sometimes the apparent strength of a curriculum can restrict it. Since it is college preparatory, the independent high school curriculum is driven by what the majority of colleges define as an appropriate secondary education. How would most college admissions offices respond if an independent school disbanded its English department, arguing that grammar, usage, and writing skills should be taught in all the other courses and that literature should be part of the social studies program? Would an independent school dare consider such a move—or one like it?

It is also the case that in some states the independent high school curriculum must include what state legislatures mandate as essential to the minds of young people about to become citizens. In the state of North Carolina, at a school where I once taught, if we did not include in the social studies curriculum a unit on economics (or, to be in strict compliance, the free enterprise system), then according to the state legislature our graduates would not be adequately prepared for the highly regarded state universities. Would that school have dared to explain to its parents that we didn't think the free enterprise system, in and of itself, fit into what we were teaching? Though the word "independent" implies great variety, the restrictions of being a college preparatory school with a tuition-paying clientele not terribly interested in political battles for the sake of education means that many schools teach the same courses, with similar textbooks, with all the work dependent upon the end of college acceptance.

Pedagogical techniques are far too often similar. If SAT scores and college admissions determine the atmosphere of schools, and if assessment practices are geared toward forcing students to memorize a certain amount of material and master certain skills, then many teachers feel limited in their choice of pedagogical methods and do not risk creative approaches. How many teachers are risking teaching to the head, heart, and hand? Aren't they instead working hard at endlessly lecturing, for example, in order to cover the material on the Advanced Placement biology exam? Or, against their own wishes, they might find themselves dominating discussions around the Harkness table,[13] perhaps unconsciously feeling the pressure to make sure students understand that "Tintern Abbey" is central to British literature and they'll be expected to know it. Teachers work harder than the students, but unfortunately they do not work hard at making students independent learners.

Given the pressure to get into college, academic standards become more important than intellectual development. A grade in a course takes precedence over what insight might have been gained. Some students fall prey to plagiarism in order to maintain the mask of individual performance instead of learning how to acknowledge and celebrate the intellectual community they are a part of. Even with new research into collaborative learning, much of the work in the classroom remains oriented toward the individual and his or her personal success. And learning is geared, as if the school were a high-class vocational institute, toward getting an acceptable profession, not toward developing an intellectual life.

Finally, keeping students at a certain grade because of their age ensures that they see their high school education as nothing more than an industrial processing of parts. If you're sixteen or seventeen, except in rare cases, you're a junior and you'll be taking junior English. Students do not advance according to their ability except within narrowly defined limits. An exceptional ninth-grade soccer player might immediately make the varsity squad, but aren't there also innumerable under-classmen quite capable of doing the work that seniors receive diplomas for? Independent schools, along with other private and public schools, are places to socialize children—they do not exist simply to reward a student's intellectual capability.

The independent school curriculum also carries with it, ironically, an anti-education bias. Educational research is only in its second generation as a science, but independent schools mistrust the work done in that field with normal schools and teacher training and so dismiss anything smacking of "education" as inferior. In the field of English, for example, research in writing techniques and in how children learn language existed for almost three decades before many independent schools even considered another method of beginning to teach writing other than diagramming sentences. Many independent schools are still stuck in teaching a traditional mathematics program, climaxing in calculus, with little knowledge of the current reform movements taking place in mathematics education.

And finally the class rigidity of independent schools also keeps the independent school curriculum from creative progress. Though the total financial aid given over the last five years has almost doubled, independent schools still have a low percentage of lower-middle-class and lower-class students.[14] The highly publicized work of a public school calculus class in Los Angeles demonstrates the possibility that the right teacher can take lower-class students and teach them what independent schools deny many of their upper-class students because they're supposedly incapable.[15] What if those same lower-class students were in an institution that made such demands on them in every course? Professor Henry M. Levin of Stanford University has devised a strategy and curriculum to accelerate at-risk students.[16] It is currently in place in networks of accelerated schools in Illinois (twenty-four schools), Missouri (six), Utah (three), and California (three). Many of Levin's ideas— school-based governance, clear sets of goals, pupil and school assessments, nutrition and health, and a heavily language-based approach for all subjects, including mathematics—are already in place or easily attainable for independent schools. And with independent schools historically thinking of themselves as the accelerated track, could they not also enhance the motivation of the disadvantaged and accelerate them with clearly taught concepts and skills such as analysis, problem solving, and applications?

There are voices interested in change. NAIS includes among its most important aims working with its client schools on gender, race, and class equity and making curriculum multicultural. The Coalition for Essential Schools, operated by Theodore Sizer out of Brown University, includes both public and private schools in a radical rethinking of school curriculum.[17] Following nine common principles, they look for a focus on a student's disposition for learning, they require at graduation a demonstration of the student's work and skills, they look toward depth instead of breadth and toward collaborative learning instead of individualization, and they see as their predominant metaphor the "student as worker." Perhaps their greatest contribution to other schools is their slow progress in making colleges and state legislatures understand that they are serious in their work and that their assessment is to be trusted and perhaps even emulated.

In shaping curriculum, independent schools are at a great advantage. They are small. People know how decisions are made. Change can come quickly. Students can learn from educators every minute of the day. At the same time, independent schools have a great responsibility to their own students, to students they have yet to include, and to education in this country. Tolstoy wrote that the fundamental method of education is experiment and the fundamental criterion freedom.[18] Simply put, independent schools must in truth be independent.

Notes

1. National Association of Independent Schools, *NAIS Statistics* (Boston: NAIS, 1990).

2. *Private School Monitor* 11, no. 4 (1990). William Howe, the guest editor for the edition, writes that "these schools are highly diverse, serving a heterogeneous and international clientele and emphasizing learning disabilities and special needs, as well as academic achievements" (p. 1). He also cites Art Powell, who argues that "the range of institutional diversity—of different types of purposeful communities—remains impressive when compared to the rest of American schooling" (p. 3). And in listing the dimensions in which independent schools are highly diverse, Howe includes "curriculum and extracurriculum (e.g., fine arts, foreign languages, work-study, and specific sports emphases)" (p. 4). In the same edition, Pearl Kane writes that "independent schools are probably more diverse than almost any type of private school" (p. 5).

3. *Private School Monitor* 11, no. 2: 9.

4. Art Powell, "Private School Responsibilities, Private School Rights," *Independent School* (Fall 1987).

5. National Association of Independent Schools, *NAIS Statistics*.

6. Sara Lawrence Lightfoot, *The Good High School* (New York: Basic Books, 1983); Arthur G. Powell, Eleanor Farrar, and David K. Cohen, *The Shopping Mall High School* (Boston: Houghton Mifflin, 1985). Two of the chapters in Lightfoot's book discuss independent schools—Milton Academy in Massachusetts and St. Paul's in New Hampshire. Powell, Farrar, and Cohen weave examples from independent schools throughout their text, but the study of "Glen" and "Carlos," pp. 198-232, makes specific comparisons between public and private schools.

7. National Association of Independent Schools, *NAIS Statistics*.

8. Conversations between the author and admissions officers at Yale, Columbia, University of Pennsylvania, and Brown.

9. E. D. Hirsch, *Cultural Literacy* and *Dictionary of Cultural Literacy* (Boston: Houghton Mifflin, 1985 and 1989, respectively).

10. Powell, "Private School Responsibilities, Private School Rights," 54.

11. James S. Coleman, Thomas Hoffer, and Sally Kilgore, *High School Achievement: Public, Catholic, and Private Schools Compared* (New York: Basic Books, 1982). See also James S. Coleman, "Social Theory, Social Research, and a Theory of Action," *American Journal of Sociology* 91, no. 6: 1309-35; James S. Coleman, "Social Capital in the Development of Human Capital: The Ambiguous Position of Private Schools" (Paper presented at the annual conference of the National Association of Independent Schools, New York, February 25-26, 1988); Richard J. Murnane, "Comparisons of Public and Private Schools: Lessons from the Uproar," *Journal of Human Resources* 19, no. 2: 263-77; and William R. Morgan, "The Analysis of NLS Youth in Public and Private Schools: Response to Coleman-Hoffer," in *Sociology of Education* 57, no. 2: 122-28.

12. Conversation with Tom Rohmberg, head of the National Center for Research in Mathematical Science Education and chair

of the National Council of Teachers of Mathematics Commission for School Mathematics.

13. In the 1930s a donor offered Philips Exeter Academy money to fund an academic innovation. The result was the Harkness table, a seminar table with a limited number of places, with fold-out leaves in order to allow examinations to be given.

14. National Association of Independent Schools, *NAIS Statistics*.

15. This work was publicized in the movie *Stand and Deliver*.

16. Henry M. Levin, "Accelerated Schools for Disadvantaged Students," *Educational Leadership* 44, no. 6; "Accelerated Schools: A New Strategy for At-Risk Students" (Paper published by the consortium of Educational Policy Studies at Indiana University and the Lilly Endowment, Indianapolis); "New Schools for the Disadvantaged," *Teacher Education Quarterly* 14, no. 4.

17. Theodore Sizer, *Horace's Compromise* (Boston: Houghton Mifflin, 1984); Kathleen Cushman (ed.), *Horace: A Newsletter* (Providence, R.I.: Coalition for Essential Schools, Brown University).

18. Leo Tolstoy, "On Popular Education," in *Tolstoy: On Education*, trans. Leo Wiener (Chicago: University of Chicago Press, 1967). "We know that our arguments will not convince many. We know that our fundamental convictions that the only method of education is experiment, and its only criterion freedom, will sound to some like trite commonplace, to some like an indistinct abstraction, to others again like a visionary dream" (p. 31).

17

A Comparison of Public and Private Schools: The Impact of Community Values

James S. Coleman and Kathryn S. Schiller

Communities in which a child's father works nearby while the mother is involved in neighborhood organizations are less common than in the past. Modern residential areas also contain two-parent families in which both parents leave each morning for work in another part of the city, single-parent families, and families that are strangers to their neighbors.

These changes in social relations have had a strong impact on the public school system. The schools no longer serve homogeneous communities where parents know each other and share similar goals for their children. Private schools have never been based on geographic communities. Their bases for community have been different. In the case of religiously grounded schools, it was the religious institution—the church or the synagogue—around which the community was built. In the case of independent schools, the community was more amorphous but was generally based on a core of socially linked families. These schools, like the public schools, have been affected by changes in family structure and in community life, but in different ways.

In this chapter, we will examine these matters through a preliminary description of the differences among eighth-grade students in public and various types of private schools. We will explore the backgrounds of the eighth graders' parents, their plans for their children's future, their involvement in the schools, and, briefly, academic outcomes. First, however, we will discuss the importance of the types of communities surrounding these schools.

Functional and Value Communities

The classic picture of the American small town from *Middletown* and *Elmtown's Youth* is one in which modes of behavior and the social structure are passed from one generation to the next.[1] These are "functional communities," defined by Coleman and Hoffer as communities in which "social norms and sanctions, including those that cross generations, arise out of the social structure itself, and both reinforce and perpetuate that structure."[2] These functional communities provide a source of support for parents beyond the boundaries of the family through a network of social interactions. Parents are able to draw on community resources to assist in supervising their children's behavior and associations. Norms that parents establish as part of their everyday activities act as important aids in socializing children.

However, these communities may harbor deep divisions just below the surface. For example, a small town might exhibit demarcations between Baptists, Catholics, and nonchurchgoers, at odds over sex education in the schools. In this case, each religious group might form its own functional community, complete with its own school, to pass its values on to the next generation.

In a larger community, there may be collections of people who share similar values but are isolated socially from each other. For example, some public alternative or magnet schools attract students on the basis of their own and their parents' values about schooling. While the students and their parents exhibit a high degree of value consistency, they are mostly strangers drawn from throughout the city. Although they cannot be considered a functional community, these parents make up a "value community" in that they share similar values about education and child-rearing. These are very loose communities based more on a common belief or action than on geographic location or social interaction.

The four types of schools compared in this chapter are usually surrounded by different types of communities ranging from functional communities lacking value consistency to value communities in which members do not interact socially. Most of today's public schools in which attendance is based on residence are faced with a number of groups holding conflicting values, each claiming legitimacy and willing to back it up by legal suits. With no dominant values to support them, school administrators walk a tightrope between competing interest groups and are in constant danger of losing community support for their claims to educational authority.

At the other end of the scale is an independent private school that has a small core of families who know each other very well but that draws many of its students from throughout the city. These "outsider" parents enroll their children in the school because they agree either with the values of the core group or the values of the school (which may or may not be the same). In between are Catholic and other religious schools whose students are drawn from families who attend the same church, which is frequently located next door to the school. These schools have the enviable position of serving a functional community, although not necessarily one based on geography, that coincides with a clear value community. Some schools with a religious foundation, however, are religiously heterogeneous and are in effect independent private schools.

We offer here only an initial description of eighth-grade students in public and private schools. Because the category of private schools is heterogeneous, the schools are divided into three groups: Catholic schools, other schools with a religious foundation, and independent private schools. There remains considerable variety, particularly among the religious schools other than Catholic, which includes some schools (such as Quaker and Episcopal schools) very similar to what we here call independent schools, as well as schools with fundamentalist and evangelical foundations. The grouping is necessary because of the relatively small number of schools of these types in the sample.

A National Survey of Eighth Graders

In the spring of 1988, the National Opinion Research Center at the University of Chicago surveyed and tested a representative sample of 30,000 eighth-grade students in American schools, along with their parents and two of their teachers. The survey was carried out for the U.S. Department of Education as the third in a series of longitudinal studies of cohorts of American students that began with 1972 high school seniors and continued with 1980 sophomores and seniors. In these surveys, the samples of schools in the private sector have progressively improved as the concept of choice in schooling has become part of public consciousness and as the assumption that elementary and secondary education is synonymous with public schools has become less reflexive.

There are a number of policy-relevant research questions for which this survey is useful. There will be additional questions as the data from a second survey of these same students in the tenth grade become available—especially since the period between eighth and tenth grade involves for most students a move from an elementary school to a high school in a different building, and for some students, a move from private to public schools, or from public to private.

However, our intention here is to give only a profile of the parents, the children, and the schools they attend. In doing so, we have truncated the sample by including only those students whose family income was $35,000 or more, in order to allow comparison among students who come from families with roughly comparable income. This includes 38.2 percent of the public school sample, 56.2 percent of the Catholic school sample, 72.8 percent of the sample in other religious schools, and 86.6 percent of the students in independent schools.[3]

Backgrounds of Parents. Restricting the sample chosen for discussion to families with incomes of $35,000 and over allows us to include substantial majorities of the students from independent and non-Catholic religious schools (79.2 and 66.6 percent, respectively) but only a minority of those from public schools (39.2 percent) and a small majority of those from Catholic schools (57.2 percent). Even with this restriction, the distribution of incomes among families of students in these schools is quite different: the public and Catholic school students are from backgrounds very similar in income, and the distributions in other religious and independent schools are quite similar to one another, but distinct from the other pair, with more families in the higher income brackets.

Similar correlations of the two pairs of schools exist when mothers' and fathers' educational backgrounds are considered, ranging from high school or less to graduate study. More mothers and fathers of other religious and independent schools have college degrees though the percentage of fathers with college degrees is not dramatically different among the various types of schools. However, the contrast is striking for graduate study: almost half of the fathers of independent school graduates have education beyond a college degree, at the graduate or professional school level, compared with less than a quarter of those with children in public and Catholic schools.

Planning for the Future. Parents were asked about the level of educational attainment they wanted their eighth-grade children to achieve. The great majority, in all sectors, wanted their children to graduate from college. However, parents of children in public, Catholic, and other religious schools were considerably less likely to want graduate or professional education for their children than were parents of children in independent schools. Consistent with this, parents of public and Catholic school children reported less money saved for their children's future education than did parents of children in other religious and independent schools. Here, the parents of children in other religious schools are somewhere between the independent school parents and parents of students in public or Catholic schools.

There is one point in plans for higher education that is surprising: in all school sectors, and in reports of both mothers' plans and fathers' plans, parents have slightly higher educational aspirations for their daughters than for their sons: 1.9 percent *fewer* parents of daughters want only a high school education for their child than do parents of sons, and 3.2 and 4 percent *more* parents of daughters want education beyond a college degree than do parents of sons. These differences are of course very small and could be due to chance, but their direction is surprising, for in earlier generations the difference has been in the opposite direction: parents wanted more education for their sons than for their daughters. This change may be due to a recognition that daughters can no longer depend on marriage for financial security but must be prepared to support themselves in adult life, or it may be due to the availability of greater career opportunities for women than in the past.[4]

The educational aspirations of these eighth-grade students were obtained via questionnaire. In response to the question "How far in school do you think you will get?", students chose among high school or less, some college, a college degree, and graduate/ professional study. The correspondence of the children's educational aims with those of their parents is quite high, but with some revealing differences. First, in every sector, there are more students than parents who think they will end their schooling without earning a college degree. Comparing children's responses with mothers' responses, there are in the public sector 7.1 percent more; in the Catholic sector, 6.7 percent more; in the other religious sector, 6.8 percent more; and in the independent sector, 3.9 percent more. This suggests that in each sector there is a set of students who are either not doing well in school or are alienated from school and whose school experiences have led them to scale back their aspirations while their parents have not done so.

Another difference between parents' and children's aspirations can be seen at the upper end of the education distribution. For three sectors—public, Catholic, and other religious—the percentage of children thinking they will go beyond a college degree is close to although smaller than that of the parents, but for the independent schools, 5 percent more children than fathers and 8 percent more children than mothers think they will go to graduate school. This suggests that the social milieu of the independent school, with nearly all students planning to graduate from college and half planning further education, is one that encourages children to think of educational goals that may be higher than those their parents hold for them—even though their parents' aspirations are already higher than those of parents in other sectors.

Involvement of Parents in the School. Parents are involved in their children's education in different ways and to varying degrees. Some of these differences show up in comparisons between school sectors. One surprising result is seen in parents' responses to the question, "Who do you think will be the most influential in deciding what courses your eighth grader will take in high school?"

Parents whose children are in independent schools are least likely to say that they will have the most influence, instead attributing more influence to teachers and guidance counselors, with 35 percent of parents attributing to them together the most influence (as compared with only 23 percent of public school parents, 31.1 percent of Catholic school parents, and 33.7 percent of other religious school parents). However, both students' and parents' reports of family discussion of high school plans show a different pattern, with the least amount of such discussion among families of public school students and the most among families of Catholic school students, with independent schools next. This suggests that for the average public school student, *both* parents and school staff (teachers and guidance counselors) play a smaller role in high school plans than they do for students in private schools, while in the differing parts of the private sector, the balance between school staff and parents varies.

This suggestion is reinforced by the data on the percentage of parents involved in various school-related activities in each of the four types of schools. Most striking is the large difference between the public and private sectors in the percentages of parents who attend school activities and are involved in parent-teacher organizations (PTOs). Far fewer public school parents visit schools, attend PTO meetings, or act as volunteers than parents of children in religious or independent schools. Catholic school parents seem to be the most directly involved with the daily life of the school, acting as volunteers and visiting classrooms.

Parents' involvement in their children's schools is related to parents' attitudes about how well the school is educating children and about school functioning. Responding to questions about whether their children are academically challenged and working hard, whether their children are being prepared for the next level of schooling, whether homework is worthwhile, and whether parents have a say in school policy and work together to support the school, parents reveal attitudes that are strikingly different between public and private-sector schools, with the independent schools at the extreme on most attitudes and Catholic schools closest to public schools. The much more positive attitudes of private-sector school parents toward their children's schools is probably in part a consequence of the fact that the child is in a school by choice of the family, not by school district assignment. The choice opportunity implies that the match between child and school will more often be satisfactory to the parent than is true in the absence of choice.

However, the differences within the private sector indicate that this factor falls far short of accounting for all the between-sector variations. Clearly, there are differences resulting from parents' experiences with the specific school their child is in, and some part of these differences lies in the degree to which the school challenges the child, at least as perceived by the parents. The parents of children in public schools are far less likely to see their children as being challenged, as working hard in school, and as being prepared well for further education. This corresponds to their attitudes about the homework assigned by the school: only 20 percent of parents of public school children strongly agree that the homework assigned by the school is worthwhile, while 36 to 46 percent of parents of children in private-sector schools have a positive attitude about homework. This probably accounts, at least in part, for the fact that slightly fewer eighth graders in private-sector schools report that their parents often check on their homework (42.2, 42.8, and 42.6 percent in independent, other religious, and Catholic schools, respectively, compared with 46.5 percent in public schools), despite the evidence that private-sector parents are more involved in their children's education.

The greater challenge experienced in private-sector schools is evidenced in the greater time spent on homework compared with the average number of hours spent watching television on weekdays. Students in public-sector schools spend the least time studying (independent school students spend the most) and the most time watching television, while independent and religious school students spend the least. The combination of these differences means that, according to the students' own reports, public school students spent over twice as much time on weekdays watching television as doing homework. Only among independent schools is the amount of time spent on homework close to equaling the amount of time spent watching television.

The difference between sectors in the effectiveness with which the schools challenge the students is in part a consequence of variations in curriculum between the sectors. Although the survey did not examine curriculum in detail, there was one differentiating course at the eighth-grade level: some schools offer algebra, and others do not. In schools that do, some students take algebra, and others do not. In the number of students reported taking algebra or another advanced mathematics course (regardless of whether their schools offered those classes), public and Catholic schools are nearly alike (44.7 and 45.4 percent), while independent and other private schools exhibit higher—and similar—percentages (59.6 and 60.1). The differences correspond roughly to the differences in parents' evaluations of their children's schooling.

The difference between Catholic and other private schools in the proportion of students taking algebra in eighth grade is especially interesting in view of results at the high school level found in the 1980–1982 survey. There Coleman and Hoffer found more mathematics taken by Catholic school students than by those in other private schools.[5] This is also true for mathematics achievement growth. The difference between these results and those obtained in this survey could be an artifact due to a poorer sample of non-Catholic private schools in the 1980–1982 surveys or a true difference reflecting more advanced mathematics in some non-Catholic private elementary schools but less success in the high schools in inducing students to continue with mathematics. The results of the 1990 first follow-up survey of these same students in the tenth grade will provide evidence on these two conjectures.

The greater challenge, the greater time spent on homework, and the more advanced mathematics in the independent and non-Catholic religious sectors are accompanied by higher achievement levels on standardized tests. The standardized tests used in this survey were especially constructed for the National Educational Longitudinal Study of 1988 and were administered to all students included in the study.

We will not attempt here to separate the achievement differences into those due to the school experience itself and those due to differences in the kinds of students in the schools and their families. The latter include differences in parents' education, income, and race or ethnicity. Students in the different types of schools differ in these background characteristics, but separating out differences due to these background factors from those due to the schools them-selves is a formidable task[6] and not appropriate for an initial de-scriptive examination of public-private differences.

There are many other differences between these schools, the students, and their parents. Beyond the descriptive differences are inferences one might make about the varying outcomes for children graduating from schools in the various sectors. It is these latter differences that are of greatest interest both to parents and to policy makers in education, but these analyses of differential effects of schools are the topics of subsequent work.

While we have made no attempts to present causal models, the results given above reinforce the descriptions of the communi-ties surrounding the different types of schools. Parents with chil-dren in nonreligious private schools seem to place greater importance than other parents on education through plans and savings for their children's future education, and they indicate more satisfaction with the school. However, these parents are less likely to report being involved in the school through participation in activities or visiting classes. These parents seem to share similar values about education but appear to have less direct contact with each other or the school.

Parents of students in Catholic schools have the most contact with the schools, suggesting the existence of a functional commu-nity in addition to a value community. Public schools tend to have the weakest communities, either functional or value. These results, of course, only describe a general tendency: individual schools in any sector may differ sharply from the tendency for that sector.

It is probable, however, that the difference between sectors in the degree to which a functional community exists requires deeper examination, particularly among private school sectors. In this study, parents were asked whether they knew the parents of their children's school friends. Answers to this question indicate that parents of public school children are least likely to know the parents of their children's friends in comparison with the three private school sectors represented in the sample and that parents of Cath-olic school children are the most likely.

The results of the study of eighth graders indicates that there are differences between public and private schools and among various types of private schools and in the ways families interact with these schools. The results also point to a need for further study of both the communities surrounding public schools and those surrounding different types of private schools.

Notes

1. R. S. Lynd and H. M. Lynd, *Middletown* (New York: Harcourt Brace Jovanovich, 1929); and A. B. Hollingshead, *Elmtown's Youth* (New York: Wiley, 1949).
2. J. S. Coleman and T. Hoffer, *Public and Private High Schools: The Impact of Communities* (New York: Basic Books, 1987), p. 7.
3. The percentages reported in this chapter are based on samples of 6,634, 1,150, 652, and 1,102 students in public, Catholic, other religious, and independent schools, respectively. The percentages given are estimates of the percentages in the respective populations of students in these schools. Differences in the population percentages in the indicated direction are very likely to exist (with probability greater than 0.95) if the differences in sample percentages are as large as the following critical values:

    *   5 percent in comparing public schools with Catholic or independent schools
    *   7 percent in comparing public schools with other religious schools, or Catholic with independent schools
    *   8 percent in comparing other religious schools with Catholic or independent schools

    These numbers take into account a sample design efficiency of about 0.5 and are based on percentages near 50 percent. If the percentages being compared are much larger or smaller than 50 percent, say as small as 10 percent or as large as 90 percent, the critical values are reduced to three-fifths of these, or about 3 percent, 4 percent, and 5 percent instead of 5 percent, 7 percent, and 8 percent.
4. Preliminary analysis of data from the General Social Survey

from 1987 suggests the last of these points, although the relatively small sample size makes this only suggestive. (The General Social Survey is conducted annually by the National Opinion Research Center, University of Chicago. Data, collected since 1972, is compiled on basic social, moral, and psychological trends.)

5. Coleman and Hoffer, *Public and Private High Schools*, p. 212.
6. See earlier publications on cohorts of 1980 sophomores and seniors: J. S. Coleman, T. Hoffer, and S. Kilgore, *High School Achievement: Public, Catholic, and Private Schools Compared* (New York: Basic Books, 1982); and Coleman and Hoffer, *Public and Private High Schools.*

18

School Culture:
Balancing Tradition
and Innovation

Terrence E. Deal

In 1980, the parents of Concord High School elected to have a role in improving their local high school by honoring teachers. In consultation with the principal and superintendent, they hosted a celebration of teaching.

When the teachers and others arrived at the high school's cafeteria, they were pleasantly surprised. The cafeteria had been transformed into a setting that resembled a top-flight restaurant. Linen tablecloths and silver candelabra softened tables from their institutional metal and formica into a more inviting form. As teachers arrived, they received corsages or boutonnieres labeled with the terms mentor, guru, or teacher. They were then escorted to a piano bar, where they drank wine and sang songs with parents until dinner was served.

Dinner was potluck; each parent furnished a dish. After dinner a choir sang, speeches were given, and the finale brought parents to their feet in a standing ovation for the high school's teachers. As the crowd started to leave, John Esty, head of the National Association of Independent Schools and a parent of a Con-

This chapter first appeared in the spring 1991 issue of *Teachers College Record* (vol. 92, no. 3). Reprinted with permission.

cord High School student, remarked: "They often wonder what private schools have that public schools often lack . . . this is it."

John Esty's remark highlights one of the unique characteristics of private schools—their emphasis on symbolic aspects of human organizations. School life is replete with symbolic figures, rituals, and events that suggest and maintain a distinct culture. The fictional Mr. Chips, for instance, served not only as a symbol of the private school master but of a way of life. This chapter will elaborate on the importance of culture in private schools by summarizing some related research, providing examples of how independent schools create meaning by attending to cultural attributes, and suggesting some potential pitfalls in moving away from tradition in response to external pressures.

Culture as a Unique Advantage

Many organizations in business, health care, and the military have rediscovered the importance of meaning in collective activity. The proposition is quite simple: people who are committed and motivated obviously work harder than those who are alienated or apathetic. Burton Clark earlier concluded the same thing about organizations in higher education. Unique private institutions such as Reed, Swarthmore, or Antioch thrived because of their stature as "beloved institutions." Each had a widely shared myth or saga, articulated by a visionary leader, maintained by a loyal cadre of followers, reinforced by distinctive practices, and supported by a loyal group of students and alumni. People were highly committed to these institutions because they believed in what they stood for and found meaning in their membership.[1]

Three recent studies extend Clark's conclusions to private secondary schools. Jane Hanaway and Susan Abromowitz compared management and cultural patterns in private schools and public schools. They found that public secondary schools were more tightly managed than their private counterparts. Public school principals, for example, spend far more time monitoring and evaluating the efforts of classroom teachers. Conversely, they found that private schools were more closely knit than public schools. In

private schools, commitment, involvement, and cohesion were reported to be significantly higher.[2]

In violation of many commonly accepted assumptions, public schools are more tightly controlled through command and rule;
private schools are more closely knit through implicit mechanisms
of social control. As Hanaway and Abromowitz relate these different
patterns to student achievement, management practices do not show
a significant effect, while cultural linkages do.[3] These results are
consistent with studies of school achievement within public secondary schools. Chubb, for example, found three powerful predictors
of high student performance in public high schools: autonomy
(freedom from bureaucratic interference from higher levels), "team-
ness" (a sense of cohesion among the various constituencies within
a school), and parental involvement.[4] All are areas in which private
schools have an advantage over their public school counterparts.

Anthony Bryk and Mary Driscoll's study comparing organizational features and outcomes of public and private (independent
and Catholic) schools arrived at similar conclusions. Private schools
displayed significantly stronger communal ties among their members, including shared values and beliefs concerning what the
school stands for and what should be learned; shared visions of what
students should become; distinctive activities to bond people to each
other and to the traditions of the school; and an ethos of caring.[5]
Bryk and Driscoll consolidate these features into a measure of communal school organization and relate this index to the sentiments,
behavior, and performance of teachers and students. Both Catholic
and private schools score more highly on the measure of communal
organization. The data show that a sense of community has positive
consequences. In communal schools, teachers are more satisfied,
enjoy teaching, and have high morale. Similarly, students in communal organizations are better behaved. They attend classes and
school more regularly and are less disruptive in class. They are more
interested in school and, as a result, are less likely to drop out.
Additionally, students in private schools appeared to learn more—
at least in mathematics.

The parallels between the Hanaway and Abromowitz and the
Bryk and Driscoll studies are striking. Their results are supported
by Susan Johnson's qualitative studies of teachers in private and

public schools. As do the other studies, she makes a distinction between community and authority, or what she terms "cultural" and "rational" bonds:

> Cultural bonds include the shared purposes, values, traditions, and history that promote harmonious behavior and a sense of community. They are internal links that draw participants together through shared meaning. They promote commitment rather than compliance. . . . By contrast, rational bonds include rules, roles, functions, penalties and formal authority that specify and regulate the behavior of individuals in organizations. They presume reluctance and dissent rather than commitment and accord. They unify participants externally by defining their responsibilities, roles, and relationships, by telling them what they can, cannot, and must do.[6]

Johnson also found that private schools are more likely to take advantage of the more efficient energy-producing cultural bonds than are public schools. Public school teachers were frequently perplexed when asked about the symbolic aspects of their schools. As one teacher noted, "I've never felt a strong community sense within the school; I've never felt a strong thing that would pull us all together."[7] Another teacher remarked, "[There is] nothing unusual—maybe that's what holds us together."[8]

The following chart highlights the differences in teachers' perceptions of cultural bonds in public and private schools. As is easily seen, there are obvious disparities in areas of goals, values, histories, rituals, and traditions.[9]

	Private Schools	*Public Schools*
Goals	We are committed to honor and excellence.	We are a ship without a rudder. No one is really sure where we are going or why we are going there.

Values	What do we expect first? Consideration and honesty.	What we need in [this school] is "Masterpiece Theater." What we have is "Let's Make a Deal."
Histories	[The school has] real roots in the community, a spirit in the parish. . . . People want to pass on what they had, hoping that their children get some of the values they knew.	Our history?
Rituals and Tradition	[Our meetings promote] a real feeling of community, of everybody coming together.	Not many, not any that I can think of. As a matter of fact, every once in a while the principal will say something like, "This is a tradition" and usually get a response of laughter.

Together these studies point to a competitive advantage of private schools. Their size, autonomy, selectivity, and stability provide conditions that encourage a reliance on cultural cohesion rather than rational rules to hold the school together. To attract clientele, private schools must create a unique identity, a set of values and traditions that sets them apart from competitors. They use their identity as a screening device for potential applicants. They rely on symbols and traditions to secure commitment and loyalty from students, teachers, and parents. Like top-performing businesses (and other organizations), they count on a distinctive culture to shape newcomers and to keep seasoned veterans in line and on fire. Like Burton Clark's distinctive colleges, many private schools are "beloved institutions," special places that capture the hearts and imaginations of their members.[10]

As a collection, these studies have important implications for schools. One implication is for public schools to emulate private schools by focusing more attention on symbols and meaning rather than on management and control.[11] Another redirects attention to private schools, where leadership must constantly reinforce cultural patterns and cautiously reshape traditions as new challenges present themselves.

Reinforcing Cultural Patterns

On the basis of the foregoing research, it would be easy for private school teachers and administrators to pat themselves on the back, but back-patting can easily lead to resting on one's laurels and becoming complacent. Complacency can quickly create chaos out of cohesion. There are many private schools that have allowed themselves to slip. In addition, there are many others that have never arrived. While, in general, private schools seem to rely more heavily on cultural bonds, others are just as rational and rule-bound as their public school counterparts.

What can private school headmasters and teachers do to reinforce cultural patterns? First, they need to agree that symbols and symbolic activity play an important role in creating a cohesive community. Second, they need to give time and attention to symbolic issues. Cultures evolve from human experience; by constantly reflecting on experience and reinforcing positive values and virtues, a school's culture can be shaped. Third, those who work in private schools need a shared framework and language for identifying cultural patterns.

By its nature, culture is elusive. It is often taken for granted and largely unconscious. While most scholars disagree on how culture is defined, there is some consensus on the meaning of the term within organization theory. Terrence Deal and Alan Kennedy argue that the culture of an organization is deeply rooted in its past history. Through trial and error a group of people separate what succeeds from what fails. These lessons are expressed in an interlocking, organic constellation of cultural elements that have a profound effect on everyday behavior.[12]

Values express what an organization stands for, its essential character. Values are typically expressed in symbols (for example, the Forest Service's "Smokey the Bear") or slogans (for example, IBM's commitment to "Customer Service, Dignity for the Individual, and Excellence in Everything We Do").

Cultural heroes and heroines personify values and provide role models for others to emulate. Chrysler's Lee Iaccoca is a larger-than-life testimony to quality and risk taking. In any organization, ordinary people doing extraordinary things comprise a pantheon of local heroes and heroines who lead by example.

Rituals provide everyday reminders of values and bond people to each other in a common quest. A public elementary school principal started bringing popcorn to the office on Friday afternoon. It has now become a regular event in which everyone participates. Rituals are expressive events, not tasks that accomplish objectives, but as the principal observed, "It's surprising what $4 worth of popcorn can do for a group of people."

Ceremonies, like rituals, are expressive events. Unlike rituals, they do not occur all the time; they mark special occasions. In ceremonies, people put the culture on display for everyone to celebrate. Mary Kay's annual seminars, for example, are extravaganzas to cultivate commitment and loyalty among the company's beauty consultants. Stories carry values. Any successful organization reinforces its identity through legend and lore. Stories about August Busch III, for example, remind even the lowest-ranking employee of Anheuser Busch's commitment to quality and pride.

Finally, the culture of any organization, large or small, is watched over and reinforced by an informal network of priests or priestesses, gossips, storytellers, and spies who operate outside formal channels to minister to communal needs, convey information, spread the lore, and conduct secret operations.[13]

Effective private school headmasters reinforce cultural bonds by articulating values, anointing and celebrating heroes and heroines, convening rituals, encouraging ceremonies, telling stories, and "working" the network of cultural players. Two examples from very different private schools illustrate the possibilities.

Al Adams is the headmaster of the Lick-Wilmerding High School in San Francisco. Founded by merging three trade schools in 1895, Lick-Wilmerding integrates college preparatory and technical training in a distinctive program that focuses on the "head, heart, and hands" of young people. The school is highly selective and has at least five applicants for each of the 330 students it enrolls. Adams models himself on George Merrill, the school's founder, who served for forty-five years and retired in 1939. Adams's initial task was to tie into the school's roots to recrystallize and articulate its vision. Today two banners fly metaphorically over the school:

"Education for the Head, Heart, and Hands" and "Private School with Public Purpose." The school's values are represented in distinctive practices. Its teachers are "action researchers." Its innovative programs are anchored in the strong traditions begun in the days of George Merrill. Heroes and heroines are kept alive and visible through an alumni video archive and a "Foxfire-like" oral history that is constantly updated through the work of current students who interview the school's alumni. Learning the ropes at Lick-Wilmerding is a hands-on experience that regularly reconnects present and past.

Today, one of the school's most important values is to maintain diversity in the student body. It does this through a "Robin Hood" tuition rate, which redefines student aid from a handout to a more value-driven concept of access and affordability.

Lick-Wilmerding is a constant stage for ritual and ceremony. At Founders Day each year, the entire school turns out to thank its founders: Lick, Wilmerding, and Merrill. All adviser groups (a teacher and ten students) bake cakes that are decorated with important themes past, present, and future. Each year the theme "head, heart, and hands" is remembered and reinforced.

In 1992, the Wilmerding family plans to hold its reunion on campus. They are renting a train to bring 200–300 people to an extravaganza that all members of the school will attend. Lick-Wilmerding, in the eyes of its current headmaster, is a ninety-five-year-old model of the integration of cognitive and hands-on learning.

From the opposite side of the country and almost another century a different example demonstrates again the importance of reinforcing cultural patterns in private schools. Frank Boyden came to Deerfield Academy in 1900. This was the beginning of a school well-known for its attractive campus, large endowment, excellence in teaching, and a commitment to nourishing the moral and social development of its students. [14]

A manuscript written in 1906 committed the school to building character and creating an intimate relationship between faculty and students. [15] Boyden exemplified the values of the school. He traveled with athletic teams and coached students on how to lose with character while simultaneously motivating them to win. He personally interviewed each prospective student. He himself was often seen walking across the campus "stooping down to pick up a piece of litter or pull a weed."[16] Boyden also knew the importance of anointing other heroes and heroines. He made sure that archetypal students appeared in photographs or came off the bus first at athletic events. He singled out people who demonstrated special character for public attention.

Boyden instilled in teachers the beliefs that "they could all build something together," that they were "there for the boys."[17] Teachers were recruited who wanted to become part of the larger enterprise and to help students develop. Those without commitment were "excommunicated." Boyden, according to a veteran teacher, was the kind of person who "exacts a fantastic commitment. If you give it, he expects more. If you don't give it, he carries you, but you don't exist."[18]

Boyden encouraged ritual and ceremony as a way of communicating values and bonding students and faculty to the school's traditions. The students ate and worshiped together. They all went to bed at a specified time. Each was required to participate on an athletic team. For many years, Boyden gave each student his grades face-to-face and made a personal comment about how well he was measuring up to Deerfield standards.

Deerfield stories are not in short supply. A specially memorable one, told again and again, focused on the life of Tom Ashley. He distinguished himself as an exemplary Deerfield student and later as a college student. After graduation from college, he returned to Deerfield as a faculty member and joined the inner circle of loyal supporters of Deerfield's values and traditions. Ashley died in France during World War I in a heroic effort to return the fire of a German machine gun. His heroism was not only decorated by the military; he also became a hero at Deerfield. His name now adorns a dormitory that he had always wanted the school to build. "He not only envisioned but also in many ways represented the potential of the school."[19] Boyden, along with other Deerfield storytellers, told and retold this story to reinforce the cultural values of the school.

In both the Lick-Wilmerding and Deerfield examples, it is easy to see and feel the power of cultural elements in shaping behavior, securing commitment, fostering loyalty, and making each school in its own way a "beloved institution." Intuitively, if not consciously, both Adams and Boyden realized the importance of attending to and reinforcing core symbols and traditions. Both seemed sensitive to the intimate connection between a school's past, its present, and its future.

Private Schools and Change

While it is important to shape and enhance values and traditions within private schools, the outside world is never static. As it changes, private schools feel pressures to keep pace. Can we remain a boys' or girls' school and survive? Can we continue to select a homogeneous group of students and expect to continue in an increasingly heterogeneous world? Can we maintain traditional methods of instruction knowing that new technology often improves instruction? How can we grow in response to new opportunities without losing that which makes the school unique?

While most organizations today feel these same pressures, private schools undoubtedly experience the dilemmas more acutely. The roots and traditions that make these schools special can also make them inflexible and highly resistant to change. In a sense, the potential reaction of faculty, students, and alumni to new instructional methods is similar to the American people's reaction to the electronic boxes that have replaced the caboose on freight trains. The new technology is far cheaper and more effective than the caboose with its human crew, but our memories and nostalgic attachment to cabooses make their superior replacements far less attractive. Deep down, we all miss the caboose and are saddened by its departure. Seeing a train pass while waiting at the wigwag just is not the same anymore.

In the same way, people form attachments to symbols and symbolic activity. Consider one person's reaction to the Catholic church's liturgical change from Latin to English:

> But now that I know that I no longer live in a Catholic world, I cannot expect the liturgy which reflects and cultivates my faith to remain what it was. I will continue to go to the English Mass. I will go because it

is my liturgy. I will, however, often recall with nostalgia the faith that I have lost. And I will be uneasy knowing that the old faith was lost as much by choice as it was inevitably lost and the Catholic Church of my youth mediated with special grace between the public and private realms of my life. Such was the extent of its faith in itself. That church is no longer mine. I cling to the new Catholic Church though it leaves me unsatisfied. I fear giving it up, falling through space.[20]

Catholic schools, like the Catholic church, have made some significant cultural changes: nuns without habits, lay teachers, an easing of religious rites, instructional materials and methods that resemble closely those in public schools. As such changes are made, it is essential to deal with the symbolic loss. In a well-known private school, for example, the chapel was recently renovated at a cost of over $1 million. Alumni, outraged at the loss of their storehouse of memories and scene of core rituals, forced the board and headmaster to return the chapel to its original state. The alumni raised the money and supervised the restoration. A similar scenario was recently enacted at Mills College. The board of trustees decided to make the school coeducational. A rebellion of students joined alumnae in opposition. In less than a week, $3 million was raised and the board reversed its decision.

Successful cultural change requires transitional rites—wakes, funerals, mourning periods, and remembrances.[21] Transition stages help people collectively let go of old forms and practices and embrace new ones with the same meaning and intensity. Otherwise, as illustrated in the foregoing quotation, people cling to old practices without meaning or satisfaction—or fall precariously through space. Private schools must be very sensitive to the balance between tradition and innovation. Unless a bridge is built between old and new, a school can easily either lose its roots or become obsolete. Lick-Wilmerding exemplifies the care and sensitivity that private schools will need in becoming modern with meaning, innovative without losing their sense of community or purpose. At Lick-Wilmerding a new building houses a state-of-the-art science center and a performing arts center. Between the two buildings is a gallery in which old pictures and artifacts are exhibited with contemporary student work. At the point of connection between the old building and the new one, Adams and the architect left a portion of the original foundation exposed. These visible roots provide a symbol of the symbolic connective tissue. In this way the school can be progressive without losing its sense of tradition.

The Future of Private Schools

John Esty was prophetic. He called attention to a competitive advantage of private schools—their emphasis on cultural bonds, rather than authority and rules, to hold the enterprise together. But cultural cohesion has its price. For one thing, distinction is not an enduring condition. Traditions, as many organizations have discovered, need constant attention, reinforcement, and reaffirmation. It takes only a short time to unravel a unique symbolic tapestry, even one woven over several decades. Private schools must be willing to devote time, energy, and resources to nourish community and tradition.

Cohesion has other potential costs. In changing times, the primary virtue of private schools can become a constricting vise. In what has been described as the "permanent white water of change," a communal raft can easily be swamped and overturned.[22] Private schools must be prepared to recognize what they have, realize what they have to do, and respect the pitfalls and opportunities in moving to where they may need to be.

The movie *Dead Poets Society* cogently depicts the dilemma of balancing innovation and tradition. It pits Robin Williams as "My Captain" against the traditional headmaster in the school. It could just as well have been a rebel confronting "Mr. Chips." The struggle between new and old, stability and change, history and progress, will always present a challenge for private schools. Like many films, however, *Dead Poets Society* offers no answers or direction for where the appropriate balance point should be. Each private school will have to determine that on a case-by-case basis, assisted by people like Esty, Adams, Merrill, Ashley, Boyden—and other leaders whose time and opportunity have yet to come.

Notes

1. Burton Clark, "Organizational Saga in Higher Education," in *Managing Change in Educational Organizations,* ed. J. Victor Baldridge and Terrence E. Deal (Berkeley, Calif.: McCullum Publishing, 1975), pp. 98–108.
2. Jane Hanaway and Susan Abromowitz, "Public and Private Schools: Are They Really Different?" in *Research on Exemplary Schools,* ed. Gilbert R. Austin and Herbert Garber (Orlando, Fla.: Academic Press, 1985).
3. Hanaway and Abromowitz, "Public and Private Schools."
4. John E. Chubb, "Why the Current Wave of School Reform Will Fail," *The Public Interest* 90 (Winter 1988): 28–49.
5. Anthony S. Bryk and Mary Erina Driscoll, *The High School as Community: Contextual Influences and Consequences for Students and Teachers* (Chicago: National Center of Effective Secondary Schools, 1988).
6. Susan Moore Johnson, *Teachers at Work: Achieving Success in Our Schools* (New York: Basic Books, 1990), p. 218.
7. Ibid., p. 220.
8. Ibid., pp. 220–21.
9. Ibid., pp. 219–33.
10. Clark, "Organizational Saga in Higher Education."
11. Terrence E. Deal, "Healing Our Schools: Restoring the Heart," in *Schools as Collaborative Cultures: Creating the Future Now,* ed. Ann Lieberman (New York: The Falmer Press, 1990).
12. Terrence E. Deal and Alan A. Kennedy, *Corporate Cultures* (Reading, Mass.: Addison-Wesley, 1983).
13. Ibid., pp. 6–7.
14. Terrence E. Deal and Kent D. Peterson, *The Principal's Role in Shaping School Culture* (Washington, D.C.: U.S. Government Printing Office, 1990).
15. John McPhee, *The Headmaster* (New York: Farrar, Straus & Giroux, 1966).
16. Deal and Peterson, *Principal's Role,* p. 73.
17. McPhee, *The Headmaster,* p. 63.
18. Ibid., p. 65.

19. Deal and Peterson, *Principal's Role,* p. 77.
20. Richard Rodriguez, *Hunger of Memory* (Boston: David R. Godine, 1982), p. 109.
21. Deal, "Healing Our Schools."
22. Peter B. Vaill, *Managing as a Performing Art: New Ideas for a World of Chaotic Change* (San Francisco: Jossey-Bass, 1989), p. 2.

19

From the South Bronx
to Groton

Johanna Vega

I think it was in the dining hall when I finally realized that my parents were going to leave me, that they weren't staying there with me. The school provided a lunch for parents before they were asked to say goodbye to the sons and daughters they were leaving behind. At the lunch table in the Groton School Dining Hall, we were sitting with a family from California, and it occurred to me that I and my parents looked glaringly different. In fact, we were sitting with serious Groton legacy material from the 1950s, and the girl next to me was the daughter of an alumnus who, as I found out later, was a schoolmate and good friend of the headmaster's. They had been on the same ice hockey team at Groton. Yes, this man and the headmaster went back, way back. He was rich, upper class, from California, and my father was sitting next to him. I remember looking at them both and wondering how farfetched a conversation would be between this businessman/Groton graduate and my father, the longshoreman from Puerto Rico. Thinking back on it now, I understand why my father rushed through his meal as he did. But I can't even begin to fathom what it was like for my mother, who barely understands English, much less speaks it. Looking around the table, I realized that not only were my parents going to leave me there, but I had nothing in common with this place and didn't really know what the hell I was doing there. My parents wouldn't have to deal with the differences because they were splitting. But I was stuck.

Later in the day, after my parents had left, we got in line for supper to get barbecued hamburgers. It was a picnic supper, probably intended to make us feel comfortable and informal. But filed in line, with preppies in front of me, behind me, and next to me, I began to feel different again. I was still wearing those Carter's undershirts that my mother ceremoniously bought for me, hoping to postpone my puberty, and the little sleeves kept popping out of my tank top so I kept pushing them back in, thinking that all these girls were probably wearing training bras. There I was, wearing the latest Bronx fashion: a Day-Glo orange tank top with my name inscribed in electric blue letters. I felt and looked like a kid, underdeveloped in every sense. All these big North American girls were taller and really developed, and maybe even socially experienced, and here I was, still my mom's little "rabito," her little tail, as she often put it—just a sheltered little thing finding out that life wasn't like home all the time, at least not anymore it wasn't.

From the moment I was born until I was eleven, I grew up in the South Bronx, in the very worst area that you can find in the South Bronx; outsiders call it Fort Apache. Then we moved to New Jersey, to the suburbs, because we weren't eligible to live in the projects anymore. My father was making more money, so we were asked to leave because we didn't need that kind of help. We went to Elizabeth, a small city next to Newark. It didn't work out there because my mother found it hard to adjust, so we moved back to the inner city and lived in the Bronx again, on the Grand Concourse. My father was mugged several times at gunpoint, his car was stolen, our apartment was broken into, and meanwhile my mother clutched at me more and more, protecting her little cub from all the dangers that lurked in the Bronx.

While I was in junior high school, we moved again, this time to Parkchester in the north of the Bronx. It was an improvement. Because it was a residential community, it was a big change, but we still had our friends, the minorities around us, plus the novelty of now living among Jews, too. However, I still went to school in the

South Bronx, where the crime seemed to worsen by the day. I remember my best friend was mugged. They ripped off a clarinet he had borrowed from school. I remember how he came into class in tears, shaking as he told our homeroom teacher what had happened. The only reason I was spared this crime was my mother's constant and doting presence. I never rode the subway by myself until I got back from Groton when I was eighteen. That was the extent to which she protected me.

Despite this environment, I was a fun-loving, perky kid in junior high and before. I was in an accelerated program designed to skip students from seventh to ninth grade. I was constantly involved in school plays, and I always had a number of friends to hang out with. I even had a clique. I hung out with kids who were in the Special Progress program—the highest-ranking class. We were the brat pack—the smarty-pants—and heck, did we know it. We were always on top, setting the highest reading and math scores for the entire district. It gave us a feeling of power in relation to the other students. I certainly developed enough of an ego in junior high to feel really confident about myself, even cocky in a way.

When I was invited to Groton to visit, I felt really great and special. My affair with Groton had actually started earlier, back in seventh grade. A Better Chance (ABC) had talked to several minority students about the virtues of prep schools, so we accepted an invitation to visit a few boarding schools. We spent a night at Groton, and I thought it was great because everything was beautiful. It was like being invited to go to camp for four years. After that visit, I had dreams about walking in the woods instead of walking on asphalt in the inner city. Groton appeared like Wonderland, and I guess I thought I could be a giant Alice.

For me it was either the Bronx High School of Science or Groton, and I already knew I wanted Groton. I had a notion that if I went to Groton the experience would somehow change me and make me a better person than if I stayed at home and lived with my family. By that time I did have a vague understanding of the upper-class white world as distinct from the lower-income Hispanic world in which I was brought up. I watched television. Television brought the elite white world into our Bronx living room, and there I learned how different my family was from the Carringtons, the

Ewings, and the oil magnate family soap operas so popular in the early eighties. As lame as it sounds, you see "Dallas" and "Dynasty" and you are influenced by the glitz and glamour. Groton looked like one of those country clubs. If I could go to Groton, I could not only get a ticket into college, I could get a ticket into that world.

Things were really bad with my first roommate right from the start because she and I weren't getting along. She had complained to the housemistress that my father kept looking at her when he helped me move into the room. She never articulated her fears directly to me. But she would ignore me in the room, and it was hard to talk to her. Her friends would come into the room; I would try to start a conversation, and they would acknowledge for a moment and then start laughing among themselves and eventually exclude me from their inside jokes. Tensions grew between us. At the time, and actually for four years, I was severely homesick. My first roommate must have thought I was a crybaby for wanting to be home with my parents, calling them every night and crying over the phone. She often told her friends that she was happy to be away from home, finally.

During the first two months in the dorms the differences between the other girls and me were engulfing my life. Underhanded references to "that Puerto Rican girl living upstairs" became a torment for me, and I cringed whenever I heard them. There were strange looks exchanged whenever I entered my room and my roommate and her friends happened to be there. I knew something was going on; to them I was a poor Hispanic and thus foreign, unapproachable, maybe even untouchable. At a dorm meeting, I exposed these feelings, telling everyone that while I might look different, I wouldn't bite their heads off. I explained to them that it was just harder for me to exist at Groton because I couldn't relate to so many things, and that they needed to know that when they approached me. In the end, however, my roommate and I had to separate, and the whole dorm ended up switching roommates as well. All this may have been typical adolescent behavior, but even so it certainly made life hard for me. My housemistress dismissed it as "going through a cruel stage." My job was to grin and bear it and wait for them to reach a more mature level, a level at which I would become more human and less "minority" in their eyes.

My best friend at Groton turned out to be the girl who became my roommate as a result of that switch. There was a lot of tension at that time because her father had lung cancer. One day she and I got into a fistfight about whether our room door should be left open or closed during study hall. Afterward, I began to admire and appreciate her, and she became my best friend. We finally let things out into the open instead of bottling them up. In a strange way that was a real relief. One of the things I appreciated about her was that she had the gall to punch me physically and not keep wounding me emotionally. At Groton there was a lot of psychic wounding and not enough relating to me as a person of flesh and blood.

As unhappy as I was at Groton, my parents were adamant about my staying there. The high schools in the Bronx are not as good, and my parents thought that I'd be tainted by the experience there. They preferred the idea of their daughter going to a very nice, clean, classy school where they wouldn't have to worry about me being introduced to drugs, sex, and all those things. My staying at Groton became more and more convenient for my parents; it was hellish for me.

The bus rides from Groton to New York always had the strange effect of empowerment for me. I remember the bus carried us into the South Bronx before dropping us off on 86th and 5th Avenues on the upper East Side, where many of the students lived. The journey had its own metamorphosis for me. The contrast between the South Bronx and upper East Side of Manhattan was as awkward as my relationship with Groton. I remember feeling a pride when the bus passed through my old neighborhood. A rush of nostalgia wrenched my heart, reminding me that it was merely a past I was now sharing with Groton on this bus. Someday, I would become as much an outsider to the Bronx as they were now. Yes, time would tell. Nonetheless, back then I couldn't grasp this, and I would tell the kids sitting around me, "See that school, the one with graffiti, where the bum is pissing—I went to school there." Those young, healthy faces looked outside the bus windows and then looked at me with astonishment and, yes, maybe a little admiration. Did I feel like the voyager, the traveled one, the insider and yet, all at once, the outsider? I suspect the Bronx they saw in passing on the bus resembled a dark forest to which only I could be admitted and welcomed. I felt powerful as I often whispered to myself, "Let's see you all try to cross the street in this neighborhood with your shiny penny loafers and Paris tweed sports jackets. Yes, let's see you find out how really powerless you are in these mean streets."

After I had been at Groton a while, I noticed that all the big girls were hanging out together. There was a separation between us that got wider and wider as time went on. You were in real trouble if you were wimpy looking, poor, Hispanic, or glaringly different. I was all those things, or felt that I was. This realization was painful because most girls there had things that I didn't have. We even dressed differently. They wore Laura Ashley dresses and I wore Lee's dungarees. I had a very limited wardrobe, while these girls seemed to have it all. I still remember the trillions of wool sweaters stacked neatly, one on top of the other, in the shelves on the walls. My shelves were always bare except for one or two acrylic sweaters that I wore alternately. Their clothes and their mannerisms made them appear more powerful in my eyes and, in the process, made me feel inferior and unworthy of attending Groton. This place was made for them, not for me.

As a result, I was stripped of my own sexuality, or perhaps I stripped myself. At Groton I didn't consider myself a woman or a man, I was a Puerto Rican—a South Bronx Puerto Rican. I couldn't conceive of any other identity. I earned my name at Groton as that; people knew what I stood for. I wasn't really treated as a girl there. There was no chance of dating, not even with the other Hispanic kid there. We were just not attracted to each other. So we were the last Hispanic boy and girl stranded on this island called Groton. Do you have to be attracted to each other just because you're from the same place? I had crushes on boys at Groton, like every young girl does, but I always knocked down those fantasies with the knowledge that it could never happen; it was taboo even to think about it for too long.

When I was at Groton, I believed that many of the kids there had been sent to tennis camps. I fantasized that there they had undergone a sort of upper-class boot camp to prepare them for prep school. I was a complete novice at this kind of life, so I kept falling behind. I was becoming lazier. For a time I didn't have enough incentive to keep going. After a while, my experience told me that being Puerto Rican somehow meant they expected less from me and led me to question why I should work harder if they didn't expect to get any results anyway. At every juncture any hope that I had seemed to be chopped down. I was behind academically and athletically. I had nothing to offer Groton. And what could Groton offer someone with no hope of catching up?

I remember the first English paper that was returned to me; the grade was a C-. I cried and cried and then went to my headmistress. I asked if I were really that bad a writer? She told me that while I had been tops in my other schools, I was now bottom. Groton was a different, tougher place, and I had a lot of catching up to do. That advice was repeated to me over and over again every year. There was no specific way to catch up, and yet the teachers kept saying that. I didn't know where to begin or where it was supposed to end. It was all very abstract. "You have catching up to do"—but in what way?

I kept my mouth shut in classes for a long time because I was embarrassed to speak up. The boys in particular were intimidating. They had a command of the language, having gone to private schools all their lives. There was no way that I could catch up to them, that I could learn their rhetoric. I didn't want to make a fool of myself in the classes so I kept quiet. I began to fall behind in all my schoolwork and could not keep up the same pace that these kids could. I was a slower learner than they were. There seemed to be so many things to do that I had never done at home. Even sit-down dinners and chapel in the morning were new and demanding.

There was one specific attempt to help, an effort that went well for a month or two though I don't remember learning anything from it because I felt so hostile toward the fact that I needed help. I was also not comfortable with the person giving me the help. My housemistress was trying to work with me, and I already had too much contact with her. The tutoring started just after the fistfight with my roommate, and all I wanted to do was get that woman out of my hair as soon as possible. Instead I saw her every minute of the goddamn day. As a result, the tutoring fell apart.

Looking back on Groton, I realize now that the teachers at Groton struggled with my whole attitude. Many of them couldn't communicate with me. That was not true of a counselor at the school. There was a different relationship between the two of us. I started seeing her when I was a ninth grader, and she became the sole support system I had at Groton. Once a week we had forty-minute sessions and I would tell her how I felt, how depressed I was, how much I hated it there, and how I wanted to leave. That went on for four years. She was wonderful. She was my savior at Groton. She gave me a lot of nurturing and love.

I suppose that every student has to find a way to survive at school, and I had to find something other than the counselor to get through Groton. Art and religion became my food there; my bread and water. A little picture of Jesus Christ that I had acquired on a pilgrimage to a religious site in the Bronx called "La Gruta" became my lucky charm, my connection to home, my psychic connection to mother and father. I saved this picture of Jesus in a little clear box and I tucked it under my pillow every night after I said my prayers. Jesus Christ and the Virgin Mary became my saviors, my dependable icons, my imaginary friends. My mother had also given me some religious medals when I was ten. I wore them all the time, even when I was jogging. I still have memories of running through the woods, hearing these medals clink together, fearful that I would never see my mother again. Even now, I can't stand this sound.

In my first year at Groton, I managed to get a part as a maid in Anton Chekov's play *The Boar*. I thought it was the most ripping thing that I had ever done, the way the audience laughed and cheered me on at the end. It was the most fun I had ever had at Groton, and I felt really proud of myself for a long time afterwards. But that was the first and last time I would appear on stage in a school production. I wanted to pursue acting, but as the years went by all the parts were taken by a certain breed of student—long and smallboned and very elegant-looking female students. Of course, I never fit into that category. I realized what was going on when an Indian girl from New Delhi also never got to act, because she was dark and didn't fit the parts. Students who looked different were lucky if they got to play the maids. This loss was very significant to me because I loved acting; one other thing which mattered to me was chopped off.

I did discover art, and sculpture in particular, at Groton. My involvement began during my freshman year with a project that we did involving food in a freshman studio art class. I made a small artichoke out of clay, since my mother comes from the south of Spain and made a lot of dishes with artichokes. My father is from Puerto Rico, so we also ate rice, beans, plantains, and other tropical specialties. My final piece was a clay sculpture of rice, beans, artichokes, and a pork chop—foods typical of my hybrid culture at home. Doing this project was just the greatest thing for me because I got to express my own cultural background to the class. It made me stand out positively, creatively, alongside the roast beef and mashed potatoes the other students made out of clay. I remember my dish was colorful and exuberant with the green artichoke next to the red kidney beans, alongside the scrupulously molded grains of white rice.

That year I also made a vase with a Mayan pattern, but it was during my senior year that I truly blossomed as an artist. By senior year I was combining my art with my politics, and I gave a complete exhibition of about seven works in the Brodigan Art Gallery at Groton. Another student described my work as "an explosion of art." That was true because I felt, during my senior year, that at any moment I might indeed explode. By then my anger had become so repressed that I poured myself into sculpture and produced an exhibition of politicized art.

Some of the faculty members appreciated it, but some of the students were less tactful about expressing their views. I can still remember walking down the stairs of the dining hall, expecting to make my daily self-congratulatory rounds at the art gallery. Instead I was greeted by closed doors and my art teacher standing in front of them, arms folded. She had been waiting for me, waiting to tell me that some unknown person had vandalized the exhibit. No explanations were necessary; it was to be expected. My art had the qualities of a time bomb; it was just waiting to explode either in my own hands or in the hands of the school.

In the process of messing around with my sculpture, it appeared that someone had broken two little figures in a clay house I had constructed after the image of my own bedroom at home. The piece was titled *"Save Your Soul,"* and I had intended to dramatize the issue of my divided consciousness at Groton. The two broken clay figures were doubles. One was seated facing the room, my bedroom, and the mirror in the room; the other was seated behind that one, looking out of the room at the viewer, facing Groton. Both of them were broken by an anonymous assailant who not only defaced my art, my two doubles, but also defaced me, the person behind the art. The symbolism was perfect! My assailant was really my accomplice; whoever broke the clay figures completed the work of art.

That little bedroom I constructed to represent me, to represent my home, contained the same picture of Jesus Christ I had tucked underneath my pillow for so many nights. The room held objects that I had to give up in order to share them with the school, to educate it about my culture as they had educated me about theirs through the community and curriculum of Groton. But in fact our relationship was not one of sharing; it was a form of cultural warfare in which my identity was to be digested by theirs. My sacrifice was symbolically completed only when the two clay figures came crashing down to represent me at Groton, to show the dissolution of my past, my culture, my own identity. Since then, I have often thought to myself that I've become the pieces of my clay figures, pieces never to be glued together quite the same way they were before I left home.

20

Diversifying Independent Schools: Examples from the Prep for Prep Program

Gary Simons

Thirteen years ago, when the first small group of Prep for Prep students arrived at Trinity School, they were greeted by a huge mural that covered much of the wall in our main assembly area. In the center of the painting was a young boy holding the world in his hands. Half a dozen scenes emanated from the boy's fertile imagination: scenes of a biochemist and an attorney, a surgeon and a professor, an engineer and an artist. The faces were brown and black, and they were intent and excited about the activity in which each of them was engaged.

The mural had been created by one of the boys in Prep for Prep's first contingent. It was titled "Be the Dream," and it said more to that first group of fifth graders than any welcome speech I could possibly deliver. What to me was so incredible about the mural was that its creator did not know any biochemist or engineer, any surgeon or attorney. In the South Bronx neighborhood where he was growing up, there were pitifully few professional role models. Yet the American dream had penetrated the ghetto and had ignited a young boy's mind.

Twelve years of teaching in the young muralist's elementary school stirred in me a sense of indignation but also a sense of hope, and Prep for Prep was born as a personal response to both. It was remarkable to me that a child of twelve growing up in a housing project in one of the nation's most devastated neighborhoods could transcend his surroundings and, through his imagination, be a citizen of the world. The myths of Greece, the paintings of Rubens, the discoveries of Galileo spoke across the centuries to him. When you encounter in a child that desire to do more and to be more in an environment that all but makes his efforts futile, you come to believe in something called the human spirit.

How could an affluent and "advanced" society offer so many of its children so very little? I worked with more than a few youngsters whose intellect and character and energy should have made college and career a fairly safe prediction, but the circumstances of their birth and their consequently limited educational opportunities made such success highly unlikely. The local junior high schools were ill-equipped to keep alive a love of learning and intellectual camaraderie, so I began to seek alternatives for the ablest of my students.

I wanted these youngsters in an educational environment that would not only challenge them academically but also nurture in them a sense of life's possibilities. Independent schools could do both. Several years of ad hoc placements in leading independent schools, however, convinced me that a good deal more was needed than a letter of admission. I was asking children to choose the other fork in the road, and they needed to have some idea where the path would lead them. With the support of Teachers College, Columbia University, I began Prep for Prep in 1978.

That first summer we had twenty-five students and three teachers. The Institute for Urban and Minority Education paid the teachers, and Project Double Discovery at Columbia provided instructional supplies and student lunches. When the grants ran out in September, three volunteers rallied to provide instruction and counseling. An enormous boon to the program was the early support of Trinity School, which provided classrooms and other facilities rent-free for the first two critical years. Eleven independent schools committed places that first year, and twenty-two students matriculated at these schools in September 1979. By the end of the first year, the New York Community Trust took note of our efforts and awarded the first of several grants it was to make to the program. This turned out to be of considerable help in gaining the attention of other foundations. In retrospect, given all the pitfalls and blind alleys and near misses of that first year, it seems a bit of a miracle that Prep for Prep survived its birth pangs. Yet it not only survived, it began to grow.

As of this writing (early 1991), there were 680 Prep for Prep students enrolled in New York City independent day schools and East Coast boarding schools, and 200 public school students attending the preparatory component of our program and aspiring to matriculate at independent schools in September 1991. About 200 Prep for Prep (and independent school) alumni are attending college, and we recently celebrated our first twenty-seven college graduates. Their journeys inspire all who have joined in this effort.

Structure of Prep for Prep

Prep for Prep has grown dramatically in size and scope, but it adheres to a set of basic premises set forth at its inception. If a successful independent school career is to be an important vehicle to develop the leadership potential of able minority students, it is best facilitated by means of a long-term, comprehensive approach that emphasizes the primary responsibility of each student for his or her own success but offers the comfort and strength and pride of earned membership in an achievement-oriented and forward-looking community.

It is just such a comprehensive approach and forward-looking community that Prep for Prep strives to be. We view the program as a partner of the independent schools that enroll our students. Although we recruit, prepare, and place students in participating schools, the major part of Prep for Prep's efforts and resources is directed at the young people already matriculated in grades seven through twelve at independent schools. We ask them to think of themselves as members of their respective school communities while simultaneously reaffirming membership in the Prep for Prep community. During their last two years in high school, we ask the students to look at their academic and potential professional success from a larger perspective. We hope they will want to make a difference, because we believe so many of them can. Other basic premises that undergird the program appear in the following description of Prep for Prep's current activities.

The Talent Search. Developing the talent of the ablest youngsters from underrepresented groups must be a high priority. A failure to provide these children with a challenging education and a sense of appropriate career options poses a risk of lost potential and perpetuates the problem of a lack of adequate minority representation in all competitive fields.

Prep for Prep seeks youngsters from minority group backgrounds who are intellectually gifted, academically oriented, and self-motivated. Despite the devastating impact of poverty (and the myriad problems correlated with it) on the educational achievement levels at many inner-city schools, there are youngsters in such schools who have the potential to compete on equal terms with privileged students even at highly selective independent schools. These students need to be identified and made aware that independent school is a viable route for them. About 350 New York City public schools cooperate with Prep for Prep to identify candidates. In 1990 more than 2,100 students participated in our talent search. The competitive selection process resulted in the admission of 155 applicants into Prep for Prep (fifth graders) and 60 applicants into Prep for Prep 9 (seventh graders; Prep for Prep 9 will be discussed in greater detail below).

A two-stage process allows us to consider a large number of initial applicants while permitting us to allocate the greater part of our resources to the intensive assessment of the strongest candidates. Eligible students first take a battery of group-administered aptitude and reading achievement tests. Group testing sessions are conducted over ten Saturdays. On the basis of performance on these tests, 25–30 percent of the applicants are invited to continue to the second level of the selection process. These youngsters are given an individually administered intelligence test.

Each child who advances to the second level of the talent search is also interviewed by members of the staff in order to assess those personal qualities that often make the difference between success and failure. Candidates are also given an opportunity to reveal intellectual and personal strengths in a writing sample. Rating scales are filled out by the children's public school teachers, and parents are requested to complete a questionnaire.

The Preparatory Component. Minority students from public schools need to acquire the academic and student skills to compete at an independent school before they matriculate, rather than be expected to play catch-up at the same time that they are adjusting to a very unfamiliar social environment.

The student undertakes a rigorous fourteen-month course of study during the intervening school year, including two intensive seven-week summer sessions, Wednesday after-school classes, and all-day Saturday classes. The academic program is departmentalized, averaging fourteen students per teaching section, and students receive several hours of homework each night. About 75 percent of admitted students successfully complete the preparatory component.

Although many students enter the program with a limited academic background, most respond well to the high expectations we have of them. Classwork addresses the need to remediate and refine skills as well as to present content that is sophisticated and advanced. Demonstrating a respect for their ability, the program asks students to grapple with ideas and issues that are complex and provoke thought and discussion. The entire curriculum, however, pays careful attention to the development of strong study skills and writing ability.

During the first summer session and the following school year, students study at least five subjects: English, American history, research skills, laboratory science, and mathematics. Many students also study Latin. During the second summer, students follow somewhat varying academic programs. Some begin French, while others begin or continue Latin. Most students take a psychology and values course to help them better understand their own development and the influences upon it. They consider the roles of heredity and environmental factors and the impact that race, gender, and social class can have on achievement. They probe the question "What is intelligence?" and debate what factors allow an individual to withstand peer pressure and societal expectations for low achievement. Many students take a course on problems and issues in modern American society. The course allows students to look at racism, poverty, the changing roles of women, and issues of life and death from multiple perspectives.

Faculty are drawn primarily from independent schools and can speak to the issue of independent school expectations. Although teaching sections are relatively small, a teaching load at Prep for Prep can be onerous, given the fast pace of classes, the expectation that students do a good deal of writing, and the emphasis on returning students' work in a timely fashion. Ever conscious that we have only fourteen months to accomplish a host of academic objectives, faculty must also confront the need to evaluate students frequently and to monitor each student's record of homework and preparation for class.

As a result, Prep for Prep seeks faculty who combine excellence in the classroom with considerable stamina and energy. Beyond this, each faculty member needs to be able to help a student distinguish between having done poor work and being a poor student. Most Prep for Prep students have excelled in other classrooms where the academic standards were lower and competition from other students was minimal. Faculty need to help students raise their expectations without crushing their egos.

Throughout the program, individual and group counseling sessions are included. At first, the sessions are geared to help the students adjust to the program. Later in the year, they focus more on adjustment to independent school. There is an emphasis throughout on relating values to the process of making decisions. Parent involvement is stressed, with monthly meetings held throughout the year and individual conferences at several scheduled points. Frequent communication with parents is maintained, but increasing emphasis is placed on each student to assume personal responsibility for academic tasks.

The preparatory component is intense. Students who embrace the challenge and complete the preparatory component gain a much higher estimation of what they are capable of achieving academically as well as a more realistic sense of the level of commitment required in order to excel.

Summer Advisory System. A special aspect of the summer session is the advisory system. Two dozen high school and college students, all of them Prep for Prep students, join our staff. Advisers are the program's eyes and ears, there to reassure, listen to, and encourage each child in his or her first experience in a truly competitive milieu. Of equal importance is the role advisers play in gathering information about the youngsters so the program staff can fine-tune their efforts on behalf of students who experience difficulties and, ultimately, make informed and fair decisions about the retention and placement of students.

Children are grouped into twelve units, and each unit has two advisers. Each unit is single-sex but includes both first- and second-summer students. Advisers meet with their units every day before or after lunch, and they also meet with each child individually nearly every day. Advisers help the new students adjust to the program and acquire the organizational and study skills needed to succeed. They also share their own experiences of life in independent schools, while helping each child feel a part of the Prep for Prep community.

Independent School Placement. Independent schools, in general, are better equipped both to challenge and to nurture able minority youngsters and ultimately to develop their leadership potential than are the public schools in New York City. At the same time, the self-interest of the independent schools should lead them to embrace such applicants. Excellence in education cannot occur in a cultural or social vacuum, and therefore diversity in the student body is one prerequisite for any school that aspires to a deserved reputation for academic excellence. Consequently, although Prep for Prep works directly with the minority students who matriculate at independent schools, the true beneficiaries of the program's efforts include the mainstream of students in such schools whose own experience is enriched and broadened by the contributions of the minority students.

Thirty-six day schools and nine boarding schools commit a specified number of scholarship places to qualified Prep for Prep candidates. Each family must demonstrate the extent of its financial need, and each candidate must meet a particular school's admission criteria. Preparatory personnel work closely with the director of placement to guide each family toward informed choices of appropriate independent schools. In providing guidance we seek to educate families about their options and to involve each child and parent in the decision-making process.

Many factors go into a placement decision. Issues of school choice (for example, single-sex versus coed school, boarding versus Manhattan school, larger versus smaller school) include strategic considerations: should a child be placed in a school with a high school or a school that terminates with grade eight or nine, which requires a second placement two or three years later? There are also competitive pressures within the Prep for Prep group: a child's chance of admission to a school depends partly on how many other Prep for Prep students choose to apply to that school. For many families, geography is an important consideration since parents are often anxious about transportation and distance. Most difficult to assess are stylistic differences among several schools of essentially equal academic standards and how subtle factors may affect the personalities of particular youngsters.

Each family is assisted through the various aspects of the process of applying to an independent school, including visits, interviews, testing, filling out applications, and applying for financial aid. The application process begins early in the fall, and each student normally knows by March to which independent school he or she has been admitted for the following year. Matriculation, however, is contingent upon the student's completion of the remainder of the preparatory component in good standing.

Post-Placement Counseling and Activities. Adjusting to the unfamiliar environment and the predominantly white and privileged student body of most independent schools is not easy even for an academically well-prepared minority student, but if he has a base of peer support, the benefits clearly outweigh the obstacles and pain. The adjustment, however, is seldom accomplished all at once at the start of a youngster's independent school career. New issues arise at various stages, and placing the whole experience into perspective takes time and maturity.

Students in grades seven through ten are served by a post-placement counseling and activities staff of seven full-time people. The program offers a home base while encouraging its students to involve themselves fully in the life of their new school communities. Each student is assigned to a counselor, who periodically visits the independent school to talk with the student and with school personnel. Tutoring is available should extra help be needed that cannot be obtained at the student's school.

A wide range of activities, including social gatherings, camping trips, excursions, theater trips, and guest speakers are scheduled by Prep for Prep throughout the year. Performing Arts at Prep enables students to share their talents with the community while expressing their feelings on social and political issues. The overall intent is to help sustain close friendships and to foster a sense of community. Involvement in such activities is voluntary, but continued communication with the counselor is expected.

Leadership Development. An increasingly diverse society needs well-educated, effective, responsible leaders who represent all segments of the population. Pragmatic considerations, as well as the hope that America eventually will live up to its ideals, require more representative leadership. Increased disaffection by large segments of the population threatens our economy and ultimately our political system.

Developing the leadership potential of able minority youth has always been the implicit and long-term goal of Prep for Prep. During the past two years, however, our emphasis on this goal has become more explicit. We have come to believe it is not sufficient that Prep for Prep enable young people to obtain a high-quality education. We need to do more than focus attention on educational achievement as a means of developing leadership potential. We need, also, to focus directly on leadership as a concept, an attitude, an ethic, and a set of skills; and we need to make available a variety of opportunities for our students to develop and enhance such skills and values. Prep for Prep attempts to develop an understanding in its students that educational achievement can serve not merely to improve their own individual life opportunities but also to help them become effective agents to improve the life conditions of others.

The leadership development component focuses on our eleventh and twelfth graders. College counseling, including overnight trips to college campuses and week-long tours during spring break, supplements the efforts of the independent schools. A projects board involves students in selecting and planning new activities intended to develop leadership skills or to promote a sense of community among Prep for Prep students. A summer jobs bank seeks to match students with worthwhile job experiences, while a mentors project pairs students with successful minority professionals.

Leadership development seeks not only to meet the students' counseling needs but also to provide a range of individual opportunities for growth as well as group projects that facilitate the development of collaborative skills. In addition, we seek ways to foster an interest in public affairs. In the past year, fifteen Prep for Prep students served as mentors to seventh graders in a South Bronx public school. Another group participated in a nine-week training program developed in collaboration with the Coro Eastern Center and has launched Students Advocating for Youth and Children, which is intended to involve public and private high school students in child advocacy projects. Many students hone important skills and contribute to the continued success of Prep for Prep by working on our newspaper, serving on the student admissions committee, or being ambassadors at fund-raising and public relations events.

In a number of projects, we are trying to determine the balance between student initiative and responsibility and the need for staff to set the parameters. We are convinced that even for those of our students who have assumed major leadership roles in their independent schools, the opportunity to reaffirm membership and maintain peer relationships in this achievement-oriented minority student community is important. The recent establishment by some of our college students and graduates of a Prep for Prep alumni/alumnae association strengthens our resolve to develop the full potential of the leadership development component.

Prep for Prep 9

The success of Prep for Prep led to the creation of a second affiliated program for somewhat older students. Closely modeled on the original program, Prep for Prep 9 identifies able and motivated seventh graders and prepares them for ninth-grade placement at boarding rather than day schools. Various aspects of Prep for Prep have been adapted to meet the somewhat different needs of the Prep

9 students. For example, two weeks of every summer session are spent as an "immersion-in-residence" on the campus of one of the participating boarding schools.

Seven of the nation's leading boarding schools joined with Prep to form the Prep for Prep 9 Consortium, which recently added two additional member schools. Although Prep 9 has developed its own talent search, preparatory component, placement procedures, and post-placement counseling arrangements, we seek to involve Prep 9's older students in the leadership development component of the original program. In this way, we hope to develop a common bond between Prep for Prep and Prep 9 students.

The Future of Prep for Prep

At times it is difficult for me to believe that the handful of youngsters who gazed up at that spirited mural in the summer of 1978 has grown to more than 1,100 students and alumni. There have been some bitter disappointments, and Prep for Prep has experienced the tensions that derive from continual growth and ever-changing organizational charts. Yet, overall, it is profoundly gratifying to realize that many hundreds of people believe in Prep for Prep and in what it represents. Some contribute financial support, others join our staff, employ our students, and disseminate information about the program. More important, there are the students, so many of whom have made themselves into remarkable young men and women. They make it difficult not to be optimistic about the future.

Yet the challenges are real. Prep for Prep's dramatic growth does not change the fact that this program and others that have been modeled on it can embrace only a minute fraction of the youngsters who need and deserve the kinds of opportunities Prep for Prep tries to provide. The demographics force upon us a constant need to remember that ultimately the public schools must educate the vast majority of children. Privately funded efforts such as Prep for Prep need to remain focused on the particular type of youngster each program is intended to involve. Yet we feel a continual nudge to reach as many youngsters as we can muster the resources to admit.

Prep for Prep continues to evolve as we come to understand

better the needs of the youngsters and the opportunities for the program to maximize its impact on them. Each year we try to gauge how many youngsters can be admitted and which needs can be addressed. Raising an operating budget of almost $2.5 million is daunting when there are no tuition payments to count on or taxes to raise.

In the early years, I was fond of telling the boys and girls, "You talk about 'the program' as though it were some entity of its own. All it really is is you, the students. You are 'the program'." A very real challenge for us is to find ways to ensure that each child we admit still feels a member of "the program."

The Public Responsibility of Independent Schools

Prep for Prep and other programs that prepare and place minority youngsters in independent schools allow these schools a nobler purpose beyond serving the private interests of the narrow strata of society that can afford to attend. Increased racial, ethnic, and socioeconomic diversity in the student body enables an independent school to guide young people from different backgrounds toward the discovery of shared values and in the process to secure several public purposes. Important as it is, the achievement and celebration of diversity is not, itself, the real goal.

I subscribe to a rather old fashioned notion, "the American dream." The implicit social contract at the core of the American dream is that each child will have an equal opportunity to develop and demonstrate his or her ability and character. The gap between the rhetoric of the American dream and the realities of American life is hardly a new phenomenon, but it is more than alarming that the disparities among children in their living conditions and prospects for achievement are increasing. If many of our children simply stand no chance of arriving at the starting gate able to compete, what is left of our most ennobling vision of ourselves?

The dismal state of many urban schools, the lack of access to high-quality education for children of poverty, and the psychological and emotional toll exacted by racism stunt the potential of many of our children. Huge numbers of American children grow up in environments in which educational achievement simply is not a viable choice. A society that puts so much emphasis on personal choice has yet to voice its outrage that for so many children, a myriad of conditions conspire to dictate poor school achievement and make a mockery of the American dream of equal opportunity.

Independent schools offer an array of advantages designed to maximize the growth potential of admitted youngsters. These include closer scrutiny of each child's academic progress, the availability of individual help and smaller classes, a wider range of advanced course offerings, more rigorous standards, more opportunities to try out leadership roles, and the promise that a child will be a known and valued member of a relatively small community. The educational advantages parents see in independent schools often compete with their belief in equal opportunity. I argue that independent schools, institutions whose very existence represents the most extreme denial of equal access to high-quality education, have a particular responsibility to serve a public purpose to help forge a national commitment to address the plight of children whose educational options deny them a chance to achieve.

Whether or not an independent school has such a responsibility, simply reinforcing the advantages of the already privileged is hardly the most noble mission a school could undertake. I would like to suggest three other purposes to which independent schools may rightfully aspire.

First, an independent school may aim to be a model of academic excellence from which less advantaged schools can learn and perhaps borrow. In carrying out this function, "academic excellence" must be defined to include training not only in critical thinking skills but in moral reasoning as well. To be more than an exercise in religious, political, or social class indoctrination, a consideration of ethical and moral issues requires participants whose cultural backgrounds and life experiences vary. To aspire to academic excellence thus requires an independent school to have achieved a significant level of diversity.

Second, an independent school can inculcate in its privileged students a sense of public responsibility. Those most likely to be influential in setting and implementing policy, whether in a corporate, public, or professional arena, are most in need of developing a sensitivity to how policies affect those segments of the population least able to influence the formulation of policy. Diversity gives a school the human resources to broaden the formal curriculum in this way.

Third, independent schools can increase the pipeline of potential leaders in government, business, and the various professionals from low-income, minority backgrounds—leaders who have been successful in environments of both poverty and privileged education. In an increasingly diverse American society, the ability to relate to people of different backgrounds is an important asset. A school environment that instills in a youngster a belief that she really matters as an individual and that there are roles she will play in society clearly enhances the likelihood of achievement. For many privileged youngsters, such a school environment merely confirms and reinforces what they have already come to believe. This is far less so for many minority students, who often have less assurance from either the media or from familial or other role models.

An independent school that views these purposes as part of its mission and takes steps to achieve them enhances its role in society and serves a public as well.

Beyond Diversity and Multiculturalism

Traditionally, a strength of independent schools has been the sense of community they engender on the part of students, families, and alumni. Collective pride fosters individual self-esteem: it is good to be a member of a winning team. While there is always a danger of smugness, the sense of belonging develops self-confidence and even a generosity of spirit as an individual extends himself for the group.

To a varying but usually significant degree, this sense of community is built on a foundation of shared assumptions about the world that people of similar backgrounds bring with them to the school. As the student and parent body of an independent school becomes more diverse, these shared assumptions can no longer be taken for granted. Many minority students, in fact, view the world very differently from the majority of their independent school classmates.

This breakdown of shared assumptions poses a threat to the

sense of community in which an independent school justly takes pride. It engenders a "we-them" mentality that perceives "our" school as being changed in ways that were unforeseen and unwanted.

As the misunderstandings mount and the tension grows, as angry minority students complain about racism and stereotypes and just plain old ignorance on the part of their classmates, school leaders take refuge in "multicultural" efforts to foster mutual understanding and an appreciation of the contributions of different groups to American life. Laudable as these efforts are, it is problematic whether they can rebuild a shattered sense of community. Unless such efforts are accompanied by a simultaneous probing for common values, shared aspirations, and a more realistic and compassionate set of assumptions about life in America on which students can converge from different starting points, multicultural efforts are unlikely to break down the sense of second-class citizenship that potentially embitters the independent school experience for many minority students.

There are no easy prescriptions to guide an independent school as it moves beyond diversity and multiculturalism to the rebuilding of a sense of community that rests upon a broader set of shared values. What may work for one school may be ill-suited for another. I offer the following observations merely as suggestions.

An individual school cannot on its own undo all the emotional and psychological hurts that racism in society still inflicts on many of our youngsters. Prep for Prep and other programs offer a collective pride that arms a student against the stereotypically low expectations that permeate the national psyche. Independent schools should not fear divided loyalties. Multiple loyalties can coexist and even reinforce each other.

We often speak of the need for successful minority students to be role models for others in "their" communities. However, the expression of such hopes can marginalize minority students by suggesting that their contributions can only be of use to "their" communities. We need the input and insights of leaders of diverse backgrounds to guide our *shared* society.

Providing a sensitive faculty member, counselor, or administrator to assist minority students is not a substitute for more widespread sensitivity training of faculty and staff. Nor should the existence of a mentor or counselor prevent the school from teaching these students how to access the range of resource people who are available to the student body as a whole.

The special tasks imposed on recipients of financial aid by some schools reinforces the notion that "we" allowed "them" to attend "our" school. This separates students according to their parents' financial status, not according to inherent qualities in the student.

Minority students who emerge as leaders in their independent schools should be allowed and encouraged to include on the school's agenda issues that go beyond the immediate concerns of the school community. The price of leadership within the school community should not be a narrowing of the student's focus to school life issues. These students can contribute meaningfully to the education of their more privileged classmates by sharing the knowledge and indignation gained from their experience of the harsh condition of life in poor communities.

Both the formal curriculum and the informal curriculum should provide students with frequent opportunities to discover their common humanity. This can be done both in the classroom and on the playing fields.

As many schools face budget challenges, they must pit financial aid allocations to minority students against rising tuitions and the need to improve faculty compensation. Racial, ethnic, and socioeconomic diversity in the student body is not a luxury to be sacrificed or eroded when the bill comes due. School leaders need to develop and maintain a consensus that such diversity is an essential ingredient in the mix of qualities that define a good independent school.

As independent schools struggle to develop multicultural curricula and services that will allow all students to feel valued and respected as members of the school community, their efforts may result in further marginalizing of minority students unless the schools go beyond the goal of achieving diversity. The true challenge that confronts schools is not simply to celebrate and respect differences. It is the chance to develop a shared set of humane values that makes diversity an imperative.

Minority students at independent schools often believe they

have either to assimilate to the majority culture or else be visible and vocal in their rejection of it. Learning how "the system" works, however, need not imply a commitment to maintain it unchanged. I would like to believe that independent schools can offer these young people a third, more viable option. If students of diverse backgrounds can be helped to move beyond a celebration of their differences to an exploration of their common humanity, perhaps together they can change enough of the rules so that "the system" adheres more nearly to America's loftiest vision of itself.

Independent schools today have an opportunity to embrace a nobler purpose beyond giving students the opportunity to attend the "right" school with the "right" people. Redefining academic excellence to include a consideration of ethical, moral, and social dimensions would be an important contribution. Developing a compassionate awareness of the life circumstances of others in privileged young people and motivating them to further the common good would ennoble a school's mission. Expanding the pool of well-prepared leaders in government, business, and the professions—an effort that represents a triumph of talent and determination over the barriers of racism and poverty—would make possible a renewed faith in the nation's highest ideals. Given the advantages independent schools have over their public counterparts, if we cannot expect an independent school to incorporate these three purposes as an integral part of their missions, what possibility is there that America can be "the last, best hope of mankind"?

21

Teaching Social Responsibility: An Interview with Robert Coles

Pearl Rock Kane

Kane: In your chapter "Entitlement," in *The Privileged Ones*, you describe the characteristics of children who are spoiled, entitled, and narcissistically entitled. Would you describe ways in which these characteristics manifest themselves socially and psychologically in adolescents?

Coles: I would respond by reminding myself and all of us interested in this subject that narcissism is by no means the exclusive property of the well-to-do—that every human being struggles with some kind of self-centeredness as a psychological and moral matter, and that this self-centeredness is actually very important to each of us. We have to learn to take care of ourselves and have an interest in ourselves or else we would not survive, we would not eat well and get enough sleep, and we would not take the necessary care of body and mind that characterizes a reasonably functioning human being.

So with that caveat, one then goes on to this question of excessive self-centeredness, and it is at this point that privilege enters the picture because privilege enables more and more appetites to be not only appeased but set in motion. Society encourages individualism and the right of every one of us to express ourselves as we wish—and this is a valuable thing politically and culturally. Nevertheless, the risk of self-centeredness accelerates with this emphasis on the individual as opposed to the community. These are some of the background influences that I was thinking about when I was describing entitlement.

Kane: I think that comes across well in the chapter. Could you describe some specific social and psychological characteristics of the narcissistically entitled?

Coles: The social and psychological characteristics include a self-preoccupation that is all too apparent to anyone who looks at the phenomenon—self-centeredness, immersion in one's own fantasies, wishes, interests, and aspirations with no redeeming interest in others, in moral and social matters that affect others in the world at large, or in the problems and needs of the world and the troubles going on in the world. The social manifestations become clear when one notices young people who lack an interest in anyone or anything other than their own particular rhythms and thoughts and fantasies. What is excluded from their lives is any contact with people outside of their own realm or any interest in having such contact. I guess what I am thinking about is what George Eliot describes as "unreflecting egoism," a kind of tug toward one's own thoughts and wishes that is not in any way impeded or thwarted by some countervailing tug toward others and their needs and concerns and difficulties.

Kane: That is beautifully stated and clarifies the concept very well. Now, how do independent schools contribute to a sense of entitlement among privileged youth?

Coles: I am going to be quite blunt and maybe uncomfortably so. The very notion of an independent school in its own way can cater just to that kind of entitlement because, after all, what is the independent school but a social version of privilege? It's a school devoted to those who have the means and the wish to separate themselves from others and get a kind of education that presumably is distinctive and better, that offers more opportunities, possibilities, and privileges. Most of us think of independent schools as centers of privilege. There are some independent schools specifically directed at overcoming particular problems—dyslexia, for example—but I am thinking of the nationally known independent schools, whether in the Northeast, where they predominate, or in other parts of the country. They are often thought of as centers of privilege and power, and the children going to them know even before they go there that a part of their privileged and powerful lives is that they have access to those schools—or, if they are from poor and working-class backgrounds, they know that those schools offer them the opportunity to obtain more privilege and power in the future.

Kane: What about children who attend public schools in places like Scarsdale, New York, or Newport Beach, California, or Greenwich, Connecticut? Do they have a different experience?

Coles: I think it is fair to say that if you come from a well-to-do background and live in Greenwich or in Lincoln or Concord, Massachusetts, you are going to have that sense of hope and possibility, whether you go to a public school or a private school. But I think going to a private school can accentuate that sense of privilege. I am not saying it has to. There are ways of dealing with this both within the home and within the school.

Kane: In what ways might schools counterbalance that sense of privilege?

Coles: It is a real struggle. The school stands for exclusiveness, privilege, authority, power, social achievement, cultural achievement, status. We have to be very much aware of the cachet those schools have for families. I do not think the families send kids to those schools only for the educational opportunities they offer. I think they are sending them in many cases for a larger purpose, which is not unlike the reason that kids go to exclusive colleges if they can get into them. Also, in the case of the well-known boarding schools, parents are choosing, for all of these reasons, to send their children away during the middle of adolescence, when in many cases the kids need to be at home and in touch with their parents rather than separated from them. My wife and I did not believe in sending our children away from home during adolescence. They went to independent schools where they could just walk or ride a bike.

Kane: Still, many schools are looking for ways to help develop a sense of social responsibility, to develop an awareness that at least affects the sense of social privilege even if it cannot totally balance it. Do you have any thoughts on this?

Coles: I know a number of schools—and some of them are public schools in the affluent suburbs—where there are very active community service programs and where there is a great deal of idealistic activity on the part of at least some of the students. Perhaps we notice it more in private schools because of the embarrassing paradox of privilege and its self-criticism. There is a dialectic here between obvious social and cultural privilege and some effort to redeem that. I am in favor of all efforts being taken in that direction.

Community service programs are important, but there are also other efforts a school can make. They can make every effort to broaden the nature of the student body to include children from backgrounds other than the upper-middle-class to wealthy segments of society. A disturbing gap results when schools actively recruit only minority students to add to their largely white, wealthy population. The ones who are not in those schools are kids from the white working class or even middle-middle-class families. And a third thing schools can do is to encourage idealism and a social and political and cultural awareness that transcends the immediate life of the student through various programs and courses, through reading, through literature especially. Old-fashioned narratives have a power to stimulate the moral imagination.

Kane: Are there any readings you would especially recommend?

Coles: A good teacher working with a Raymond Carver story or a Tillie Olsen story or a William Carlos Williams poem or story or a Richard Wright story or the Ralph Ellison novel *Invisible Man* can do a lot to help students think of others and also to think of themselves and what they both possess and lack. Some movies can do this too. I'm thinking of a film called *Nothing but a Man*—a not very well-known film about black life in the South and an ordinary family's struggle just toward the beginning of the civil rights period.

It's important also, of course, that the teacher using the literature or the movies ask for a comparable kind of self-scrutiny on the part of the students and on the part of the institution itself. A frank, open discussion of the ironies and paradoxes you and I are discussing can help all of us try to figure out how to live our lives in this society. And a lot can happen to young people when one couples such teaching with community service.

Kane: What do you say if your students at Harvard ask you why you teach there rather than in some other institution which has a different population of students?

Coles: I answer as candidly and honestly as I know how to answer them. I tell them about my own experiences, my preferences, my weak spots, and the enjoyment I get out of being a part of that particular community. I also tell them that sometimes after spending a long day talking with children in Roxbury, which is a ghetto of Boston, or working with migrant farm children, that I have to get out of there, that I need some other kind of working life. I feel I ought to just put the matter on the table. This is a part of the dilemma many of us struggle with. I also tell them that I wish more people could live the way I do and more people could go to better schools and this is part of what I'm struggling for in my work. I don't think we get anywhere by covering up the essential and sometimes cruel ironies and paradoxes that face us, the inconsistencies in our lives.

I also tell them about conversations I used to have with Dorothy Day. I worked in one of her soup kitchens on the lower East Side in New York when I was in medical school. She never tried to tell other people how they should live. She herself was living all the time on East First Street, down there among the poor of New York, when she could have lived otherwise, and yet she always pointed out to me how her position was still that of infinite privilege because she had her own room, she had books that were hers. She was a writer, people knew her, they came to visit her. So it is very hard to deny the aspects of success and privilege that you have. Dorothy Day had no desire to deliver sermons to people on Park Avenue to make them feel they were the damned and she was the saved. I think it's a very important point for all of us not to let righteousness become self-righteousness. When we start pointing fingers at others, pretty soon we are seriously undercutting our own purposes and maybe making a travesty of them.

Kane: Yes, I think many of these dilemmas you talk about are dilemmas that independent school faculty confront. I work with a lot of young faculty members, and they struggle with wanting to make a difference although they work in country club environments. They work very hard and care very deeply and try to do some of the things you suggest in terms of making students aware of people who live differently from themselves. It is certainly a problem that troubles them.

Coles: What matters is an honorable effort accompanied by an honorable conversation with one's self in which all of these matters are faced squarely, with the hope that we have some sense of what we are trying to do and that we try to do it with as much success as we can.

I hope that independent schools think of qualities such as these—a capacity for self-scrutiny—when they are hiring. It's very important that they hire the person, not the credentials. In my opinion there's nothing more important in education than development of character, because intellect without character is a disaster.

Kane: Do you know of any examples of teachers who were particularly successful in trying to deal with character development?

Coles: I remember a particular teacher who taught my children that what mattered to him was not only the grades they got on tests but how they behaved with one another on the playing field and in the corridors and in the classroom. He did a remarkable job of showing the distinction between a careerist's success on the one hand and moral behavior on the other. Similarly, I remember a conversation I had with a chemistry teacher at Phillips Exeter who reminded me that some of her best students in terms of grades were not necessarily the students she felt were the best human beings and the ones most worthy of going on to the so-called best universities. She looked for students who could reach out to help someone who was having difficulty with an experiment, for kids who cooperated with others. And she tried to help her students see that elbowing others out of the way to achieve their own particular goals was not a definition of success.

There are all kinds of possibilities for encouraging moral

sensitivity in the everyday life of a school teaching character—including the power of teaching by example. To be courteous and thoughtful and sensitive as a teacher is perhaps the biggest lesson any of us can offer students. It makes me sad to have to say that I've seen arrogance, self-importance, snobbishness, and mean-spiritedness in any number of teachers in independent school, in public schools—and, I might add, in universities, including my own. My worst thought is that there may be schools who want those qualities—and that people like me are all too ready to oblige!

Kane: Can schools change values initiated in the home, such as excessive competitiveness? Are there problems associated with changing values initiated in the home?

Coles: I am arguing for putting all our moral and cultural dilemmas and contradictions and inconsistencies squarely before all of us teachers, headmasters, "paying customers"—namely, parents—and not least the students. I think we have to have enough confidence in our own purposes to be willing to be self-critical and to take the most embarrassing questions from our students and from their parents. All of these issues we're talking about call for a kind of Augustinian self-scrutiny that is perhaps more relentless than even the kind of psychoanalytic self-scrutiny that people like me pursue professionally. I think the existential questions that are asked by Camus and Dostoevsky and Walker Percy and Flannery O'Connor and Elie Wiesel—these are the questions that we ought to ask of ourselves as teachers, and the questions that presumably parents ought to be asking of themselves.

Kane: So you are talking about educating parents as well.

Coles: Certainly. Parents need self-reflection—all of us need to stop and take a hard look at who we are and what we believe in, occasionally. Why not, on a parents' day, ask parents to come to school prepared to discuss one of the pieces of literature I mentioned earlier? Could parents not have a discussion that reflects the same kind of serious reflection being held among students? What would happen if they read carefully and took to heart Walker Percy's novel *The Moviegoer?* This novel offers a searching philosophical and moral discussion of life's meaning rendered through a main character who is a stockbroker and therefore not atypical of many of the parents who can send their children to private schools. There are plenty of independent school teachers who would be willing to do this, I think, with a group of parents.

Kane: I like that idea, and I know that schools are looking for ways to deal with the issues we are discussing. Schools also grapple with the question of how to communicate with parents about their children. Do you have any recommendations for ways to do this effectively?

Coles: Well, you know we have college advisers for students, and we have school psychologists who are concerned with the emotional difficulties of particular students. We have athletic advisers. I just wonder if there could not be advisers who are basically concerned with the students' moral and spiritual and personal being—with the character of the students. I know this is difficult because we quickly get into all sorts of difficulties, such as being sure about the character of the adviser—and yet the mission of independent schools from the beginning has centered on the question of character, and I don't want to think that mission has been lost.

   I remember from my own high school experience a particular teacher who was not only my English teacher but a wise and thoughtful person who looked after us in an old-fashioned moral way. He was a man who had wisdom and was willing to share it with us and was willing to help us measure up to that wisdom. Again, I'm going back to that question of teachers who care about not only what we know on tests but how we behave with one another. Our schools today need to do more than pay lip service to that word "character." We can try to implement character development in the way students are advised and the responsibility teachers feel toward their students. I wonder if schools can't find ways to connect with students in such a manner that their altruism and their compassion and their thoughtfulness might be encouraged and taken note of—just as all good schools try to take note of individual students' academic progress or athletic skill in a particular sport. Couldn't information about such qualities—or their absence—be shared with the students first and then the parents?

Kane: Yes. I was thinking that what really counts for students and for parents is what we evalutate in the comments we send home.

Coles: That is right, and I regret to say that in all the years of my children's education, I got very little from teachers evaluating their character. I would get statements evaluating their performance in English and math and history. Or I would get a psychological statement such as "Your child seems happy" or "He is functioning very well." These are all mechanistically psychological comments and cliches. I'm really asking for an old-fashioned character evaluation of students—and of faculty. I remember a particular teacher who was a very, very able teacher of languages, a brilliant man, but he was also in many ways callous, insensitive, rude, even mean-spirited. We all know that this kind of thing goes on in schools, and what are we to make of it? If we as parents tolerate it and say that one has to go through this kind of thing in life, it's a kind of moral surrender. The kids learn the lesson that rudeness and callousness and insensitivity and unfairness are simply part of life. It's not too long then before they begin to impose these qualities on one another, and it is a terrible tragedy. Where are the school mechanisms for eliminating this kind of behavior in teachers?

Kane: We're back to the question of the importance of hiring the person, not the resume.

Coles: I think schools should place an enormous emphasis on applicant interviews. I would make telephone calls to references, not just get written reports from them, and maybe I would hire by trial with a clear understanding that one wants to get to know the person better and is not bound to any agreement for too long a period of time. If a school's officials are really interested in the character of the person they are going to have teaching, they can find the ways to find that out.

It is a question of the school's values. Is the school interested in what the Hebrew prophets Isaiah and Jeremiah and Amos and Micah had to say? Is it interested in Jesus and how he lived his life and with whom and for what purposes? Is it interested in the kinds of ironies that Shakespeare gives us in *Macbeth* and in *Hamlet* and in *King Lear* and in *Othello?* Is it interested in what Dostoevsky and

Tolstoy were struggling with? Or the issues in Dickens or in Hardy, in his *Jude the Obscure*—the young country boy Jude finally sees Oxford University in all of its arrogance and insensitivity? Or is it interested in its own social and economic and political power and in the number of students it gets into X, Y, or Z college? These are decisions that have to be made, and they all have practical consequences for teaching.

Kane: How powerful do you think a school can be in molding a student's values?

Coles: I believe it can be very powerful, because I have seen the process work. I have seen students come from one kind of family and seen those students change in school—and again I'm also including public schools—under the influence of particular teachers who become an extremely important part of the life of particular young men and women. I find students in college still remember not the school as such but a particular teacher who has become part of the conscience, the ideal parental and human figure in the life of the young man or woman, and this lives on. This is the best hope a teacher has—without it, we might as well surrender. A teacher stands for certain values and principles, no matter what academic subject he or she is teaching. This is true even in subjects such as math or physics, which are to some extent removed from moral and spiritual matters. Nevertheless, the great people in physics were people such as Einstein, who connected science to the larger questions of life and its meaning.

I want to touch again on the question of a school deciding what its values are. Are those values centered on concern for others? Think of the various biblical traditions from which many of these schools take their names. What is St. Paul's School? In a literal sense, it belongs to St. Paul. Is the school living up to that name? And St. Mark's. Mark was a fisherman, was he not? An ordinary humble person—he did not check into the equivalent of the Ritz-Carlton Hotel, he did not go to the equivalent of Harvard College—but he did stand for certain very important moral and spiritual matters. It's questions like these that I'd like to see a headmaster and a group of students and teachers discuss at great length.

Kane: I know you're familiar with the move in many schools toward racial diversification. Recent statistics place a minority population, which includes Asian-Americans, African-Americans, and Hispanics at 13 percent of independent school populations, with schools which have greater endowment having a significantly higher percentage. How do you think this change has affected the nature of schools?

Coles: Well, it is all to the good, but the really important question is what happens to both the minority students who come to those schools and to those who are not in the minority. In a school which does not examine its own moral purposes, it is possible to take in students from minority groups and encourage them in unpleasant traits possessed by some members of the majority. It's quite possible to indoctrinate students with self-importance, smugness, self-satisfaction, arrogance, thoughtlessness, and crude or rude ambition. The best situation exists when a school can teach respect for everyone's background and for what everyone has to offer. It's good when students can feel respect for a wide range of people in this country, not just for those who are eminently and visibly successful in an economic or a social sense.

Kane: I know you wrote a review of Sam Anson's book *Best Intentions,* and it comes to mind as you are talking. Are there ways that Exeter might have done things differently to change the fate of Edmund Perry, for example?

Coles: One wonders whether the school confronted some of the difficulties he brought to the school, or maybe, that the school brought to him. It is one thing to be at Exeter, and it is quite clearly another thing for him to return to his home in Harlem, New York. Maybe if the school had made an effort with all of its students to indicate the discontinuities that can take place between school and home, and to bring that topic up for discussion and contemplation, things might have been different.

I am thinking not only of that particular young man and his Harlem life, but of some of the students who leave schools like Exeter and go home not to Harlem but to very, very rich neighborhoods where a different kind of discontinuity takes place. I'm not equating arrogance and smugness and insensitivity with street murder, but those qualities can result in killing, hurtful, mean-spirited ways between people. That ought to be discussed as well. Moreover, some youths will learn how to behave in a different way as a result perhaps of certain friendships, certain involvements with teachers—learn to be more introspective morally—and then they go home and are up against forms of behavior and values that really offend them, and they are told, if they object to those forms of behavior and values, that they are going through an adolescent rebellious stage. In other words, psychology is used to put them down—a very interesting mechanism, by the way, in our contemporary culture. So their moral and spiritual struggles are either reduced to psychology and dismissed or fought by parents and relatives, and in a curious way this is not totally unlike what went on with that young man who went back and forth between Exeter and Harlem.

Kane: That is an excellent point.

Coles: The old tradition that Salinger evokes in *The Catcher in the Rye* is very important for schools to contemplate; namely, a kind of sensitive adolescent moral awakening that the school ought to treasure and work with and encourage, and the possibilities that moral awakening offers not only the students but the teachers and the school itself, and the difficulties that moral awakening encounters in all sorts of neighborhoods. I would encourage candid discussions between teachers and students in which the students are given some authority by the school to be heard and understood. This is a matter of tone, a hard word to define, but when it is there, it is there—and when it is not there, it sure is not there.

Kane: Who sets that tone?

Coles: It ought to be set by the headmaster and the board of trustees. There ought to be some effort to reach out and have good old-fashioned bull sessions with some of the kids and let them speak candidly and openly and learn from them, so that the regular structure of authority somehow does not have all the say.

Kane: What kinds of roles do you think the head of school should play?

Coles: The headmaster should not be an austere, aloof, authoritarian figure but someone who can be part of the life of the school and the life of the students. There are social mechanisms for headmasters, all kinds of informal get-togethers or meals, not only with teachers or trustees but with students as well. If the headmaster wants to break out of confinement, he or she will find a way. If the headmaster does not, I regret to say he or she will also not find a way.

Kane: Is it useful for heads to teach, to be actually in the classroom?

Coles: I think that is a great idea; to teach and to learn how to demythologize themselves just enough to get nearer to the psychological and moral truth available when such undercutting and demythologizing take place. And the learning the headmaster does will be just as important as the teaching. What matters most is the headmaster's tone, the feeling he or she conveys to students about interest in them. In that sense it's not too different from some of my concerns about students' attitudes in doing community service. Let me talk for a minute about the distinctions between noblesse oblige and social responsibility. We are dealing here with intangible words like tone and intent and meaning—very important words, hard to quantify, and one would not even want to quantify them. They are essentially qualitative and moral judgments. I can imagine someone doing something responsible, socially and politically and morally responsible, but doing it in such a way that the whole intent is undermined by the manner and the attitude and the subjectivity of the particular person involved.

Kane: Could you be specific?

Coles: Well, I think sometimes we patronize other people, and a certain kind of smugness or arrogance comes across to the person we intend to be helpful to. The helping, the interest we have in the person is undermined by some of our own problems of cockiness and smugness. We are all too sure of ourselves and all too unwilling to reach out to another person in such a way that we can be of most help to them. At times, I think we all have to worry about this because of our own motivations. There is a kind of egoism that is tied up with a desire to help others; this is natural and even normal. It is what we do with it that matters. My mother used to tell me that when you try to help someone, it ought to be balanced by a desire to learn from that person, and to this day I find that I do not have anything better to offer myself or anyone else.

Kane: That is a very useful way to think about any kind of community service within or outside of the school.

Coles: My mother was the one who suggested to me when I was in college that I work as a volunteer tutor with children. When I was in medical school and wanted to pull out because I thought I was not getting anyplace and I did not have the kind of mentality that most medical students have, she always urged me to go and do work. She was the one who urged me to get to know Dorothy Day and work in the Catholic Worker movement. But the *way* my mother gave me the advice, that was all-important: she said, "You desperately need to get out of yourself, you need to find out about others whose travail maybe will humble you and give you some perspective." She would add the caveat that there is a danger of using other people in order to find your own way. There is a blindness there, and so she would add this further bit of advice, because she herself was a schoolteacher—as, by the way, is my wife, so both of them have straightened me out a lot—that I should remember that there is much to be learned by those we want to teach and there is much to be learned from those we teach—and from those we want to help. Now, years later, when I am talking with children and find myself bored or patronizing, I hear her voice urging me to stop imposing on them, to stop patronizing them. I can hear my mother's voice telling me to regard those children as individuals who have a lot to tell you about their own lives, about the lives of their families, about life in general as they are experiencing it.

This is all very complicated and requires a continual conversation with ourselves. I go back to my phrase "Augustinian self-scrutiny." We have to be on the alert about our own purposes, our own blind spots, our own privileged lives, and the occupational hazards that go with privilege. Like any state, it's a mixed blessing. Poverty is certainly nothing any of us want, yet the kind of voluntary poverty that Mother Teresa or Dorothy Day, or for that matter the Hebrew prophets and Jesus, had, that kind of voluntary poverty in the face of arrogance and privilege and power can have its own grace.

Kane: I wonder how what you're saying applies to community service, because sometimes schools require community service, and students just go out and do things, and there is little or no analysis or reflection on the experience.

Coles: There's a delicate balance involved here. One does not want to push these children into a kind of overwrought self-analysis that paralyzes them. On the other hand, one does not want a kind of self-importance being imposed on others whose vulnerability serves as an excuse for our egotism. These are tightropes we walk— psychological tightropes, moral tightropes—and we have to some- how figure out, each of us, how to walk these tightropes in a way that a decent side of ourselves does not deteriorate into an arrogant kind of noblesse oblige. How did Henry James refer to difficulties like these? "We work in the dark, we do what we can, we give what we have, our doubts become our passion, and our passion becomes our task. The rest is the madness of art"—and teaching, I believe, is an art.

Kane: I'm thinking with sadness about schools that say you have to do fifty hours of community service this semester and then just set the kids free.

Coles: No, no. I think it is very important to sit down with those kids and talk candidly—not in that gratuitous way that some of us in the social sciences can have, but from the heart. When I talk with students at Harvard who are doing community service, I sit down with them and tell them frankly abut my mistakes and the difficul- ties I have had, and I try to indicate how one can learn from expe- riences that help one avoid some of those mistakes the next time around. The hope is that if we share some of our mistakes and our blind spots and our self-criticism, maybe we can help one another along as we do this work.

Kane: What kinds of mistakes?

Coles: I remember working with a youngster who wanted to be a welder. I saw in him certain mathematical gifts, and so I was pushing him toward college. In a way, I never really looked at him and his family and his life and what he wanted to be. Who am I to tell him not to be a welder? Who am I to patronize this occupation? It was very unfortunate.

Kane: Are you referring to imposing our standards?

Coles: Yes, our standards and our values. There is nothing wrong with being a mathematician or a scientist either, but I was just failing to see who this young person was and what he wanted and what his family was about. It took me some time to sort out what I wanted of him as opposed to what he wanted of himself. Again, there's the question of a kind of tightrope. You want to avoid the danger of imposing on them what you want them to be, but on the other hand you want to avoid the danger of not trying hard enough to work with them in a way that they find some hope and purpose and meaning in life. Some of them have been hurt badly and constricted by life and have not been able to form dreams and aspirations that the rest of us have. But if they have dreams, we need to try and hear them before we start trying to impose our dream on them.

Kane: Some of what you are saying may have applicability for some children we take into our schools and how we deal with them.

Coles: Right. It's fitting that a teacher have dreams for them of literacy and competence and intellectual progress. But on the other hand, we want to respect what they have to offer and want to work with them on their own terms as well as on ours. By the way, I was very moved and impressed with the book *Small Victories*. Of all the books I have read about schoolchildren, that in a way is the best, because that teacher, Jessica Segall, was working against great odds and yet she intuitively had a wonderful capacity for self-criticism and self-reflection. I was very moved by that and by her particular struggle with those children. And I think her success with those children is not unconnected to her self-critical humility as she worked with them.

Kane: How can we make the experience of opening up our schools to children of diverse backgrounds a better experience for everyone?

Coles: First of all, those in charge at the school want to make sure they are not just buttressing their statistics and perhaps expanding their pride. Questions such as "What are we trying to do?", "Why do we want to do it?", and "How are we going to go about doing it?" need to be asked. Perhaps some of the teachers in these schools ought to go and meet these children on their home turf and learn from the neighborhoods and from the children and be part of their lives. After all, many teachers are very much on the home turf of a lot of the other students—considering the location of the schools and the recruiting process and the parents. Let us be a part of all of this effort toward diversity! We would learn from it and figure out with these youngsters what it is we are trying to do.

Kane: What should we be trying to do?

Coles: Presumably, we are trying to give these children the best possible education, but I repeat that we ought to learn where they are coming from. Going back to Jessica Segall, I was astonished that she seemed to know the personal lives and the neighborhood lives of every child. I wonder if our private boarding schools can take that kind of interest. The ideal environment, it seems to me, is a day school which has the willingness to integrate itself into the lives of these young people.

Kane: How do they integrate?

Coles: This is what Ned O'Gorman is doing with his Harlem Storefront Learning School. That is a private school.

Kane: But doesn't that school have a 100 percent population of disadvantaged children?

Coles: The Manhattan Day School has made a strenuous effort to integrate both sides.

Kane: But most schools are not in a financial situation to do that. Most of the schools I know can only offer limited numbers of places for disadvantaged children.

Coles: They ought to think very carefully about which children to admit and what they are trying to do. An admissions committee has to be very careful about its purposes; and I hope that admissions committees are equally careful about who they are taking in on the other end of the economic spectrum. Look at some of the wealthy white students in private schools who really do not belong there but are admitted by virtue of being legacies. Some of these kids present major psychological and emotional and intellectual hurdles to these schools. Some of them are disasters. We talked earlier about Edmund Perry's antisocial behavior, but some of these kids are very antisocial. They have lied, cheated, stolen, been delinquent—and they come from very wealthy families. The newspapers do not write this up, and books are not written about these kids. This is an important point.

Kane: Financial privilege doesn't mean problems are alleviated.

Coles: Some are extremely disturbed children. They have been abandoned in certain ways emotionally by their parents. They are troublemakers who come into these schools and terrorize teachers and headmasters because their parents are powerful and rich. This is thus far an untold story in the private schools. It ought to be put on the table for perspective when we think about the troubles of some of our ghetto kids in these private schools. A little context here is very important. Some of the kids who come from wealthy and powerful families are alienated, disturbed, very unhappy in the private schools they are sent to. For them, being sent there is the final rejection against a background of psychological betrayals and emotional abandonment. Let me repeat that some of these kids create havoc for teachers, for classmates. They are delinquent, they drink and use drugs, they lie and cheat, and they should be expelled, but sometimes they are not because of the parents' power and influence. I know this as much as I know the troubles of ghetto kids in some of these private schools.

Kane: I don't think anyone has made that point as powerfully.

Coles: There have been dozens and dozens of documentary studies of poor, vulnerable populations but very few studies of rich and powerful people. Of all the books I have written—and I have written a lot, maybe too much—the one that is least attended to in its implications is *The Privileged Ones.*

Kane: That is my favorite of your books! Would you say that the independent school has the potential to fulfill the democratic ideals that the common school was originally intended to serve? I'm referring to the fact that it can equalize, to some degree, conditions of birth in offering all students the same curriculum. There is no differentiation into vocational and academic tracks; the schools don't decide that kids have different destinies and thus must learn different things. The schools have not diluted the curriculum to keep the students interested but ask that students rise to the level of the curriculum.

Coles: Right. What I value about the private schools is that they hold on to Latin and Greek, hold on to intense education in mathematics right through calculus, hold on to the most demanding kind of education with respect to literature and history and make no compromises in that respect. They might introduce *Invisible Man* or *Their Eyes Were Watching God,* for instance, not because they were adding "new cultures" but because these books are examples of the highest form of literature. In that sense writers such as James Allen McPherson or Ralph Ellison or Zora Neale Hurston are not important as black writers but as enormously talented American writers. This I value—and I am willing to stand up for it in my rights as a teacher and as a parent. As I mentioned earlier, I respect Ned O'Gorman of the Storefront Learning School for teaching children in Harlem Latin and Greek, starting at the junior high school level. I love Latin and Greek, had six years of one and four of the other, and I wanted to see my children educated that way. This is what private schools have in the academic sense that is most valuable. If they start diluting that, I think they are making a serious mistake.

Kane: Can this intense academic emphasis be combined with an emphasis on character development which we were discussing earlier?

Coles: Both are extremely important. I love that old-fashioned emphasis on character development that I have seen with certain headmasters and certain teachers. I would be very worried if the academic emphasis was lost, and I would be very worried if an emphasis on character development was lost.

Kane: In addition to the important role of the individual teacher and of a candid discussion of moral issues, do you have other thoughts on how private schools might best carry on this education in character development?

Coles: They can stand up for spiritual and moral values that might be controversial or even illegal in the public schools. They can take the Bible out and really pay attention to it, both the Old and the New Testaments, without fearing a suit from the ACLU. They can stand up for a whole tradition of moral strictness. They can encourage self-criticism in teachers and students alike in a way that may be difficult for the public schools. They can encourage a kind of—dare I use the word?—puritanism that I find preferable to some of the extremes of psychological self-consciousness and some of the moral laxity one sees in this society as a whole.

Kane: How do you see that moral self-consciousness being generated in students?

Coles: With some very firm principles constantly enunciated among the teachers themselves. Let me give you an example. I find it a little worrisome that more and more of the private schools are buying into what Christopher Lasch calls the "culture of narcissism," including the psychiatric aspect of it. Some people interested in psychological awareness become so involved with the problems of the kids that they suspend their standards of behavior.

Kane: They become too therapeutic?

Coles: Too therapeutic and not sufficiently sure of themselves with respect to the values of character and standards of behavior.

They do not demand enough—and, yes, I'll say it, they do not punish enough. Rather, they become overly attentive to what they would call "needs" or "problems."

Kane: Every case becomes an individual case.

Coles: Precisely. There is an army of psychologically aware teachers and consultants, but the school fails to delineate its standards and values. This is a sad, sad development. Not everything should be thought of as "problems" that need to be "resolved." The irony of it is that a lot of the people in the private schools will listen to me on this score because I am part of the very faddish therapeutic culture I am denouncing. They will listen to me for the wrong reasons. Psychologically sanctioned permissiveness is a scandal.

Kane: What exactly do you mean by that?

Coles: I mean using psychology and psychiatry and psychoanalysis as a means of constantly "understanding" impulsive, aberrant, smug, self-satisfied, self-indulgent behavior and refraining from moral judgments and punishment when moral judgments and punishment are desperately needed.

Kane: Do you think the schools are getting somewhat soft because of the financial situation? Are they failing to stand for principles because of the fear of losing students?

Coles: Well, then they might as well go out of business and, in my opinion, should go out of business as independent schools! If they are independent only in the sense that they are not run by a town or a city, and if they are basically chasing the dollar and subverting their moral and intellectual mission to that, then they might as well just call it quits. An independent school that makes every decision based on financial considerations has lost its own mission and lacks the integrity of the public school, and therefore has the worst of both worlds.

Kane: That is an ugly picture, but I think the point needs to be made.

Coles: It is an ugly picture. And I fear the point *does* need to be made. But I hope that some of the better-known schools that are enormously well endowed will stand for something that gives them a sense of their own purpose and meaning—something that will enable them to stand up to the worst aspects of the secular culture. I'm talking about standing up to the notion of "value-free" education or to junk talk such as "values clarification"—an absurd phrase! "Anything goes!" "You have your ideas and I have mine!" Schools need to offer firm moral values, a bedrock moral culture that one will stand up for and be willing to be unpopular for.

I return to my valuing of particular teachers in private schools who maybe would not last in a public school because of their idiosyncrasies and their old-fashioned values and their tough insistence that children learn, learn, learn. Some of those teachers are extraordinary in their moral urgency and their intellectual urgency and in their willingness to share both with students. Even in this day and age they want their students to know Latin and Greek and the Bible and ancient history and calculus. They will not move aside for the social sciences or for television, and good for them! And good for the schools that will support them!

By the way, one of the saddest things to me is private schools in which the old chapel has been lost, or the old church that was part of the school has given way to secular meetings and voluntary chapel. I know the difficulties, but these are private schools. A lot of them do have a religious and spiritual history, and I think they could make all students—Catholic, Jewish, Protestant, agnostic—comfortable with that history. I find it sad when they abandon that history.

Kane: I agree. It adds another important dimension to the school that reinforces what schools stand for.

Coles: Let me be specific. I love the chapel at Groton. It is not only aesthetically beautiful, but it stands for something. In my experience, in students of all faiths or of no faith, there is a certain awe, a kind of transcendence that they feel when they go to those services, and I hate to see that yield to secularity.

Kane: I think schools are bending more to family wishes than they used to and are more sensitive to the diversity of constituents.

Coles: They can still stand for a certain kind of transcendence and awe in spiritual and religious traditions. To have that tradition diminished to "school announcements" and to make no effort to bring the school together around certain civic virtues and cultural values and traditional principles is very sad. For instance, at Exeter, which certainly does not have the kind of spiritual tradition that Groton—with some qualification—clings to, I was impressed that they asked the male students to put on coats and ties for the assembly at which I spoke. A simple thing like that can give some larger meaning in context to an educational experience. A feeling of dressing up in a certain way at a certain time, a sense of having some reverence at some agreed-upon moment, a combination of music and poetry, or even speeches that become sermons—all these things can connect us to our religious and spiritual and philosophical roots.

The Greek tragedians, the biblical prophets, the wise novelists like George Eliot and Leo Tolstoy, struggle with spiritual matters mightily. So do poets such as T. S. Eliot and even nonreligious poets like William Carlos Williams or Philip Larkin. They give us a sense of mystery and awe that is very important.

Kane: Are there any ways you could suggest that private schools might work more collaboratively with public schools? Do you see that as their mission in any way?

Coles: I think in curriculum development, and maybe even working with public school teachers, exchanges might be of some use, depending on how they are done.

Kane: What do you think of supplemental programs where financially underprivileged public school students come to the private schools on Saturdays or during the summer to do intensive academic work?

Coles: They can be helpful to particular kids, but it does bring up a moral issue for the independent schools. What does it mean to say that we do this only in the summer as a separate activity? These matters of inequity haunt all of us, and I think we are morally dead if we aren't concerned about them. Maybe one of the great things about the private schools is that some of these questions still haunt a significant number of human beings! I think these difficulties are the subject, really, of what you are concerned with and the questions you put to me, and I assume of your book. I think that in itself is important—the acknowledgment of difficulties and paradoxes—and may distinguish independent schools from a lot of ordinary suburban schools where these matters are not discussed at all. "Who deserves to be where?" This is a big question for all of us, and it is what children ask in their own moral and philosophical moments. I just sent forth to the world that book of mine, *The Spiritual Life of Children.* In it you see again and again children asking questions such as, "Why am I living this way and someone else is living some other way?" "How is it that I have this kind of good luck and someone else has bad luck?" "Why did I not get sick but my brother or sister did?" These are the powerful existential questions we all by our nature ask.

Kane: You make me feel more positive about the potential. I think that making children think about uncomfortable questions is not a bad thing.

Coles: It is an important mission, and schools that promote such thinking should have confidence and assurance about assuming that responsibility, rather than trying to get rid of any uneasiness or shame or guilt.

Kane: Certainly what you have said is helpful for me because I work with young teachers every summer. They are all bright people from liberal arts colleges. We read the Edmund Perry book and discuss the public responsibility of private schools, and many of them have this sense of guilt about working in independent schools. I think the response to give is the one you gave—that feeling uncomfortable is OK.

Coles: Questions like these—the notion of how to live an honorable life amidst the privileges of the richest and in one of the freest countries in the world—are an important part of education. This is what Ralph Waldo Emerson struggled with all during his life; it's in his letters, in his essays—and it's great that they struggle with that.

Kane: The task is a huge one. I know the small percentage of students who attend independent schools disproportionately have leadership positions because they are so well educated and because they have access to jobs through social networks. But if those young people can become morally sensitive and do their jobs with great humility, I think we will accomplish a great deal.

Coles: I hope so. Private schools must have self-respect, a sense of respect for their own mission and purpose, or they will lose their sense of integrity and purpose. The school must decide first what it is about, and it has to be willing to discuss openly the contradictions and inconsistencies and vulnerabilities that it has along with everyone else. If we can teach in such a way that more and more students begin to think more and more about life's moral issues, this country will gradually become a better country. If the independent schools of this country can give the important moral questions a forum and an incarnation, they would do a lot, I think, to justify their existence.

Part Three

CHOICE,
PUBLIC POLICY,
AND INDEPENDENT SCHOOLS

HOW CAN THE BEST ASPECTS OF INDEPENDENT SCHOOLS DESCRIBED IN the preceding chapters, available to relatively few, be amplified and made available to the many in public schools? Historically, independent schools have been virtually omitted from public policy debates on school improvement. In recent years, there has been increased recognition that aspects of private schooling may offer solutions to public school problems. Chief among them is the issue of giving parents choice in schooling. This section focuses on aspects of choice and related proposals for privatizing public schools that are currently being hotly debated by policy makers, teachers, and administrators.

Unlike school reforms of the past, the choice issue brings into focus the distinction between the purposes of public and private schools. Public schools were established to serve the broad democratic interests of society as a whole and to contribute to the economic welfare of the nation. The individual interests of parents, students, and teachers have been, at least in theory, subordinated to broader societal aims such as equity and pluralism. Public schools are accountable to state and federal authorities as a way to ensure that the interests of society are being served. Private schools were established to serve the particular values or religious orientations of individuals and are accountable only to the families they serve. Many public officials fear that the exercise of choice will give greater decision-making power to the individual, threatening the balance between individual interests and the interests of the community.

Choice in public schooling has been supported by different groups for various reasons. Initially, choice was viewed as a means to desegregate schools through the development of magnet schools, which were intended to bring together families with common interests in particular types of schools, overcoming obstacles of racial segregation. Choice in schooling is also regarded as a way to give poor families what wealthier families have always enjoyed: options in schooling. Families who can afford it have moved into residential areas where their children could attend good public schools, or they have elected to send their children to private schools. More recently, as the move toward restructuring schools has become a popular strategy for improving schools, choice has been regarded as a catalyst for bringing about dramatic change. The first four chapters in this section present models of choice and responses to those proposals. The last chapter deals with factors related to achievement in public and private schools.

Some find choice objectionable in the public sector because it turns parents into consumers of education, but that is exactly what makes private schools better according to authors John Chubb, a senior fellow at the Brookings Institution, and Terry Moe of Stanford University. Chubb and Moe would replace the current system of public schools with a system of choice in which schools would compete for markets and have the freedom to decide how best to serve their students and parents. But they would not stop there. The authors would dismantle our current system of public education and free schools of the bureaucratic constraints of government. They believe that only when the institutional context of public schools resembles the autonomous governance of private schools will America's schools improve. Chubb and Moe base their recommendations on results obtained from analyzing achievement scores of a national sample of high school students and a national survey of teachers and administrators.

President of the American Federation of Teachers Albert Shanker laments the current crisis in education but is not prepared to embrace Chubb and Moe's proposal for abandoning democratic governance of public schools for market control. Shanker and his assistant, Bella Rosenberg, argue that implementing Chubb and Moe's plan raises insoluble problems of equity and access. Since markets differentiate by product and price, they would be inherently antithetical to the common school notion of education that brings together all classes, races, and creeds. Shanker also challenges the empirical grounds that are used to support the case for market control of schools, concluding that while our particular form of democratic control has shortcomings, Chubb and Moe have failed to prove that effective school organization is a leading cause of student achievement.

California Superintendent of Public Instruction Bill Honig considers Chubb and Moe's plan for the radical deregulation of schools and the imposition of market control risky and dangerous. Honig contends that complete choice and deregulation would breed chaos and corruption and undermine the equity that mass education has achieved. The data used to support Chubb and Moe's thesis are, according to Honig, based on tests administered before the current reform movement was initiated. He believes that recent gains in student achievement in California public schools are evidence that the existing system can work, making radical restructuring unnecessary.

Public schools, not just public funding as Chubb and Moe advocate, are essential to our nation, argues Deborah Meier, principal of Central Park East schools in District 4, New York City, where choice has been implemented to improve schools. Meier, whose school has been used to popularize the concept of choice, demonstrates that choice is a necessary part of a much larger strategy to radically improve public schools. In District 4, choice coupled with self-governance provided the means to stimulate fundamental changes in curriculum and pedagogy, and it allowed schools to build small, cohesive communities. Since choice already exists for parents who are able to use their private power for the advantage of their children in public and private schools, Meier says we need to ensure that all parents can have what is now available to only a few. The alternative to privatizing education must be good public education.

Will independent schools be included in the growing movement toward choice in schooling? Isolated experiments such as the pilot program in Milwaukee, Wisconsin, which allows 1 percent of the city's students to attend private schools, may be an omen of the future or it may demonstrate the futility or unpopularity of such plans. The purpose of this section is not to promote one type of schooling over another but to debate various possibilities. As our nation searches for better models for educating all children, we need to consider different ways of thinking about schooling. Independent school approaches may be useful alternatives for consideration.

22

Why Markets Are
Good for Education

John E. Chubb and Terry M. Moe

Do private schools really outperform public schools, and if so, why? These have been among the most controversial questions addressed by educational research over the last decade. Researchers disagree vigorously over why private schools regularly post higher test scores than public schools. Some researchers attribute the difference to the special student bodies that private schools allegedly have and to the control—through admission and expulsion policies—that private schools exercise over them. Others argue that students achieve more in private schools because of the schools themselves. Private schools are said to have stricter discipline, higher academic expectations, and stronger bonds with families and students. Researchers also heatedly dispute what their findings imply for school reform. If private schools are indeed more successful than public schools, it may be good policy for the government to promote private school attendance through vouchers or tuition tax credits, which supporters of public schools despise.

In our view, private schools *are* more effective than public schools in promoting student achievement among comparable stu-

This chapter is adapted from John Chubb and Terry Moe, *Politics, Markets, and America's Schools* (Washington, D.C.: Brookings Institution, 1990), chapter 2, by permission of the publisher.

dents. And private schools *do* offer solutions to problems in the public schools. But our view of these matters, while controversial, is actually quite consistent with much of what education research has been finding about school performance in recent years, and our recommendations are increasingly within the mainstream of education reform.

In essence, we believe that private schools outperform public schools because they are more effectively organized—they have clearer goals, stronger leadership, more professional teachers, higher academic expectations for all students, and a coherent, team approach to education. We also believe that private schools are better able than public schools to develop these qualities because they are less constrained by the kinds of bureaucratic rules and regulations—personnel policies, curriculum specifications, and the like—that can easily undermine effective school organization. Neither of these beliefs is especially controversial. The first is consistent with countless studies of effective schools. The second is consistent with longstanding critiques of excessive centralization and bureaucratization in America's schools.

It is only a third and final observation that we make about public and private schools that is truly controversial. We believe that public schools are at a decided disadvantage in building effective organizations and at gaining autonomy from external constraints because of the political context in which they now operate. The political institutions that currently govern and control public schools work systematically and routinely, despite everyone's best intentions, to burden the schools with excessive bureaucracy, to discourage effective organization, and to stifle student achievement. In the final analysis, private schools outperform public schools because private schools are not directly subject to these political institutions. Private schools operate in a fundamentally different context that is structured not by politics but by markets. And markets work systematically and routinely to promote school autonomy, effective school organization, and superior student achievement.

If we are correct, then, private schools have a very important lesson to teach public schools. If public schools are to improve— if they are to become more autonomous, better organized, and more effective—they must be freed from the political institutions that now control them and be subjected to the discipline of the market. Ultimately this is what makes private schools work, and it can make public schools work too. This is not to say that private school attendance should be promoted or that public schools should be encouraged to compete with private schools. In our view, public education itself should be fundamentally reformed. Public schools, like private schools, should be made to function in a marketplace where parents can choose among them and where each public school can decide how best to serve its students and parents. The current system of public education should be replaced, in other words, with a system of public school choice.

The purpose of this chapter is not to propose a specific reform, however. It is rather to show why reform of the public system should be based on an understanding of the private system. We have just completed a nationwide study of public and private high schools—*Politics, Markets, and America's Schools*—involving some 500 schools and over 20,000 students, teachers, and principals. Here we would like to highlight the differences between politics and markets—what each implies for school organization and performance—by contrasting public and private schools.

Authority and Decision Making

The place to begin in comparing politics and markets is with the distinctive ways in which the public and private sectors allocate authority over their schools and prescribe how it can be exercised. These properties set the foundation for educational decision making, determining who has the right to make what kinds of educational decisions in what ways.

The public sector is built around public authority. Democratic institutions allocate decision-making rights by attaching public authority to elected and appointed positions of government—for example, school board seats and superintendencies—and by setting out rules that specify who has a right to occupy these positions and how the authority attached to them must be exercised. The "winners" under these rules—including, implicitly, individuals and groups whose interests the officeholders represent—have the legal right to make public policies and to devise governmental structures that are binding on everyone in the polity. The "losers" have the obligation to accept and help finance these policies and structures however much they may be opposed to them.

In this sense, democracy is essentially coercive. The winners get to use public authority to impose their policies on the losers. On some issues, for example, teachers' unions might prevail over the opposition of administrators or parents. On others, business groups might succeed in imposing reforms fought by the unions. What makes this peculiar form of coercion broadly acceptable is that public authority does not belong to any individual or group. Anyone who plays by the rules and gains sufficient popular support has the same right as anyone else to take control of public authority and to specify the legitimate means and ends of public policy for everyone.

Public authority is also important for market institutions, but its role is far less central to decision making. For markets to operate, governments must create a legal framework that specifies and enforces property rights. They must use their public authority, in other words, to impose a system of rules for determining who owns what property and for assigning to owners the authority to make certain choices about its disposition. Once such a framework is created, individuals are free to enter into exchanges with one another as they see fit, and markets take over.

Effective authority within market settings, then, is radically decentralized. In private-sector education, the people who run each school decide what they will teach, how they will teach it, who will do the teaching, how much to charge for their services, and virtually everything else about how education will be organized and supplied. Students and parents assess the offerings, reputations, and costs of the various schools and make their own choices about which to attend. No one makes decisions for society. All participants in markets make decisions for themselves.

The kind of authority that market participants exercise, while public in origin, is extremely limited in scope. The owners of a school have the legal authority to create whatever kind of school they please, but they cannot require anyone to attend or finance it. They have authority over their own property, not over the property of others. Similarly, parents and students have the right to seek out whatever kinds of schools they like. But they cannot force schools to adopt specific courses, hire certain teachers, or pursue certain values. Nor can they force schools to grant them admission. They make decisions for themselves, not for the schools.

The key elements that supply the motivational foundation of democratic politics—the tremendous value, wide availability, and coercive power of public authority—are essentially absent from the marketplace. In markets, individuals and groups try to achieve their ends through voluntary exchange with others, and the benefits they receive arise from these transactions. In the private sector, the key to success—for school, parents, and students alike—is having something to offer that other people want.

Constituents and Consumers

Most everyone's first impulse is to think that the purpose of schools is to provide children with academic training, with essential information about society and the world, with an understanding of citizenship in a democracy, or something of the sort. On reflection, however, it should be apparent that schools have no immutable or transcendent purpose. What they are supposed to be doing depends on who controls them and what those controllers want them to do.

In the public sector, schools are controlled by whoever controls public authority. Popular myth, of course, lauds the role of local citizens and their elected school boards, but this is misleading. The public schools are not really locally controlled and are not supposed to be. The authority exercised by local governments is delegated to them by the states and can be modified or revoked at the states' pleasure. More generally, public authority over schools is legally vested in democratic institutions at all levels. State and federal governments—and their constituents—have legitimate roles to play in financing schools, setting standards, and otherwise making and imposing educational policies and organizational structures. This means that citizens everywhere, whether or not they have children in school and whether or not they live in the local school district or even the state, have a legitimate hand in governing each and every local school. They are all controllers.

The heterogeneous interests of all these constituents do not automatically find faithful reflection in the policies and structures of government. Democracy, like all other institutions, works imperfectly. Political resources are unequally distributed. The interest group system is biased in favor of some interests over others (the organized over the unorganized, especially). Politicians and administrators sometimes pursue their own interests at the expense of citizens' interests. And so on. As a result, who wins and who loses in politics is not necessarily representative of what ordinary citizens actually want.[1]

These are well-known problems that plague all democracies in one way or another, and they are the sorts of things that attract attention from many critics of American public education. They think the education system would be vastly improved if democracy's imperfections could somehow be overcome. Even if this were possible, however, the fact remains that democratic politics would still be a competitive struggle for the control of public authority. It would still be a game of winners and losers. On any given issue, the winners might include various combinations of interests: those of teachers' unions, associations of professionals, book publishers, ideological groups, or factions among the citizenry at large. But everyone cannot win, and the losers have to take what the winners dish out. This is the single most important thing to know about how interests get represented in a democracy. It is not an imperfection. It is what democratic control is all about.

Notice that we have said nothing so far about parents and students. The myth that parents and students are uniquely special in all this—that the schools are somehow supposed to be what parents and students want them to be—goes hand in hand with the myth of local control, and it is equally misleading. The proper constituency of even a single public school is a huge and heterogeneous one whose interests are variously represented by politicians, administrators, and groups at all levels of government. Parents and students are but a small part of this constituency.

A frequent complaint is that parents and students are not well enough organized to be very powerful. In the struggle to control public authority, they tend to be far outweighed by teachers' unions, professional organizations, and other entrenched interests that, in practice, have traditionally dominated the politics of education. This is true enough. But what it implies is that parents and students would get the kind of schools they want if they could somehow gain appropriate clout—if democracy, in other words, were less imperfect and did a better job of reflecting their interests. And this is simply not the case.

The fundamental point to be made about parents and students is not that they are politically weak but that, even in a perfectly functioning democratic system, the public schools are *not meant* to be theirs to control and are *not supposed* to provide them with the kind of education they might want. The schools are agencies of society as a whole, and everyone has a right to participate in their governance. Parents and students have a right to participate, too. But they have no right to win. In the end, they have to take what society gives them.

In the private sector, the situation of parents and students would appear to be worse still. There they have no legal right to control the schools at all. The authority to control each private school is vested in the school's owner—which may be an individual, a partnership, a church, a corporation, a nonprofit agency, or some other form of organization—and the owner has the legal right to make all the decisions about policy and structure that, in the public sector, are matters for "the people" and their representatives to struggle over. Despite the formal dominance of owners, however, markets work to ensure that parents and students play a much more central and influential role in private-sector education than they do when democracy gives them formal rights to govern. There are three basic reasons for this.

The first is that those who own and run the schools have a strong incentive to please a clientele of parents and students through the decisions they make. This sort of responsiveness is perhaps the most obvious path by which markets promote a match between what parents and students want and the kind of education the schools provide. It is not necessarily the most important, however.

The second arises from a basic prerequisite of market choice: people have the freedom to switch from one alternative to another when they think it would be beneficial to do so. If parents and students do not like the services they are being provided at any given school, they can exit and find another school whose offerings better meet their needs.[2] Even if schools were entirely unresponsive to their clienteles, then, this process of selection and sorting would tend to encourage a match between what parents and students want and the kind of education they receive.

The third arises from a basic property of markets that operates on the population of schools as a whole: natural selection.[3] Schools that fail to satisfy a sufficiently large clientele will go out of business (or, if subsidized, become an increasing burden to their patron organizations, generating pressures that work in the same direction). Of the schools that survive, those that do a better job of satisfying consumers will be more likely to prosper and proliferate. They may be joined or challenged at any time, moreover, by new schools that enter the marketplace to offer similar services in a better way, or perhaps to appeal to specialized segments of consumer demand that are not being met adequately. The dynamics of entry, success, and failure, driven by the requisites of parent-student support, all tend to promote the emergence of a population of schools that matches the population of parents and students.

A standard claim about public schools is that there are strong forces, including quasi-market forces, that tend to promote this kind of matching in them as well.[4] For instance, although the local public school is usually a monopoly, in the sense that all children living in a designated geographical area are typically assigned to a particular school, parents and students can still exercise exit and choice by taking account of school quality in deciding where to live. If they like the schools, they can move into the area. If they do not like them, they can move out.

It is true that residential mobility does tend to promote the kind of matching that occurs in markets, but it is a very rough and inadequate approximation to the real thing even for those citizens affluent enough to move where they want when they want. In general, residential decisions involve many factors in addition to education—proximity to work, quality of housing, availability of public services—and, once they are made, the financial costs and personal adjustments entailed by moving are quite high. Low or declining educational quality need not keep parents from moving into an area, and it is even less likely to prompt existing residents to pick up and leave.

It might prompt them to consider a private school—another exit option that would help drain off the disgruntled and improve the average satisfaction of those who are left in the public sector. But here parents confront a major disincentive: public schools are free, private schools are not. Because of this cost differential, the perceived value of private schools must far outweigh that of public schools if they are to win students. To put it the other way around: public schools, because they are relatively inexpensive, can attract and hold students without being particularly good at educating them.

Lacking feasible exit options, then, whether through residential mobility or escape into the private sector, many parents and students will choose a public school despite dissatisfaction with its goals, methods, personnel, and performance. Having done so, they have a right to try to remedy the situation through the democratic control structure. But everyone else has the same rights, and the determinants of political power are stacked against them. Democracy cannot remedy the mismatch between what parents and students want and what the public schools provide. Conflict and disharmony are built into the system.

While this is an inherent feature of democratic control, we do not mean to imply that markets are somehow capable of perfectly satisfying parents and students. Obviously, they are not. Markets are inevitably subject to all sorts of real-world imperfections—monopolizing, price fixing, uninformed consumer choice—just as democratic institutions are. These imperfections cannot be eliminated, though through government actions they can be reduced.

But it is a mistake to place too much emphasis on market imperfections, just as it is a mistake to be obsessed with the imperfections of democratic control. When it comes to the basic issue of whose interests find reflection in society's schools, these two systems clearly function under real-world conditions to promote very different social outcomes. Under a system of democratic control, the public schools are governed by an enormous, far-flung constituency in which the interests of parents and students carry no special status or weight. When markets prevail, parents and students are thrust onto center stage, along with the owners and staff of schools; most of the rest of society plays a distinctly secondary role, limited for the most part to setting the framework within which educational choices get made. These differences are absolutely fundamental to the two systems, however imperfectly each may work in practice.

Bureaucracy and Autonomy

So far, we have discussed how democratic control and markets allocate authority and attach weight to social interests. These are rather abstract concerns that may seem to have very little to do with something so concrete as the organization of schools. But in fact they have a great deal to do with it. To see why, let's turn to what many educators view as the most fundamental organizational issue facing the schools today: the issue of bureaucracy versus autonomy.

Markets: Decentralization and Discretion. While markets decentralize effective decision authority to the suppliers and consumers of services, they do not automatically give rise to organizational structures that are themselves decentralized. The economic system obviously boasts all sorts of organizational forms, some of them highly centralized bureaucracies in which subordinate levels of organization have little discretion. Presumably, an educational market system might do the same if centralized organization were an efficient way to supply educational services that satisfy parents and students.

As a rule, however, this is unlikely to be so. One very basic reason has to do with the technical requirements of producing educational services. Because education is based on personal relationships and interactions, on continual feedback, and on the knowledge, skills, and experience of teachers, most of the necessary technology and resources are inherently present in the school itself, and thus at the bottom of the organizational hierarchy (if there is one). Higher-level administrative units have much less to contribute.[5]

It is no accident, for example, that so much attention in both the academic literature and the policy-making process has focused on teacher professionalism. For true professionalism requires not simply that teachers be experts in their subject matters and the methodology of learning, but also that they have the autonomy to exercise discretion in applying it to the infinitely varying individuals and circumstances that make up their jobs. The widely accepted notion that education would be better if teachers were treated as professionals is but another way of saying that the schools already have (or should already have) what it takes to provide quality education—they just have to be allowed to use it.[6]

A second basic reason that centralization is unlikely to be efficient has to do with the purely administrative requirements of controlling education from above. Effective bureaucracy is commonly built around rules that specify appropriate behavior, rewards and sanctions that encourage such behavior, and monitoring to ascertain whether goals are being met, whether rules are being followed, when rewards and sanctions are called for, and whether rules and incentive systems need to be adjusted. All are rendered highly problematic in education because good education and the behaviors conducive to it are inherently difficult to measure in an objective, quantifiable, formal manner.[7] The measurement problem makes it difficult or impossible for education administrators to know what they are doing—and their controls, as a result, threaten to be ill-suited to the ends they want to achieve.

While virtually everyone in a given school typically knows who the good teachers are, for instance, their assessments arise from actual experience and judgment, not from formal tests of teaching competence. As teachers are quick to point out, there are no formal tests that can adequately tap the intangible qualities that make someone good or bad at the job, it is impossible to hand down a set of rules from on high that will somehow transform bad teachers into good ones, and it is organizationally counterproductive to reward and sanction teachers on grounds of merit.[8] For the most part, the people at the bottom of the hierarchy do not have a serious measurement problem. They essentially solve it without really trying, just by taking part in the everyday life of the school. The people at the top are the ones with the measurement problem. The organization as a whole has a serious measurement problem only to the extent that there are people at the top who try to control the people at the bottom.

A third reason why centralized organization is unlikely to

prove efficient arises from the market constraint that schools must, above all else, please their clients. The school staff members who interact with students and parents day in and day out are in a far better position than administrators to sense whether their clients are happy with the services they are getting. They are also better able to devise and implement whatever adjustments might be necessary to enhance the school's appeal. Again, they know what administrators cannot because it is a natural, integral part of their work in the schools.

A common assumption on the part of parents and students is that students need to be treated and understood as individuals if they are to make the most of their educational experience. Given the variety of human personalities and family environments, this happens to make good scientific sense as well.[9] Principals and teachers can get to know their students, gain a sense of their special needs and talents, and respond accordingly. Administrators cannot. Administrators "know" students in terms of numbers, categories, rules, summary statistics, theories, and methods, all of which leads to precisely the kind of treatment that parents and students do not want: treatment that is insensitive to what is different or special or unique about them. Bureaucracy inherently requires equal treatment for people who are in fact very different. Schools can recognize and respond to those differences—as long as they are unconstrained by bureaucracy.

In a market setting, then, there are strong forces at work—arising from the technical, administrative, and consumer-satisfaction requirements of organizational success—that promote school autonomy. Organizations that want to build and nurture successful schools will have incentives to decentralize authority to the school level. Similarly, schools that exist on their own, as well as individuals and groups that want to start schools from scratch, will tend to find that the requirements of success do not entail a highly bureaucratic organization—and indeed militate against it.

Politics: Bureaucracy and Hierarchical Control. In the public sector, the institutional forces work in the opposite direction. The raison d'être of democratic control is to impose higher-order values on schools and thus to limit their autonomy. The schools are not in the business of pleasing parents and students, and they cannot be allowed to set their own agendas. Their agendas are set by politicians, administrators, and the vast democratic constituencies that hold the keys to political power. The public system is built to see to it that the schools do what their governors want them to do—that they conform to the higher-order values their governors seek to impose.

Bureaucracy arises naturally and inevitably out of these efforts at democratic control. While most everyone seems to complain that the public schools are overly bureaucratized, American political institutions give all the major players strong incentives to pressure for more bureaucracy, not less, when official decisions get made about what the schools ought to be doing, who should be doing it, and how. The same people who complain about bureaucracy find that it is their dominant political strategy.

To see why, we must first recognize that public authorities do not have the luxury of creating an organization de novo. The Constitution and countless federal, state, and local laws made pursuant to it already set out a structure of democratic authority—a massive, fragmented, multilevel "organization" blanketing the entire country—in which various offices have certain rights to impose decisions on the local schools. There is no analog to the private-sector owner who exercises concentrated authority in designing an organization. Instead, there are multiple "owners"—authorities at the federal, state, and local levels—who all have legitimate roles to play within the existing "organization." They all have some authority to shape and control the schools, and they all come under pressure from organized groups and constituents to put their authority to use. The question is not whether they will use their authority, but how.

Consider the situation from the standpoint of those who exercise authority at the federal level. They are in a position to impose higher-order values on the schools through policies of their own choosing. For federal authorities to succeed, however, they must somehow ensure that their policies—which many people in local communities may flatly disagree with—get implemented as they want. They do not have any choice but to exercise hierarchical control. In doing so, they face some of the same technical problems—the bottom-heavy nature of education technology and the difficulty of measuring school performance—that private owners face. But they also face, as all government authorities do, two other kinds of problems that are especially severe because of the democratic "organization" in which their control efforts must take place. [10]

First, they cannot assume that principals and teachers will expertly harness their energies, talents, and resources toward federally imposed policies. If they had the authority, federal policy makers could act like private owners and choose their own principals and teachers on grounds of philosophy, personal goals, expertise, or even loyalty. But they do not have that authority, and they are unable to do much of anything to guarantee that their policies do not end up in the hands of school personnel who disagree with their goals, who find the prerequisites of effective implementation to be burdensome or objectionable, or who are simply not competent enough to be effective. [11] The misuse of federally granted discretion, therefore, can easily be serious and widespread. To make matters worse, federal authorities are far removed and cannot directly observe what is going on in each and every local school around the country. Thus they cannot easily tell where or when their grants of discretion are being put to bad use.

Second, these dangers of noncompliance and ineffectiveness are rendered far more threatening by the presence of multiple authorities within the democratic "organization." Any discretion left in the hands of school personnel is subject to legitimate influence and control by other democratic authorities at the state and local levels. These authorities have their own groups and constituencies to look out for and their own political interests to pursue. Given the opportunity, they can be expected to turn discretionary programs and federally supplied resources toward ends that may be at odds with federal intentions.

Given the widespread incentives and opportunities for noncompliance, the most attractive solution is simply to bureaucratize the implementation of policy. Through bureaucracy, federal officials can strategically reduce the discretion of school personnel by specifying the kinds of behaviors they want—and requiring them by law. They can insist on the adoption of specific practices, procedures, and decision criteria they think are most conducive to federal policy goals; they can impose information collecting, reporting, and monitoring requirements as means of holding schools accountable for their performance; and they can impose sanctions for noncompliance. It is no surprise that federal education programs are constantly criticized by lower-level authorities for being excessively bureaucratized.

The incentives to bureaucratize the schools are somewhat different for different levels of government. Those who exercise authority at the federal (especially) and the state levels, for instance, are farther away from what actually happens within the schools, have much larger and more diverse populations of schools (and personnel and competing authorities) to worry about, and are probably more prone to extensive formal controls than districts and other local governments are. But even at the local level, where consolidated city and county school systems serve large populations—sixty-two different school districts now serve at least 50,000 students each—there will still be strong incentives to pursue school-level compliance through an array of bureaucratic controls.

The general point is the important one: all public authorities, in seeking to impose higher-order values on schools—values that many in society, including many in the schools, may not embrace—face serious control problems that are endemic to the larger democratic "organization" in which they are forced to operate. They cannot solve these problems by granting the schools lots of discretion. Discretion is the very source of their problems. The best means of ensuring that their values get implemented is to engineer the schools' behavior through formal constraints—to bureaucratize.

From a technical standpoint, of course, this is far from ideal. Given the bottom-heavy technology of education and the measurement problems inherent in trying to control it, bureaucracy is a clumsy and ineffective way of providing people with educational services. Within the context of American democratic institutions, however, those who seek to impose higher-order values through public authority have no better options. Discretion and autonomy are out of the question. Bureaucratizing the schools is their best strategy.

The Organization and Performance of Schools

Now let us move from the general to the particular by considering what all this means for the specific features of school organization. To simplify school organization, we will take a look at four dimensions that are obviously quite basic and important to the performance of schools: personnel, leadership, goals, and practice.[12] These dimensions, like almost any others we might have employed, are bound up together and cannot be understood in isolation from one another. Nonetheless, we purposely begin our discussion with personnel, for it raises a fundamental distinction between political and market institutions—the role of teachers' unions—that we have yet to deal with explicitly, and, for reasons that will become apparent, it has a special role to play in promoting strikingly different syndromes of organization across sectors.

Personnel. In the public sector, principals are likely to find that their control over who works at their school and how staff incentives are structured is significantly limited. The reason is that personnel decisions are constrained, if not dictated, by formal rules designed and imposed by higher levels of government.

For the most part, these rules have two concrete sources. First, they arise from tenure laws, certification requirements, and other civil service–like protections enacted by public officials over the years to insulate teachers from political influence. These reforms—which, for reasons inherent in the democratic struggle, have long been widely endorsed by groups, politicians, and bureaucrats of all political stripes—put an end to the early use of schools for political patronage. They also ensured that principals would have limited discretion in choosing or motivating school personnel.

The second source of formalization is teachers' unions. When party machines reigned supreme in politics, teachers' unions were resisted by politicians wedded to spoils. But as the old arrangements of power broke down over time and party politics gave way to interest group politics, unions found powerful allies—and success. Organized teachers could offer money, manpower, publicity, and votes to politicians eager for electoral support; and, especially in state and local elections, where turnout is typically very low, these proved to be attractive inducements indeed. The transformation took decades, but eventually the vast majority of public school teachers came to be unionized, and unions came to be an established power in the politics of education.[13]

Most personnel matters are now subject to collective bargaining between the unions and the relevant public authorities, usually those representing the school district. Through collective bargaining, unions make demands for more pay, fringe benefits, and vacations. But they also demand that economic rewards be governed by formal rules that specify who gets what and when and that remove as many employee incentives as possible from the discretionary choice of "management." The notion that rewards might somehow be linked to merit is anathema, since merit cannot be measured objectively and any subjective assessment of merit threatens to put discretion in the hands of principals and other superiors.

Collective bargaining leads to formal contracts that specify, usually in excruciating detail and at spectacular length (a recent Philadelphia agreement ran 133 pages), the formal rights and obligations of both parties and the formal machinery by which these rights are to be implemented and enforced.[14] This translates directly into bureaucracy: rules governing organizational incentives, rules governing what teachers do, and rules governing how basic educational decisions must get made and who gets to make them. Unions use their power in collective bargaining to formalize public education and to eliminate managerial discretion.

The formalization of personnel has consequences for school organization that are so pervasive that their importance would be difficult to exaggerate. The alleged leader of the school, the principal, is purposely prevented from staffing the organization and arranging incentives according to his or her best judgment. The principal may value expertise, enthusiasm, collegiality, communication skills, creativity, facility in dealing with parents, special sensitivity to student problems, or any number of qualifications related to the school's goals—but the principal is prevented from taking effective action to obtain teachers who possess these qualifications and to eliminate those who do not. For the most part, the principal is stuck with the teachers the system provides. They are stuck with the principal. And the teachers are stuck with one another.

Serious disabilities are easy to anticipate. Aside from ham-fisted attempts by administrators to measure expertise, the qualifications crucial to good teaching—and the kinds of characteristics principals tend to value in building an effective staff—may have little to do with the formal criteria that determine who ends up teaching in a given school. And even if public officials and unions were moved to try to include these qualifications, they would find them impossible to formalize anyway. People at the school level know collegiality, enthusiasm, and sensitivity when they see them, but there is no way to devise a formal test that would take such assessments out of the domain of discretionary judgment. In a bureaucratic system dedicated to the elimination of discretion, especially on matters of personnel, all of the intangible properties so necessary for effective performance are ruled out and cannot be recruited or mobilized for the pursuit of school goals. The bureaucratization of personnel tends to ensure that public schools will lack the proper mix of talents on which effective education inherently depends.

It also tends to leave the school organization vulnerable to disunity and disarray. Teachers may reject the principal's leadership, dissent from school goals and policies, get along poorly with their colleagues, or fail to perform acceptably in the classroom—but they nonetheless have formal rights to their positions. Because personnel is likely to be heavily bureaucratized, there is no systematic way to screen out people who are bad fits, nor is there a systematic way to recruit and retain the kinds of people who would fit and function well together as a team. To make matters worse, principals are unlikely to be granted the formal tools of leadership that might allow them to create a team out of the motley crews the bureaucracy gives them.

In a market setting, things tend to be very different. The most general reason is that market forces give the owners of schools strong incentives not to organize bureaucratically but to grant their schools substantial autonomy instead. Now that we have considered in more explicit terms just how serious and far-reaching the consequences of bureaucratization may be, it is easier to appreciate why these incentives are as strong as they are. In the marketplace, where other schools compete for support and clients are free to go where they want, the bureaucratization of personnel is a good way to create an organization fraught with disabling problems, incapable of effective performance, and destined to fail.

Consider how different the organization of schooling is likely to be when personnel decisions are decentralized to schools and left to the discretion of principals. Under these conditions, principals can systematically recruit the kinds of teachers they want and weed out those they do not, giving weight to whatever qualifications have a direct bearing on organizational performance, regardless of how intangible or resistant to formalization they might be. Through this selection process, principals are in a position to create and maintain what can meaningfully be called a team—a group of teachers whose values, talents, backgrounds, and personalities mesh well together and promote the cooperative pursuit of organizational objectives.

All this can be systematically reinforced through the incentive structure: when the principal is able to make jobs, job assignments, and the rewards associated with them contingent on performance (in all its aspects, however intangible), teachers have strong incentives to be good team players on a continuing basis. This applies to all teachers, whatever their true qualifications. Teachers who initially lack expertise, finesse, or sensitivity in the classroom will be motivated to improve. Their motivation, moreover, will focus on actual performance and its determinants—not on "paper qualifications" like formal degrees and tests. These will tend to be seen for what they are: largely meaningless.

It might seem that teachers are destined to be the classic subordinates in this arrangement and principals the classic bosses, but this is not so. In the first place, owing largely to the technology of education, principals have incentives to grant teachers discretion in their work: the effectiveness and success of the organization are heavily dependent on their expertise and professional judgment. In the second place, and perhaps ironically, it is the principal's concentrated authority that frees him or her to do this aggressively and on a grand scale. Precisely because the principal is able to build a hand-picked team of "right-thinking" teachers whom he or she respects and trusts, teachers are not a threat to the principal's leadership. They are on the principal's side. And knowing that they are, the principal has every reason to take full advantage of what teachers have to offer by granting them substantial autonomy in their own spheres of expertise, encouraging their participation in decision making about important matters of school policy, and promoting a context of interaction, exchange of ideas, and mutual respect. The principal has every reason, in other words, to treat teachers as true professionals—and, indeed, to build the school around their professionalism.

The bureaucratization of personnel tends to rule out this distinctive form of organization and all its tremendous advantages, substituting a very different form plagued by serious, debilitating problems. The basic paths to formalization in the public sector—civil service protections and unions—therefore have little appeal to decision makers in the private sector. As a market strategy to attract good teachers, private schools could choose to offer tenure and other civil service-like protections, particularly given that public schools already offer these benefits. But if private schools can offer true professionalism and other attractive educational benefits—and there is every reason to believe that they can—they can attract good teachers without relying extensively on tenure or other formal protections. [15]

Similarly, teachers are free to join unions if they want to, and unions are free to try to organize them for collective bargaining. But unions operate at a serious disadvantage in a market setting. Teachers who are team players, who have lots of autonomy in their work, who routinely play integral roles in school decision making, and who are treated as professionals are hardly good candidates for union membership. On those occasions when a union does succeed in organizing a school, moreover, its achievements threaten to translate into higher labor costs and the bureaucratization of personnel, both of which take their tolls on the school and put it at a competitive disadvantage in the educational market. Unions do best in noncompetitive, protected, regulated settings—like government—where costs can simply be passed on and ineffectiveness has almost nothing to do with organizational survival. [16]

The extent to which personnel decisions are bureaucratized, then, is largely a reflection of the institutional settings in which schools find themselves. Because institutions of democratic control prevail in the public sector, personnel decisions for the public schools tend to be heavily bureaucratized. Because market forces are so important in the private sector, personnel decisions for private schools tend to be informal and discretionary. These institutional differences, in turn, have enormous consequences for schools—consequences that shape and pervade almost every important aspect of their organizations and combine to generate distinctly different organizational forms across sectors.

Goals. Although we will still use the terminology, it is a bit misleading to say that the public schools have goals. They are public agencies, and, as the word "agency" implies, their role is to take action on behalf of others: the citizens, organized groups, politicians, and bureaucrats who have the authority to specify what the schools should be trying to accomplish and how. The schools do not really set their own goals, especially in an institutional system dedicated to reducing their discretion on all matters that really count. Their goals are largely contained in the laws and regulations by which the higher-order values of their democratic authorities are formally imposed on them.

What can we say, then, about the nature of these goals? First, they are almost countless in number. Schools are legally bound to honor and be constrained by all laws and regulations on the books—local, state, and federal. Many of these explicitly deal with educational policies and practices. But many have nothing directly to do with education at all—those dealing with due process rights, for instance. In sheer magnitude, the set of goals that schools are expected to pursue is overwhelming.

Second, there is no necessary coherence to the overall structure of school goals. In politics, whoever gains public authority can impose almost anything on the schools, regardless of what has been imposed by others in the past or might be imposed in the future. Schools can therefore be asked to move in every direction at once, from sex education to psychological counseling to the socialization of immigrants to vocational training to desegregation to mainstreaming of the disabled to bilingual education. Somewhere in all this, they are also expected to provide students with academic excellence.

Third, school goals will tend to be weak and watered-down, owing to the huge, heterogeneous constituency of public education and the necessity for political compromise. Thus schools will be directed to pursue academic excellence, but without making courses too difficult; they will be directed to teach history, but without making any value judgments; they will be directed to teach sex education, but without taking a stand on contraception or abortion. They must make everyone happy by being all things to all people—just as politicians try to do.

None of this has anything to do with public school principals and teachers lacking standards or somehow having no sense of what good education is all about. It is an institutional matter, a matter of authority and constituency. Principals and teachers do not have the authority to set basic school goals—far-flung, diverse constituencies do. School goals therefore tend to be piled on until they are so numerous, incoherent, and diluted that they provide teachers and principals with no clear sense of mission and no foundation for working together as a team. When schools lack mission, when there is no meaningful way of saying what it is they are supposed to accomplish—how is it possible, even in principle, for principal and teachers to create an effective organization? Effective for what?

In the private sector, schools do not have to be all things to all people. To be successful, they need to find their niche—a specialized segment of the market to which they can appeal and attract support. The obvious way to do this is through the strategic design of their curriculum. They might offer a broadly based liberal arts education, for instance, or they might specialize in math and science, in the dramatic arts, in the humanities, in vocational education, or in almost anything else that a clientele of parents and students might value. They are also free to target their appeals to other value dimensions: discipline, religion, theories of learning, the socioeconomic and ethnic makeup of the student body, school or class size, athletics and other extracurricular activities, perspectives on personal growth, sensitivity to particular cultures and languages—the list could go on until it exhausts the educational concerns of parents and students.

As a population, schools in a market setting tend to reflect a full, heterogeneous range of educational concerns. The goals of individual schools, however, tend to be far simpler, clearer, and more homogeneous than those of the typical public school—for they are intended to appeal only to a portion of the market, and perhaps a very small and highly specialized portion. Their goals are also more likely to have true intellectual coherence—for they are not ad hoc collections of value impositions but packages that are consciously designed to constitute an integrated whole. The market allows and encourages its schools to have distinctive, well-defined missions.

This vastly simplifies the job of organizing an effective school. Schools know what they want to accomplish, and they can consciously design their organizations in ways that appear best suited to accomplishing it. They can match organizational means to organizational ends. They may make mistakes in the process, but they have strong incentives to try to correct these over time by moving toward structures better suited to their goals—and if they falter, the marketplace will penalize them and ultimately put them out of business.

Leadership. Much of what we need to know about leadership is already implicit in our discussions of personnel and goals. Private school principals are likely to be in a position to lead their organizations. They may not succeed, but they should have the tools and the flexibility to do what leaders need to do. Public school principals, on the other hand, are systematically denied much of what it takes to lead.

It may be better to think of the public school principal as a lower-level manager than as a leader. In the public sector, the principal is a bureaucrat with supervisory responsibility for a public agency. Most of the important decisions about policy have been taken by higher authorities: they set the goals, and the principal is expected to administer them. Many of the important structural decisions are also taken by higher authorities: the principal is bound by all sorts of formal rules and regulations that dictate aspects of internal structure. And many of the important personnel decisions are imposed from above as well: the principal is unlikely to have much control over the choice of teachers or the incentives that motivate them. The real leaders of the public school are the authorities, not the principal.

Most of the high-level rhetoric about the importance of the principal's leadership role is essentially just that. The fact is that those who succeed in exercising public authority want principals to behave more like bureaucrats than leaders. Authorities want principals to ensure that formal hierarchical directives are put into effect; they do not want principals to exercise real discretion. The public system is set up accordingly. The position of principal is a bureaucratic office in a recognized hierarchy of offices. People who desire advancement within the educational system begin as teachers—the lowliest of bureaucrats—then advance up the ladder to assistant principal, then principal, then into the district office as assistant superintendent, and so on. They are on a career track, and the principalship is one step along the way. Doing a good job as principal qualifies one for advancement.

The nature of the job and its career path inevitably generate a process of selective attraction. People who like administrative work and who desire advancement in an administrative hierarchy tend to be attracted to the job, while people who want to be genuine leaders tend to be turned off. Once in the job, moreover, the incentives promote behavior that is classically bureaucratic. Doing a good job, and thus doing what is necessary to get ahead, requires playing by the rules, implementing them as faithfully and effectively as possible—and staying out of trouble. The easiest way to get into trouble is to launch bold, aggressive, innovative moves: discretionary acts of leadership that are bound to be threatening to the interests of someone, somewhere, in a position of political power.

In a market setting, the basic forces run the other way. For all the reasons that bureaucracy in general is discouraged, the role of principal tends not to be a bureaucratic one. While important policy decisions may still be taken by owners or governing boards, they have incentives to decentralize and thus to grant principals the discretion and resources necessary for leadership. What successful leadership calls for, in terms of specific behaviors, will vary with the circumstances. A school that occupies a stable, supportive niche in the parent-student environment may call for a conservative emphasis on continuing the package of offerings, structures, and personnel that have worked in the past. A school whose niche is in flux, however, or that has attractive opportunities to move into new niches, may require more dynamic, innovative leadership.

While the hallmarks of effective leadership can be expected to vary, the technology of education and its market setting should tend to impose an important uniformity. Principals, like their own superiors, will have incentives to exercise leadership by decentralizing—which means, as we have discussed, building a team based on professionalism, high interaction, and shared influence. Another way of putting this is that effective leadership in a market setting should be heavily oriented toward teaching. Team-building requires that principals know their teachers well, know what happens in the classrooms, understand what good teaching is all about, and employ the substantial—but largely intangible—human capital of teachers to the school's best advantage. Success does not call for a power struggle. Nor does it call for a supreme administrator. It calls for effective leadership—which, in turn, calls for a firm anchoring in the profession, culture, and everyday experience of teaching.

Practice. "Practice" refers to what principals and teachers, especially the latter, do in the performance of their jobs. It refers to the various behaviors by which programs are carried out, services provided, and children taught. It therefore includes most of the activities within a school that are directly related to education and is the most immediate determinant of a school's effectiveness. From the standpoint of the people involved, not surprisingly, it tends to be regarded as the crucial difference between success and failure: "practice" is what education is all about. Given the bottom-heavy technology of education, we can only agree. But we must add a caveat: the form that educational practice takes in any given school is not simply a matter of what seems to work best but is largely a reflection of the other aspects of organization we have already discussed—personnel, goals, and leadership—and the institutional setting that shapes them all.

In the public sector, the whole thrust of democratic politics is to formalize and constrain educational practice. As public authority is captured and put to use by various interests over time, the discretionary exercise of professional judgment is systematically curtailed, and the practice of education is transformed into an exercise in administration. Because technical concerns remain important to those who make political decisions, all discretion is not eliminated. Moreover, because so much technical and operational knowledge is concentrated at the lower reaches of the organization, in people whose professional sensibilities are violated by formal constraint, hierarchical control is inevitably imperfect: teachers will subtly be able to evade some of the rules without detection or punishment.

Nonetheless, the public world of educational practice is a world of rules imposed on the schools by local, state, and federal authorities. Some of these specify what teachers are to do and how they are to do it—rules about curriculum, about instructional methods, about the design of special programs, about textbooks, about time spent on various activities, about what can and cannot be discussed. In addition, there are all sorts of rules—monitoring and reporting rules—designed to ensure that teachers are doing these things and not evading hierarchical control. Thus teachers are doubly constrained in their efforts to perform their educational tasks as they see fit. First, they are required to follow rules that cause them to depart from what they might otherwise do, and thus to behave in ways that contradict or fail to take advantage of their professional expertise and judgment. Second, they are required to spend time and effort documenting, usually through formal paperwork, that they have in fact followed these rules. The combination may leave little room for them to do the kind of teaching they think they ought to be doing.

In a market setting, principals and teachers are likely to have a great deal of discretion in determining school practices. In putting that discretion to use, they need not be driven to adopt practices whose major justification is that they avoid offending anyone. Schools can be clear, bold, and controversial in the practices they adopt as long as they attract a specialized clientele that values what they do. They are free, in particular, to adopt whatever practices they consider most suitable to the effective pursuit of the school's mission—and they have strong incentives, as we have seen, to do just that by building an organizational team that enables a school to take advantage of the expertise and judgment of its teachers.

Given the segmentation of market demand and the diversity of views among professionals, the population of private schools is likely to reflect a rich heterogeneity of educational missions and practices. Some schools may base their appeal on academic rigor, but others may put their emphasis elsewhere—on personal growth, say, or artistic expression—and their practices may vary quite dramatically as a result. Similarly, schools that pursue academic rigor may choose to approach it in different ways—some through a highly structured curriculum and lots of homework and discipline, others through more fluid, open-ended processes encouraging discovery and creativity. Amidst all this organizational diversity in the marketplace, however, the hallmark of the individual school is likely to be organizational coherence: a coherent mission, a coherent set of practices, a close and productive fit between the two—and a professional dynamic that continuously seeks to maintain their intellectual integrity.

Conclusion: The Institutional Perspective

The theoretical road we have traveled in this chapter has been rather long and complicated, taking us from the institutional foundations of politics and markets to their general implications for bureaucracy and autonomy in schools to their more specific implications for personnel, goals, leadership, and practice. The purpose of all this, however, has been to say something quite simple and general about how schools can be better understood—and how, on that basis, they might be made more effective.

Schools, we believe, are products of their institutional settings. America's public schools are governed by institutions of direct democratic control, and their organizations bear the indelible stamp of those institutions. They tend to be highly bureaucratic and systematically lacking in the requisites of effective performance. Private schools, on the other hand, operate in a very different institutional setting distinguished by the basic features of markets—decentralization, competition, and choice—and their organizations bear a very different stamp as a result. All things being equal, private schools tend to possess the autonomy, clarity of mission, strong leadership, teacher professionalism, and team cooperation that public schools want but (except under very fortunate circumstances) do not develop.

The primary lesson to be drawn from this comparison is not that private schools are inherently better than public schools. For—as we explain in the conclusion to our book—there is every reason to believe that, with the right governing institutions, the public schools could be disposed to develop these same effective school organizations. The differences between schools in the two sectors do not arise from immutable public-private differences. They arise from institutional differences. And this is the primary lesson. It is a lesson about the pervasive ways in which institutions shape the organization and performance of *all* schools, about the value of understanding schools from an institutional perspective—and about the crucial role that institutions and institutional reform ought to play in the thinking of those who want to improve America's schools.

Notes

1. The reasons for this are the basis for many now classic works on interest group theory, such as Mancur Olson, *The Logic of Collective Action: Public Goods and the Theory of Groups* (Cambridge, Mass.: Harvard University Press, 1965); Grant McConnell, *Private Power and American Democracy* (New York: Knopf, 1966); and Theodore J. Lowi, *The End of Liberalism: The Second Republic of the United States,* 2d ed. (New York: Norton, 1979).

2. The concept of exit is developed generally in Albert O. Hirschman, *Exit, Voice, and Loyalty: Responses to Decline in Firms, Organizations, and States* (Cambridge, Mass.: Harvard University Press, 1970).

3. The importance of natural selection in economic markets was first explicated in Armen A. Alchian, "Uncertainty, Evolution, and Economic Theory," *Journal of Political Economy* 58 (June 1950): 211–21.

4. See Charles M. Tiebout, "A Pure Theory of Local Expenditures," *Journal of Political Economy* 64 (October 1956): 416–24; and Paul E. Peterson, *City Limits* (Chicago: University of Chicago Press, 1981).

5. On the crucial importance of what goes on inside of schools—and on how little is known about this by administrators and policy makers—see especially John I. Goodlad, *A Place Called School: Prospects for the Future* (New York: McGraw-Hill, 1984); Michael W. Sedlack, Christopher W. Wheeler, Diana C. Pullin, and Philip A. Cusick, *Selling Students Short: Classroom Bargains and Academic Reform in the American High School* (New York: Teachers College Press, 1986); and James

P. Comer, "Educating Poor Minority Children," *Scientific American* 259 (November 1988): 42–48.

6. On the importance of professionalism, see especially Carnegie Forum on Education and the Economy, Task Force on Teaching as a Profession, *A Nation Prepared: Teachers for the 21st Century* (Washington, D.C.: Carnegie Forum on Education and the Economy, 1986); and Holmes Group Executive Board, *Tomorrow's Teachers: A Report of the Holmes Group* (East Lansing, Mich.: Holmes Group Executive Board, 1985).

7. On the measurement problems in regulating teaching and schooling, see Sedlack and others, *Selling Students Short*, chap. 8; and, especially, Eric A. Hanushek, "The Economics of Schooling: Production and Efficiency in Public Schools," *Journal of Economic Literature* 24 (September 1986): 1141–77.

8. The experiences of school districts with merit pay illustrate the difficulties of arriving at performance measures that are mutually agreeable to school authorities and teachers. See, for example, David K. Cohen and Richard J. Murnane, "The Merits of Merit Pay," *Public Interest* 80 (Summer 1985): 3–30.

9. This is especially true where family circumstances deviate from the professional mainstream, such as in ghettos. See especially Comer, "Educating Poor Minority Children."

10. These problems and the measurement problems referred to earlier are problems of agency. See, for example, Oliver E. Williamson, *The Economic Institution of Capitalism* (New York: Free Press, 1985); and Terry M. Moe, "The New Economics of Organization," *American Journal of Political Science* 28 (November 1984): 739–77.

11. We should point out that, because of tenure laws, civil service restrictions, unions, and collective bargaining agreements, officials at state and even local levels find themselves in much the same bind.

12. The importance of these dimensions is stressed in "effective schools" research, as surveyed in Stewart C. Purkey and Marshall S. Smith, "Effective Schools: A Review," *Elementary School Journal* 83 (March 1983): 427–52.

13. On teachers' unions, see Myron Lieberman, *Beyond Public Education* (New York: Praeger, 1986); and Susan Moore John-

son, *Teacher Unions and the Schools* (Cambridge, Mass.: Harvard University, Institute for Educational Policy Studies, 1982).

14.   "Agreement between the Board of Education, School District of Philadelphia, and the Philadelphia Federation of Teachers, Local 3, American Federation of Teachers, AFL-CIO, September 1, 1985–August 31, 1988" (Philadelphia Federation of Teachers).

15.   According to our data, tenure is offered in only 24 percent of Catholic high schools, 39 percent of elite high schools, and 17 percent of other independent and sectarian private high schools. John E. Chubb and Terry M. Moe, "Politics, Markets, and the Organization of Schools," *American Political Science Review* 82 (December 1988): 1065–87, cited on p. 1075.

16.   While most public schools are unionized, only about 10 percent of all Catholic schools are unionized. Other private schools appear to be not unionized at all. Chubb and Moe, "Politics, Markets, and the Organization of Schools," p. 1075.

23

Politics, Markets, and American Schools: A Rejoinder

Albert Shanker and Bella Rosenberg

There is no question that America's public education system is in need of fundamental reform. In fact, there is unusual agreement that the system is not producing citizens who can perform at the levels they and this nation need to be successful. Businesses complain that recent graduates can't read, write, reason, or even behave well enough to do the work they've been hired for. Colleges and universities bewail the enormous number of freshmen who need remedial classes before they can begin college-level work. The nation's governors and President Bush are so alarmed about the economic consequences of poor student achievement that they convened an unprecedented "education summit" in September 1989 and issued a set of national education goals, the first in our history. And lest anyone doubt the basis for this widespread concern, a stack of national and cross-national test results confirms these low estimations of the achievement of American students.

So this much is clear: public education is in bad shape. But what exactly is the reason for our crisis in educational productivity? And what do we need to do to overcome that crisis?

In "Why Markets Are Good for Education" and, more elaborately, in their book, *Politics, Markets, and America's Schools*, John Chubb and Terry Moe claim they have the answers to these vexing questions. The reason for our education crisis is nothing less than our system of democratic control of public schools, which, they argue, leads "naturally and inevitably" to bureaucratization and thus works "systematically and routinely, despite everyone's best intentions" to thwart effective school organization.[1] And the reason we ought to be so alarmed about this impact of democratic control on school organization, Chubb and Moe contend, is because effective school organization is a leading cause of high school student achievement; in fact, they say, it even explains why private schools outperform public schools. It follows that if democratic control is antithetical to effective school organization, then overcoming our crisis in educational productivity means abandoning democratic control. Public schools, Chubb and Moe conclude, "must be freed from the political institutions that now control them and be subjected to the discipline of the market. Ultimately this is what makes private schools work, and it can make public schools work too."[2] They call the plan they devise "public school choice." It is more commonly known as privatization at public expense.

This is bracing and powerful stuff. America has been struggling for generations to find the explanations for poor student achievement and the keys to school improvement. During this seven-year period of education reform alone, hundreds of policy initiatives were justified or attacked on the basis of one or more of the dozens of prevailing explanations for our low educational productivity. Now, however, the search may be over, the debates resolved. For Chubb and Moe have cut through all the competing explanations like Occam's razor. They've found one root cause, democratic control of schools, and therefore one root reform—the "panacea" they call it—market control of schools.

The question is, are they right?

The answer depends on a number of things. First, does our system of democratic control of schools thwart effective school organization? Second, does market control also have inherent defects—an issue that Chubb and Moe dismiss—or is democratic control the only system that inevitably produces problems? Third, have Chubb and Moe empirically demonstrated, as they claim to have done, that effective school organization is a leading cause of high student achievement? And are they correct that private schools outperform public schools, and, if so, that the reason is their more effective organization? In sum, have they proven their case that we ought to embrace market control of schools because that will yield us higher student achievement and a solution to our educational crisis?

Does Democratic Control of Schools
Undermine Effective School Organization?

Effectively organized schools, Chubb and Moe believe, are marked by clear goals, strong leadership, professional teachers, high academic expectations of students, and a coherent, team approach to education. They further believe that if schools are to develop and maintain these qualities, they must have autonomy or freedom from bureaucratic rules and regulations. To the extent that our system of democratic control of schools encourages bureaucratization—and Chubb and Moe say it is a considerable extent—it discourages effective school organization.

It is easy to agree with the proposition that bureaucracy inhibits the development of effective school organizations. Running schools according to centrally promulgated rules and regulations elevates following procedures over thinking about the outcomes of those procedures. One result is a rigid, one-size-fits-all system that does not happen to fit the vast majority of our kids because they don't happen to conform to the model's specifications. Another result is to make creativity, flexibility, and responsiveness—thought itself—seem like maverick activities instead of standard, professional behavior. And the end result is a system that does not work very well for either the students or the staff in our schools.

This realization is behind the most recent stage of our education reform movement. It is behind the movement to "professionalize" or "empower" teachers. It informs the latest round of decentralization efforts. It is the rationale for experiments with school-based management and shared decision making. And it is the foundation of recent discussions about establishing outcome levels for schools, experimenting with incentives, and leaving virtually all decisions about the way to run schools in the hands of school personnel.

One would think that Chubb and Moe would approve of

these developments, consistent as they are with their beliefs about effective schools. And they do mention a number of them approvingly. But in the final analysis, they say, these efforts will fail. The officials of a democratically controlled school system may grant greater autonomy today, but they are sure to withdraw it tomorrow, or whenever the first inevitable complaint or problem materializes. No matter how promising the reform, they say, our system of democratic control of schools will end by bureaucratizing and, finally, destroying it.

How does this system work? On the local level, democratic control means that school board members who are interested in holding onto office have to respond to pressures from various constituencies. The "winners"—both the school board members who achieve office and the constituencies with the most power—get to impose their policies on others, while the "losers" have to live with (and help finance) the results.

So how does this inevitably lead to bureaucratization and ineffective schools? To make sure that the people in the schools carry out the mandates of the successful groups, Chubb and Moe explain, there have to be programs embodying the mandates, regulations specifying how these programs are to be carried out, and a bureaucracy to administer the programs and check on compliance with the regulations. In time, there will be new demands and new winners and losers in school politics and, therefore, new programs. New programs, however, rarely displace old ones altogether. Instead, the new programs, with their new goals, new mandates, and new regulations, take their place beside the old ones and create additional bureaucratic snarls and instructional knots. Inevitably, too, in politics, demands conflict with each other and compromises are made, so that programs are likely to embody a little bit of everyone's goals or no clear goals at all. One result, then, of democratic control is to make schools responsible for implementing multiple, contradictory, and vague sets of goals, programs, and regulations. Another result is a severe constraint on the autonomy of school personnel. And the ultimate results are ineffective school organizations and thus ineffective schools.

There is no question that Chubb and Moe have provided one of the most lucid and powerful accounts of public school governance. Their descriptions, especially of local school politics, ring true to experience. Their analysis uncovers a clarifying logic to the illogical world of educational policy making. And the relationship they reveal between our system of democratic control and the capacity of school organizations to be effective breaks new ground in explaining why there are so many changes in schools but real change is so difficult to achieve.

Still, uncovering the limitations of our *particular* system of democratic control of schools is not the same thing as proving that democratic control per se is incompatible with effective schools. Nor does it justify the conclusion that democratic control is unreformable and must therefore be abandoned for market control of schools. Indeed, rather than endorsing market control, Chubb and Moe's analysis might just as logically have concluded that the way to protect schools from the pernicious effects of direct democratic control is to shift control of schools to larger and more distant units of government.

For example, why not get rid of local school boards and put schools under the authority of mayors or county executives? It is true that these officials have to get elected, just like school board members must. But mayors and county executives, unlike school board members, are not elected for education alone. And because they're responsible for a broad range of services, they are able to take some heat on any one of them, especially if they're doing pretty well in other areas. Moreover, they are able to give their appointees greater autonomy and protection from the day-to-day interference from interest groups. In short, many of the problems Chubb and Moe attribute directly to democratic control may instead be a result of the unusual accessibility and vulnerability of schools. And this is something that can be altered without resorting to market control.

Similarly, Chubb and Moe's analysis might just as well be used as an argument for changing the operation and powers of local school boards. Suppose that instead of meeting once or twice a month, school boards met once or twice a year to set and evaluate broad policies? This is something like the way the boards that run universities or corporations or private schools work, and with few apparent difficulties. And suppose these boards turned the other operations of the schools over to the people who worked in them instead of micro-managing? Or suppose state boards of education worked this way and local school boards were merely an administrative arm of state boards? And suppose further that individual schools had discretion over how to implement higher-order policies and needed only to report on outcomes?

Perhaps none of these ideas would work, but that is not the point. Rather, it is to illustrate that democratic control operates on a continuum. In this view, our present system of school governance is at one, near extreme end of that continuum, while different systems of democratic control, here and abroad, represent other points on the continuum. To pretend, then, as Chubb and Moe do, that we either have to live with the poor performance of our present public schools or plunge into the bracing, uncharted waters of market schools is not only irresponsible, it is dangerous.

It is also apparent that not even Chubb and Moe are entirely convinced that direct democratic control is the major culprit in our educational crisis. If our system of democratic control inevitably leads to bureaucratization, and if this is why public schools don't develop effective organizations and thus don't produce high levels of student achievement, then we would expect the effects of our system to be near universal. Yet this turns out not to be the case.

Take the example of democratically controlled suburban school districts. Suburban public schools, Chubb and Moe tell us, have more effective organizations and thus higher student achievement than urban schools. So why doesn't direct democratic control work its inherently pernicious effects on suburban school systems and schools?[3]

The answer Chubb and Moe give is instructive: suburban schools operate in relatively homogeneous, stable, and problem-free environments, so they are far less bureaucratized than urban schools. Suddenly, then, it is not direct democratic control per se that inevitably produces bureaucracy, ineffective school organizations, and poor student achievement. Instead, diversity and problem-laden environments are responsible! Chubb and Moe put it this way:

> The nation's large cities are teeming with diverse, conflicting interests of political salience—class, race, eth-

nicity, language, religion—and their schools are plagued by problems so severe, wide-ranging, and deeply rooted in the urban socioeconomic structure that the situation appears out of control and perhaps even beyond hope. Urban environments are heterogeneous and problem filled in the extreme. . . . It is important to stress that the capacity of some public schools to develop reasonably healthy, effective organizations does not imply that all public schools can somehow do so. The fact is, suburban schools are lucky. They are more likely to be blessed with relatively homogeneous problem-free environments, and, when they are, their organizations should tend to benefit in all sorts of ways as a result.[4]

To those who value America's diversity and pluralism and who believe that it is extreme poverty rather than heterogeneity that bedevils its cities, this is shocking stuff.[5] It does, however, help explain why Chubb and Moe never consider alternative forms of democratic control of schools and insist that market control is the only solution to our educational problems. And that is because markets, by their very nature, strive to separate diverse individuals into homogeneous groups.

The Nature of Markets

This bald statement about markets is something that any economist or businessman would confirm. It is the way markets are supposed to and, by and large, do work. By its very nature, then— and not by overt discriminatory policies—market control of schools would separate students by class, race, political power, level of achievement, or behavior.

Chubb and Moe are fully aware of the differentiating effect of markets but give it only a benevolent spin. They write repeatedly about how market control enables private schools to "please" their clients, "satisfy" them, "fulfill" their "interest," "tastes," "needs," and "wants." And, by advocating a publicly funded market school system, they are saying that the primary purpose of taxing American citizens for education should be to fulfill private interests rather than to pursue the public interest. Furthermore, they note repeatedly how market control gives private schools incentives to stake out a particular niche because that is the way you attract particular clients. They observe disapprovingly that democratic control forces public schools to try to be all things to all people— and, in an environment of diversity, that's all too many different people and things. And they tell us approvingly that private schools are under no such obligations: they merely must please their targeted segment of the school market.

But how is this done in private schools? As is the case with market control in the economy, it occurs by differentiating product and price. But unlike market control in the economy, where generally only the customers choose, market schools also get to choose their customers using admissions policies that operate according to different criteria, depending on the school. Thus, while anyone whose needs or tastes in cars run to Rolls-Royces can buy one so long as he can pay the price, not everyone who can afford the price of admission to a particular private school can get in. You may have to be the right religion; you may have to be a high achiever; you may have to produce evidence that you're not a discipline problem; you may have to pass muster as someone who can "fit" with the school's philosophy, curricular emphasis, or existing student body. To be sure, unlike the Rolls-Royce customer, you may not have to be able to afford the price of tuition because scholarships sometimes are available. But you *must* meet the school's objective and subjective criteria.

Private schools must exclude, either in whole or in part, the types of students and parents that will not fit well with their existing student and parent body—their market niche—lest their established clientele leave. This is not mean-spiritedness; this is business, and to do otherwise is to incur a risk. The Rolls-Royce manufacturer and dealer may have a similar concern, but if, for example, they worry that their product will be socially devalued if too many of the wrong kinds of rich people drive their car, they can't legally do a thing about it; private schools, on the other hand, are under no such constraints. And this capacity to exclude, through admissions criteria, as well as by product and price, is central to their existence.

Is this the type of public school system Chubb and Moe are after? Yes, although they do not say so directly in their article. All their readers are told is that "private schools have a very important lesson to teach public schools" and that the "current system of public education should be replaced . . . with a system of public school choice."[6]

Now, "public school choice" is a widely used phrase these days. To most people it conjures up a policy of allowing parents to choose which *public* schools their children will attend rather than being forced to accept a public school assignment based on residence. Typically, the only constraints on such a choice are space available and, if applicable, racial balance. The major exceptions to this rule are the few public schools that require entrance examinations and some thematic magnet schools. But by and large, public schools under a public school choice scheme must continue to be open to all students, and all of them must continue to observe federal, state, or local laws or regulations pertaining to school personnel, students, academic curriculum matters, and so on.

As their book makes explicit, however, this is not exactly the kind of public school choice system Chubb and Moe are recommending. To begin with, their plan is not confined to public schools. Any existing or future private school that wishes to accept public funds may do so; they need only meet the new criteria a state would establish for what constitutes a "public school" under the new system. "These criteria," write Chubb and Moe, "should be quite minimal, roughly corresponding to the criteria many states now employ in accrediting private schools"—in other words, practically none.[7]

Although many Americans would call this policy privatization, Chubb and Moe reject this label. Participating private schools, they say, simply would be reclassified as public schools, although they would be subject to no more, and perhaps less, public regulation and accountability than they were before. But what exactly do Chubb and Moe mean? "Our guiding principle in the design of a choice system," they say, "is this: public authority must be put to use in creating a system that is almost entirely beyond the reach of public authority."[8]

Telling as this statement is, it still does not tell us whether Chubb and Moe's new "public" school system would be able to operate like the private school system. We already know it would differentiate by product, which public schools of choice may also do. But would it also exclude both by price and through admissions criteria? The answer is not exactly so in procedure but almost identically so in principle and effect.

Take the example of how this new "public" school system would be funded. According to Chubb and Moe, local arms of a state "Choice Office" would give these new "public" schools, along with any public schools that district governments may continue to run, scholarship money based on the number of students that chose them; scholarships would be an aggregate of local, state, and federal funds. Chubb and Moe then make some worthy recommendations for an equalization approach to funding that would guarantee students in all districts, and not just wealthy ones, "an adequate financial foundation."[9] They even recommend that, for the sake of equity, parents not be allowed to supplement their children's scholarships with personal funds and that students with special educational needs be given larger scholarships (albeit using state and federal funds already targeted to these students).

But then they begin to backtrack. "Complete equalization," they say, "strikes us as too stifling and restrictive. A reasonable trade-off, we believe, is to allow for collective add-ons (much as the current system does). The citizens of each district can be given the freedom to decide whether they want to spend more per child than the state requires them to spend. They can then determine how important education is to them and how much they are willing to tax themselves for it. This means that children from different districts may have different-sized scholarships."[10]

Neutral language notwithstanding, what this really means, as we know from its direct analogue in the current system, is that even if poor and wealthy districts value education equally and tax themselves at the same rate (a hardship for poor districts), the result will be fatter scholarships for children from wealthy districts. Apparently, then, there are certain features of the present system of democratic control of schools that Chubb and Moe do like, and one of them is the public cousin of the private market: the greater purchasing power that wealthy districts possess.

Chubb and Moe also recommend that the schools themelves be permitted to set their own tuitions.

> They may choose to do this explicitly—say, by publicly announcing the minimum scholarship they are willing to accept. They may also do it implicitly by allowing anyone to apply for admission and simply making selections, knowing in advance what each applicant's scholarship amount is. In either case, schools are free to admit students with different-sized scholarships, and they are free to keep the entire scholarship that accompanies each student they have admitted. This gives all schools incentives to attract students with special needs, since these children will have the largest scholarships. It also gives schools incentives to attract students from districts with high base-level scholarships. But no school need restrict itself to students with special needs, nor to students from a single district. [11]

Just like private schools, then, the new "public" schools will be able to differentiate not only by product but through price. Indeed, the only difference between this "public" school system and private schools, or any other markets as we know them, is that *individual* parents would not be permitted to spend their personal funds on tuition. And if these "public" schools can differentiate by price much as private schools do, then by the inherent logic of the market they will differentiate in other ways, as well.

They will recognize that children with special needs cost a lot to educate, probably even more than the amount represented by their "larger scholarships." Or if they believe they can do this within costs, the thought will occur to them that if they cut down on services, they can use student scholarship funds for other purposes, like advertising for more students or supplementing staff salaries or buying nice furniture—all of which is perfectly legitimate in Chubb and Moe's plan. Or they may even decide that it does not pay to attract students with special needs at all, no matter how large their scholarships, because doing so may repel students with higher base-level scholarships, who are likely to be from wealthier districts and thus likely to pose fewer problems and challenges and be less costly to educate. They will note that Chubb and Moe's plan says they must adhere to nondiscrimination laws,[12] so if they want to avoid trouble, they had better be circumspect about rejecting students who fall under the protection of those laws. (It is instructive that in the closest thing to Chubb and Moe's plan we have, the Milwaukee choice program that includes private schools, private schools were exempted from having to accept students with special needs, a decision that was upheld by the federal Department of Education.) But they'd quickly realize that they wouldn't face this issue if those students never sought admission in the first place. And so if the niche these schools carved in the market did not explicitly extend to those students, and if their advertising and other materials were not targeted at them, this group of children would be less likely to show up.

On the other hand, there are bound to be some "public" schools that will decide that their niche is serving some category of students with special needs, and they will aggressively pursue this market. There may even be some "public" schools that decide their niche is offering a common school experience, where children of all classes, races, and creeds sit side by side and learn through a common curriculum. This, however, is not likely to be typical, because the capacity of a market school system to differentiate both by product and price means that it would be inherently antithetical to common schooling; the incentives are all lined up in the opposite direction. This is not a flaw; market schools, like markets in general, are *supposed* to work this way: they are supposed to organize diverse individuals into separate, relatively homogeneous groups.

Chubb and Moe's book also tells us that students and parents would not be the only ones making choices. Their "public" schools would not only determine their missions and tuitions, they would also get to choose their students. As it turns out, some students and parents would have no choice at all. As Chubb and Moe put it:

> Schools will make their own admissions decisions,
> subject only to nondiscrimination requirements. This
> is absolutely crucial. Schools must be able to define
> their own missions and build their own programs in
> their own ways, and they cannot do this if their student
> population is thrust on them by outsiders. They must
> be free to admit as many or as few students as they
> want, based on whatever criteria they think relevant—
> intelligence, interest, motivation, behavior, special
> needs—and they must be free to exercise their own,
> informal judgments about individual applicants. . . .
> Schools must also be free to expel students or deny
> them readmission when, based on their own experi-
> ences and standards, they believe the situation warrants
> it (as long as they are not "arbitrary and capricious").[13]

And what happens to the leftover students, the youngsters
whom no schools want? They will get the leftover schools, the
schools that few students and parents want.

The conclusion is inescapable: Chubb and Moe's plan may
improve some students' chances of having their educational needs
and wants fulfilled, but it also would further reduce other students'
chances of doing so. Similarly, market control may increase the diversity of offerings in America's schools, but it also would add to our
supply of separate and unequal schools and decrease the diversity of
the student body within our schools. And while market control may
result in a new batch of good schools, it would not diminish, and
might even increase, our supply of mediocre and bad schools.

After parsing its central elements, we thus find a "public"
school choice plan that Americans more typically, and accurately,
call privatization at public expense. Indeed, Chubb and Moe's insistence that theirs is a public school choice plan seems rather dis-
ingenuous, for there is little in it that is public and nothing at all
that respects the historic role and social ideals of public education
in a democratic society.

Chubb and Moe might dismiss this observation as the defen-
siveness or blinkered vision of public school advocates. Yet it is
consistent with their own explicit rejection of any higher purpose for

public education. As they say themselves, "It should be apparent that schools have no immutable or transcendent purpose. What they are supposed to be doing depends on who controls them and what those controllers want them to do."[14] The problem, at least for them, is that about 200 years ago this nation decided that public schools were *supposed* to have a transcendent purpose. That is why America created a public school system financed out of public funds in the first place, and that is why public schools were placed under direct democratic control; not only to enable individuals to pursue their particular academic and vocational interests in education, but, first and foremost, to pursue the public interest in education—what Chubb and Moe call "higher-order values." Some of those values have remained consistent over time, while others have changed or been elaborated to include Americans once excluded from the vision of equal educational opportunity. But this fundamental principle and rationale of free public education in America has endured.

That conception of public education, Chubb and Moe believe, has outlived its usefulness. Indeed, that is the central, most significant, and most radical message in their work. The reason they give is straightforward and utilitarian: "The raison d'être of democratic control is to impose higher-order values on schools, and thus to limit their autonomy."[15] This makes it difficult, and sometimes impossible, for schools to have effective organizations and thus produce high student achievement. This is the cause of our educational crisis, and that crisis will endure so long as we persist in democratic control of schools.

The question then is, is effective organization the leading cause of superior student achievement, that is, the chief variable that is within our control, as Chubb and Moe claim? And is this the reason for the "fact" that private schools outperform public schools, as Chubb and Moe further claim? Does their case for market control of schools rest on the solid empirical grounds they say it does?

Is Effective School Organization the Cause of Student Achievement?[16]

Chubb and Moe base their case for market control of schools on the High School and Beyond 1980 Sophomore Cohort First

Follow-Up (HSB) and the HSB's Administrator and Teacher Survey of 1984 (ATS). Their central question is: what caused the difference in the number of questions answered correctly on a 116-item test the HSB sample of high school students took in their sophomore and senior years? (How well a random sample of up to thirty-six students in each of 389 public and private high schools did on this five-part, sixty-three-minute test in their senior year relative to their score on the same test in their sophomore year is what Chubb and Moe mean by student achievement.)

On average, the sophomores answered 62 of the 116 questions correctly. In their senior year, these same students answered, on average, 6.6 more questions correctly—an appallingly modest gain after two years of high school. However, when the average student results are broken down, a more interesting picture emerges. The lowest quartile of students answered, on average, 4.66 *fewer* questions correctly in their senior year, while the top quartile answered 18.13 more questions correctly. The gap between the bottom and top groups of students was therefore almost 23 correct answers wide by their senior year.[17]

A number of features of the HSB test and the way Chubb and Moe handle its results should be noted because they further undercut the credibility of Chubb and Moe's analysis. First, the HSB test is not geared to the diverse curriculums and standards of the diverse public and private schools that make up our high school system (or, rather, nonsystem). Unlike every other advanced industrial nation, we do not have national high school curricula or common educational standards. Equating the results of the HSB test with what American students learn by virtue of attending a place called high school is therefore problematical because different students are taught different things in different curriculum tracks in high schools whose practices are shaped by different state and district requirements and principals' preferences.[18]

Second, the most notable finding about the HSB test results was the shockingly poor average gains registered by students between their sophomore and senior years—6.6 more questions answered correctly on a 116-item test. If this is the average amount of student learning being produced in American high schools, then we are in even more serious trouble than we thought.

Now, the very modest level of student learning that occurs between the tenth and twelfth grades, at least as measured by the HSB test, is not news.[19] Even Chubb and Moe mention it briefly. But small test-score gains do not make for bold policy recommendations and media headlines; Chubb and Moe never again mention the small gains.

Moreover, not only does the issue of the small additional number of correctly answered test questions disappear, these small student gains get dramatically exaggerated because Chubb and Moe transform them into *years* of student learning. Thus, the average student test-score gain, a mere 6.6 additional correct answers between the sophomore and senior years, becomes two years of student learning; the 4.66 fewer correct answers given by the lowest student quartile group become a *loss* of 1.4 years of learning; and the average gain of the highest student quartile group, 18.13 additional correct answers, becomes 5.46 years of learning accomplished during the last two years of high school. And in the end, the difference between the highest and lowest student quartile groups is a staggering 6.86 years of learning![20]

At the school level, transforming the variation in student achievement into years of learning produces equally dramatic results. That is how very small average test-score gains become dramatically large differences in student achievement and school performance. That is why Chubb and Moe's results look like "major" findings with "profound" policy implications. And that is how a book that devotes almost half its pages to statistical analyses that few people are trained to understand becomes the hottest and most covered educational "news" in the popular press.

The big surprise after all this is not that Chubb and Moe proved their hypothesis but that they didn't: their analysis fails to make the case that student achievement is largely caused by school organization. In fact, *all* the variables they put in their model to explain student achievement—family background, peer group influence (school socioeconomic status, or SES), school economic resources, school organization, and a correction for selection bias (due to sample attrition)[21]—taken *together* don't explain more than 5 percent of the differences in student achievement! In order of importance, the influences on high school student achievement they found were, first and foremost, student ability (prior student achievement), "followed by family SES and school organization, each roughly two-thirds as influential as student ability, and school SES, about one-third as influential as student ability."[22]

Chubb and Moe themselves concede that "all of the influences appear to be small." But undaunted by the failure of their model to explain much of anything at all, they proceed to say, in effect, let's see how much more a student would learn in high school if he had his family background or school organization or prior academic record raised from "the median of its lowest quartile to the median of its highest quartile."[23] Statistical wizardry and leaping quartiles notwithstanding, the results once again turn out to be trivial—not, to be sure, according to what Chubb and Moe tell us, but according to what their analysis doesn't tell us.

This time around, as before, prior achievement is the strongest influence on a student's achievement gain in high school. But now closely behind in importance and of almost equal magnitude are family background and school organization, followed distantly by the student body composition of the school. Even after jumping an average student from the 12.5th percentile of school organization—a very poorly organized school indeed—to the 87.5th percentile, the achievement gap of 6.33 years gets closed by only a half year. And according to the measure that Chubb and Moe have by now long dropped from sight, that actually means no more than 1 or 2 more correct answers on the 116-item IISB test! Moreover, when Chubb and Moe control for the effects of students' curriculum track (academic versus general or vocational), 30 percent of the influence of school organization on student achievement disappears. Being in an effectively organized school thus ends up yielding the average student as little as 1 more correct answer, or a fraction thereof, on the 116-item test!

Clearly, then, even if Chubb and Moe's data base were unproblematical and their methodology unassailable, a fraction of 1 more correct answer on a 116-question test is not exactly solid proof that school organization is a leading cause of student achievement. Nor does this fractional improvement make it worth abandoning democratic control of schools and embracing market control. Although Chubb and Moe have failed in the first instance to prove that effective school organization is a leading cause of student achievement, lest anyone still believe that market control of schools is the panacea for our educational crisis, let us take up the issue of public-private school differences.

Do Private Schools Outperform Public Schools?

The case that is likely to be—indeed, has been—most damaging to public education (and therefore to democratic control) is that of Catholic schools, where most of the nation's private school students are to be found. Many privatization advocates, and not a few researchers, have contended that Catholic schools are most like public schools in the students they enroll. So if Catholic school students outperform public school students, the argument goes, it is because Catholic schools are better.

This contention has been particularly prominent in discussions about the differences in student achievement between urban public schools and urban Catholic schools. Urban Catholic schools, like urban public schools, enroll poor and minority youngsters, many of whom are not Catholic. Yet when the performance of these Catholic-school youngsters is compared with that of their peers in public schools, public school critics claim the Catholic schools come out ahead. Public schools, they conclude, must therefore account for their inferior student outcomes relative to Catholic schools, particularly in urban areas.

The fact is that this accounting has long been available. Indeed, it exists in the very HSB/ATS data that Chubb and Moe analyze to tout the superiority of private schools. And what it reveals is that things are not at all equal between public and Catholic schools (not to mention other private schools), and not even remotely so.

First, there are very few Catholic schools located in cities. The overwhelming majority of them are in the suburbs, while the majority of public schools are rural. Second, regardless of where Catholic and public schools are located, the socioeconomic mix of students in public schools is substantially poorer. As John Witte notes, "There are almost no Catholic schools that fall in the bottom SES quartile of schools. On the other hand, 70 percent of the Catholic suburban schools (by far the most prevalent type) are in the highest SES quartile."[24]

Moreover, when the socioeconomic backgrounds of students in urban public schools in particular are compared with those in urban Catholic schools, it also turns out that some popular wisdom is wrong: urban public schools are not at all like urban Catholic schools because the public schools are educating far more disadvantaged students. For example, whereas only 9 percent of urban public schools are in the highest student SES quartile, 16 percent of Catholic schools fall in this category; and whereas 42 percent of urban public schools are in the lowest SES quartile, only 17.5 percent of Catholic schools are. Represented another way, only 26.5 percent of urban public schools are in the top half of SES, while 73.4 percent of these schools are educating students who are in the bottom half of SES. In sharp contrast, 55.1 percent of urban Catholic schools are in the top half of SES, and only 44.8 percent of them are in the bottom half.[25] As Witte summarizes it, "Public schools are thus educating the lowest socioeconomic students wherever they are located," and they also "teach more minority children wherever they are located."[26]

What about the poor and minority students that Catholic schools *do* educate? privatization advocates might insist. Don't Catholic schools nonetheless do a better job with them than public schools do? But the notion of "all thing being equal" between public and Catholic schools turns out to be ludicrous on these grounds, as well. Again, the reason is revealed in the very data Chubb and Moe employ to argue that private schools are superior by virtue of their greater autonomy and more effective organizations. What that data demonstrate is that Catholic schools simply do not permit either low-achieving students or youngsters with a prior record of discipline problems to enter their doors.[27] Urban Catholic schools may indeed admit some poor and minority youngsters, but, unlike public schools, they are only admitting the ones who are the cream of the crop.

Contrary, then, to what some people would have the public believe, public and Catholic schools are worlds apart when it comes to their student bodies because they are worlds apart in their student admissions criteria. The most important admissions criterion in public schools is the residence of the student. In overwhelming and decisive contrast, the most important admissions criteria in Catholic schools—the private schools that presumably are most like public schools in the students they serve—are student academic and discipline records and the results of achievement and aptitude tests.

So do private schools outperform public schools? By now, it would be hard to imagine that they wouldn't, given the initial advantages they enjoy from their students. However, the amazing fact is they don't. Indeed, even those studies that have concluded that student achievement is higher in Catholic than in public schools, "all things being equal" (in terms of measurable student background characteristics), result in only a small advantage for Catholic schools. Moreover, the differences in achievement they have found are so small that, as the latest review of this literature notes, "We can draw almost no conclusions from [these differences]."[28] Finally, when researchers employed statistical controls for student tracking and course-taking patterns between the two school sectors, they found no difference in student achievement between public and Catholic schools at all.[29]

Perhaps Chubb and Moe should have said that the way to get effective school organizations and superior student achievement is not through market control but rather through enabling schools to select their student bodies. And, of course, in effect Chubb and Moe did say that. But that is not the way public schools are supposed to operate, nor do we wish them to operate that way. Indeed, even if Chubb and Moe's analysis had come close to proving the case for market control, we confess that we would have been resistant to the idea of abandoning democratic control of schools and the American common school idea.

Notes

1. John E. Chubb and Terry M. Moe, *Politics, Markets, and America's Schools* (Washington, D.C.: Brookings Institution, 1990).
2. Ibid.
3. Apparently, direct democratic control works differently in rural areas, too. Here there is no bureaucracy to speak of, yet

student achievement is nonetheless very poor. If this is because of rural schools' ineffective organizations, then it can't be blamed on bureaucracy, which is how Chubb and Moe say elsewhere in their book democratic control works its insidious effects. Here, Chubb and Moe tell us that the ineffectiveness of rural schools is due to their problem-laden environment. It seems that Chubb and Moe's analysis is having a hard time accounting for the problems in most of America's schools, which are primarily rural or suburban and therefore relatively nonbureaucratic.

4. Chubb and Moe, *Politics, Markets, and America's Schools*, pp. 64–65.

5. Chubb and Moe then go on to argue that "the fundamental obstacle to effective organization among urban public schools is not their conflictual, problem-filled environments. It is the way democratic control tends to manage and respond to such environments" (p. 65). We agree that some of the responses to the problems of urban schools exacerbate their problems. But the fact is that Chubb and Moe's analysis is foundering on the question of causality, an issue we raised at the beginning of this chapter. There's a big difference between arguing that direct democratic control, through bureaucracy, undermines schools' organizational effectiveness and therefore depresses student achievement and, on the other hand, saying direct democratic control does a poor job of responding to schools that are already in trouble in terms of organizational effectiveness and student achievement.

6. Chubb and Moe, *Politics, Markets, and America's Schools*, pp. 2–3.

7. Ibid., p. 219.

8. Ibid., p. 218.

9. Ibid., p. 200.

10. Ibid., p. 220.

11. Ibid., p. 222.

12. Ibid., p. 224.

13. Ibid., pp. 221–23.

14. Ibid., p. 30.

15. Ibid., p. 38.

16. The analysis in this section draws heavily on the work of F. Howard Nelson, American Federation of Teachers, Department of Research; John F. Witte, "Understanding High School Achievement: After a Decade of Research, Do We Have Any Confident Policy Recommendations?" (Paper delivered at the 1990 annual meeting of the American Political Science Association, August 30–September 2, 1990); and Bella Rosenberg, "Response to Chubb and Moe," *Educational Leadership* 48 (December 1990/January 1991): 64–65.

17. Chubb and Moe, *Politics, Markets, and America's Schools,* pp. 73–74.

18. Chubb and Moe comment on this point, as well, in a footnote. "There is a possibility that the tests do not adequately measure high school curricula and therefore under-represent student learning. But since all high schools are equally disadvantaged if the tests have such a shortcoming, the tests will still provide valid comparative measures of performance" (p. 291). We, however, do not believe that all high schools are equally disadvantaged. As Chubb and Moe themselves note, private schools are overwhelmingly academic in their orientation and focused on getting students into college. So are many public high schools, but many others are not. And most public high schools are "comprehensive," that is, they have an academic track and a variety of nonacademic tracks that are either chosen by students or chosen for them. Put another way, the likelihood that most of the randomly sampled students in a private high school were in an academic program is far greater than the likelihood that most of the randomly sampled students in a public high school were in the academic program. This, as other researchers have repeatedly shown, has an influence on test results.

    Chubb and Moe give somewhat more of a nod to the tracking issue. They control for tracking in their *preliminary* analysis and then don't raise the issue again until they get to their appendixes (pp. 92–95; 252–58). We are not persuaded by their discussion that the controls they employ for tracking are adequate. Interestingly and unsurprisingly enough, they do find that academic track has an influence on student achievement. They then minimize this finding and attribute it to school organization. Moreover, we believe that the effect they found for tracking would have been even larger if they had examined course taking more rigorously, which other researchers have found has a significant influence on achievement. We should also point out that if a school's tracking policies or course content are in part a reflection of school organization, then they are also—and perhaps more so—a function of the pre-high school achievement levels of the students a particular school takes in. In other words, the students a high school gets influence the school's decisions about curriculum tracks—if and how to track and the level and nature of course content. They often also influence a district's decisions about what requirements to impose on its high school(s). And a student's pre-high school achievement clearly influences what a student decides to take and do in high school—a decision over which he or she has considerable latitude in most American high schools. Clearly, too, private schools do not face these issues to the extent public schools do.

19. James S. Coleman, Thomas Hoffer, and Sally Kilgore, *High School Achievement: Public, Catholic, and Private Schools Compared* (New York: Basic Books, 1982); James S. Coleman and Thomas Hoffer, *Public and Private High Schools: The Impact of Communities* (New York: Basic Books, 1987).

20. Chubb and Moe, *Politics, Markets, and America's Schools*, pp. 73-75.

21. Ibid., p. 260.

22. Ibid., p. 128.

23. Ibid.

24. Witte, "Understanding High School Achievement," p. 28 and Table 10.

25. Ibid., Table 10.

26. Ibid., p. 28.

27. Ibid., pp. 28-29 and Table 10.

28. Ibid., p. 27.

29. Ibid., p. 28.

24

Why Privatizing Public Education
Is a Bad Idea

Bill Honig

Theoreticians John Chubb and Terry Moe propose to transform our public schools from democratically regulated to market-driven institutions. They argue that the past decade has seen the most ambitious period of school reform in the nation's history, but gains in test scores or graduation rates are nil. Their explanation: government, with its politics and bureaucracy, so hampers schools' ability to focus on academic achievement that improvement efforts are doomed.

Using data from the early eighties, Chubb and Moe contend that freeing schools from democratic control boosts performance a full grade level. Thus, they would give students scholarships for any public, private, or newly formed school; prohibit states or school districts from establishing organizational or effective curricular standards or assessing school performance; and allow schools to restrict student entry. They assert that parent choice alone will assure quality.

What's wrong with their proposal to combine vouchers with radical deregulation? Everything. Chubb and Moe misread the evidence on choice and claim it is the *only* answer. I believe that we should give public school parents more choice, either through magnet schools or open-enrollment plans. Choice builds commitment in parents and students and keeps the system honest. But limits are necessary to prevent skimming off of the academic or athletically talented or furthering of racial segregation. More importantly, where choice has been successful, such as in East Harlem, it has been *one component* of a broader investment in quality.

A Plan That Jeopardizes Students

Chubb and Moe's proposal most certainly jeopardizes our youngsters and this democracy. Any one of the following objections should be enough to sink their plan:

- The proposal risks creating elite academies for the few and second-rate schools for the many. It allows schools to exclude students who do not meet their standards—almost guaranteeing exacerbation of income and racial stratification. We had such a two-tiered system in the nineteenth century before mass education helped make this country prosperous and free. We shouldn't go back 100 years in search of the future.
- Cult schools will result. Nearly 90 percent of American youngsters attend public schools, which are the major institutions involved in transmitting our democratic values. By prohibiting common standards, Chubb and Moe enshrine the rights of parents over the needs of children and society and encourage tribalism. Is it good public policy to use public funds to support schools that could teach astrology or creationism instead of science, inculcate antiminority or antiwhite attitudes, or prevent students from reading *The Diary of Anne Frank* or *The Adventures of Huckleberry Finn?* Absent democratic controls, such schools (which already exist in the private sector) will multiply.
- Their plan violates the constitutional prohibition against aiding religious schools.
- The lack of accountability and the naivete of relying on the market to protect children is alarming. In the nineteenth century the slogan was "Let the buyer beware," and meat packers sold tainted meat to consumers. In the twentieth century deregulation produced the savings and loan crisis. Nobody seriously proposes rescinding environmental safeguards—why should our children not be similarly protected? In fact, look at private

trade schools. Regulation is weak and scholarships are available. The results: widespread fraud and misrepresentation. Similar problems occurred when New York decentralized its school system. Corruption and patronage surfaced in its local boards of education. All across the nation there are calls for *more* accountability from our schools, not less.

- The plan would be tremendously chaotic. Vast numbers of new schools would have to be created for this plan to succeed; yet most new enterprises fail. Many youngsters will suffer during the transition period, and with no accountability we will not even know if the experiment was successful.

- Taxpayers will have to pay more. Chubb and Moe maintain that competition will produce savings, but they offer no proof. A potent counterexample: colleges compete, yet costs are skyrocketing. Furthermore, if this plan is adopted nationwide, a substantial portion of the cost of private school students—about $17 billion—currently paid for by their parents will be picked up by taxpayers (unless public school expenditures are reduced 10 percent, which would make the plan doubly disastrous).

In addition, the proposal includes expensive transportation components and the creation of a new level of bureaucracy—so-called Choice Offices. These offices will include Parent Information Centers, where liaisons will meet with parents to advise them on what schools to choose. But how many employees will be necessary for this process if parents are to receive the information they actually need in a timely manner?

Schools Post Impressive Gains

Furthermore, Chubb and Moe's basic charge that current reform efforts have not succeeded is dead wrong and, consequently, the need for risky and radical change unjustified. While their data say something useful about the dangers of rigid bureaucracy and overpoliticization of education, their findings cannot be used to judge the reform effort, since the students in their study were tested before reforms began. More recent evidence points to substantial gains.

Consider our experience in California: in 1989, in reading and math, seniors scored *one year* ahead of seniors in 1983, the exact magnitude of growth that Chubb and Moe say their proposal would achieve and just what they argue couldn't be accomplished within the existing system.

Also, from 1986 to 1990, eighth graders improved an average of one-half grade for all subjects.

The pool of seniors from which we draw most of our professional and business talent—those who score above 450 on the verbal portion of the Scholastic Aptitude Test and above 500 on the math portion—has grown by 19 percent in verbal and 28 percent in math from 1983 to 1989. One out of five seniors now reaches these levels. Thirty-six percent and 43 percent more, respectively, score above 600 on the verbal and math tests.

In California, these gains have been made despite a pronounced demographic shift among test takers. During the past five years, ethnic minorities have increased from 35 percent of the test takers to 45 percent. The number of test takers who are ethnic minorities has grown from 36,000 to 52,000.

This phenomenon results in the seemingly paradoxical situation that occurred in the state this year: combined verbal and mathematics SAT scores went *down* 2 points, but each major ethnic group's scores went *up*. In addition, 13 percent more students are taking the tests, a factor that normally lowers scores. The number of test takers has increased from 102,000 to 115,000.

In addition, the number of Advanced Placement courses taken and passed during the past five years has more than doubled, to over 57,500. And the high school dropout rate has shrunk from an estimated 24.9 percent to 20.4 percent, an 18 percent decrease between 1986 and 1989.

Between 1984 and 1989, 63 percent—or 16,000—more students enrolled in physics, bringing the total to 41,000 students. The rate of enrollment in chemistry increased by 53 percent—or 34,000 students—to 97,000 students. About 37 percent—or 59,000—more students are taking advanced mathematics, for a total of 211,000 students.

These improvements have occurred even though our schools have had not only to accommodate an annual enrollment growth of 140,000 students but also to deal with deteriorating social conditions. The number of youngsters living in poverty has doubled since 1979, as has the number of students limitedly proficient in English.

Nor are these good results limited to California. Nationwide, a recent U.S. Department of Education report found that the percentage of high school dropouts has shrunk by one-third since 1979, and that the rates for blacks are almost comparable to those for whites. Nearly one-half of the dropouts eventually graduated or received a graduation equivalent.

The pool of college-bound students scoring above 450 on the verbal portion of the SAT has grown by 9 percent in six years. Eighteen percent more scored above 500 on the math portion. Scores above 600 have increased by 15 percent in verbal and 27 percent in math. Some commentators argue that even though there has been some improvement in the past seven years, combined verbal and math scores are still 80 points below what they were in 1963. Actually, one can make a good argument that schools are performing a little better now than then. In that year, only 16 percent of the graduating class took the test; in 1989, 40 percent did—a much less elite group.

According to recent research on adjusting SAT scores for the percentage of students taking the test, a 1 percent increase in test takers will lower combined scores by 2 points. Thus, two-thirds of the gap results from the rise in the percentage of test takers. The remainder is more than accounted for by demographic changes in the test takers. As confirmation, when the Preliminary Scholastic Aptitude Test was given to a representative sample of eleventh graders in 1960, 1966, 1974, and 1983, verbal and math scores were stable. Of course, doing a little better than we did in 1963 is not good enough for the realities of the 1990s.

Other gains are also apparent nationally. The number of Advanced Placement exams taken nationally has more than doubled between 1983 and 1989, from 211,000 to 455,000. Between 1982 and 1987, the number of students taking chemistry grew by 45 percent to nearly one out of two students, and the number taking physics expanded by 44 percent, to one out of five students. College-going rates have increased to an all-time high of 59 percent, up from 51 percent in 1982.

In terms of achievement, the National Assessment of Educational Progress found that in 1988 virtually 100 percent of seventeen-year-olds reached the two basic reading levels: demonstrating proficiency in carrying out simple, discrete reading tasks, and comprehending specific or sequentially related information. It also found that the number who did not reach the third or intermediate level declined by 27 percent from 1980 to only 14 percent in 1988, and that the number who read at the "adept" level necessary for advanced technological jobs—the next-to-highest level—increased from 38.5 percent to 41.8 percent. Problems appeared at the advanced level in reading, where students were asked to synthesize and learn from specialized reading materials. Problems also appeared for thirteen-year-olds; and in writing, including persuasive writing and reporting on events.

In math, almost every seventeen-year-old reached the first three levels, and the number able to handle moderately complex problems—the fourth level—grew between 1982 and 1988 from 48.3 percent to 58.7 percent—a 22 percent increase. In science, the number who did not reach the third level shrank from 24 percent to 14 percent, and those who reached the fourth level grew from 37.5 percent to 44.6 percent, or a 19 percent boost. Students who reached the top levels grew by 20 percent in math and 14 percent in science, though only a small percentage of students attained these goals. These results were achieved even though the number of students still in school increased by 9 percent as dropout rates fell.

Certainly, these gains are not sufficient to prepare our youngsters to enter the changing job market, to reach their potential, to participate in our democracy, or to keep up with international competition. We still have a long way to go. But that is not the issue. Educators are being challenged on whether we have a strategy that can produce results. We do, and this nation should be discussing how best to build on this record and accelerate the pace of reform—not how to dismantle public education.

California's Comprehensive Strategy

The crucial question, of course, is: what caused these gains?

In California, we believe the answer lies in how we approached the reform effort and the steps we are taking to ensure its success. First, a reform strategy must be comprehensive and strategically aligned, and it must spring from an understanding of what needs to be learned and how best to teach it. We started with the belief that virtually all children can learn to think, understand democracy and the culture around them, and become prepared for the changing job market. We worked hard to obtain agreement that our young people needed a more demanding curriculum to meet these goals. We reached a consensus that the ability to abstract, conceptualize, and solve problems is becoming increasingly important, even for traditionally blue-collar jobs; that academics, broadly defined, are the best vehicles for teaching such skills; and that instructional methodologies stressing the integration of theory and application and encouraging cooperative learning are crucial to success.

Second, using experts in each field, we defined the kind of curriculum and instruction necessary to reach these higher goals. We obtained consensus without watering down the bite of reform. These agreements were embodied in our state frameworks and curricular guides, which are widely available and *used*. The guidelines are sufficiently precise to have a definite point of view—for example, reading instruction should include literature—but open enough for teachers to figure out how best to organize their instruction.

Third, we changed our state tests to reflect the altered curriculum. We tested in science and history, evaluated writing samples, and assessed for higher levels of understanding in reading and math. We also instituted an accountability system that set specific targets and gave each school and district information on how it was doing. We publicized the results annually.

Fourth, we devised implementation strategies in each curricular area to get the word out on what the changes were and the reasons for them. For example, in shifting to a more literature-based English curriculum, we developed training through the University

of California at Los Angeles Literature Project and created numerous documents to support our efforts.

Fifth, and crucial to the whole enterprise, a tremendous effort
was made to get superintendents and board members to buy into
this vision of reform and devote substantial dollars during tight
fiscal times to staff development. Unfortunately, in many political
circles, the obvious strategy of heavy investment in teacher development smacks of a boondoggle. But without that investment, large-
scale improvements will not occur.

Schools devote pathetically few resources to staff development, and education remains one of the lowest-capitalized enterprises in the country. In California, we designed training programs
consistent with our revamped curriculum. Because of limited funding, however, only a small fraction of teachers have been able to
participate.

Sixth, California spends nearly $315 million a year for site
planning and implementation through our "school improvement
program." This effort provides resources for teachers and principals, with the community's advice, to take the general reform ideas
and devise specific approaches.

Seventh, we put into place strategies aimed at improving the
quality of instructional materials, enhancing leadership of principals and superintendents, and involving parents.

We formed strong working relationships with the business
community, higher education, and law enforcement; and we have
initiated hundreds of partnership programs. We are revamping each
special program—such as vocational education, bilingual education, and programs for children at risk of failure—so that each
becomes more supportive of the regular program. We also embarked
on a multimillion-dollar program for introducing technology.

The impressive gains produced by these aligned initiatives
can be seen in our junior highs. In 1985, when it was apparent that
eighth-grade performance was lagging, we produced a report calling for strengthening academics, increasing attention to students,
and making organizational changes in schools. Almost every California junior high and middle school is attempting to implement
these recommendations.

To further their efforts, a Carnegie Corporation grant established a support network of 100 middle-grade schools. We also obtained from the legislature and governor $5 million for planning grants of $30 per student for one-third of our junior highs (as of 1991, all will receive funds), and local districts devoted substantial resources to middle-grade improvement. We also strengthened our testing program.

The comprehensive approach worked better than any of us had expected. Our eighth graders now perform an equivalent of about half a grade level higher than eighth-grade students four years ago on California Assessment Program tests. The critical elements of such massive change should provide a serviceable blueprint for other efforts: a vision of quality specifically defined; assessment procedures that reinforce that vision; activities to allow people at schools to work through those ideas and plan site-tailored responses and organizational changes; massive investments in staff development; and school and district alignment of curriculum, assessment, and training in a coordinated effort.

These improvements in California and in the nation clearly demonstrate that this country has an incredible opportunity to build a world-class school system. Many educators not only are prepared to improve schools but have already started to do so.

We need to continue working with our national leaders to build further upon these gains and invest selectively in those strategies with a high potential for leveraging the whole system. These strategies are much better investments than Chubb and Moe's fanciful idea.

Model Programs

A perfect example of a successful program made possible by a small initial investment that incorporates every critical component of our effective reform strategies is Project 2000 in the Kern Union High School District in Bakersfield, California. Ford Motor Company and several other corporations are putting up the initial capital, $400 per student (approximately 10 percent of the state's annual per-pupil expenditure) for 100 students at each of four high schools.

The project concentrates on the average child, encouraging

that student to take more, and more difficult, academic courses and to go to college. Students and parents must commit to the project. A team of four teachers (English, science, math, and history) at each school plans the curriculum and organizational changes, with the principal's participation, and stays together during the school year with the 100 students. Teachers have common preparation periods. Each school receives a classroom of Macintosh computers, and the program stresses word processing and writing for the freshmen. Students are provided with role models and heavy counseling support. Substantial funds are provided for staff development, and teachers tackle the problems of how to make complicated subjects accessible to the average student.

Similar projects, such as AVID (Advancement Via Individual Determination) in San Diego, have doubled or tripled the college-going rates of minority youth and completely transformed their schools' atmosphere by changing the attitude of many previously apathetic students. The same strategy has worked for potential dropouts in the California Partnership Academies program, which has enjoyed substantial success in increasing graduation rates and community college attendance.

As a final example of what we could do if we reached agreement on a few comprehensive reform strategies, let us look at mathematics achievement. The participants at the president's "education summit" in 1989 established a goal of catching up with the rest of the world in math and science. Educators agree with that goal. The University of Chicago has analyzed international textbooks and has determined exactly where we fall short in math. We waste one-half year in second grade by delaying introduction of some topics; we review too much at the fourth grade; and we flounder in junior high school by assigning too much review and failing to cover measurement and applied problem solving. By the eighth grade our students are two years behind where they should be.

There is a consensus on what to do about this situation. The National Council of Teachers of Mathematics has issued a new set of standards; the University of Chicago has figured out how to teach these complicated standards to the average child; and a major textbook publisher has incorporated these ideas in new materials.

Eighth graders who have used these books have grown *four* grade
levels in one year.

Here on the West Coast we have initiated the university-
sponsored California Mathematics Project, which has designed a
promising training network and delivered effective training for
teams of teachers in successful ideas, methods, and materials. So far
only 5 percent of our teachers have been reached. We are ready to
go statewide if given the green light. New Jersey's PRISM (Partnership for Radical Improvement of School Mathematics) Project has
initiated a similar strategy. If our political leaders want to improve
math instruction in this country, we have already devised the curriculum and implementational strategies. What we need is a modest
infusion of investment capital for significant training and on-site
implementation of these plans.

Currently, the United States spends approximately $195 bil-
lion annually on public schools. Only $12 billion of this amount
comes from the federal government—1 percent of its budget. If we
provided an additional 5 percent of the $195 billion—$10 billion a
year—and invested it in the right activities for five years, we could
substantially improve our schools' productivity and influence the
future well-being of our country. A return worth hundreds of bil-
lions a year is not a bad payoff for a $10-billion-per-year investment.

Public schools have turned the corner, educators have developed an effective game plan for the nineties, and promising ideas
to encourage further flexibility within a context of vision and accountability are being implemented. If our leaders support that
game plan, our children will enjoy the schools they deserve as we
enter the twenty-first century.

25

Choices:
A Strategy for
Educational Reform

Deborah W. Meier

When I first entered teaching, and when my own children began their long trek through urban public schools, I was an unreconstructed advocate of the zoned neighborhood school. I knew all about choice: the favorite tactic of racists fleeing desegregation and of elitists avoiding responsibility for their neighbors. There were even moments when I wished we could legally outlaw any selective public or private institutions, although I could readily see the risks—not to mention the political impossibility—of doing so. That is no longer the case. I have changed my mind.

Because I have spent the past sixteen years in a public school district in East Harlem that has pioneered choice and have founded a network of small elementary schools of choice in that community, my change of heart naturally grows out of personal experience. There are today more schools in East Harlem that have put the rhetoric of reform into practice than in any other comparably sized community in the United States. This has been done despite the fact that the community of East Harlem possesses few obvious advantages for reformers, serving as it does nearly 15,000 largely poor Latino and African-American youngsters from kindergarten through junior high in one of the most bureaucratic systems in the nation. (High schools still fall under the jurisdiction of the New York Central Board rather than its thirty-two Community School

Districts.) District 4's fifty-three schools (in twenty often old and dilapidated buildings) are all small, largely self-governing (through what is now called site-based management and shared decision making), and pedagogically innovative. They are schools with a focus, with staffs brought together around a common set of ideas and given the freedom to shape a whole set of school parameters in accord with these ideas. How did this happen?

Choice as a Prerequisite for Change

It would have been impossible to carry out this ambitious agenda without choice. Choice was the necessary, however insufficient, prerequisite. It was an enabling strategy for a superintendent who wanted to get rid of the tradition of zoned, factory-style, bureaucratically controlled schools that have long been synonymous with urban public schooling. He wanted to replace it with a wholly different image of what public education could mean. The "District 4 way" was deceptively simple. While it required no vast ten-year blueprint, between 1974 and 1984 the district changed the way families related to schools, professionals worked within them, and children were educated. Superintendent Anthony Alvarado sidestepped the resistance that has made reform seem so daunting elsewhere by building a parallel system of choice, until even its opponents and holdouts found themselves benefiting from reform.

To begin with, Alvarado initiated a few model schools open to parental choice. Given the financial straits facing the city in 1974, he located them within existing buildings where space was available. He could not offer additional funds, but he insisted from the start that these schools needed the broadest possible autonomy if they were really going to break with past practice. For openers, Alvarado sought educators who would create schools that looked excitingly different, that would have a loyal—if small—following among families and a strong professional leadership. Central Park East (CPE) and the East Harlem School for Performing Arts were the result. The East Harlem School for Performing Arts grew out of the work of a District 4 teacher integrating the arts and academics. It began with grades five and six and turned into a 300-student intermediate school for grades five to nine. Central Park East was the creation of a unique invitation. Alvarado invited me to come into District 4 to "do what you believe in, Debby." That was the only mandate. I brought with me five colleagues from around the city whose work I knew and liked. We spent a few months planning together, spreading the word to prospective parents in the neighborhood, and gathering necessary materials from our attics and closets. We spent the summer painting walls and building lofts and dreaming. When we opened our doors in September we had almost a hundred youngsters, ages five through seven. Our students were recruited out of local Head Start groups, were directed to us by other schools and local agencies, or were brought to us by parents desperate for something different.

Alvarado gave each of these new schools extraordinary initial support, primarily in the form of flexibility. He encouraged us to experiment with regard to staffing, use of resources, organization of time, and forms of assessment. He hired a former principal, Sy Fliegel, to hold our hands, alert us to dangers, run interference for us with the Central Board, and look for other prospective school innovators to join our ranks. When people in the regular schools complained of favoritism he assured them that he would happily favor them too if they had ideas they wanted to try. Each year, he added more new schools initiated by other teachers with their own wonderful ideas. He made it clear that he liked risk takers and did not expect immediate results. The new schools generally started with a few classes, and the largest grew to slightly over 300 students. Some stayed as small as 50. When Central Park East graduated its first class of sixth graders, it had already grown so popular that we decided to start a second school, Central Park East II. CPE II was located in a different building, as was River East, which opened a few years later in response to continued popular demand. All three stayed small, never exceeding 275 students. The decision to stay small allowed all three CPE schools to be internally flexible and easily governable. It meant that everyone knew everyone else and could respond quickly and humanly to crises. While the three CPE schools remained connected philosophically and organizationally, each had its own director, parent association, and staff, and the freedom to develop its own version of a commonly held viewpoint.

By 1980, six years after the first school of choice was launched, most of the students in District 4's junior high grades were attending an alternative school. The focus on junior high was intentional since these are the grades where dissatisfaction with the status quo has traditionally been greatest. In addition, about a fourth of the elementary-age students were attending alternative schools by 1980. In the process, schools were no longer equated with buildings: each building now housed several independently governed schools. It became harder and harder to differentiate between the regular and the alternative schools. In less than ten years, the same twenty buildings that had once contained twenty schools now housed fifty-one different schools, plus two district schools that were located in a nearby high school building. The schools housed together in shared buildings often overlapped age groups, with early-childhood and junior high students often sharing a location. Stage one was now complete.

Only then did the superintendent announce stage two: henceforth no junior high would serve a specific catchment area. Choice would reign from grade seven up. All families of incoming seventh graders would have to choose. The district provided sixth-grade parents and teachers with lots of information to assist their choosing, although probably word of mouth was the decisive factor (as it is in private schools). The original sixteen neighborhood elementary school buildings, unlike the four former junior high buildings, continued to house the traditional neighborhood schools (plus alternative schools). Space in such schools went first to families residing in the old designated zones, but Alvarado promised that even in the case of elementary schools, parents were free to shop around for the school of their choice if space existed. Thus elementary school parents now had a choice among the sixteen regular neighborhood schools, the fifteen new alternatives (including seven bilingual schools), and their zoned school. As a result, the neighborhood elementary schools became, like their alternatives, smaller and, in effect, schools of choice. Alvarado even enticed a former independent (private) elementary school to enter the public sector and left intact its parental governing board.

Educational Reform Through Choice

A majority of the new schools were pedagogically fairly traditional, although more focused and coherent in terms of their themes (music, science, journalism, and so on). Significantly, they were all more intimate and family-oriented due to their small size. Small size also meant that regardless of the formal governing structure, all the participants were generally at least informally involved in making decisions about school life. Most of the schools were designed by small groups of teachers tired of compromising what they thought were their most promising ideas. As a result, there was a level of energy and esprit, a sense of co-ownership, that made them stand out.

A few schools (such as our three Central Park East schools) used this opening to try radically different forms of teaching and learning, testing and assessment, school-family collaboration, and staff self-government. Few of these ideas seem so radical today, and in fact most have become (at least rhetorically) mainstream. In 1974 the use of "whole language" approaches to learning to read and write seemed daring and risky; today they are the accepted mode. The CPE schools were organized around inter-age classrooms so that children would stay with the same teacher for two years and to encourage what today is considered essential to good practice—peer teaching and collaborative learning. Children with special needs were mainstreamed in regular classrooms, as specialists were used not to pull youngsters out but to provide inside support to the regular teacher. Classrooms were organized so that teachers could be coaches, not performers, and students could be active learners, not passive recipients of information. New forms of what is now called "performance assessment" were pioneered, and parent-staff conferences included students so that the conferences could become planning sessions rather than just quickie checkups between parent and teacher. The schools engaged in a continual reexamination of the roles of the director and of parents in schools operating on a more democratic, staff-run basis. Visitors thought we looked more like a New York City independent school: children seemed not only cheerful, but purposeful, articulate, and courteous. Everywhere there were books on display and in use, evidence of children's writing abounded, and there was lots of conversation between teachers, between students, and between teachers and students. Projects were the major learning mode, art was produced in every room, parents were everywhere welcome, and everyone was on a first-name basis with everyone else.

Ten years before the word *restructuring* was invented and fifteen years before it became nearly a cliche, the CPE schools were exploring all the issues now on the reform agenda—and they were doing so not against the grain but with it. District 4's unique organization is what made this possible. The district abandoned the idea of standardization, seeing it as an obstacle to high standards. Instead it promoted the needed freedom for self-selected faculties to develop coherent communities with commonly held assumptions and priorities. This meant that the schools were not expected to be the same. This meant that all the participants were in a position to choose "in" as well as to choose "out." When change is sought in schools that exist within a system still ruled by archaic regulations designed to keep everything in place, and when innovators face resistance (if not sabotage) from members of the staff and parent body who do not want any part of change, it is unlikely to occur. The temptation to retreat is enormous even under the best of circumstances. The CPE staff were often tempted to slide back into accustomed habits, not make waves, not face another battle; after all, we were not always sure we were right or that all would work out well, and innovation always demands more time and effort. To break the mold as far as we did we needed the strength and support of our united community. Voluntarism helped us build and maintain that unity.

In this one district, noted only a decade earlier as one of the worst of the city's thirty-two local districts, there were by 1984 dozens of highly distinctive schools with citywide reputations and stature, alongside dozens of others that were decidedly more humane, where children were less likely to fall between the cracks and teachers were enthusiastic about teaching. A few did not work and had such serious problems that the district phased them out of existence or merged them with other, more successful schools. The decision to phase a school out was usually triggered by the clear absence over a period of time of either students or staff interested in attending or working in such a school, confirmed by the professional judgment of district personnel that efforts to help the school get on its feet were not succeeding.

The consensus from the streams of observers who came to see our schools, and those who studied the data, was that the change was real and lasting. What was even more important, however, was that the stage was now set for trying out even more radical educational ideas as professionals had the opportunity to be more directly involved in decision making, and as parents and children were no longer unwilling captives of any particular group of professionals. It was not a cost-free idea, but the extra money needed was small compared with amounts for many other much-heralded reform efforts: less than one additional teacher for every newly created school.

If this were the best of all possible worlds, the next ten years would have been used to launch stage three. The district would have studied what was and was not happening within these fifty-three small schools, examined more closely issues of equity, followed graduates to see how they fared in high school, studied the families' reasons for making choices, and looked for strategies to prod schools into taking on tougher educational challenges. Meanwhile the Central Board would have worked out ways to legitimize these wildcat schools, while also encouraging other districts to follow a similar path. Under the leadership of Alvarado's successor, Carlos Medina, District 4 began stage three.

It was not, however, the best of all possible worlds, and for reasons that had nothing to do with the education going on in the fifty-three schools the district's focus on education, much less innovation, came to an end. It became increasingly involved instead in interminable political disputes over turf between school board factions and between the district and the Central Board bureaucracy. Finally Medina's leadership came to an end amid largely misleading charges of financial irregularities and overspending. Such infighting—not unknown, I might add, in the private sector—paralyzed further initiatives for several years.

Today, District 4 stands at another crossroads. With new leadership both within the district and at the Central Board, it is once again in a position to launch stage three. That our schools have survived so many years of at best benign neglect and at worst systematic harassment in a system that never officially acknowledged their existence is a tribute to the loyalty and ingenuity that choice and co-ownership engendered. In fact, in the midst of the political turmoil, the district initiated an ambitious secondary school of choice, which required cooperation among the district, the Central Board, and the high school division. Central Park East Secondary School (CPESS), of which I am now principal, is one of the best-known pilot schools in Ted Sizer's Coalition of Essential Schools, and the first of a number of seventh- to twelfth-grade secondary schools of choice now being planned in other districts in New York.

Risks and Advantages in Choice

It is understandable that this extraordinary experience in District 4 has made me an advocate of choice as a tool for reforming public education. For the district, however, the objective was change, not choice. Alvarado and Medina used choice to stimulate fundamental change, to shake up the status quo and create a new set of school choices. Theirs was not a laissez-faire strategy. It did not depend on abstract market forces but on conscious activism and public leadership.

Unfortunately, providing citizens with choices still scares most public school advocates. They think it is too risky. While our schools, they point out, are seriously undereducating all our students, they are failing some more than others. Choice as a strategy for dramatically and rapidly improving education for those others is too risky a business. The risks they fear are dual: first, that choice will become a vehicle for creating an elite set of schools that will increase—not narrow—the gap between the haves and have-nots; second, that choice will be used to undermine public education itself via vouchers. Since I believe the United States badly needs both a more equitable system and a strong and vigorous public one, these dangers must be addressed. If they are not addressed, choice, like any other reform, will be co-opted to serve the most powerful at the expense of the least powerful. District 4 will prove the exception, not the rule.

Equity Concerns. Broadly stated, Americans have long supported two levels of schooling. Whether schools are public or private, the social class of the students was and continues to be the single most significant factor in determining how a school works and the intellectual values it promotes. The higher the student body's status, the meatier the curriculum, the more open-ended the discussion, the less rote and rigid the pedagogy, the more respectful the tone, the more rigorous the expectations, the greater the staff autonomy. Goodlad's vast investigative data on classroom life, Jeannie Oake's study on tracking, and Ted Sizer's reportage on American high schools are benchmark confirmation of a simple fact: the biggest difference between schools (as well as between programs within schools) is not their publicness or privateness but the social and economic status of the students who attend them. What we need, if we are to educate all children to standards previously expected of only an elite few, are strategies for giving to everyone what the rich have always valued. The rich, after all, have had both good public schools and good private schools. The good public ones looked a lot like the good private ones. The bad ones have looked alike, too. The difference has mainly been a question of the clientele the schools were intended to serve. If we intend to use choice to undermine this historic duality, then the *kind* of choice plan that is adopted will be more important than Chubb and Moe acknowledge.

Choice has its natural attractions, of course. Its popularity in opinion polls is hardly surprising. The right to choose seems elementary, an extension of democracy. People in authority generally take choice away only with trepidation. Yet public school advocates rarely ask what compelling reasons ever led us to take such choice away in public education. We know full well that even if medicine were a pure science, no two doctors would be interchangeable. Our neighbor might like Dr. Z, but we would not go to him for all the world, if we had a choice. We would find it intolerable to accept a baby-sitter by assignment, even if we knew the sitter had passed a qualifying exam. At the college level, we take choice for granted. Why does all this seem unreasonable when it comes to the right of parents to select a school for their youngsters?

Historically, it was not a concern for equity that led to the concept of the geographically zoned school. After all, until 1954, so-called neighborhood schools excluded neighbors of color, and many continue to do so more subtly even today. Thus while elitism, sexism, and racism are concerns among current opponents of choice, the original reasons for curtailing choice were not based on any desire for racial or social class integration. In small-town and rural communities egalitarian ideals may have been promoted by neighborhood schools. In urban communities, however, the poor, the children of immigrants, and racial minorities rarely were schooled together with those from more favored circumstances. Even when they occupied the same buildings, internal practices generally ensured that they remained in separate worlds.

A full account of the history of public schooling might help us understand why the single-zoned school developed, but it will not tell us if that was the only possible route public education could have taken—or could take in the future. It may well be that compulsory public education could have developed equally well without eliminating the right of families to choose one particular school rather than another, or teachers to exercise similarly greater discretion over their job placement. The notion that one's address determines one's school placement is not, as District 4's story suggests, necessary to the survival of public education. The zoned public school may have been a convenience, and in a time when schooling itself was a minor factor in the development of our youth with minimal impact on employment opportunities, this happenstance of history may have had only a trivial impact. This is no longer the case: today, the school a student attends has a great impact on that student's potential for development and advancement.

Behind the opposition to choice lies an understandable fear that it will lead ultimately to either the demise of public education or its marginalization as the program of last resort for losers. However, if public schools are so incapable of responding to the demand from policy makers for rapid wholesale change, and if choice can be such a useful tool for change as the District 4 story suggests, why worry so much about the risks of privatization inherent in many choice plans, including some that Chubb and Moe support? Worrying about privatization will surely slow down the adoption of choice plans, and thus hinder reform. Just such desperation has led a number of African-American educators and political activists to give up on public schooling, given its appalling record of miseducating black children. Could they be right that the risk of privatization is well worth taking? If public education is so inept, and so difficult to change, why all the fuss to save it? Why not let the chips fall where they may?

The question is a good one. If we want to preserve public education as the socially accepted type of schooling for most citizens, then we must proclaim important and positive reasons to do so, reasons that are compelling not only to parents and teachers or to those most at risk but to the broadest public. Chubb and Moe have made a case for choice. While they claim to make it as friends of public education, it is clear that public funding, not public education, is what they are concerned about. They make no case for public education itself. In this time of educational crisis neither has our president, nor the leaders of either party. This silence is deafening. It coincides with a general climate of cynicism about public institutions. Nor can we afford to rest our case on nostalgia for the past, especially at a time when we want our schools to break with nostalgia. The public needs positive reasons to support public education.

The rationale for education reform has been made, but not in a manner that augurs well for public education. To effect meaningful reform of public education we must go beyond the problem employers face in recruiting sufficient numbers of competent and reliable workers, or our chagrin at finding the United States at the bottom in test scores for math and science. These arguments, however important, do not offer a sufficient justification for preserving *public* education. In fact, on the basis of such data a compelling case might well be made to turn our schools over to employers!

Civic Concerns. The argument against privatization is strongest when we consider the role education plays as a tool in reviving and maintaining the fabric of our democratic institutions. While public education may be useful as an industrial policy, it is essential to healthy public life in a democracy. Never has this been clearer or more critical than it is today.

More than half of our citizens, and particularly the youngest members, have voted with their feet against democracy, or at any rate with indifference toward it. No doubt, if asked, they would tell pollsters they favor democracy, but in their own lives few give democratic institutions much of their time or energy, not even the few minutes needed to register and vote. They act on the belief that virtually all important decisions are no longer made in public spaces, and that the power of the dollar, exercised through some kind of mysterious marketplace (or, less mysteriously, in collusion with political power brokers), is far more weighty than any bill in Congress, any petition of citizens, or any other public act of citizenship. Wealth is the only kind of power, political or economic, they acknowledge. These beliefs are a danger to the raison d'être of democratic life. While the economic market has its place in democratic life, it is not a substitute for collective political decision making, for acting like a community of equals. That is a declaration of belief, resting on convictions and values regarding the merits of democracy. But is it credible to most of our students? If not, what is the role of education in making it credible?

While making individual decisions based on private calculation about what is best for oneself has its place in democratic life, so does considering one's neighbors' welfare, and even that of the other fellow citizens who are not our neighbors. Democracy assumes political discourse across divisions of race, class, neighborhood, and ideology, in which citizens hear each other and are heard by each other. Participation in public life is undertaken in the belief that such mutual discourse leads to collective democratic decisions of importance, and that such decisions are not merely academic but are capable of being carried out and of making a difference. If we sever the connection between discourse and power, then democratic life is a charade, an empty ritual. If there is power in that conversation, then public education provides a critical link. It becomes the place to learn *how* to carry on such an informed conversation. Equally important, it becomes a topic *about which* such public conversation takes place.

A society that gives up its right to a collective voice in educating its young has little else important to talk about. Why debate what direction we want the future to take if we cannot influence the institutions that shape the citizens of the future? The skills, values, and habits of mind of the young have never been more important. An intellectually disarmed public is a dangerous thing. It is too bad that proponents of the right to bear arms are not more concerned with the disarming of our minds.

A school system in which students must come together with others who are different may or may not further any individual's life goals, but it furthers our common goals as a democratic society. A school system that demands that young people consider issues from multiple perspectives may not make any individual student richer, but it makes society as a whole safer. A society that eliminates all its commonly cherished arenas of life and divests itself of all need to think about what is good for others is on the slippery road to losing its democratic pretensions. There is a necessary tension between individual and communal interests that we are in danger of losing sight of in glorified rhetoric about the marketplace.

The issue of a shared public responsibility for our children is more critical today than ever. The institutions, both formal and informal, that once were accessible to children and that grounded them in a society of responsible adults are no longer there for too many children. Stable communities, extended and intact families, strong and active churches, solid neighborhood institutions, and that whole myriad of face-to-face institutions such as political clubs and union halls have lost much if not all of their vitality. Many young people are rarely exposed to a range of working adults (except teachers) who could serve as role models. Because such institutions and personal interactions between adults and young people are disappearing, schools of necessity play a larger role than ever in the lives of students. To become minimally self-supporting, young people are now required to spend at least thirteen years in steady school attendance, and eighteen if they want to earn a decent living. The school as gatekeeper has never been more powerful. The student who is deemed inadequate ("not the academic type") cannot sit it out for six to eight years and then move into the "real" world or work at the age of fourteen or sixteen as so many once did. Getting any kind of job, even getting a driver's license in some states, now requires staying the whole route. Quite aside from its intellectual potency, or its certificating role, the school marks youngsters deeply with its explicit and implicit system of values. Establishing a rank order of merit that can leave lifetime scars, schooling has a far greater—and often more devastating—impact than ever before on young people's sense of worthiness and self-esteem.

Reasons for Advocating Choice

The contemporary fragility of our democratic institutions—the existence of widespread cynicism about civic pursuits—makes public education more critical than ever and every attack on it dangerous. This is why the argument about choice cannot be divorced from the question of the impact choice will have on our already endangered public schools. The answer is that some choice plans will help to kill it and others will help to revitalize it. To argue that the impact of schooling in America is an issue best resolved by one single act—"Let them choose"—is reminiscent of Marie Antoinette's blithe and bewildered "Let them eat cake!" The picture conjured up by marketplace advocates is as far from reality as Marie Antoinette's statement, and its proponents are often as removed from real life. Our belief in the value of public education and equity will not be well served, however, if we just stand firm and say no to choice. The answer is to *use choice wisely*.

In part my response to those who oppose choice out of concern for equity is personal. I am irritated by the fact that so many concerned policy makers who oppose choice because of its impact on equity are already exercising choice for their own children. They are generally among the millions of well-intentioned citizens who have chosen private schools, gotten their children into selected or specialized public schools, moved to more affluent communities where the schools are better, or taken whatever measures were needed to see that their children qualified for classes for the gifted. Despite their recognition that such choices have negative consequences, they cannot resist. Writ large, however, such individual acts have already fatally damaged most of our neighborhood schools and made change of the sort advocated by policy makers in place of choice nearly impossible. The system we have today is—despite all the rhetoric—chock full of choices that are not going to go away by our saying no. There is little chance that we will eliminate the right of parents to select private schools. There is little chance that parents with the means to do so will not shop around for neighborhoods with schools they find congenial. There is little chance that more advantaged parents will not do their best to get their youngsters into existing public schools of choice on the basis of influence or merit. There is no chance that parents with the power to do so will not use their advantage to get the best programs, classes, and teachers for their children within whatever school they find themselves. That is what being a good parent is all about: doing the best you can for your child. Efforts to limit parental power always face the ugly alternative: such families can simply withdraw their children from the public sector along with their political and economic influence.

The more serious the impact of schooling on young people's future options, and the more critics decry the quality of the existing schools, the more parents will use their private power of choice. Once we acknowledge how widespread the current impact of choice is, we will recognize that we cannot stem the tide by saying no to choice. What we must do instead is to shape the concept of choice into a consciously equitable instrument for restructuring public education so that over time all parents can have what the favored few now have. This is the District 4 way. The alternative to privatization must be not change for its own sake but good public education, and it must be offered just as fast as we can put it into place. While choice is not a silver bullet, it is an essential weapon in that effort.

A second reason for advocating choice is simpler: there is no other way to carry out radically new pedagogical practices. Until we implement such practices on a sufficiently large scale and over a sufficiently long period of time, we will not be able to make a convincing case for their efficacy. While people argue over what went wrong and why, there is a considerable and powerful consensus that pedagogy must change, and change fundamentally. The recommendations of task force after task force would, if actually carried out, be revolutionary. Proclaiming the need for revolution is not a strategy, however, nor is mandating that schools get dramatically better results or else. Such top-down mandates go only so far, and we have pretty much reached their limits. The kinds of major restructuring that deal with teaching and learning practices and the relationships among teachers, students, and families are least susceptible to mandates and most dependent on changes in the quality of the relationships among people in schools. Choice, as District 4's story suggests, turns out to be the single most efficient strategy for rapid and dramatic restructuring when it comes to such changes, precisely because it undercuts the natural layers of resistance that threaten each and every specific proposal for change. Public policy makers vastly overestimate the readiness of parents, students, or school staff to doing things differently. The majority of citizens still want schools to stay the way they are but to work better—and cheaper. The saboteurs of change are not just the big bad bureaucrats. Everyone wants change, but. . . . Choice helps us undercut the "buts."

Furthermore, such resistance to change should not be seen as mere crotchetiness. There is a bit of fraud in any claim that we now know "what works" in education. We do not. There continues to be substantial dispute; there may always be. Education, like child rearing, depends on so many minute variables, so many intuitive interactions, so many conflicting agendas and priorities, that the idea that we can ever find the one best way is illusory. There is, after all, a good reason for the fact that human beings have argued about education for thousands of years. There is a reason, too, for the fact that so many of the very latest educational ideas appear familiar. As soon as we discard one set of educational innovations, they reappear wearing slightly new clothes. What seems to me indubitable strikes an intelligent colleague of mine as ridiculous. Educators are not peculiar in this regard. Medical diagnosticians and practitioners trained in the same traditions of Western medicine reach wildly different conclusions based on similar evidence. They too rediscover old nostrums, dressed up in new medical jargon. Lawyers disagree on the best way to handle a case or conduct a trial. Such disagreements do not separate the good from the bad but exist among equally prominent and successful doctors, lawyers—and educators. Only yesterday social promotion was declared the cause of our educational ills, yet today it is coming back into style under a new name, based on what appears to be new, ironclad data. Even were we to make decisions in education on the basis of such research, we would easily find a basis for defending contradictory theories.

If we expect to create conditions that produce a better-educated citizenry, we will need to allow for such differences and even to encourage them. We will need to scrutinize the impact of different practices on a wide range of indicators and to look not only at immediate effects but at long-range ones as well. We need variety for its own sake, because people are different and desire different kinds of school experiences, and we need variety for the sake of progress in order to learn better ways. As school staff are given greater power to put their knowledge into practice, to explore ways to improve the intellectual competence of their clientele, the profession will gain the confidence to establish new norms. Some quarrels will remain, but others will be settled. We do have new knowledge about teaching and learning, but the implications for daily practice are quite another matter. Choice can, if we allow it to, free practitioners to take advantage of a climate more conducive to putting their experience to use, to developing a more reflective and thus scientific approach to their practice. Different practitioners will explore differently, and the trade-offs they make will not all be understood at first, nor will they be equally palatable to all students and their parents. Just as doctors often lay out options to patients based on less than fully understood prognoses, so too must educators. While doctors have been loathe to acknowledge that fallible human judgment must still rule the day, educators cannot afford to hide their fallibility.

It is hard even to imagine how the kind of large-scale experimentation that is presently needed can occur without allowing parents (and teachers) to make choices. Once we publicly admit that School X and School Y are doing things very differently, how can we ignore parental tastes? Besides, it is a lot easier to be successful if the teachers and their constituents are not fighting one another.

If we cannot mandate such changes for an unwilling and unready public or profession, it is an illusion that the marketplace will stimulate this kind of massive reform. The private marketplace may encourage livelier marketing practices, but, in general, history shows that private schooling has proven as convention-bound as public schooling. Private schools do differ, but mostly either in an invidious way or cosmetically. The biggest differences depend on the school's placement in the social hierarchy. The choosiest schools, which attract students from families with higher social status and talent, are imitated in a steadily watered-down fashion as their clientele's status (and resources) decrease. With a few notable exceptions, schools differ mostly on the basis of socioeconomic means and expectations. The dual system has remained alive and well in the private sector, and innovation is the rare exception.

Public Policy and Incentives for Change

To induce change in schooling for all children will require conscious outside intervention in the form of altered public policies. Schooling has to matter to society as a whole, not just to families with children in school. Toward this end choice, while important, is only one of the necessary elements. We will also, for example, need money. While few reform advocates believe that throwing money at schools will do the trick, the affluent have never argued that money was not important to the education of their children. Furthermore, change itself requires extra resources, just as does retooling an industry. Retooling a labor-intensive industry such as education may be even more expensive. If we claim that *all* children can develop the intellectual competence we once expected of only the top 10 percent, we are launching a revolution that cannot be completed on a lean-and-mean budget.

Money will be essential, but a variety of federal, state, and local initiatives that stimulate districts to adopt one or another variation on the District 4 story are necessary. For one thing, we need to provide incentives to districts to break up large schools and redesign them into many small schools, easily accessible to families on the basis of choice. Small size is a major factor in improving schools and an absolutely essential one for the kind of pedagogical exploration we are talking about. Schools might be given more funds, not less, if they are smaller. Maximum sizes might even be mandated—300 for elementary schools and 500 for high schools, for example.

Once we think small, we can imagine locating new schools in available public and private spaces, near workplaces as well as residences, in places where young people can interact with adults going about their daily business. Local and state policies that make it more difficult to use such flexible physical spaces need to be reviewed and changed.

While no system of rules and regulations can ensure equity, public policy must address the critical ways in which choice might adversely affect the least advantaged. Methods to ensure equitable resource allocation must be developed. We will need guidelines that promote social, ethnic, racial, and academic diversity. This is important not primarily for the sake of the disabled, poor, or slower students, but for the sake of society as a whole. At the same time, trying to plan in advance for all the rules needed to attain this goal in the varied settings that exist will ensure that such schools never get off the ground. Rather, we need to be alert to particular local circumstances.

Schools of choice will, of course, have to be monitored regarding health, safety, and fiduciary responsibility. An agreed-upon list of indicators—regarding attendance, turnover, graduation rates, achievement, and so forth—can be used to suggest when and if intervention is required. We should, however, no more expect perfection from public schools than we do from private institutions (such as schools supported by vouchers would be). A large portion of the bureaucracy in public institutions, which we all decry, has been created through our anxiety to ensure against every contingency, to respond to each outcry over waste or mismanagement. We need to resist the temptation to waste public money trying to prevent every conceivable form of public waste. The cost of current vigilance is both too high and counterproductive. If we do not alter our mind-set on this score, then smaller schools of choice will merely triple our monitoring costs! Small schools in which all the constituents have a strong sense of ownership, backed by legislative requirements for openness and access, may be the best protection against gross abuses. It is hard to hide in a small and familiar setting. While a conspiracy on the part of all the parties is possible, it is highly unlikely.

Regarding purposes and goals, schools need to be far more explicit than they are today. Top-down mandates in this area are of limited value unless they are few and compelling. Some general statements regarding educational purposes and outcomes will do far better than long laundry lists of "what every student should know." Some standardized performance assessments regarding school outcomes may help reassure us, but more critical is the creation of a well-endowed inspectorate system that makes accessible to all interested parties information and judgments on how well schools are doing. Such an inspectorate's task must include raising the consciousness and standards of a community by a lively, even contentious dialogue about what is and what could be, based on reliable and honest information. Our current massively regulated and numerically documented system tells us little that we need to know and much that is misleading.

Critical as monitoring or data collection may be, the bulk of funding must go straight into the schools. This is an area where legislative mandates may be effective. Chicago today operates under such a reform rule, requiring that no more than 5 percent of the budget go into central and district administrative oversight and support services.

These kinds of measures would free innovators already eager to "restructure." As these first hardy pioneers got going, others more cautious or less experienced would be able to explore change on a more limited basis. The number of families interested in dramatically altered schools probably will closely match professional willingness to take the plunge. Such a strategy would enable us to use our limited carrots judiciously: to support, protect, and encourage successive waves of slightly less courageous innovators and risk takers. For some time the students, teachers, and families in the schools in the forefront will be swimming uncomfortably against the tide. They will be the research-and-development labs for education. This imposes special obligations on us toward such innovators since their subjects, however willing, are not guinea pigs but children. Creating schools different from what we are familiar with, that run counter to the previous experience of most families and teachers, requires giving schools the extra means—in time and resources—to learn quickly from their experiences and modify practices accordingly.

That school staff, like parents, are naturally conservative and reluctant to change their habits is both expected and healthy. It is not necessary that they sign up at once. What is needed fairly quickly is a range of models, examples for school staff and the public to scrutinize and learn from. Credibility will require a critical mass of such schools—how many is hard at this stage to know.

We do know that we can go only as fast and as far as those who bear the burden of change can tolerate. Putting more money into schools cannot by itself create change, but it is one of those variables that can both stimulate and ease the way, thus accelerating the pace of change. Budget cuts will slow the rate of change. The urgency of school reform will be reflected not by our rhetoric but in how generously we fund this massive retooling effort.

Choice is a necessary *part* of a far larger strategy, not itself the solution. Creating smaller and more focused educational communities, enhancing the climate of trust between families and schools, developing workable models of self-governance, increasing the heterogeneity of a school's population, and using pedagogies that respond to diverse learning styles and student interests are all factors that current research suggests correlate with improved school outcomes. All of these are far easier to accomplish in small schools of choice, and it is possible that many of them can be accomplished only in such a setting. But choice itself will not produce a single one of them! It is a vehicle for allowing us to move ahead more efficiently, not a guarantee that we will do so.

There is something nice about the idea of choice. There is something galling about being stuck in a particular school unless you are rich enough to buy yourself out of it, but if compulsory zoned schools worked, we would put up with the gall. They do not. That is why we must try choice. What is not necessary is to buy into the rhetoric of the rigors of the marketplace, the virtues of private schooling, and the inherent mediocrity of public places and public spaces. Choice can be used to avoid watering down educational reforms until they satisfy everyone—and thus no one—in an endless process of political compromise. Public decisions do not always require us to settle on one answer. A majority vote is not always necessary or appropriate: sometimes both sides can have their way. Public life can embrace publicly supported differences. Choice can be a proactive strategy for meeting changing social and educational needs, not a desperate defensive measure, nor a retreat from democratic ideals. Public choice can be a golden opportunity to engage citizens in consciously inventing schools that answer the most important of all questions any society can ask: by what means and to what ends are we educating our young?

Epilogue

Future Challenges
for Independent Schools

Pearl Rock Kane

The patches of a community quilt are carefully sewn to convey the ideas of the individual contributor. In the same way the chapters composing this volume define and interpret various perspectives on independent schools. And just as those individual patches form an overall design, each in interaction with the others, so too do the disparate voices of practitioners, students, researchers, and policy makers in this book reveal a thematic pattern that describes what is currently transpiring in independent schools. These themes emerge as paradoxes: the schools are different and similar; the schools serve the interests of families and the needs of society; the schools respect traditions and respond to change. An exploration of these paradoxes may hint at the future of independent education in America.

Differences and Similarities

Among the characteristics that most distinguish independent schools is their right to define themselves. Freed of the encumbrances of a central bureaucracy, each school has been able to develop as it chooses. Various independent schools have different missions and employ different approaches. What works in one school, or with a particular child or group of children, is never considered the blueprint for all schools or all youngsters in independent schools. Among the various types of schools are day and boarding schools, single-sex and coeducational schools, highly competitive and relaxed schools, experimental and traditional schools, and schools that focus on the arts or teach the entire curriculum in a foreign language. Because the schools offer options to parents, it is not uncommon to find children within the same family attending different independent schools. In localities where families can choose from several schools, both families and schools attempt to fit the needs and interests of the child with the optimal school setting. As various types of independent schools have evolved, they have not concerned themselves with a search for the one best approach to schooling or the one best system.

Within the range of differences that characterize the schools are core values that the schools hold in common. From the founding of the first academies in the eighteenth century, a dual focus of independent schools has been educating the minds and building the morals of the young. The constitution of one of the earliest secondary schools, Phillips Exeter Academy, written in 1781, leaves little doubt about the school's purpose:

> But, above all, it is expected, that the attention of instructors to the disposition of the minds and morals of the youth, under their charge, will *exceed every care;* well considering that, though goodness without knowledge is weak and feeble, yet knowledge without goodness is dangerous, and that both united form the noblest character, and lay the surest foundation of usefulness to mankind.[1]

Responsibility for educating the head and the heart requires a conception of learning that gives equal attention to formal and informal interactions between adults and students throughout the school day. Small classes, an environment in which teachers get to know students well, a recognition that learning takes place on the playing field as well as in the classroom—these are characteristic of the independent school. Because teachers are charged with the development of the mind and the spirit, hiring practices tend to appraise the candidate's character and overall personality as well as the academic record.

Families and Society

Researchers James Coleman and Thomas Hoffer have described public and private schools as having different orientations. Public schools are oriented to represent society: in the ideal, they are viewed as a way to transcend the constraints of family social origins. In a sense, the public school serves to emancipate the child from family limitations. The schools are also intended to provide a forum for developing understanding and respect among people of various classes, religions, and ethnic groups. In contrast, according to Coleman and Hoffer, independent schools are oriented to serve the direct interests of families and to reinforce family values.[2]

A school that operates as an extension of the family may fail to serve the best interests of society. Parents may prefer an independent school where they feel comfortable, often one where the families are similar to their own. They may have little regard for exposing their children to socioeconomic or ethnic or religious diversity. Because most independent schools rely on tuition and contributions for survival, and because the schools are governed by boards composed largely of parents and alumni or alumnae, it is not surprising that a certain sameness can be perpetuated within any one school. Some students whose values and backgrounds differ markedly have found such schools oppressive. Schools are attempting to confront that problem.

In recent years independent schools have attempted to recruit a more diverse student body, often over the objection of conservative forces within the school community. Enthusiasm for expanding the social mission of the school may come from faculty or administrators, especially from those who grew up in the idealism of the sixties. Although many of the faculty of former years were independently wealthy, today's faculty members are largely from middle-class families, and many attended public schools where they were exposed to diverse populations. Similarly, enlightened boards have become convinced that independent schools benefit from increased diversity, that students are better prepared to function in society when they respect and can communicate with all people. On a pragmatic level, board members understand that schools may be financially compelled to diversify as America becomes increasingly a nation of people of color.

Since most independent schools are tuition dependent and thus do not have ample funds for financial aid, they are not likely to change dramatically, but schools are increasingly receptive to diversity and to accepting a larger role in societal change. As independent schools consciously expand their mission beyond the values of the immediate families they serve, they more closely approach the original mission of the public school. There is also a growing movement in public schools to allow parents to choose the public school their child attends. Choice may appear to subordinate the traditional mission of the public school and to approach more closely the ideology of the private school. Public schools, however, may find that choice enhances commitment and is a necessary condition for achieving educational goals at the same time as independent schools discover the advantages of serving the broader interests of society.

As public and private schools become more alike, independent schools may find themselves engaged in stiffer competition for students. In fact, models are likely to emerge that include features of both types of schools. These new school models may mix funding and mission elements from private and public schools. For example, some public schools may receive some private funding, such as state-sponsored boarding schools for students gifted in mathematics and science, or private schools may receive public supplements to serve poor children who typically attend public schools. The voucher experiment in Milwaukee, Wisconsin, which provides state-funded tuition supplements for a small percentage of children from low-income families, is an example. More schools have evolved in recent years that combine aspects of public and private schools, and parents appear to be increasingly receptive to these hybrid models.

Tradition and Change

In many independent schools the age and architecture of the buildings and the deference accorded alumni and alumnae remind students and faculty that they are part of a noble and established tradition. Rituals and celebrations regularly punctuate the calendar of independent schools, exerting a powerful influence on the way people think about their institution and their own role within it. The respect for alumni and alumnae, though likely to be influenced by incentives for the school coffer, underscores the fact that students who attend the school are part of an esteemed heritage. At the same time, the cultivation of graduates serves as a leveling influence in attempts to change.

The omnipresence of the past and the freedom from state-imposed dictums partially explain why independent schools have not responded to the waves of external changes that have swept through public schools. The internal structure of independent schools at the secondary level, where teaching disciplines are organized into departments that set their own curriculum and often become territorial, also ensures that curricular change is more likely to be resisted than fostered. Since most curricular modifications in independent schools require democratic participation and faculty consensus, changes will continue to occur slowly and only after careful deliberation.

In part, independent schools have not changed dramatically because they have not had to change. As compulsory education obliged public schools to accept large numbers of students with different abilities and attitudes toward learning, the state schools did what they could to accommodate themselves to their changing clienteles. Public schools diversified the curriculum to hold students' attention and lowered standards as a way to discourage students from dropping out. In contrast, independent schools did not have to change because they were able to select youngsters who were likely to benefit from their school program. This may no longer be the case. Recently, demographic factors, social conditions, and financial constraints have conspired to bring about more substantial change. There are four areas in which change is occurring in independent schools.

First is the changing configuration of independent schools, specifically, the movement away from single-sex education to coeducation. Parents today are less inclined to send their boys to single-sex schools despite benefits claimed by their proponents. Whether out of financial need or philosophical conviction, most of the boys' schools have elected to become coeducational. Although some research suggests that schools for girls have advantages not available in coeducational environments, it is becoming increasingly difficult to convince parents of their merits. Marketing approaches that encourage schools to communicate their strengths and distinctive qualities in school publications, in meetings with prospective parents, and in public media may allow more single-sex schools to exist.

Ironically, schools that are already coeducational may learn from following the process that several single-sex schools have recently employed in becoming coeducational. Entire school communities have developed greater sensitivity to gender differences as they prepared for coeducation, engaging in a process of study and self-assessment that might be of benefit to schools that have been coeducational for years.

Second, different kinds of students are being recruited and accepted by independent schools. As discussed above, children of color are increasingly represented, and boarding schools are making a greater effort to recruit children from international communities. In recent years children with different learning needs have been welcomed. Many independent schools that once had the luxury of being highly selective in their admissions are now obliged to be more receptive to students with different learning styles and special learning needs. Because independent schools are unlikely to make significant changes in curricular goals, the schools will have to provide additional support for these students and be more resourceful in using a variety of pedagogical approaches, a burden that will fall largely on the shoulders of classroom teachers.

Third, whether driven by social commitment or by a need to accommodate a more diverse clientele, independent schools are beginning to respond to a mandate for a more inclusive curriculum for all students, altering the core curriculum based in Western civilization to include non-Western studies and works by women and people of color. Since independent schools often follow curricular trends in the established colleges, where major shifts in curriculum are already taking place, it is likely that these changes will continue to gain momentum. Such innovations have occurred and will continue to occur incrementally, constrained only by the weight of tradition and the slowness of democratic governance.

Finally, the composition and expectations of the faculty have changed. The independently wealthy teacher, mythologized as the "dollar-a-year man," is an anomaly in today's independent schools. Most faculty must support themselves on their income and are or expect to be married and have families of their own. They expect decent salary and benefits. Even in the case of dual working couples, economic conditions usually require the income of both. Schools can no longer depend on paying meager salaries to spouses of professionals. Faculty demands are being spurred by increased salaries in the public sector. Boards are finding it necessary to be attentive to these and other financial demands.

Higher costs, changing demographic conditions, and a commitment to diversity and increased financial aid have conspired to create greater competition for diminishing resources. John Ratte, chairman of the board of the National Association of Independent Schools and head of the Loomis Chaffee School, has warned that only if independent schools become more sophisticated in their administration, more professional in dealing with families, and more convincing in their claim of offering high value relative to cost will their financial survival be assured. Ratte also cautioned that the schools are only as good as their teachers. They must continue to attract the kind of faculty "who share a romantic view of youth and love the subject matter they teach."[3] Indeed, excellence in teaching may be more crucial than in the past. In the years ahead, the demands of educating a new clientele requiring modifications in curriculum and pedagogy will tap the efforts and skill of the best teachers.

Any forecast for independent schools must be posited in the context of financial viability. Schools consumed with problems of survival may avoid risk taking and render themselves incapable of responding to an enlarged social mission. In the future, independent schools may have to search aggressively for ways to promote their schools to the larger community while they work to persuade the conservative elements within their own community of their expanded mission. The broader mission that independent schools are addressing may help to convince parents, alumni and alumnae, corporations, and foundations that the schools are worthy of increased support. In the face of financial challenges, an enlarged vision of the future role of independent schools is a noble one. Seldom in the history of independent education have the schools been so severely challenged, and seldom has the mission been so worthwhile.

Notes

1. John Phillips and Elizabeth Phillips, the original deed of gift to Phillips Academy, in Phillips Exeter Academy, *The Charter and Constitution of Phillips Exeter Academy* 17 May 1787 (Exeter, N.H.: Phillips Exeter Academy, 1980), p. 37.
2. James S. Coleman and Thomas Hoffer, *Public and Private High Schools: The Impact of Communities* (New York: Basic Books, 1987), pp. xxvi–xxviii.
3. John Ratte, interview held at Teachers College, Columbia University, November 29, 1990.

Name Index

Subject Index